Professional
Catering

The Modern Caterer's Complete Guide to Success

Stephen B. Shiring, Sr.

DELMAR
CENGAGE Learning·

Australia • Brazil • Japan • Korea • Mexico • Singapore • Spain • United Kingdom • United States

Professional Catering: The Modern Caterer's Complete Guide to Success, 1st edition
Stephen B. Shiring, Sr.

Vice President, Careers & Computing:
Dave Garza

Director of Learning Solutions: Sandy Clark

Senior Acquisitions Editor: Jim Gish

Managing Editor: Larry Main

Senior Product Manager: Anne Orgren

Editorial Assistant: Sarah Timm

Vice President, Marketing: Jennifer Baker

Marketing Director: Wendy E. Mapstone

Senior Marketing Manager: Kristin McNary

Associate Marketing Manager:
Jonathan Sheehan

Senior Production Director: Wendy Troeger

Production Manager: Mark Bernard

Senior Content Project Manager: Glenn Castle

Senior Art Director: Bethany Casey

Cover and Interior Design: Mike Stratton,
Stratton Design

Large tent image: ©iStockphoto.com/ Scott Cramer, China and Alexa image Courtesy of HLC Inc., Apples image Courtesy Eat'n Park Hospitality Group, Proper Measurement image courtesy of Diemo Video Picture

Library of Congress Control Number: 2012950879

ISBN-13: 978-1-133-28078-1

ISBN-10: 1-133-28078-1

Delmar
5 Maxwell Drive
Clifton Park, NY 12065-2919
USA

Cengage Learning is a leading provider of customized learning solutions with office locations around the globe, including Singapore, the United Kingdom, Australia, Mexico, Brazil, and Japan. Locate your local office at:
international.cengage.com/region

Cengage Learning products are represented in Canada by Nelson Education, Ltd.

To learn more about Delmar, visit **www.cengage.com/delmar**

Purchase any of our products at your local college store or at our preferred online store **www.cengagebrain.com**

Notice to the Reader
Publisher does not warrant or guarantee any of the products described herein or perform any independent analysis in connection with any of the product information contained herein. Publisher does not assume, and expressly disclaims, any obligation to obtain and include information other than that provided to it by the manufacturer. The reader is expressly warned to consider and adopt all safety precautions that might be indicated by the activities described herein and to avoid all potential hazards. By following the instructions contained herein, the reader willingly assumes all risks in connection with such instructions. The publisher makes no representations or warranties of any kind, including but not limited to, the warranties of fitness for particular purpose or merchantability, nor are any such representations implied with respect to the material set forth herein, and the publisher takes no responsibility with respect to such material. The publisher shall not be liable for any special, consequential, or exemplary damages resulting, in whole or part, from the readers' use of, or reliance upon, this material.

Printed in the United States of America
1 2 3 4 5 6 7 16 15 14 13 12

DEDICATION

To R. William "Bill" Jardine, a pioneer in the contemporary catering profession, a dear friend and mentor, this book is in your honor.

Contents

Foreword

Dr. Stephen B. Shiring has crafted one of the finest primers for both the catering industry and for the classroom. *Professional Catering* provides not only the critical know-how, but also offers valuable tips and inside information into the world of catering. Business plans for entrepreneurial development and growth will guide home-based caterers into successful and popular event suppliers. Furthermore, on-premise caterers will benefit from the tactical basics of management functions, to the execution of menus, and the professional handling of clients.

Special events are moments in time when people come together to celebrate and enjoy life. The event industry is not able to support these types of experiences without quality foods and creative banquet and event services. The catering industry is the business of satisfying guests' culinary needs while creating an ambiance of sensory experiences to enhance their celebrations and special events.

Today's tablescapes also reflect various cultures and cuisines which must be embraced to provide feasts for the most "plugged-in" consumer. Dr. Shiring's manuscript is a total presentation of the responsibilities, goals, and methods of operations for one of the most fascinating aspects of the hospitality industry. The world of catering is both an art form and a business science that must be mastered over and over again due to the changing nature of the event industry.

Social events, such as weddings, birthdays, and other personal milestones, have no reset button, and the expectations of professional caterers go far beyond those of most event suppliers. To adequately prepare, deliver, and serve memorable foodservice experiences and banquets is not for the faint of heart. The extensive body of knowledge concerning foods, wines, and beverages as well as their proper and safe handling is only the beginning. Today, innovative caterers are evermore creating customized, engaging, and artistic environments for clients which in itself is emerging as new business opportunities and supplemental revenue streams for today's catering professionals. Floral, linens, entertainment, and many other event elements are areas of familiarity a first-rate caterer must intimately know.

Please take the time to prepare yourself within the pages ahead to empower yourself for this fast-paced and rewarding arena of foodservice. Cheers!

Dr. Mary Jo Ross, CSEP, CPCE
University of Central Florida
Orlando, Florida

Preface

OVERVIEW

Catering education has undergone a drastic series of changes over the past 100 years. It continues to change as industry and business also experience change. Catering education today demands new approaches to teaching and new directions for learning. *Professional Catering* is a practical, hands-on text written to help you become more efficient and effective as a professional caterer. The student will embark on a journey to learn more innovative catering methods and their application. With the demand of America's eating habits, the need for qualified caterers will always be on the rise. The job market will enable any individual with an interest in catering to start their own business or work in hotels, restaurants, and institutions around the globe. Each catering opportunity will create unique experiences with food, beverages, and individual development. However, the need for further research in the catering industry remains a driving motive for the continued development of catering professionals.

Professional Catering structurally applies by design key essential and emerging management, marketing, and strategic management concepts empowering the student, practitioner, event planner, chef, or aspiring entrepreneur with the appropriate knowledge, tools, and Tips from the Trade to start and position within the marketplace a competitive catering business.

The three parts of this text are divided into 18 easy-to-read chapters. Each chapter explains how to plan, organize, implement, and execute a catering function. The format of the text complements the author's direct approach to the subject matter. General Objectives and a list of Key Terms at the beginning of each chapter explain what should be accomplished before proceeding to the next chapter. Ingredients for Success, listed in most chapters, emphasize fundamental catering rules and reinforce general standard operating procedures necessary to build a successful catering career. Tips from the Trade, found throughout the text, apply real-life situations to the topic being discussed. These tips present critical problem-solving skills demonstrated by leading professionals in the market today. Handy forms and checklists being used in the industry are interspersed throughout the text to aid comprehension of processes. Review Questions are presented at the end of each chapter, along with Putting It All Together exercises for students to apply what they have learned. The text also includes a glossary, containing all the highlighted key terms. Carefully selected pictures visually show the real-life catering environment and are used to compliment and reinforce the content material.

Part One of the text identifies the different types and aspects of catering. An overview of the catering industry, how the caterer creates a relationship with their client, choosing the right client, and using social media strategies to forge a loyal clientele is provided. Part Two of the book explores the seven critical functions in the dynamic catering environment as it applies to the central role food and beverage play in an event. A detailed explanation of how a caterer plans, organizes, implements, and controls an event is revealed. Attention to specific catering tactics to properly keep food at the correct temperatures is emphasized. Next, a revealing explanation on the type, kind, and quantity of catering equipment is given. Procurement strategies inform where and how to buy catering equipment. A detailed use of standard operational procedures adhering to OSHA guidelines to prevent and limit risk is furnished. An overview of insurance, the use of contracts, and other related legal issues is addressed. Part Three focuses on gaining a competitive advantage in the catering industry. A caterer can distinguish him- or herself by creating a distinctive operational competency through the effective resolution of conflict, creating a sustainable catering business, hiring the right employee, and by following appropriate beverage management strategies.

Ancillary Materials

Instructor Resources

- The instructor resources to accompany *Professional Catering* include computerized test banks in ExamView® format, PowerPoint® lecture slides, and the Instructor's Manual. The Instructor's Manual offers several features that allow the instructor to specifically tailor the course to curriculum requirements, including a suggested course syllabus, chapter summaries, and answers to the Chapter Review questions. In addition, a comprehensive and fully integrated case that applies and reinforces information gleaned from each chapter is provided. This case simulates for the student the seven critical catering management functions performed when planning, organizing, implementing, and controlling a catering event. The instructor resources are available online and on CD.

CourseMate

CourseMate is available for *Professional Catering.* This CourseMate includes:

- an interactive eBook, with highlighting, note taking, and search capabilities
- interactive learning tools, including:
  - Quizzes
  - Flashcards
  - Videos
  - and more!

To learn more about this resource and access free demo CourseMate resources, go to http://www.cengagebrain.com, and search by this book's ISBN (9781133280781). To access CourseMate materials that you have purchased, go to login.cengagebrain.com, enter your access code, and create an account or log into your existing account.

ACKNOWLEDGEMENTS

To write a contemporary textbook on catering is a Herculean effort. I am proud to say this effort was enthusiastically supported by many professionals, family, and friends who unselfishly gave their patience, expertise, time, and willingness to share their personal life experiences so others can learn of the complexities, challenges, and joys of catering.

I thank my wife, Tammie, and daughters, Samantha and Elizabeth, for their love, encouragement, and support. My son, Stephen Jr., for editing the manuscript, his photography, insight, and pictures. This task could not have been accomplished without the many long walks with Excalibur, our Yorkshire Terrier, who kept me focused on the task. R. William "Bill" Jardine and his wife, Joyce, for their support, encouragement, expertise, guidance and friendship over the past 25 years. My friend Richard J. Mills Jr., PhD, and certified chef of the American Culinary Association, for his professional perspective, continued friendship, and encouragement on this project. The project team at Delmar Cengage Learning. Jim Gish, senior acquisitions editor, for his vision on the project. Anne Orgren, senior product manager, for her meticulous guidance, instruction, inspiration, and friendship. Anne certainly made this project an exciting and a memorable journey. Kathryn Kucharek, Kristin McNary, Casey Kirchmayer, and Sarah Timm for their professional and creative effort on this project

To my parents, James and Laura-Valasek Shiring, thank you for your love and encouragement. A special remembrance for Isabel and Sam Galzerano—thank you for your love and for having a wonderful daughter. My brothers James Jr., Erick, and Scott and sisters Laurie and Letitia for their support. My Uncle Tony Valasek and Aunt Babara Valasek for their support.

To my current and former students, many of whom are now practicing the art and science of catering, restaurant and hotel management, and special event planning, thank you for expressing your enthusiasm, sharing your expertise, and taking the time to participate in this project. To my industry friends, I will always remain grateful for your Tips from the Trade and energy you devoted to this project.

Bill Jardine, Jardine's Farm Restaurant & Catering, Sarver, PA

Richard J. Mills, Jr., PhD, and certified chef of the American Culinary Association, associate professor, hospitality and tourism, Robert Morris University, PA

John Smith, chef and co-owner, All Occasion Catering, Inc., Pittsburgh, PA

Debbie Smith, president and co-owner, All Occasion Catering, Inc., Pittsburgh, PA

Vicky Baronyak, All Occasion Catering, Inc., Pittsburgh, PA.

Chris Garofalo, territory manager, US Foods, Greensburg, PA

Michael Tkach, director of ceramic engineering, The Homer Laughlin China Company, Newell, WV

John Marino, specialty sales manager, The Homer Laughlin China Company, Newell, WV

Dan Williams, director of marketing, The Homer Laughlin China Company, Newell, WV

Robert Shuman, The Homer Laughlin China Company, Newell, WV

Jamie Moore, director of sourcing and sustainability, Eat'n Park Hospitality Group, Pittsburgh, PA

Bill Jones, catering director, Parkhurst Dining Services, Inc., A Division of Eat'n Park Hospitality Group, Carnegie Museum of Natural History, Pittsburgh, PA

Bryan Gorton, Sous Chef, Waldorf Astoria Hotels and Resorts, (Arizona Biltmore), Phoenix, Arizona

John Daloisio, CPPC, CLU, of The Daloisio Agency, Kittanning, PA

David Curran, President of Curran-Taylor, Inc., Canonsburg, PA, founding member and Board of Director and Treasurer of PRIDE, founding member and Management Committee of the online equipment site Foodservice Warehouse

The Honorable James J. Panchik, Judge, Court of Common Pleas, Armstrong County, PA

David Piper, PhD, Department of Employment and Labor Relations, Indiana University of Pennsylvania, Indiana, PA

Leah Riegel, Human Resource Coordinator, Wyndham Grand Pittsburgh Downtown, Pittsburgh, PA

Michael Korns, PhD, Department of Employment and Labor Relations, Indiana University of Pennsylvania, Indiana, PA

Scott Decker, PhD, Juris Doctor, Department of Employment and Labor Relations, Indiana University of Pennsylvania, Indiana, PA

Daniel Walters, Graduate Student, Department of Employment & Labor Relations, Indiana University of Pennsylvania, Indiana, PA

Gregory Timmons, York, PA

Diemo Video, York, PA

Rafael A. Rivera-Vigo, Interstate Hotels and Resorts, Tampa, Fl

Bob Pleva, Vice President of Operations, Hoss's Steak and Sea House, Duncansville, PA

Ben Cavallaro, Unique Limousine, Harrisburg, PA

Tracy L. Salinger, General Manager, Unique Limousine, Harrisburg, PA

Steve Steingart, CP-FS, Chief, Department of Health, Food Safety Program Allegheny County Health Department, Pittsburgh, PA

Henry Holthaus, Certified Executive Chef/Instructor, Culinary Institute of the Pacific Honolulu, HI

Keith Boyer, University Photographer, Indiana University of Pennsylvania, Indiana, PA

John W. Wilson, Jr., Assistant Director of Food Service, Monongalia General Hospital, Morgantown, WV

Jeffrey Miller, Assistant Professor, Department of Hospitality Management, Indiana University of Pennsylvania, Indiana, PA

Shannon Dickerson, student, Department of Hospitality Management, Indiana University of Pennsylvania, Indiana, PA

Jeffrey C. Brunermer, student, Department of Hospitality Management, Indiana University of Pennsylvania, Indiana, PA

Nellie Henigin, student, Department of Hospitality Management, Indiana University of Pennsylvania, Indiana, PA

Kelsey Lorenz, student, Department of Hospitality Management, Indiana University of Pennsylvania, Indiana, PA

Victoria Cassar, student, Department of Hospitality Management, Indiana University of Pennsylvania, Indiana, PA

Irish Amora Epondulan, student, Department of Hospitality Management, Indiana University of Pennsylvania, Indiana, PA

John Hunsberger, student, Department of Hospitality Management, Indiana University of Pennsylvania, Indiana, PA

Leah Angott, student, Department of Hospitality Management, Indiana University of Pennsylvania, Indiana, PA

Eileen J. Dudik, student, Department of Hospitality Management, Indiana University of Pennsylvania, Indiana, PA

David J. Calao II, student, Department of Hospitality Management, Indiana University of Pennsylvania, Indiana, PA

Christina Lynn Mesko, student, Department of Hospitality Management, Indiana University of Pennsylvania, Indiana, PA

Adel Albalushi, student, Department of Hospitality Management, Indiana University of Pennsylvania, Indiana, PA

Marty Horn, President/CEO, FOODgalaxy.com, Parsippany, NJ

Nikko John Leitzel, Owner, North Country Kettle Corn, Ridgway, PA

Jennifer Currie, Owner Operator and Event Planner, Practically Perfection, Pittsburgh, PA

Jennifer Braughler, Marketing Manager, ARAMARK Campus Dining, Indiana University of Pennsylvania, Indiana, PA

Lesley Orlousky, Indiana, PA

Rachel Russell, Indiana, PA

Corinne Elizabeth Miller, Catering Sales, Hotel du Pont in Wilmington, DE

Jennifer Babaz, Assistant Wedding Coordinator, Skytop Lodge "Very Special Events" Skytop, PA

Robert Baldasassari, Director of Sales & Marketing, Skytop Lodge, Skytop, PA

Adam Baumbach, Catering Manager, Legends - York Revolution, York, PA

Natalie Dunlap, Catering Sales Manager, The Chestnut Ridge Golf Resort & Conference Center, Blairsville, PA

Andrea Stoddard, Corning Incorporated Culinary Services, Corning, NY

Suzy Miller, Senior Sales Manager, SHERATON STATION SQUARE, Pittsburgh, PA

Jordan M. Kovalcik, Assistant Beach Club Manager, Club at Mediterra, Naples, Fl

Sara-Lynn Hunter, Banquet Server and Assistant Event Coordinator, Marriott Pittsburgh North, Cranberry Township, PA

Bruce Schmidt, President/Owner, Holstein Manufacturing, Inc., Holstein, Iowa

Brian Keller, Catering Manager, Marriott Pittsburgh North, Cranberry Township, PA

Dianne Herzog, Catering Manager, Hyatt Orlando, Kissimmee, FL

Michelle Albright Lennox, Catering/Convention Services Manager, Hyatt Orlando, Kissimmee, FL

Kenneth P. Darling, Executive Pastry Chef, Heidi's Gourmet Desserts, Tucker (Atlanta), GA

Michael P. Simon, Jr., Great Lakes Region Manager, MasterFoodServices™, A Division of Uncle Ben's, Inc., Houston, TX

Dan Miller, Manager, Springfield Restaurant Group, Mercer, PA

Chris Gowdy, Director of Marketing, Mount Vernon Mills, Inc., SC

Phillip A. Ali, Cafe Manager, Restaurant Associates/Corporate Real Estate, Richmond, Virginia

Mary Jo Ross, PhD, Assistant Professor, Rosen College of Hospitality Management, University of Central Florida, Orlando, Fl

Pete Turner, Regional Sales Manager, Kunzler & Company, Inc., Lancaster, PA

Kathy Marshall, Senior Sales Manager, Levy Restaurants, PNC Park, Pittsburgh, PA

Mike Rhoten, General Manager, Springhill Suites Washington, Washington, PA

Courtney L. McKenna, Human Resources Director, Andaz 5th Avenue, New York, New York

National Advisory Committee on Microbiological Criteria for Foods (NACMCF), Courtesy of the US Food and Drug Administration

US Food and Drug Administration

Video Interview Series

Bill Jardine, Jardine's Catering, Sarver, PA

John Smith, Chef & Co-Owner, All Occasion Catering, Inc., Pittsburgh, PA

Michael Tkach, Director of Ceramic Engineering at The Homer Laughlin China Company, Newell, WV

John Marino, Specialty Sales Manager, The Homer Laughlin China Company, Newell, WV

Jamie Moore, Director of Sourcing and Sustainability, Eat'n Park Hospitality Group, Pittsburgh

The Honorable James J. Panchik, Judge, Court of Common Pleas, Armstrong County, PA

Bob Pleva, Vice President of Operations, Hoss's Steak and Sea House, Duncansville, PA

Daniel Walters, Graduate Student, Employment & Labor Relations, Indiana University of Pennsylvania, Indiana, PA

Natalie Dunlap, Catering Sales Manager, The Chestnut Ridge Golf Resort & Conference Center, Blairsville, PAv

Steve Steingart, CP-FS, Chief, Department of Health, Food Safety Program Allegheny County Health Department, Pittsburgh, PA

Chris Garofalo, Territory Manager, US Foods, Greensburg, PA

Jeffrey Miller, Assistant Professor, Department of Hospitality Management, Indiana University of Pennsylvania, Indiana, PA

Justin Keiser, Food and Beverage Supervisor, Rivers Casino, Pittsburgh, PA

Training Video Series

To put together the catering how-to videos required extensive planning, enthusiastic attention to detail, specialized expertise, team work, and the skilled proficient delivery in the execution of the featured tasks. I thank the following for their contributions to this effort.

Jim Gish, senior acquisitions editor, Delmar Cengage Learning, for championing the video project

Anne Orgren, senior product manager, Delmar Cengage Learning, for coordinating the video project

Glen Castle, senior project content manager, Delmar Cengage Learning, for his support on the video series

Ann Sarah Colangelo, student, Department of Hospitality Management, Indiana University of Pennsylvania, Indiana, PA for her role as the "Chef" and as a "Server" in the video series

Mike Gibbons, student, Department of Hospitality Management, Indiana University of Pennsylvania, Indiana, PA for his role as a "Server" in the video series

Mr. Jeffrey Miller, Assistant Professor, Department of Hospitality Management, Indiana University of Pennsylvania, Indiana, PA for his customer service expertise in dining room etiquette

Sara Saplin for her expertise and guidance in monitoring and adhering to each step-by-step task procedure as outlined in the scripts for the video series

Lori Staples for her know-how and skill in operating the camera to capture in detail the featured tasks being performed in the execution of each task

Chris Conto for his ability to coordinate each individual's performance in this project to forge a cohesive team effort in creating the video series

The Vista at Van Patten Golf Club, Clifton Park, NY, for hosting the video shoot and providing equipment and supplies

US Foods for providing equipment used in the videos

Tom Van Dyke, Ph.D, Chairperson, Associate Professor, Department of Hospitality Management, Indiana University of Pennsylvania, Indiana, PA for his support on this project.

The author and Cengage Learning would like to thank the following reviewers: Kimberle Badinelli, Virginia Tech; Philippe Garmy, Oklahoma State University; Iris Gersh, CHA, CHE, Fairleigh Dickinson University; Karl Guggenmos, Johnson & Wales University; Ron Koetter CEC, CCE, AAC, Faulkner State Community College; Victor Moruzzi, Culinary Arts Institute, Hudson County Community College; Dr. Peter Ricci, CHA, Florida Atlantic University; Sheila Scott-Halsell, PhD, Oklahoma State University; and James Taylor, MBA, CEC, AAC, Columbus State Community College.

Professional Catering

The Modern Caterer's Complete Guide to Success

Part 1

What Is Catering?

Courtesy of HLC Inc.

Chapter 1

The Catering World: Types of Catering

Objectives

After studying this chapter, you should be able to:

1. Discuss the catering industry.

2. Identify catering segments.

3. Define on-premise and off-premise catering.

4. Explain the different types of catering events held on-premise and off-premise.

5. Provide examples of the different kinds of on-premise and off-premise operations.

KEY TERMS

bin system

catering management

commercial segment

convention catering

customer appeal

distinct competence

dual-restaurant catering

exclusive caterer

high school catering

home-based caterers

hospital catering

military segment

mobile catering

noncommercial segment

off-premise catering

one-stop shop

on-premise catering

packing list

private or nonprofit caterers

private-party catering

seasonal niche

supermarket catering

university/college caterers

CATERING INDUSTRY

Catering is a multifaceted segment of the food service industry. There is a niche for each type of catering business within the segment of catering. The food service industry is divided into three general classifications: commercial segment, noncommercial segment, and military segment. **Catering management** may be defined as the task of planning, organizing, leading, and controlling. Each activity influences the preparation and delivery of food, beverage, and related services at a competitive, profitable price. These activities work together to meet and exceed the customer's perception of value.

CATERING SEGMENTS

Catering management is executed in many diverse ways within each of the three segments. The first, **commercial segment**, traditionally considered the *for-profit* operations, includes the independent caterer, the restaurant caterer, and the home-based caterer. In addition, hotel/motel and private club catering operations are also found in this category.

The **noncommercial segment**, or the *not-for-profit* operations, consists of the following types of catering activities: business/industry accounts, college and university catering, health care facilities, recreational food service catering, school catering, social organizations, and transportation food service catering. The **military segment** encompasses all catering activities involved in association with the armed forces and/or diplomatic evens. Figure 1.1 illustrates how the food service catering industry is segmented.

ON-PREMISE CATERING

There are two main types of catering (on-premise and off-premise) that may be a concern to a large and small caterer. Figure 1.2 illustrates the different types of catering events. First, **on-premise catering** indicates that the function is held exclusively within the caterer's own facility. All of the required functions and services

Figure 1.1 Modern American catering categories.

FOOD SERVICE CATERING INDUSTRY		
Military Segment	**Commercial Segment**	**Noncommercial Segment**
Military Functions Diplomatic Functions	Independent Caterers Hotel/Motel Caterers Home-Based Caterers Restaurant/Catering Firms Private Clubs	Business/Industry Accounts College and University Catering Health Care Facilities Recreational Food Service (amusement and theme parks, conference and convention facilities, museums, libraries, stadiums, and sport arenas) School Catering Social Organizations (fraternal and social clubs, associations, and fire halls) Transportation Food Service Catering (in-flight catering)

catering management Tasks of planning, organizing, influencing, and controlling each activity involved in the preparation and delivery of food, beverage, and related services at a competitive, profitable price that meets and exceeds the customer's perception of value.

commercial segment Traditionally considered the "for-profit" catering segment, it includes the independent caterer, the restaurateur and caterer, and the home-based caterer whose financial goals include a profit gained from revenue minus expenses.

noncommercial segment Traditionally considered a "not-for-profit" catering segment that operates on a break-even basis where revenue equals expenses. Catering and services are provided as an adjunct service to complement the catering required by a business and industry account, college and university account, health care facility account, recreational food service account, school account, social organization account, or transportation food service account.

military segment The catering segment that encompasses all catering activities involved in association with the armed forces and/or diplomatic events. Traditionally operates on a break-even basis, with revenue equaling expenses.

© Cengage Learning 2014

on-premise catering
When all of the tasks, functions, and related services that the caterer executes in the preparation and implementation of food and service for the client are done exclusively within the caterer's own facility.

Figure 1.2 The catering event.

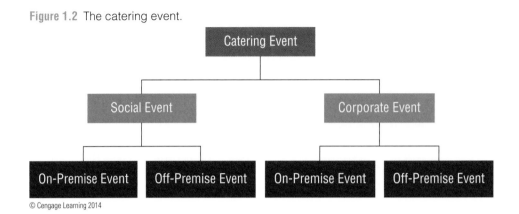

© Cengage Learning 2014

that the caterer executes are done exclusively at their own facility. For instance, a caterer within a hotel or banquet hall will prepare and cater all of the events without taking any service or food outside the facility. Many restaurants have specialized rooms on-premise to cater to the *private-party* niche.

A restaurant may have a layout strategically designed with three separate dining rooms attached to a centralized commercial food production kitchen. These

Figure 1.3 Catering in the armed forces.

separate dining rooms are available at the same time to support the restaurant's operation and for reservation and overflow seating. In addition, any of the three dining rooms may be contracted out for private-event celebrations and may require their own specialized service and menu options.

Hospital Catering

An example of **hospital catering** is an on-premise catering operation for events that occur within a hospital's environment. It is very rare for a hospital to sponsor an off-premise event. One exception could occur if the hospital is sponsoring a fund raiser.

There are great demands placed on the food service department within a hospital environment when an active catering service is used. Special functions are held by the internal hospital associations. There are many *visible* and *invisible* associations conducting business within a hospital's environment. Associations having special requests for internal catered functions (Figures 1.4 and 1.5) may be the medical technologists in the laboratories, ladies' auxiliary, physicians' meetings, nurses' organizations, employees in all departments, or x-ray departments.

Many hospitals have beautiful dining rooms that are primarily used for catering internal events. In addition, they may have other dining areas to have breakfast meetings, luncheon events, and special dinner events in a private setting.

hospital catering Primarily on-premise catering operation that occurs within a hospital's environment servicing internal associations and/or a department's special needs.

High School/Elementary School Catering

It is very unlikely that a high school would cater an on-premise event for a customer who is not associated with the school. **High school catering** operations service events exclusively for the high school population; high schools frequently cater athletic banquets, teachers' meetings, events on the football field for fall and spring celebrations, and other sporting events. They may hold a catered event anywhere on the school property, but the preparation of the food is done in the high school cafeteria. One logical reason for this policy is that insurance and liability costs would escalate, and therefore be prohibitive.

high school/elementary school catering An on-premise catering service offered by the food service director exclusively for the school's own population.

Private or Nonprofit Caterers

Why does a school cater internal events by using its on-premise food service facilities? There are certain advantages for maintaining an on-premise food service: catering its own activities provides an exceptional opportunity to increase profits and raise profit margins for the purpose of strengthening its internal fiscal health. The school directors can lower operational food costs in the cafeteria or use the additional revenue to expedite the purchase of new pieces of production equipment.

Usually those facilities can provide food and service for less cost than an independent caterer because they have the facility, labor costs are built in, and they are not paying certain kinds of taxes. Churches, fraternal organizations, and fire halls are other examples of where an entirely on-premise catering operation may take place. Not many **private or nonprofit caterers** will cater off-premise events because they lack the expertise and equipment to do so; these organizations usually provide the hall,

private or nonprofit caterers A catering segment that operates on a break-even basis where revenue equals expenses.

SPECIAL CATERING FUNCTION REQUEST

Name of Group/Department/Association _____

Contact Person _____ E-mail _____ Extension _____

Group/Department/Association Location _____

Function Day and Date _____ Function Location _____

Number of Guests _____ Beginning Time _____ Ending Time _____

Menu

Appetizer

Entree

Sandwich

Starch

Vegetable

Salad

Dressing

Bread

Butter/spread

Dessert

Beverage

Other

Special Services

Flowers _____

Decorations _____

Entertainment _____

Napkins _____

Table Seating and Arrangements

☐ Classroom   ☐ Conference   ☐ Theater   ☐ Banquet   ☐ Sit-down   ☐ Buffet

Invoice To _____

Deposit Required $ _____

Cost Per Person $ _____

I agree to the arrangements as outlined on this special function request form.

_____ Date _____

Figure 1.4 A hospital special catering function request form.

CATERING SCHEDULE					
Time	Location of Function	Group or Association	Number of Guests	Contact Person E-mail/Extension	Menu
7:00 A.M.					
8:00 A.M.					
9:00 A.M.					
10:00 A.M.					
11:00 A.M.					
12:00 P.M.					
1:00 P.M.					
2:00 P.M.					
3:00 P.M.					
4:00 P.M.					
5:00 P.M.					
6:00 P.M.					
7:00 P.M.					
NOTES					

Courtesy of Monongalia General Hospital

Figure 1.5 Hospital catering schedule form.

food, beverage, and servers for an occasion. They employ catering as a supplement to their internal financial budgets to help raise money to fund special projects.

These organizations have three strategic advantages over the independent caterer.

1. They have no labor costs because the labor is "donated" by the members themselves.
2. They do not pay taxes.
3. Many of them do not incur the expense of carrying any kind of liability insurance.

These organizations can charge $20 per plate for a meal and generate a profit. In contrast, the independent caterer would have to charge at least $30 per plate for the same job because of the above costs and responsibilities. Since it is difficult for the independent caterer to compete against these organizations on price, they must find another means of competition. They may become a specialist, create a proficiency, strengthen a concept, or create a distinction that leads to satisfying and exceeding customer expectations in ways other organizations cannot do.

Customer Appeal

customer appeal Professional expertise, such as proper food preparation techniques, sanitation procedures, attractive thematic presentations, and related amenities offered by the professional caterer.

Fire halls are not decorated and do not offer many fine accompaniments. This is one area where the independent caterer may show individuality and thus compete with a nonprofit group. They can expend resources on a continual training program resulting in superior customer service. Whereas fire halls have volunteers serving the client, they may not be well trained in proper food preparation techniques or proper sanitation practices. The independent caterer can provide **customer appeal** by offering more variety, attractive presentations with china and glassware, and a higher quality of food and expertise. This may assure the caterer that the customer will come to the independent caterer rather than a nonprofit group.

For example, at Christmas time, the decorations supplied by the independent caterer would be more elaborate and could be tailored to fit the clients' tastes and needs. The caterer strives to be a specialist and to satisfy the customer's needs. If the caterer is able to satisfy more needs, one benefit will be a broader customer base. Ultimately, the caterer will achieve success because more customers will recommend him or her to do work for their friends and other associates.

University/College Caterers

university/college caterer On-premise catering service primarily responsible for providing food and related services to the students, faculty, administrators, and guests.

The management of college and university food service is either contracted to a company which specializes in food management services or handled internally by the institution itself. Regardless of the type of management selected, **university/ college caterers** are responsible for providing food and related services to the students, faculty, administrators, and guests.

College or university campus facilities are often utilized for on-premise catering. Universities and colleges have a myriad of activities happening simultaneously by many diverse organizations. Campus organizations, individual departments, educational conferences, or other independent groups on campus make it necessary for the college or university to maintain an active on-premise caterer. The caterer can supply food and beverages ranging from cheese and crackers to buffets and elaborate dinners. On-campus requests for catered events can be held 7 days a week, 24 hours a day, and range from such locations as individual classrooms to faculty clubs, renovated historical locations, and open-air functions.

The campus caterer will offer the client a choice from a standardized menu book or will customize a menu to fulfill special requests and needs. Functions held on a campus will include dessert receptions for visiting dignitaries, pre-meeting dinners for the members of the board of trustees, and special requests for the university president. The on-campus caterer is the **exclusive caterer** for the president and his or her activities. The president may request weekly or monthly meal plans that will provide breakfast, lunch, or dinner. The catering services are available for the president and visiting dignitaries.

exclusive caterer A caterer owns the sole rights to all catering functions held at a specific facility.

The caterer will also be involved in special university events. Graduation ceremonies, homecoming activities, and sporting events such as football games are important to the university. For homecoming activities, the caterer may set up tents to support both food and beverages for the president and the school's alumni. For football games, the caterer will prepare elaborate pre-game buffets, and during the game may provide food, beverages, and service for the president and his or her invited guests in his or her personal box.

The university caterer only services functions on campus for university personnel. Not many events are catered outside the university property for the local community since the university does not want to compete against community caterers.

Catering in Cultural Institutions

Defining Cultural Institution

A cultural institution is defined as a museum, zoo, historical home, or a venue for the performing arts. Although the primary mission of a cultural institution varies, it often houses, protects, preserves, and displays historical artifacts, art, and antiquities. Furthermore, these institutions support exploration and research, and foster community activities. It is important to understand a cultural institution does not exist, nor was it originally designed, to provide venue space for catered special events. However, an increasing trend is for cultural institutions to host corporate and/or social events on their property.

The cultural institution's primary purpose is to house the holdings or exhibits for public display. However, from a caterer's perspective, the actual building is but the protective shell and the space within is the "playground" which is offered to clients. The caterer "sells" this designated revenue producing space along with a separate contract package for food and beverage to the client. According to Bill Jones, catering director, Parkhurst Dining Services, Inc., A Division of Eat'n Park Hospitality Group, Carnegie Museum of Natural History, Pittsburgh, Pennsylvania, cultural institutions find it attractive to host catered events on-premise for the following reasons:

1. Create memorable, unique client and guest experiences.

2. Generate a "forecasted" incremental revenue stream, resulting in supplementing the cultural institution's operating budget, as government funding for cultural institutions continues to decrease.

3. Enhance positive public relations within the community; cultural institutions house world-class artifacts and have worldwide reputations, and catering on-premise helps to solidify brand awareness regionally.

4. Reinforce and strengthen the marketing message; the benefits of allowing catered events on-premise include promoting guest interaction with the property's unique environment and reinforcing the institutional marketing plan's advertising and promotional message.

5. Drive incremental guest exposure and participation year round. A guest attending a special event may not have had the intention to visit a cultural institution's exhibit on his or her own. This exposure empowers the guest to return with family and/or friends to the exhibit, thus creating positive word-of-mouth advertising.

6. To secure new sponsorship and donations for the property.

Creating the Event

Usually, the first step in offering space for catering events on-premise is for the property's board of directors to designate internally appropriate areas for catered events. Next, specific policies, procedures, and rules for the use of these spaces will be created. The primary purpose of these policies, procedures, and rules is to protect the institution's assets. These policies will frame the constraints and restrictions the caterer must operate within while serving food and beverage to the client. Therefore, the caterer will plan and implement each event framed within these policies. As there is no universal law requiring a cultural institution to "rent" space, the caterer and host property can be selective in the type of client they select for use of the property. Not all business is good business, and not all business is acceptable in cultural institutions.

Jones offers the following examples of specific policies, procedures, and rules that guide caterers in cultural institutions:

1. No service of red wines or dark liquors is permitted. If spilled, these beverages produce unforgivable stains that must be avoided.

2. The cultural institution is a museum (zoo, aquarium, etc.) first, and a venue for catered events second.

3. No open flames are permitted. This includes no use of fuels such as butane or propane.

4. No service of food and beverage is permitted close to the exhibits. This will, of course, limit the available square footage the institution offers for the service of food and beverage.

Unique Challenges

Cultural institutions face unique challenges in operating their food and beverage service (FBS). The type, kind, and variety of FBS offered will depend on the specific cultural institution itself. The food service provider responsible for the catering operations will be responsible for managing the retail food outlets on-site as well. On-site food service outlets may include full-service sit-down restaurants, cafes, mobile carts, vending, or any combination of "grab-and-go" options.

The guests visiting the cultural institution will also vary. Guests may be members of the institution. Guests vary by age, gender, income, ethnicity, and interest. Their reason to be on site may differ as well. A guest may be visiting the exhibits or may be a local businessperson conducting a meeting over lunch in the restaurant. Often, members of the board may host potential donors over lunch in the institution's restaurant. Remember, cultural institutions are open to the public and guests need to have food and beverage options while in house.

Self-Operated Versus Outsourcing

Cultural institutions commonly use one of two different food service management systems. One system is called an internal self-operation management system. The second system uses an invited external management company, such as a contract management company, or an independent commercial caterer, to provide the management of all food and beverage options.

A self-operation FBS is when the cultural institution operates all food service and catering services using its own employees and management staff. In addition to the cultural institution managing the cultural exhibits, it must also handle all management functions associated with providing food and beverage services to visitors, members, clients, and their guests. This means the FBS options are managed by the institution itself. All tasks involved in providing the FBS are managed internally by the institution. Most cultural institutions do not use a self-operated system, since they lack the specialized knowledge, expertise, and time to manage their own FBS.

Outsourcing, the invitation to an external hospitality management company to provide FBS in a cultural institution, is the most common form of management used.

A contract food service management company can be hired as exclusive to the property or designated as a recognized preferred caterer deemed acceptable by the institution. To become a preferred caterer, formal approval by the institution against a set of established standards is required. These standards include a current certificate of insurance, operating from a health department approved commercial kitchen, and having an appropriate level of experience. The institution will only permit those approved and their own in-house caterers to provide FBS.

Internal and External Food and Beverage Service

The caterer's defined role in a cultural institution varies according to need. Caterers service both internal and external event functions. Internal event functions are FBS for all in-house functions. These types of functions commonly include small, informal coffee breaks for two in the president's office, department-sponsored lunch meetings, Very Important Persons (VIPs) meetings, exhibit openings, and perhaps, a four-person director reception. These types of internal functions may pop up 30 minutes before they are needed, or may be planned 24 hours in advance. Most of the time, however, these internal functions are driven by uncontrollable outside forces and a caterer must be ready to respond to them.

In addition to the mandatory day-to-day retail operations and in-house catering needs, caterers will provide FBS for outside or external clients. External catering services are those external to the institution. These external clients may or may not be related or associated with the institution. These types of events can be both social, such as weddings and birthday parties, and/or be corporate in nature. The caterer will control all aspects of these externally driven, on-premise special event functions. Unlike internal demands thrust upon a caterer for last-minute food and beverage requests, external catering functions most often have the luxury of being planned over a longer time frame. It is not uncommon, for example, for a catering management team to plan a menu and set a preliminary budget 2 years in advance of a large art gallery's opening night. Often, these events forecast 800–1,000 attendees for the preopening reception with an additional 300–400 people filtering in later that evening to see the exhibit. Even though this function has a longer time frame for planning, it still would not be unusual for the client to call 10 days to 48 hours before the actual event to make changes to the "final count."

The unique challenges of catering in a cultural institution create the continuous need for the formulation of innovative service strategies to exceed the client's expectations. The demand is to plan, organize, implement, and control an event, while exceeding a client's stated needs and wants, while adhering to the specific rules of the property, within a predetermined event budget. A key to succeeding is innovation and the use of technology. One challenge occurs when several events or when a single client is using multiple locations on-premise at the same time. For example, it may not be uncommon to have 2,000 guests attending a special catered event occupying nine different locations on-premise using three different floors. A versatile tool a caterer adopts into these events is technology. Cell phones, hand-held radios, and wireless access to the Internet to obtain e-mail messages are vital tools that ensure successful events. But in the end, thinking on one's feet to provide superior quality, customer service, and implement solutions to unique problems are the keys to success.

Design

The infrastructure housing cultural institutions was originally designed to protect and display historical artifacts, art, and antiquities to the public. It was not designed to provide on-premise food and beverage options to guests. Unlike a specifically designed catering/banquet hall, these properties may be logistical nightmares, as inefficient structural designs for food service applications will cause caterers grief when planning an on-premise event.

Often, when the decision is made to move forward with selling space for catering events, some cultural institutions may need to be renovated. Renovations require the installation of commercial kitchens and other added on features to provide on-premise food service options. For example, according to Jones, due to the original configuration of the building, the installation of commercial kitchens may not be in a central location. The caterer might find the heart of the operation two to three blocks away, plus two floors down, and buried within the cultural institution. The flow of food from receiving to waste removal may be a challenge. Keeping hot food hot and cold food cold becomes an event-specific performance issue and a Hazardous Analysis Critical Control Point challenge.

A caterer must be aware of these structural design flaws and know how to navigate them. When these design flaws are known, the caterer can formulate flexible solutions into the pre-event plan to address these constraints. For example, logistical constraints in the movement of food and equipment will most certainty add increased time that translates into additional labor cost to the event.

It is during the formulation stage of creating the pre-event plan where the catering team identifies these constraints and addresses the additional time needed for employees to make their way through a maze of halls and rooms, or use inadequate public elevators, or navigate long hallways, steep stairs, and narrow doorways, when moving from production to service.

In addition, the use of forklift trucks, carts, or other transport devices is not likely permitted due to the delicate nature of the flooring materials used in the cultural institution. At times, on-premise catering in these facilities is not always as easy as one might think.

Time

When catering in cultural institutions, the availability of time is a significant critical constraint. Cultural institutions are open to the general public. Therefore, a caterer must silently work during the institution's hours of operation in preparation for an event. Most of the time, setting up for an event will only begin after the institution has been officially closed to the public. This often gives a caterer only a 2-hour window from setup to event. It is critical to be extremely organized and guided by a detailed, well-thought-out event plan.

Bill Jones terms this operating window as "Organized Chaos." One successful operating strategy he uses to manage this window is to adopt an "assembly-line mentality" for the event. This is done by working backwards through the event. For example, Jones creates his event-specific time-line plan by working backwards from the completed setup to his beginning point. To help him achieve this process, he answers the following questions:

(1) What is needed for the final room/function setup?

(2) What are the individual tasks/steps needed to arrive at this final setup?

The purpose is to create a simple sequence of critical steps that lead backward from the final event design to a predetermined, committed starting point created to minimize the impact of a time constraint.

Jones suggests as a typical sequence working backwards to be:

6:00 P.M.—setup completed

5:45 P.M.—final inspection of the event area

5:30 P.M.—place and fill water glass on table

5:15 P.M.—set flatware on table

5:00 P.M.—set cover plate on table

4:45 P.M.—set the floral arrangement/centerpiece on each table

4:15 P.M.—place the linens on each table

4:00 P.M.—erect the tables into the correct configuration

(B. Jones, personal communication, May 24, 2011, and July 16, 2009)

Subcontractors

The use of subcontractors for an event creates additional planning needs. When using subcontractors for an event, it is necessary to coordinate their arrival time and contracted service tasks into the event plan. For example, Jones says if renting linens and working with a florist on an event, the caterer must coordinate their arrival times for them to gain access into the building and have enough allotted time to complete their tasks without creating a bottleneck. "What time do I schedule the linens to be delivered?" "How much time will the linen company need to set the linens down on each table?" "What time will the florist be able to gain entry into the building?" "How much time will the florist need to set each centerpiece on a table after the linens have been set down?"

Collective Bargaining Agreement

If operating within a union property, an understanding of the collective bargaining agreements is a must! For example, if security begins their shift at 7:00 a.m., then of course it would be useless to schedule deliveries before 7:00 a.m.

OFF-PREMISE CATERING

off-premise catering
The caterer transports all of the food, equipment, and personnel to an external location to execute the event.

The second type of catering, **off-premise catering**, is accomplished exclusively by the caterer. The off-premise caterer transports all resources (e.g. food, equipment, personnel, supplies) to a location other than the commissary where the food is prepared. Planning the logistical operations of an off-premise event is a critical management function. Physically visiting and surveying the event site prior to planning ensures a successful event. The vital task for all off-premise caterers is accessing the appropriate equipment to safely prepare, transport, and hold the food prior to service on location (a review of catering equipment is provided in Chapters 10 and 11).

Tips from the Trade

Catering in cultural institutions is a rewarding, challenging, creative, and restrictive unique job that requires one to constantly think on one's feet. The job offers both intrinsic and extrinsic rewards. The opportunity to interact with a diverse group of people and be the first person to see an art exhibit as it opens, are tremendous rewards. The job contains many warm and fuzzy positive things, but it can also be emotionally draining at the same time.

The caterer is constrained by time, a client's budget, operating hours, location, equipment, infrastructure, and the rules of the institution.

Exceeding guest expectations by delivering exceptional Food and Beverage Service in a cultural institution includes all of the unrivaled services a client expects from a large scale hotel, a country club, exhibit hall, convention center, theater, conference and meeting facility, or a concert hall. Always remember the caterer operates in someone else's building—merely an invited guest who must play by their rules.

Courtesy Parkhurst Dining Services, Carnegie Museums of Pittsburgh

Maintaining food at the proper temperatures, below 41°F and above 140°F, is critical. Caterers use refrigerated trucks and/or other purposely designed equipment to keep food hot or cold. In addition, transportation for staff to get to the site may be provided. Some off-premise events are so large a caterer will rent buses to transport staff. This ensures they all arrive at the same time dressed in the proper uniforms. Off-premise caterers use equipment rental services (Chapter 11) to fulfill their client's needs.

Storage

Off-premise caterers work from a commissary or central location. Catering resources typically are stored at these sites in "cages." Storage cages are usually located in out-of-the-way spaces, such as the basement or a side room. Separate cages are used to store similar resources, thus making it easier for the staff to locate the item. A typical storage scheme may have one cage to hold the chafing dishes, trays, pitchers, and miscellaneous items. The second cage stores the china, silverware, and elevation tools, such as ice blocks. It is important to note that regulations guiding the proper storage of flatware and silverware must be followed. One strategy is to marry resources together in bundles of 10 units. Therefore, 10 spoons are bundled and held together using plastic wrap. Then, 10 forks are bundled and held with plastic wrap. By bundling resources together, it enables packing to be more efficient and protects the clean and sanitized resource from becoming contaminated. A third cage stores the linen, tray jacks, specialty drinks (e.g. Perrier and tonic water), and cabinets that hold small items such as salt and pepper, sugars, and baskets. A separate storage room is used to house the alcohol and related supplies. It is good management practice to limit access to the alcohol storage room.

A common practice is to utilize every inch of space for storage. In some instances, the hallway within the building is used to store glass racks perched on their wheel racks and covered by plastic to keep them sanitized (make sure all emergency exits have clear access). Storage areas also hold table numbers, holders, buffet card holders, and even decorations. Common food serving utensils might be stored in the kitchen.

Keep an accurate count or inventory of all resources in storage. Accurately verifying the resources are available, as needed, will avoid last minute "surprises."

Challenges of Being an Off-premise Caterer

Off-premise events present unique challenges and obstacles. Off-premise catering is certainly different than on-premise catering since it requires the caterer to relocate with the equipment, food, and staff. A common challenge is always the unexpected. Working in different atmospheres, lack of familiarity with the party site, its layout, resources (electrical voltage, sockets, and circuit capabilities), and usable space make the logistics challenging for any caterer.

A word of advice is to take each situation in stride, create an organized plan, focus on delegating tasks, and control each step to ensure a successful off-premise event. It is extremely important to be completely organized when implementing an off-premise event due to the single most important

Tips from the Trade

A packing list must include every little detail down to the liner napkins for the silverware baskets. Here is an example of a packing list for a 50-person beverage station (soda, water, and juice), and cheese and fruit platter. This list will cover the packing of the beverages for the break, and all that is needed to consume and serve the beverages and the snacks:

12 pack of regular and diet soda

6 caffeine-free sodas, 6 caffeine free diet sodas, 6 ginger ales

1 case of water

Assortment of orange, apple, and cranberry juice

Basket for forks

5 black napkins

Cocktail napkins

2 tongs

60 salad forks

Ice bin

Ice

Lemons

60 bread and butter plates

Ice scoop

50 water glasses

2 black 90s linen table cloth

As for the setup, begin by taking your black 90s and "box-skirt" the tables. Once covered, place at the left end of the table the water glasses, flipped upside down. Set the ice bin behind them to conserve space. Next the beverages are placed in a row starting with water, regular caffeine soda, diet soda, diet caffeine-free soda, ginger ale, and juices, following in their specific category. If table space is limited, display what you can of each item, stocking as needed throughout the service break. Also take one bread and butter plate (B & B) and place lemon slices (cut in half moon form), arrange nicely, and place a service fork on it. Position two platters and set service tongs with each. Fold a napkin within a basket to cover its interior. Neatly lay forks inside the basket. You could also stagger the forks in a nice pattern on the table top. Unwrap and check each B & B plate for cleanliness. Stagger the plates in two stacks set immediately before the food and just following the beverages. Position cocktail napkins at both the beverage end and at the food end of the table.

The packing list is an excellent management tool. It helps the off-premise caterer to stay on task. It keeps everyone informed as to the correct resources needed for the event. It ensures everything needed to implement the event, on location, is delivered, on time.

Andrea Stoddard, Corning Incorporated Culinary Services, Corning, New York

fact—travel. When moving resources from one location to another, once a caterer leaves the home base, returning to get something left behind is not an option. The next consideration is packing all resources for shipment and delivery to the new location.

The Packing List

Off-premise caterers create standard operating procedures to manage the movement and transportation of their resources. A standard checklist called a "packing list" (see Chapter 2, Figure 2-3a and b) is created to organize each event. The packing list is an all-inclusive standard form that will:

1. show the resources (food, equipment, supplies) needed to successfully implement the off-premise event on location

2. be organized by resource location (storage cage)

3. list by category and subcategory each specific item

4. exactly specify the type and quantity of resource required

5. be a communication tool to inform what has been packed and loaded for transport (see Tips from the Trade, Chapter 2, Chef Henry Holthaus, for his explanation on using a checklist).

Caterers match the packing list against the Banquet Event Order (BEO), which is derived from the proposal and contract (see Chapter 14). The BEO details the resources and diagrams the site layout, as specified by each client through the sales department. The packing list verifies that the resources ordered by the client will be delivered on time to the event site.

packing list A standard operating tool detailing the list of equipment, supplies, food and such needed to execute the event.

Transportation

Moving one's staff can pose unique logistical problems. Off-premise caterers usually have one vehicle or several vehicles to transport staff to the site. It is common practice to have either a large van(s) or a specially designed vehicle to transport the staff. In addition, the culinary team will usually have refrigerated and nonrefrigerated trucks to transport the food and other related resources.

The logistics for organizing resources and moving them to an off-premise site is a key management responsibility. Often, one specific employee is delegated the responsibility and granted the appropriate authority for packing resources for an event. Specific job responsibilities include assembling resources, packing them together in usable form, loading them onto the transportation vehicle, and, if necessary, driving the vehicle and delivering the resources to the site in a timely manner. If it is a large event, the resources can be delivered in advance.

Otherwise, the entire staff can be involved in the packing and loading task. After the staff is briefed at their pre-event meeting, packing lists and event sheets (BEOs) are distributed. Staff obtain from the storage cage areas the resources for the event. Staff can use a variety of different types of carts, such as supermarket carts, to assist in the internal movement of the resources to the loading area or other central location. The van/truck will be delivered to the loading area where the resources are loaded and packed for transit.

Temperature Control

Temperature control is a critical challenge in transporting and holding food at an off-premise location. Monitoring appropriate storage temperatures is a key factor in promoting safety and sanitation for the client and their guests. Adhering to a carefully formulated Hazardous Analysis Critical Control Plan (HACCP)

Tips from the Trade

There are good methods to follow when loading resources onto a transportation vehicle. First, understand loading and unloading a vehicle takes effort, time, and can be exhausting. Staff may be wearing their service uniforms, so care must be taken to keep everyone neat and presentable. All items should be checked, double-checked, or even triple-checked as they are loaded onto the vehicle. Tightly pack all items either in a crate or a bus bin, or contain them in a small or a large storage bin. All soda, water, alcohol, trays, and jacks are left in their natural state. Glassware is transported to and from the vehicle on wheeled cart racks and covered by plastic. Rule one is to never stack something higher than you can see above it. Rule two is always secure all items. Do not just throw loose resources anywhere inside the vehicle. Loose items may fall or harm someone either while driving or when opening the vehicle doors.

My method of loading a van is to place the resources you will need to remove last away from the vehicle doors, and the resources you will need first upon arriving at the site near the doors. This method works great when unloading the vehicle into an event room immediately after arriving at the site.

Otherwise, if you're unloading into a staging room at the off-premise location, one strategy is to load the resources into the vehicle in the reverse order of when they will be used. Place the resources you will need last from the on-site staging room near the vehicle doors, and load them last onto the vehicle. They will then be positioned as the first resources to be removed after your arrival at the site. They will be placed in the staging room first and be out of your way. Some resources can be unloaded directly to where they will be consumed at the site. Others will need to be moved to the staging area and stored for future use. Always try to move the resources directly to where they are needed or where they will be used.

When loading a vehicle to its fullest capacity, I like to load the glass racks in the far back, stacked, and place the wheel rack upside down on top of them. Then I place stackable items such as soda and/or alcohol neatly. I then load the bins and crates next, as they are also stackable, and will allow more space for the other items. If ice is needed, I load it next. I make sure to leave enough room for the flat beds and double-decker carts. Once all the resources and carts are loaded, I carefully secure the trays and tray jacks into the vehicle. I like to place the trays and jacks into the vehicle last because they are very loose items that can fill in space just about anywhere.

Andrea Stoddard, Corning Incorporated Culinary Services, Corning, New York

(Chapter 7) makes sure standards are being properly followed for an event. The temperatures of the hot and cold food are monitored to guarantee the prevention of food-borne illness, which can lead to many problems. A review of the proper hot and cold food transportation and service equipment is provided in Chapters 10 and 11.

Another logistical challenge faced by an off-premise caterer is the available space one has to work with at the event site. Space is needed to store the resources, such as the extra food and the serving utensils, as well as an area designed for the staff. When catering an off-premise event in a client's home, the following critical questions must be answered in the planning stages: Where does the caterer store the equipment and extra utensils? Where do the staff prep the food? Where are the drinks prepared? Where is the assembly location for the staff to gather until needed?

Many homes are not capable of hosting a party of 50 or more guests plus have the extra space to store the caterer's resources. In certain situations, some homes may have a separate private prep kitchen or may have a large enough garage to store the extra food and other resources. Even sites such as parks and other outside areas can create challenges when trying to implement an event, due to the lack of adequate space required for food storage, staging areas, and guest tables.

Always be cognizant of the challenges confronting the off-premise caterer. Be prepared. It is important to always survey the off-premise site before the event. Planning in advance on how to handle these unique situations will ensure a successful event.

Off-premise Site Setup

A typical sequence is usually followed when implementing an off-premise event. The caterer arrives and unloads the resources into the staging area. Next, the resources are moved from the staging area to set up at the main location. Usually the event tables will be preset with chairs, as well as the tables for beverage service and/or a buffet line. Depending on the site, laborers within the building will set the tables and chairs prior to the caterer's arrival. If not, the caterer is responsible.

Every off-premise event differs in style. However, one can categorize them into two main styles: formal and buffet.

For a formal event, a common setup technique is called the **bin system**. Each packer will use one bin to set two tables. Each bin will be loaded with the correct quantity of resources needed to set dining service for exactly the number of guests sitting at those two tables. The content in each bin will include: linen, table stands, table numbers, silverware, china, salt and pepper, and menus if being used. Staff will set all the tables via the bins, resulting in a quick and efficient room setup. Once the setup of the main function room is completed, the staff establishes an organized behind-the-scene service staging area. This area will include coffee, water, and possibly a wine station on each wing, water glasses filled with ice and water, trays and tray jacks covered with linen. If there is a need for a service bar, the designated bartender will set it up. For example, Andrea Stoddard, Corning Incorporated Culinary Services, the exclusive caterer to and within the Corning Museum of Glass, Corning, New York, says, "if the off-premise event is scheduled in the auditorium at the Corning Museum of Glass, staging is done from dressing room one and the resources are then moved to the auditorium."

For a buffet setup at an off-premise site there is a different approach. Stoddard describes a standard buffet setup procedure for a typical event being held at Corning's main research center, Sullivan Park, in the Atrium.

"We drive up to the entrance and unload the resources directly into the Atrium. We distribute linens to each location as needed. The linens are used to cover the tables and to 'box-skirt' the buffet and beverage tables. As we set the guest tables and buffet, we empty the packing bins and crates. A standard buffet would be set in the following sequence: stacked and scanned plates, all

bin system An inventory control method used to organize and store a set quantity of resources needed to set a tabletop guest cover for dinning service.

cold items, chafers in order from least to most expensive food, soup station, if applicable, dessert (if on the same table) with its appropriate plates, and rolled silverware at the end, if used.

"Buffets can differ in many ways and are dependent on the client's needs and the catering company's policies and procedures. This is a standard setup procedure that I have learned over the years. At a buffet event there is commonly either a beverage table or the service of drink orders. At the Atrium in Sullivan Park, we stage out of a side entrance and use folding screens to conceal our prep area. In the staging area we set a clearing station. We organize all resources. For either formal or buffet off-premise styles, the culinary team will arrive approximately 1 to 2 hours in advance to establish their preparation area as needed.

"Load what is not being used back onto the van. Repack the resources at the conclusion of the event following the same guidelines as loading it. Back at our home base, it is common practice to unload the vehicle, clean and sanitize all equipment, and return it to storage. Update the inventory list so it's available for the next function."

How to Work with a Banquet Staff

When executing off-premise events, it is necessary to develop a certain strategy when working with staff. Most catering teams consist of approximately three managers who will supervise a staff of between 20–30 employees. Some caterers will have a smaller number of employees depending on the size of their facility; however, most caterers, like exclusive or corporate, will need to have a substantial number of employees to implement huge events.

When staffing employees, know the type of event being planned. This will determine the number of employees required to complete the delegated tasks in a timely and efficient manner. Caterers have their own system for scheduling staff; whether it's utilizing a database enabling an employee to access their schedule online or posting work schedules outside of the catering office. Good communication, having no barriers between the caterer and staff, is a key management skill. Always schedule the appropriate number of staff for the given function or day. If a smaller event, a good rule of thumb is the ratio of one manager to three–five staff members. If it is a corporate event or a group of 50 or more guests, then extra staff would be required. If a change (increase) in the number of guests for a given event occurs, always inform the staff before to avoid confusion on the day of the event. It is not uncommon for assigned staff not to show up, potentially disrupting the continuity and timing. Not having enough staff for an event can be hectic.

Communicating the proper uniform is a key management task associated with scheduling the event. The appropriate uniform can be addressed either directly on the schedule or communicated and reinforced through employee training. A training module explaining the appropriate uniform or specific dress requirements per event should be reviewed with all employees. Most new employee orientation modules will answer the question: "What do I wear when. . . ." Usually, if the staff works in the morning, the uniform is white and black. If they work at night, for a formal event, then a "tuxedo" reminder can appear on the schedule. The standard tuxedo consists of black pants, socks, nonslip shoes, and a white long-sleeve button-up shirt with a black bow tie. Each staff member needs to know the appropriate uniform for each event.

Properly trained employees understand the caterer's service philosophy, the standard operating procedures to implement and execute a function, and the conceptual view of how the business operates as a complete unit. Specifically, staff needs to know that tables use different-sized linens, what is the appropriate china to use (see Chapter 11, Obtaining Catering Equipment), what kind of chafers are needed, and how to set a buffet table.

High employee turnover rates are a concern in catering. An astute caterer continuously trains their mature and new staff. Properly trained staff properly performs the tasks as needed. The caterer's staff will be in direct service contact with the client and guests.

A staff must look and behave in a professional manner, and always have a positive attitude and cheerful personality. Be respectful to the client and their guests. When operating in a client's home, respect the host's personal belongings. The staff must know where they are permitted and not permitted in the home. If a staff member is unwilling to cooperate, problems and client complaints can ruin or tarnish an event.

One fact of off-premise catering is the reality that one works in different locations on a daily basis. When you arrive at the off-premise site, immediately assess the type of atmosphere. Second, conduct a pre-event meeting with the banquet staff to discuss the following:

> The type of event being implemented
>
> Is it an alumni or corporate dinner, president's event, or an athletic event?
>
> What style of service is being preformed?
>
> Is it ballet or synchronized service?
>
> Review the service standards and procedures.
>
> What is the service delivery system and timeline?
>
> What is the service?
>
> Explicitly review the menu.
>
> What food is being served during the event?
>
> What is the entree?
>
> What ingredients were used to make the meal?

Getting to know the catering staff on a personal level and by acknowledging their hard work (whether working long hours or challenging events) and accomplishments will help forge a bond that can bring the business together and create a synergy leading to a greater success. Happy employees create a positive atmosphere.

How to Work with a Hotel Staff

When working with a hotel staff or another caterer's or employer's personnel, understand their guidelines and rules associated with their own events. Hotel personnel are usually trained a certain way by their management team. When catering from a new or different off-premise location, conduct marketing research beforehand on that establishment. What does the establishment expect from the caterer after he or she arrives?

The staff should report early before the event starts. This provides time for a pre-event meeting. The function room should have been set prior to the caterer's arrival. In most hotels, depending on scheduling and logistics, this is usually done by the hotel staff one day before the event. The caterer may have to set favors and/or other little necessities for the event, like placing the bread and butter on B&B plates. The caterer will review the set menu and the times for each presentation, unless buffet style. The hotel staff usually does synchronized service for an event and will deliver food accordingly. Hotels usually employ more staff than a caterer, therefore, tight supervision will make sure tasks are done properly and at the right time. It's not just about serving food but refilling drinks, restocking stations, and clearing tables. They must look and behave professional at all times (attire is usually the typical banquet tuxedo outfit). Typically, it is similar to working with a regular banquet staff except there are more employees to supervise and the event may be larger.

Jardine's Farm Restaurant & Catering provided a huge chicken barbeque for a corporation's 50th Anniversary. This special event celebration included all of the corporation's employees and their families, totalling 13,500 guests. The caterer had approximately 100 employees working that day to support the effort to provide exceptional customer service. The event was held on a very hot August day. Two buses were chartered to transport the employees to the location. An agreement with the bus company was made to keep the buses running all day with the air conditioners on so that if the employees became physically exhausted from working in the August heat, combined with the heat from the charcoal grills, they could go into the motor coaches and get refreshed and cooled down. With this size event, located 30 miles from a centralized location, the caterer had to be organized. Attention to details and planning were the keys of the game. The contract with the corporation was made 9 months in advance and the caterer worked on organizing this event continually up to the last minute through planning and focusing on all the details. The caterer had to answer questions such as: "How much coleslaw is needed for 13,500 guests?" "How much charcoal would be needed to prepare the food?" "How was the caterer going to set up stations to expedite the service of the food?" With the details and planning process, the caterer eventually determined how many people they could serve per minute.

Bill Jardine, Jardine's Farm Restaurant & Catering, Sarver, Pennsylvania

supermarket catering A traditional supermarket prepares food in their deli department. The customer will purchase this food and carry it themselves to the event location.

Supermarket Evolution into Catering

Supermarkets are also attracted to the opportunities associated with the catering business. Supermarkets have staff and facilities to get into the business with very little additional costs. However, **supermarket catering** is usually limited to what can be served, not what can be prepared.

The evolution of the supermarket and its ability to provide catering service began when they first started offering cheese trays, vegetable trays, and items that people could pick up and take home while shopping in the store. Some of the more upscale supermarkets deducted that since they already had kitchen production facilities for the preparation of hot and gourmet foods, they could easily diversify into other related food items.

Supermarkets also use many of the value-added or convenience foods available in the market today. With the use of prepared foods, a menu can be built entirely around these prepared food items. A shopper can conveniently purchase prepared salads and heat-and-serve entrees. Since many of these supermarkets are already serving these items in their deli departments, they can increase their sales by offering similar foods to people who come in and pick up their food and take it home with them. Another development in the prepared food departments in supermarkets is the hiring of highly trained, certified chefs. Certified chefs now manage supermarket gourmet departments, providing an upscale and professional touch to the preparation and presentation of the food.

Dual Restaurant Catering Operations

Many restauranteurs will cater on-premise special events and pursue off-premise opportunities. One strategic reason for **dual restaurant catering** is that restauranteurs have invested in professional production equipment and can thus increase efficiencies. This effort will lower the overall fixed costs of the operation. Another reason to pursue off-premise catering functions is to increase incremental gross sales without having to incur a capital expenditure of expanding either the dining room area, the kitchen area, or building another restaurant.

Restaurant facilities have a fixed capacity-sized dining room and are only limited by increasing incremental sales while serving more customers within a given time period. Therefore, a strategy is to serve more people off-premise because they lack the space to hold two functions simultaneously. By complementing an on-site location with off-premise catering, a restauranteur can gain greater efficiencies in the use of production equipment and professional staff, lower overall fixed costs of business, incrementally increase gross sales, increase cash flow and profits, achieve better efficiencies in purchasing, and gain a much broader customer base.

dual restaurant catering When a restaurant operator evolves into catering services to strategically increase the efficiencies of the base operation.

> Hoss's Steak and Sea House, founded in 1983 by Bill Campbell, is a 36-unit regional chain located in Pennsylvania and West Virginia. The restaurant concept is very much entrée-driven around steaks, seafood, and chicken, complimented with an unlimited soup/salad bar and dessert station, which is a big part of our business.
>
> Our banquet business is primarily done within the restaurant's four walls. Occasionally we will cater some outside special events, if needed, as we are really not set up to do off-premise events.
>
> The size of our buildings is really a benefit for us. We are able to service the banquet guest, private meetings, and our restaurant guests quite well, all at the same time. If we know in advance, we can reserve the banquet room, and sufficiently staff both the restaurant and the banquet area.

(continues)

(continued)

We have the benefit of being able to host large groups whereas other restaurants can't or may not want to handle the volume. Other restaurants are not set up to handle large groups. Their dining areas are equipped with two, four, and/or six-top tables that turn over during the course of service. It's a different operating philosophy of business, but it works well for us.

Our banquet services are used by a diverse group of guests. We host sporting banquets, wedding receptions, and funeral banquets, which are typically arranged through the funeral home.

The logistics of an on-premise function can be very detailed when planned in advance. Sometimes groups just show up, so we have to wing it, and do the best we can in the restaurant. In that case, the unexpected guests would just order from our restaurant menu.

We can create, for each client, a special banquet menu based on their needs. We also offer a standard banquet menu. It is more convenient for groups to use the standard banquet menu, especially if the event is billed on one check. A funeral banquet is a good example of a preplanned event billed to one check. In this case, we get a guaranteed guest count prior to the event and prepare accordingly. Although we try to suggest a special banquet menu, it depends on the group. Some groups like for their members to select an entree based on their own preference from our restaurant menu.

The competitive advantage of having the banquet space, especially if the guest uses a banquet menu, is to permit us to serve large banquets in prime time. We are able to prepare the banquet food in advance, and then serve it when the guests arrive. If we have a lot of people arrive without prior notice and order from the restaurant menu, then our service staff and kitchen may not be able to execute it well.

Both food and labor cost are two factors that affect banquet pricing in our restaurants. Because we have an unlimited salad bar with soups and desserts, we cannot always exactly control what our food cost is going to be, so we average it as best as we can. When we plan a banquet, we exercise more control over our cost of food because we serve portions and individual needs. Banquets help us to control our overall food cost in the restaurant.

Last year approximately 4 percent of total sales were derived from our banquet business. Banquet sales provide a real benefit for us. First, it helps us to accomplish our sales projections and financial goals. Second, we know the business is coming. Third, anytime we can do more business, it helps to drive down our labor and the fixed or overhead costs of doing business. Fourth, it brings first-time guests into our restaurants who then become loyal customers. Fifth, it helps us to operate our restaurants at full capacity.

Courtesy Robert Pleva

EXCLUSIVE CATERING RIGHTS

One of the most important strategic decisions for a successful off-premise function is the design of the menu. It is necessary to create a menu that will complement the equipment in the kitchen facility. Many caterers serve both on- and off-premise catering quite successfully. All Occasion Catering, Inc., is an example of a caterer who has facilities to handle both on-premise and off-premise functions simultaneously, catering off-premise events from 50 to 1,000 people.

All Occasion Catering, Inc., maintains exclusive dining rights in off-premise catering locations at local museums, cultural centers, grand halls, centers for the arts, historical mansions, conservatories, and social halls. Our market niche for off-premise functions is quite specialized: banquets and weddings, business meetings, exhibits/trade shows, private/corporate picnics, senior citizen functions, military and government events, and personal celebrations have all experienced our expertise.

Distinct competence in off-premise catering has given us a strategic advantage over many other caterers in the market. When a caterer is able to define a target market, a competitive advantage is developed that is difficult for others to copy. Because of our expertise, All Occasion Catering, Inc., is often called upon to service significant military, government, and other special community activities. Our ability to define our market and work toward exceeding our customer's needs has brought us several awards of honor.

Permission of John R. Smith

distinct competence
This is achieved when a caterer defines their target market exclusively and hones their skills to enable them to do something uniquely better than the competition. It also provides a competitive advantage that is difficult to copy or penetrate.

ON-PREMISE AND OFF-PREMISE COMBINATIONS

Although a distinction between on-premise and off-premise catering does exist, actual operations blend both types of catering so there is some fluctuation between on-premise and off-premise catering services. Many caterers may prepare their foods within their own facility and possibly use labor from another. Hotels and small restaurants may prepare food in their production kitchens and transport food off-premise to another location to serve their guests.

In many instances, a caterer may be selected to provide either off-premise or on-premise work. For on-premise catering to be successful, the caterer must know how many people can be comfortably seated in their facility. Can *entertainment* be provided? Can a wide variety of *menu items* be prepared efficiently at the last minute? The capabilities of getting food off the grill or out of the oven is a serious consideration. However, going off-premise to a facility may find the caterer feeding many people inside a building, 25 or 30 people in a *private home*, feeding two or three hundred people at a *church* facility, or even outside for a picnic or fundraising event. These are issues a caterer must consider.

A caterer must decide and determine, in advance, the specific *clientele* for their business. It is imperative that a caterer understands the relationship between the potential clients' needs, the caterer's knowledge base and skill levels, the event's labor requirements, and the facility's capabilities and availability.

Advantages and Disadvantages

While there is an advantage for both on-premise and off-premise catering, some inherent problems may occur. The distinct advantage of catering a banquet on-premise for 150 people is that everything is within reach. If an unforeseen problem strikes, a better opportunity to create a successful alternative may be implemented.

If a customer receives a steak they do not like, a caterer can immediately prepare another one. If serving at an off-premise location, this may not be an alternative. Because every job is different, experience teaches what has worked in similar circumstances in the past and will most likely work again in the present.

Private Parties

private-party catering
Many restaurants have separate rooms that can accommodate small groups for private parties such as bridal showers or retirement and award dinners. Off-premise caterers can service private parties at an individual's home.

Many restaurants will do on-premise work, but the size of the event they can accommodate depends on how many seats they have available. Some restaurants have separate rooms where customers can have private parties catered. If it is a small restaurant, they may offer **private-party catering** for 25 or 30 people. They could cater bridal showers, a small retirement dinner, or a small awards dinner for a special occasion. If the caterer did off-premise work, he could provide the same services by catering the event at an individual's home. The caterer might provide a mini menu such as hors d'oeuvres and sandwiches. If the caterer has access to a hotel where there is seating for hundreds of people, the options are completely different. This opens a window of opportunity for the caterer to offer multiple services for large weddings, business meetings, conventions, or trade organizations. Meetings can be held in one section of the hotel, while dinner and dancing can take place in another. These types of events are quite profitable for hotels and very important to the overall function of the facility.

Conventions and Weddings

convention catering One of the most profitable types of catering events. Distinguishing feature is the ability to simultaneously prepare and serve food and beverages to support professional, business, and social activities of a large group of people. These events are held in a closed environment, at a hotel or convention facility, using multiple meeting rooms and/or a large banquet or ballroom.

Wedding and **convention catering** are two of the most profitable events for caterers because of all the extra purchases that can be incorporated into a single event. A wedding will usually require wine and champagne, which is provided by the caterer; in addition, the caterer may also provide the wedding cake, the floral service, and the limousine service. The challenge for a caterer is to understand both the Jewish and Christian wedding ceremonies. Many caterers have a bridal consultant on staff to assist the prospective bride in her decisions. Often, caterers can receive a percentage of the money from those outside suppliers working with them, providing the caterer with additional profit. These multifaceted events are quite important for the caterer.

One-Stop Shop Catering

one-stop shop catering
A full-service catering operation that supplies the client with a choice of a variety of services designed to satisfy their needs, wants, and demands.

When building an off-premise or on-premise business, many caterers evolve into a full service or **one-stop shop** for the client. The caterer will work with rental companies to provide tables, chairs, tents, and limousine service (Figure 1-6). The client appreciates this worry-free service provided by the caterer.

Today, caterers can provide many additional services based upon the needs of the client. Many caterers will provide entertainment, photography, videography service, invitations, ice sculptures, and any other services needed for a memorable occasion. In addition, some caterers provide a champagne toast for the bridal party, disposable cameras placed on each table or at key locations around the reception area with same day development, wedding favors, personalized take-home money

Figure 1.6 Limousine vehicles vary in size, amenities, luxuries, style, and color, although most are black or white.

boxes, and flower preservation. A caterer may have worked out a program for a large corporation picnic to provide services such as entertainment for the children, registration of guests, and valet parking. The keys to success are understanding the customer's needs and determining how the caterer can better satisfy those needs.

The limousine industry has evolved over the past 100 years, and it continues to change to meet the needs of its riders. The first limousine appeared in 1902 and the stretch limousine was designed in 1928. Stretch limousines were often referred to as "big band buses" as their primary purpose was to transport bands and their equipment. Nowadays, limousines have multiple purposes. They are used for any and every occasion, such as proms, weddings, birthday parties, or simply a shopping day with the girls. Many different sizes and types of limousines are used today.

All limousines are bought as stock automobiles and are sent to a stretch company to be modified. Very few limousines are sold brand new to a private person. Limousines are traditionally longer but are mainly considered to be any chauffeured vehicle. This is why the vehicles vary so much in size, amenities, luxuries, style, and color, although most are black or white.

Five main styles of limousines exist: each is unique and serves a different purpose. The first is the traditional limousine. This vehicle has a longer frame with a rear oversized passenger compartment, offering a substantial amount of foot room. This larger area provides for a more comfortable ride. Some examples of traditional style limousines are London's Black Cabs and the Lincoln limousine that was used by the President of the United States.

(continues)

(continued)

A newer style of the traditional limousine is the modern limousine. Modern limousines can be created from just about any car model. These are designed to offer a more luxurious form of travel providing additional amenities. Some of the more popular car types used include Hummers, Mercedes-Benz, Jaguars, Bentley, Lincoln, and Rolls Royce. Unlike traditional limousines, modern limousines feature amenities such as flat screen televisions, disco balls, and bar areas. While modern limousines can be very costly, they are popular forms of transportation for proms, weddings, and celebrities.

The next style is a stage limousine. The stage limousine is technically not considered a limousine because of its design. A stage limousine has multiple doors that allow access to the forward facing seats. This style is mostly made from sedan cars and station wagons.

One of the more high-end limousine styles is the exotic limousine. This is the "ultimate" stretch limousine that adds special amenities to make its design unique and special. For example, some designs feature an additional supporting rear axle to support the weight of a hot tub. The exotic limousine is made from very luxurious and fast cars, such as Bentley, Cadillac, and Lexus. The larger limousines, such as Hummers and Lincoln Navigators, are stretched out to accommodate more people and larger parties. Exotic limousines are among the most expensive and are typically rented by celebrities or very important people.

The last style of limousine offered is the novelty limousine. The difference between novelty limousines and another style is that they are used for a specific purpose, such as transporting the bride and the groom from their wedding ceremony to the reception. They are typically very unique, one of a kind vehicles, often designed from older, restored antique cars. This style may also include remodeled trolleys to transport entire wedding parties.

Courtesy Benjamin Cavallaro

Mobile Catering

mobile catering A caterer who employs one or a fleet of trucks specially equipped to support an assortment of food and beverages for customers located at diverse locations, such as construction sites.

Another interesting facet of the catering segment is mobile catering. **Mobile catering** employs trucks that are equipped with a body that has built-in facilities, such as gas-fired coffee urns (Figure 1.7). Many mobile caterers have developed a seasonal menu and a picnic table concept on the back of their truck. It is necessary for their units to be approved by the local health department because of the many sites and types of foods they serve. Mobile caterers keep hot soups in the winter, and their fleet of 25–30 trucks are dispatched to a variety of sites and locations from construction sites to automobile dealerships. They furnish a wide assortment of hot or cold sandwiches, beverages, soup, coffee, doughnuts, bagels, burritos, and other menu items for the construction workers or mechanics to eat.

Seasonal Niche

seasonal niche Special events that may occur during a specific time or season of the year. One example is a county fair.

Off-premise catering opportunities will also enable many restaurants and hotels to develop a **seasonal niche**. Based upon the time and season of the year there are special events, some that occur on an annual basis, of which the caterer should be aware. These events may involve food such as barbequed chicken and ribs that are prepared at a restaurant or hotel and served off-premise. An advantage of this type of special event is that the restaurant gains publicity that will help build their client base.

Figure 1.7 Mobile catering units supply a variety of hot and cold items to their patrons.

Another advantage that a restaurant can experience by doing off-premise catering is the opportunity to serve more people than they can at their facility. A county fair might attract thousands of people requiring a great deal of planning, organizing, and menu writing. It is not impossible for a small restaurant that seats 40 people during the week to do an off-premise event serving 5,000 meals every Saturday at a fair or public event. The most important aspect to consider when planning and organizing this kind of service is the design of the menu.

The caterer arrives at the menu based on the needs of the client and what the kitchen equipment is designed to do in food preparation. A caterer cannot expect to do much sautéing without adequate burner space, or roasting without the necessary oven capacity. A caterer must understand that the design of the facility determines the ability to cater at an off-premise location and must be sure the food items on the menu match the production capability of the kitchen. Before selecting the type and categories of food for the menu, the caterer must have a clear understanding of the relationship between the equipment, production capability, and production scheduling.

Summer Outdoor Events

When catering summer off-premise jobs a caterer must be prepared in advance for the unexpected. Is the caterer prepared with the necessary resources if inclement weather threatens the event? The caterer needs to consider having tent rentals available for the day of the event, especially if the client does not have a rain date. Tents will be needed to protect the guests and the food. Additional production details must be coordinated to the type of menu and style of preparation.

QUESTIONS CATERERS NEED TO ASK

A caterer must make a decision to work with a client. Every caterer must develop a standard set of questions that will assist them in making this determination. See the Client Checklist below for a list of questions that may help a caterer decide whether or not to accept a function.

Location Considerations

To illustrate the importance of location in off-premise catering, a caterer agreed to cater an off-premise event at a familiar banquet hall. Unfortunately, days before the event, a fire erupted at this facility, rendering it unusable. The event was shifted to another location. At this new location, the function was held on its third floor. Therefore, the job became more difficult and demanding. Food, china, equipment, and supplies had to be transported up and down two flights of stairs. After this experience, the caterer never catered another event in this facility. This is a good legal example for a caterer to cite when including a clause in the contract that allows them to assess an extra fee.

Client Checklist

1. Is the location of the event conducive to the caterer's capabilities to produce the food and service necessary to satisfy the guests' needs?
2. Is the caterer comfortable with the management at the hall or facility? Is the caterer comfortable with the client? Is the caterer comfortable with the personalities?
3. Can the caterer work within the quoted budget specified by the guest?
4. Is the caterer's staff compatible with the hall's staff?
5. Was a background check completed on the financials of the hall and client?

When catering social events, especially in the client's home, the caterer must determine if there is enough area to effectively handle the invited guests. If 40 or 50 people will attend the event, is it possible to work in the home with that many guests? What is the size of the kitchen? Is room available to prepare the food and to get the food served properly and expeditiously?

HOME-BASED CATERERS

home-based caterer
A caterer who operates from their home facility.

One of the most challenging aspects of the catering business is the presence of **home-based caterers**—caterers who operate from their own homes. In many instances, these caterers may have limited experience, smaller insurance policies, and less knowledge in proper sanitation techniques. Operating out of the home may limit storage facilities, adequate refrigeration, proper food production, and equipment for holding hot food. Many of these home-based caterers are forced to learn techniques on the job. They have a small margin for error.

Tips from the Trade

To ensure food safety standards, the first thing a caterer needs to do is to understand the rules and regulations. It really does not matter if you are involved in Allegheny County, the state of Pennsylvania, or in the state of Nevada. It is all basically the same because we follow the Federal Food Model Code (http://www.fda.gov) regulations from the Food and Drug Administration (FDA). Those regulatory standards are guidelines. The regulations we enforce follow those FDA guidelines. First thing I have to say, other than following the FDA rules and regulations, is for caterers to get a license. There are a number of caterers who go into business and do not purchase a license. Once we find out about these caterers, I mean the regulatory authority, we have no other choice than to close them or to make sure they come up to standards. How do we get alerted to people catering from their homes? Well, we get calls from their clients or guests who have become sick from their catered event. Our first step is to identify the caterer. We try to look up the caterer in our records. When we find they are not registered with us, then we know they are working a catering business from their home. Now we get into legal action. We may have to take them to court because they are operating a business without a license. The first thing you need to tell a student who is studying catering is to do the right thing by getting a license.

There is a new emerging industry called the cottage industry. People who want to bake goods in their home kitchens and resale these baked goods to the public. Currently, health departments in the United States are in the process of writing regulations that will permit certain items to be baked in people's homes, such as cookies, brownies, jams, and jellies, and then allow them to sell these items to the public. Will they be required to operate with a license? At this time, probably not, as long as the home-based business owner registers with their local health department. We get approximately 20 calls each month from people who want to start a small business from their home.

Permission of Steve Steingart

Equipment

Home-based caterers are required by the FDA Food Code (http://www.fda.gov) and enforced by local health departments to have a separate kitchen in their homes. A private home, a room used as living or sleeping quarters, or an area directly opening into a room used as living or sleeping quarters may not be used for conducting food establishment operations. In fact, food prepared in a private home may not be used or offered for human consumption in a food establishment. This may be a disadvantage to the amount of money necessary to start, but on the other hand, may be an advantage because of the amount of equipment a home-based caterer can purchase. Their equipment may consist of a four-burner stove and a small domestic refrigerator. They may lack a commercial dish machine to sanitize the equipment. The local health departments have a concern over these sanitation issues. If the home-based caterer is preparing mayonnaise-based salads in the summer time, how will he or she hold it at the proper storage temperature (below 41°F)? What kind of transportation equipment will he or she use, a car or pick-up truck? A professional, licensed, insured caterer will most often own a refrigerated truck and will rent more as demand necessitates.

Professional Training

Another potential weakness of a home-based caterer is a lack of professional training for his or her staff. Many do not have the time or resources to adequately train staff in professional service techniques. In addition, they may not have workman's compensation coverage for their staff.

Home-based caterers can do a good job catering out of their home and charge less money than a licensed, professional caterer. They can handle small jobs between 50–100 people at less cost per plate than the licensed caterer. Many, however, are not equipped to handle large events.

Unfair Competitive Advantage

Home-based caterers are sometimes viewed as unfair competition to a licensed caterer because the professional caterer is required to have a license, must be inspected by the proper authorities, must conform to the rules and regulations of the health department, and many must have on-staff personnel certified in sanitation. The home-based caterer does not have these expenses or the overhead of having commercial equipment, professionally trained staff, and the required insurance coverage to compete in today's market.

Finally, it is important to understand that food prepared in a private home may not be used or offered for human consumption in a food establishment.

Summary

Restaurants and hotels are holding banquets on-premise, which permits these events to flow smoothly. The functions may be completed with fewer problems at an on-premise facility than an off-premise location because an on-premise event allows a caterer to have all the equipment at his or her complete disposal. At an off-premise event, a caterer has to know who is responsible for any cooking, if there is equipment available to heat the food, if the kitchen is large enough to get the food out to serve the guests, and if it is a dinner or stand-up cocktail party. The off-premise catering challenge does give a caterer more hassle, but many times the intrinsic reward and personal satisfaction of completing the event and satisfying the customer is well worth the effort.

Review Questions

Brief Answers

1. Identify and discuss features that distinguish on-premise catering from off-premise catering.
2. Define *catering management*. Discuss and provide examples of how catering fits into three general classifications of the food service industry.

3. Identify and discuss different types of catering events which may occur on-premise and/or off-premise.

4. Identify eight ways restauranteurs benefit from catering off-premise events.

5. Discuss how private or nonprofit caterers have a competitive *advantage* over the independent caterer.

6. Explain competitive *disadvantages* a private nonprofit caterer has compared to an independent caterer.

7. Identify the types of catering events a university-based caterer would execute on campus.

8. Discuss the role a *one-stop shop caterer* provides for a prospective bride and groom when planning their wedding.

9. Identify eight ways off-premise catering events can contribute to increased profitability for the restauranteur.

10. What are the key questions caterers must ask themselves before accepting off-premise functions?

11. Explain why the home-based caterer may be viewed as a competitive threat to the professional caterer.

Multiple Choice

Select the single best answer for each question.

1. Which of the following catering businesses would be found in the commercial segment of the food service industry?

   a. business/industry accounts

   b. college and university

   c. health care

   d. independent caterer

   e. diplomatic functions

2. When all required tasks, functions, and related services the caterer executes in preparation and implementation of the food and service for a client are done exclusively at the caterer's own facility, that is called _____ .

   a. off-premise catering

   b. on-premise catering

   c. corporate catering

   d. social catering

   e. recreational catering

3. Restauranteurs will pursue off-premise catering opportunities for which one of the following reasons?

   a. It raises the overall fixed costs of business.

   b. It incrementally increases gross sales.

   c. It will decrease cash flow.

   d. It will decrease the customer base.

   e. It will decrease purchasing efficiencies.

True or False

Read each of the following statements and determine if it is true or false.

1. The commercial segment of catering management represents the not-for-profit operations, which include business and industry, health care, and private clubs.
2. The evolution of supermarkets and their ability to provide catering service began when they first hired highly trained, certified chefs to upscale the food.
3. Off-premise catering is accomplished when the caterer transports all the food, serving products, and personnel to a location other than the building or facility where the food was prepared.

Putting It All Together

Visit an independent caterer, the catering department of a hotel or restaurant, a health care facility, college/university, or a home-based caterer. Identify and discuss the different types of catering events they have executed in the past year. Identify how their facilities benefit from catering off-premise events. Discuss how private or nonprofit caterers may have a competitive advantage over the independent caterer. Write a short report summarizing your visit.

Chapter 2

The Caterer and the Client

Permission of John R. Smith

Objectives

After studying this chapter, you should be able to:

1. Explain why a caterer's reputation may influence a potential client's decision.
2. Explain how clients select caterers.
3. Describe why referrals are important to a caterer.
4. Explain how developing a market, targeting it, and working toward it creates success.
5. Explain why a caterer may refuse catering jobs and clients.
6. Provide examples of unanticipated inconveniences a caterer may confront.
7. Provide examples of how a caterer can be safeguarded against unanticipated problems.
8. Explain corporate and social catering.

KEY TERMS

amusement park catering

corporate catering

creativity

fund-raising events

hidden costs

personality conflicts

primary caterer

referrals

reputation

secondary caterer

social catering

word-of-mouth advertising

Ingredients For Success

1 "Every customer served at the event is a possible referral."
2 "We cannot be all things to all people."
3 "Research every job."
4 "Build a relationship of trust."
5 "Everything must be 100 percent, 100 percent of the time."
6 "Never confuse being a nice person with being an astute business person."

WHY CLIENTS DECIDE ON A CATERER

It is important for a caterer to understand how the potential customer's decision-making process works. A potential client looking for a caterer who has the capabilities to do both on-premise and off-premise catering is certainly beneficial. There are many advantages that ultimately attract a potential customer. The caterer must understand how the needs of the customer will influence their decision to select the *right* caterer.

Reputation

reputation The character of the caterer, whether favorable or not, that is held by a customer. A customer's expectations predicated on the past performance of a caterer. One of the most important considerations a client uses to select a caterer.

One of the most important considerations a client uses in the decision-making process is a caterer's **reputation**. It is imperative that the caterer is reliable. There are four requirements when choosing a caterer:

1. Is the caterer well respected and well known?
2. Does the caterer do most of the catering in the client's area?
3. Are the customers satisfied?
4. Are clients recommending the caterer to others?

If all these issues are answered satisfactorily, the client can be confident in this decision-making choice (Figure 2.1).

POTENTIAL CLIENTS WILL SUBCONSCIOUSLY REVIEW THE FOLLOWING QUESTIONS FOR INFORMATION

1. How many people will attend the event? What is the maximum and minimum number of guests ever to attend their catered function?

2. Is the location convenient?

3. Will the caterer be able to serve the party in a timely manner?

4. Can the caterer take care of any unexpected needs?

5. Can the caterer exceed expectations? (A portfolio of pictures, testimonial letters, and thank you cards can be requested.)

6. Can the caterer solve problems? What procedures exist for emergencies?

7. Is the caterer reliable? Will the caterer supply references?

8. Does the caterer serve quality food and provide exceptional service? What are the prices?

9. Does the caterer use a contract? What are the policies?

10. How many years has the caterer been in business? How many years has the caterer been at this current location?

11. If the function must be canceled, what will happen to the deposit?

12. Can the food be sampled at a private taste-testing session?

© Cengage Learning 2014

Figure 2.1 Criteria for selecting a caterer.

The client must also meet and interview the caterer. This interview will help answer such questions as:

1. Is the client comfortable with the caterer?
2. Is the client comfortable with the caterer's personality?
3. Is the client comfortable with the caterer's suggestions and promises for the event?
4. Where does the client need the caterer to execute the function (location)?

When the client selects a caterer who has been in business for a long time, the caterer need not make false promises. His or her reputation, based on the business's track record, should be proven by a satisfied clientele.

Referrals

Referrals may be a caterer's best vehicle for advertising his or her skills and expertise. A referral in the catering trade occurs when a customer is satisfied with the quality and workmanship of the caterer. If the caterer satisfies their needs, clients will share their experiences with friends and associates.

referral(s) When a satisfied customer recommends a caterer to others.

> Jardine's Catering turned down numerous requests by prospective clients who were located too far from the location. We believed that the distance would hinder a successful job. One of the customers I worked for was an international cosmetic company. I did an upscale job for them in Pittsburgh, Pennsylvania. The company was so pleased with the work that they asked me to consider traveling to Washington, DC, to cater a breakfast or a brunch. It was to be a much larger job. This was just totally out of the question for Jardine's. It was their opinion that I could successfully execute this function 4 to 5 hours away in a different state, at a different facility. I recommended they select a caterer from that area. I believe they were trying to save money by having us do the job in addition to being pleased with our work.
>
> *Bill Jardine, Jardine's Farm Restaurant & Catering, Sarver, Pennsylvania*

Referral Concerns

Referrals also bring other issues to the caterer. One concern is when a referral is searching for something inexpensive. A good operator must rely on personal attributes and strengths in the preparation of food and delivery. The caterer must avoid competing with other organizations solely on price, but in contrast compete through his or her own expertise. There is always one client who is looking for a service that the caterer cannot provide for the price the client has in mind. For example, the client may prefer less service to satisfy preconceived cost estimates.

Satisfied clients who recommend a caterer to others become a caterer's best advertising agent (Figure 2.2). Remember, we cannot be all things to all people, and therefore it would be extremely difficult to attract a client who is shopping for a caterer with only one dimension: price. Those customers may be attracted to a caterer's competitor, the nonprofit organization.

Permission of John R. Smith

Figure 2.2 Satisfied customers will share their experiences with others.

Word of Mouth

word-of-mouth advertising A type of referral when a satisfied customer recommends the caterer to others.

Word-of-mouth advertising is the best type of advertising for a caterer. If the client is bragging about the job executed by a caterer, the person in need of a catering service will get excited. A potential client may believe that the caterer is as good as a friend says. Satisfied customers are always willing to recommend a caterer they are excited about. Current functions, as well as future jobs, offer the opportunity to attract new customers from the guests in attendance. This introduces *Ingredient for Success 1: "Every customer served at the event is a possible referral."* Guests can be impressed with the food, service, or the caterer's attitude displayed during the function. For this purpose, it is important for the caterer to project a positive attitude regarding the presentation of food and related services. A satisfied client will potentially tell at least three friends, family members, or business associates.

Many caterers are successful at creating new business through referrals from their current clients. Several jobs were acquired because a pleased CEO, who was golfing with his peers, bragged about the exceptional job a caterer had done for him. This kind of recommendation is a compliment to the caterer and ensures continued business growth. It is estimated that one satisfied customer will relate this experience to 3 others; however, an unsatisfied customer will tell 11 other people.

DECIDING WHETHER TO TAKE THE EVENT

An important rule to guide your decision to pursue taking on a catering function is *Ingredient for Success 2: "We cannot be all things to all people."* This ingredient cannot be stressed enough.

A caterer must determine, in advance, the specific market niche to establish for the business, then develop the market, target it, and work toward it. Since caterers cannot be all things to all people, it is imperative to understand the relationship between potential clients and their needs, the caterer's knowledge base and skill levels, labor requirements, and facility resources and availability. Developing a market, targeting it, and working toward it will help the caterer create the best plan and contribute to his or her success as a caterer.

We must recognize that a caterer can perform different on-premise tasks more easily than can be performed at an off-premise location. One must attempt to understand the natural characteristics of food. Foods differ in how they are handled, stored, prepared, and served. A caterer must know the effect heat will have on the quality of food while being held on a hot serving line or in refrigeration. A sauce should never be made that cannot withstand the required holding period for an off-premise function (See Chapter 7). Because of the nature of some foods, they are better if they are prepared at the last minute. If catering a breakfast event, it is best to do "eggs to order" rather than preparing them ahead of time and transporting them to an off-premise location.

Personality Conflicts

There are times when a caterer must refuse jobs based on lack of comfort with the client. **Personality conflicts** *will* exist. The caterer must also follow intuitive feelings when it is obvious how impossible it would be to meet a client's expectations because of extreme demands. Therefore, when a caterer develops a potential customer list and client base, mutual respect should be perceived on all levels.

personality conflicts An unexplainable dislike of the client based on the intuitive feeling of the caterer, formed by the initial interview, that causes the caterer to refuse the function.

Unanticipated Inconveniences

A caterer must always be vigilant and mentally prepared when confronted with unanticipated inconveniences while executing an off-premise assignment.

Bad Politics

One unanticipated inconvenience a caterer may experience is the unpleasant sting of *bad politics*. The following illustration best describes this situation. A caterer is contacted to provide the food for a client who has rented a hall for their special event. The caterer is a third party to the event. The caterer prepares for the event and arrives at the facility with the understanding the caterer is to have full use of the kitchen and production area. Upon the caterer's arrival, the caterer discovers that the kitchen and production areas are locked. Apparently a dispute between the client and the facility's management caught the caterer in a bad position. The caterer must develop creative alternatives to serve the food and provide the best service possible.

Hidden Costs

Another potential problem occurs when the off-premise caterer encounters additional *hidden-to-the-client* expenses from the rented facility's management. These **hidden costs** are not usually discussed with the client who rents the catering hall or banquet facility.

The client has made a contract with the management of the banquet hall and has paid the rental fee for its use. The management of this facility contacts the caterer and demands an additional *catering fee* per plate while they are in the

hidden costs Any unknown (to the client) costs levied against the caterer for providing food and related services in a third-party owned catering hall.

banquet facility. The caterer may have already agreed to the price per plate with the client. The client has already paid the rental for the facility but the management levies an additional charge on the caterer for doing business in the hall. If the caterer is overwhelmed with these hidden charges, they have one of two choices: the caterer can absorb the additional cost per plate or can modify the client's original contracted agreement. At this point, the contract must be voided and renegotiated to accommodate the additional charge. This could anger the client, who has already paid for the hall and was not informed of any additional costs.

Gratuities

Another dilemma may occur when people are looking for financial compensation that was not included in the contract. When the caterer is contracted by a third party to enter a banquet hall and serve the food, often the catering hall uses their own service staff and/or bartenders to serve the food or beverages. The caterer is notified by the hall's management to contribute a gratuity for the bartenders and servers. This additional fee, however, could be kept by the management team and never find its way to the servers.

What Experience Teaches

How can a caterer safeguard against these poor business practices?

Explore Options

Caterers have to explore all options. Someone will say that they have cooking facilities, but their idea of cooking facilities may be a two-burner hot plate. Touring the facility before the event is scheduled is important to help determine what options are available at an off-premise facility. Make sure all things are in place *before* the event to avoid getting caught in an unsatisfactory situation.

Research the Job

Caterers have to research every job. ***Ingredient for Success 3: "Research every job."*** The caterer must be aware of and understand all situations that can potentially occur at the event. Food service, personnel, the type of service be it buffet or sit-down, and the china must be decided in advance. A well-planned catered function should include a schedule that specifies when the event will happen, where the event will happen, and how jobs will be completed.

Experience is the best teacher. Experience of handling food teaches one, over time, how much effort is required for each recipe being prepared. This is how to determine the prep work. The caterer may have to schedule prep work the day before or even on the same day of the function. Other factors that affect prep work include the quantity of food being prepared; type of production equipment available; amount of storage space, including cold storage; and complexity of the recipes.

Avoid problems by being completely organized, especially if it is an off-premise catering function. If something is forgotten, it may be difficult to return to the premise. To eliminate that potential problem, make checklists of what you have to do.

Everything is generated from the menu, based on what you are going to cook. You start with a list of all ingredients for every item to be cooked. The first list is a shopping list. The next list is the prep list. The prep list is very important, especially when you are working with inexperienced help. I have prepared these recipes so many times that I have everything stored in my head. Although I know what needs to be done, my staff needs direction. I have to make a prep list and itemize what needs to be done for each recipe. The list will be based on the pre-prep required for both the day before and the day of the event.

For example, we catered a fund-raising event for a political candidate at an off-premise location. We set up 12 action stations for 600 people. It was a lot of volume for each one of these stations. Depending on the recipe and the menu, the amount of prep work varied. One item served was a goat-cheese wonton. We made this item the day before the event. The goat cheese mix was very easy to make and we assembled the wontons. We had a lilikoi (also known as passionfruit) wasabi dipping sauce that was prepared the day before and stored. Everything was ready the day before, completing the prep work. So you have your checklist done. Everything on that checklist is out of the way. Now, on the day of the event, all you have to do is get to the event, set up, and cook. This becomes another checklist.

Based on the recipe, what equipment will you need to take to the event? To make the equipment list, I recommend building your equipment from the floor up! To begin, I need three banquet tables. I need tablecloths and skirting. I need a big, thick cutting board because the burner holding the wok that is cooking the wontons will burn through the table cloths into the table without it. What is next? What type of safety equipment is needed? You should have a first-aid kit in case someone gets burned, and a fire extinguisher in case of fire. Either bring a fire extinguisher with you or make sure one is close by at the cooking site. Always make sure you are permitted to have an open flame at the site. Next, the caterer transports the cooking oil to the event in a clean plastic container, but how will the caterer bring it back? This cooking oil is now at 300°F. When you are finished with the event, you will want to leave right away. You do not want to wait 3 hours for the oil to cool down. A very large pot should be added to the equipment list. This pot must be larger than the amount of oil needed to transport back. Pour it into the pot and cover it. Make sure the pot is not filled more than one-third.

An important catering task is to make these checklists. First, the food, then the prep work, next the actual cooking, and finally, the equipment list. On the day of the event, make sure you have the checklist. As everything is being packed into the truck or van, it should be checked off. This job should be assigned to one person. Each time I have an event, this job is mine because I want to make sure that I am not going to be missing anything. I do not take anything for granted. Many times I have heard employees say "Yes, we got it, let's go, let's go." Then you get to the site, and the employee says "Oh, I must have forgotten it, Chef." Then you go back to the home base and find it sitting on the loading dock. I prefer a *double checklist*. One checklist that verifies that I have procured the item from the storeroom or kitchen, and the second checklist is used to verify that I actually saw it get on the truck. This system helps to ensure that everything you need gets on the truck including hand towels, fuel, lighter, and matches. I have forgotten matches to light the fuel for the chafing dishes many times. You get to the site and guess what? No one has any matches if no one smokes. Making sure everything is on the list is the best way to prevent a last minute crisis. Then, if you have last minute problems, they are usually surmountable and you can deal with them.

Henry Holthaus, Certified Executive Chef/Instructor, Culinary Institute of the Pacific, Honolulu, Hawaii

Wedding Packing List

1. Table cover * Always check to see if an alternate color is being used.

2. Plates – Salad bowls – Fruit Cups – Cake Plates – Coffee Cups

3. Caterwrap Rolled cutlery Kit or Reflections

4. Basket of Cake Forks

5. Fan folded Napkins and White linen napkins for Bride and Groom

6. White Napkins for Cake – Bev Naps for Cookie Table

7. Ashtrays

8. Bud Vases with Flowers *Always check the invoice to see if needed

9. Linen cloths and Skirting * Check skirt chart for sizes needed

10. Greenery – Candelabras – Candles

11. Real Silverware for people at Head Table

12. Champagne Glasses for Head Table

13. Waitress Trays or Oval Trays if cake is to be served

14. Trays and Doilies for cookies. * Check to see if party is having cookies.

15. Scissors and Tape

16. Business Cards – Comment Card – Reserve Signs (if requested)

17. Chafing Racks – Water Pans – Lids – Sterno – Matches

18. Serving Utensils and Cake knife

19. Crocks – Ladles and Tongs for Tossed Salad (check menu)

20. Coffee Urn (make sure all parts are in urn)

21. Bags of Coffee – Coffee Filter

22. Basket of Tea Bags – Pot to boil and serve hot water

23. Baskets for Rolls – Butter – Condiments – Sugar – Creamers

24. Tray for bread if a deli tray is ordered

25. Salt and Pepper Shakers (**2** sets fairly full)

26. Bowl of parmesan cheese with spoon (if needed)

27. Take Out Containers – Foil – Saran – Plastic Serving Spoons

28. Soap – Towels – Scrubbies – Rubber Gloves – Thermometer

29. Garbage Bags

30. Pots for scooping – extra ½ pans ect. (check with cooks for what you will need)

31. Pots of Gravies or Sauces with Ladles

32. If Hor d Oerves were ordered get Picks – B&B's – Bev Naps

Food Items

1. Sugars – Sweet & Low – Creamers
2. Butters
3. Dressings
4. Champagne (1 bottle per 8 p.p. at Head Table)
5. Rolls or Bread
6. Mustard and Mayo (if needed)
7. Food Items *Always use invoice when loading food.

Check to see how we are to handle the cake parts after you cut the cake.

Packing List for Plate-Ups

1. Table Cover (if tables are not covered)
2. Plates – Salad Bowls – Fruit Cups – Cake Plates – Coffee Cups (Masterpiece if ordered)
3. Forks – Knives – Napkins – Spoons – Cake Forks (Reflections if ordered)
4. Basket of Teaspoons for coffee table – Basket of Cake Forks
5. Extra Napkins for Desserts
6. Bud Vases with Flowers (if needed)
7. Coffee Urn (check for all parts) & coffee (if ordered)
8. Pots for Tea Water
9. Plastic Drink Cups – Ice Bucket and Scoop (if pop was ordered)
10. Trays and Doilies for Desserts
11. Serving Utensils – Cake Knife – Extra Utensils for Desserts
12. Crocks – Ladles – Tongs (for tossed salad if ordered)
13. Salt and Pepper Shakers
14. Baskets for tables for rolls and butters
15. Baskets for Creamers – Sugar – Condiments (for coffee table)
16. Scissors – Tape (if needed)
17. Business Cards – Comment Card
18. Disposables – Foil – Saran – Plastic Serving Spoons
19. Soap – Towels – Scrubbies – Rubber Gloves – Thermometer
20. Garbage bags

Figure 2.3b Sample catering packing list for plate-up service.

Food Must Be Checked with Invoice

Check each rack to insure that all cold food items on your invoice are included.

Know the Customer

Caterers need to get to know their customers. It is possible to cater a dinner with fine china, glassware, silver, and no facilities out in the middle of a meadow as long as the caterer is prepared and willing to do so. The key to doing these events is to design some kind of checklist to organize and plan all activities and equipment needs before arriving at the event. Figure 2.3 illustrates examples of checklists that a caterer may use.

Date:

Name:	Hot Entrees:	Cold Entrees:
People: Time:		
Type:		

Name:	Hot Entrees:	Cold Entrees:
People: Time:		
Type:		

Name:	Hot Entrees:	Cold Entrees:
People: Time:		
Type:		

Name:	Hot Entrees:	Cold Entrees:
People: Time:		
Type:		

Permission of John R. Smith

Figure 2.3c Kitchen bulletin board worksheet.

TYPES OF CATERING

Professional caterers have distinct types of catering functions in which they can become involved. We can identify all catering functions and place them into two categories, known as *off-premise* and *on-premise*. All catering functions can be identified further as either corporate catering or social catering. One advantage of a catering business is the caterer can decide in advance on the kind of catering function and the clientele to be serviced. A caterer can have the opportunity to aggressively pursue either category. The caterer is in control to select the preferable kind of catering function.

Corporate Catering

Corporate catering is a wonderful form of catering where the professional caterer will build a clientele comprised of large or small corporate and business accounts. These corporate catering events can vary depending on the situation. Many caterers decide to specialize in corporate catering.

One corporate caterer named his business *Strictly Business Catering*. His business strictly caters breakfasts and lunches to small business organizations. This type of caterer does not do any socially catered events. Examples of corporate catering events encompass employee training sessions, board of directors' luncheons, and company-specific picnics for employees and their families.

Organizations will select a caterer based on specific needs and the function they must perform. One advantage of corporate catering is a continual need for food at corporate sponsored events.

One cannot stress enough the importance of *Ingredient for Success 4: "Build a relationship of trust."* Corporate accounts will usually notify the caterer to prepare for an event in 30 or 60 days for 100 people and instruct them to "just invoice us with the costs." This is one advantage of building a relationship based on *mutual trust.*

Relationships Built on Mutual Trust

A second advantage for the caterer is avoiding a bidding war against other caterers. Once the business relationship has been established, and the customer knows what can be done, the client will usually call and give a date. This is done to avoid the hassle of putting the event out for a bid. The building of trust is a mutual process based on what the caterer can do for the client and what the client can do for the caterer.

A disadvantage of having to bid on events against other caterers happens because one caterer will provide "extra" things, such as service, that another caterer is not equipped to do.

corporate catering The professional caterer's target market is a clientele of corporate and business accounts such as meetings, ceremonies, anniversaries, recognition dinners, training sessions, seminars, conventions, and other related events.

Jardine's Catering began its service to the corporate segment with a picnic for 1,800 guests attending a banking organization's function. Eventually they merged with another bank and Jardine's began to supply food for employee training programs. Jardine's Catering usually catered lunch for between 50 and 100 employees involved in each training class. In addition, at the end of each one-day training program, Jardine's would serve them a steak dinner. Often, they would be contracted to provide two and sometimes three meals a day for the bank's employees. On many occasions, Jardine's also provided either a continental breakfast or a full

primary caterer Handles approximately 75 percent of a client's total catering need.

secondary caterer This caterer manages approximately 25 percent of a client's catering needs. Often maintained to back up the primary caterer.

Financial Security

Money is another advantage of catering to the corporate segment. The profit is better and is more guaranteed than in social catering. It is very seldom that a caterer ever loses money when catering for a corporation. Caterers pursue corporate accounts because of the willingness of the corporation to issue money up front to the caterer in the form of a deposit. Once a relationship built on trust is created, deposits will become a part of the standard operating procedures that a caterer will establish with the client as part of the business agreement.

Corporate Fund-Raising Sponsorship

Another important catering segment is the power of corporate support. It might be an advantage for a caterer to participate in certain types of corporate **fund-raising events** where food and related services can complement their efforts. Usually, corporate accounts support their fund-raising activities at different times during the year. Once they establish an event, it will be supported annually and often continues to grow in size each year. The following illustration describes how many caterers are able to grow their businesses by catering fund-raising events.

One caterer may be the primary caterer for a charitable organization. A cultural event, such as a concert, may be held in the summer in any city. The production area would be set beneath a huge tent and the caterer would provide the food, related services, and equipment. The caterer may even be required to supply drinking water. Everything can be supplied in relationship to tents, tables, linens, and silverware. A caterer must understand costs because tent rentals and related services will drive up the price per person for this type of event. It is not unusual for a specialized corporate event to cost as much as $100 per person.

The cost of such an event varies based on many factors. The client can spend a lot of money for a very elegant event. A caterer may charge up to $40 per person depending upon the charitable organization's budget. The fund raiser probably

fund-raising events Usually catering services are required to support various fund-raising events sponsored by the corporate community. These provide excellent business opportunities for a caterer.

generates about a 50 percent profit based on the ticket prices. Many charitable organizations raise ticket prices depending on response.

A corporate caterer may also cater events such as corporate-sponsored family picnics, employee meetings, and corporate appreciation dinners. Sometimes these more elaborate events incur a huge cost for the caterer so the corporate clientele should be made aware of all costs. They will pay the agreed upon price for a caterer to come into their facilities and satisfy their needs. For the corporate account, money is often no object as long as they are getting value for their dollar with no surprise costs.

Creativity and the Caterer

The corporate caterer can also enjoy success by weaving **creativity** into each event. Creativity is used to exceed the customers' needs and satisfaction. The art of being creative is important in catering. It is especially important when the caterer builds a relationship with a corporate account. A primary caterer is challenged to create enthusiasm for the guests attending a corporate function. They must often fascinate the same group of people.

The primary caterer for a corporate account must anticipate and plan for the evolution of the relationship. The expectations will change as the client's needs change. A subtle pressure to reinvent each function will challenge the caterer as their relationship with the client evolves.

The first event will probably be a typical dinner. The menu may offer a choice of chicken or roast beef. After a few similar events, a comfortable relationship is built on trust. The primary caterer's challenge is to keep the client's event successful. To remain the primary caterer, the excitement and the participants' anticipation for the event must be maintained. The next step in the evolutionary process is for the primary caterer to plan the function around a theme-based dinner.

The next corporate event may be a fund-raising dinner on Saint Valentine's Day. The primary caterer may use the Saint Valentine's theme and have the wait staff dress in tuxedos with red cummerbunds and bow ties. Approximately 250 people will attend the fund-raising event. Instead of having a formal dinner, as was common practice in past years, the primary caterer can design food stations, designed to provide food and desserts, at various locations in the banquet facility. One station may offer only assorted appetizers; another station, a variety of entrees including carving stations. A variety of delicious desserts may be offered at another station. These stations will be staffed and restocked with food and beverages all night. An orchestra, dancing, and entertainment will complement the food stations. The guests can dance, select food, and mingle for an active, successful event.

One can imagine the excitement for the very next fund-raising event. The client so enjoyed the theme-based dinner that he wanted it to continue. The primary caterer was now further challenged. The customer's needs and expectations had been changed by the innovative caterer. A good caterer will strive to exceed customer expectations and will educate the client. A caterer must continue professional growth.

The primary caterer's employees can play an important role in the development of these theme-based dinners (Figure 2.4). Innovation and creativity will excite the staff as well as the client. Research the topic. Ask for employees' ideas—have a general brainstorming session. It is important for a caterer to have someone on the staff with decorating talents to create those memorable, unusual events.

creativity Combination of imagination, ability, and understanding customer needs to create excitement, wonder, and anticipation for the client attending a catering event.

Figure 2.4 Creative catering ideas evolve from a common theme.

> Every event is different. Every client has a different vision of what they want their event to look like. As the event coordinator, you must listen to the client and visualize their needs. The coordinator must be able to translate the guest's wishes into an operations procedure to realize the event. Occasionally, a client may have a very vague sense of what they are looking to achieve. It is the coordinator's responsibility to guide them toward a look, which includes a decor and room setup to satisfy both the client's needs and the event itself. This may require you to think outside of the box. To be effective, one must have a very clear understanding of food, beverage, service, and design options to offer the client. Being able to customize your services creatively to exceed the client's needs creates a valuable negotiating tool.
>
> *Courtesy Skytop Lodge*

During the brainstorming stage, employees may suggest the following themes: a county fair, a circus, a hobo camp, dinner on a dining car, the Roaring '20s, or opening day at the baseball stadium. The next fund-raising theme selected by the client may be the circus theme. The circus theme can be featured throughout the entire event. Clown outfits may replace the official uniform. Each table may have a carousel horse as its centerpiece. The *medicine wagon* will serve as the beverage display. The guests may pass through the midway on their way to tables under the big top. They can stop and play games. The music of the calliope steam organ, and the aroma of popcorn, cotton candy, and fresh food will certainly elevate the guests' desire to participate in the event. The fun house will surprise and amuse.

The following year, the client may select an old-fashioned farm hoedown theme. The caterer may emphasize the fact that the event is being held in the middle of a farm. Set the theme in the catering hall as if the event was being held "in the middle of a meadow." The old buckboard may be used as the beverage station. Decorate the buffet table with wild flowers and miniature bales of hay. Decorate the service area with antique farm equipment and tools, such as an old-fashioned plow. Every detail is planned to simulate a farm environment with straw hats and overalls replacing the official uniform.

Chamber of Commerce

A caterer can begin building a client base by contacting the local Chamber of Commerce. The Chamber of Commerce usually sponsors events such as membership drives, golf outings, and fund raisers. These events help the caterer get established. A caterer can establish relationships and develop a reputation from these events. It takes a professional, organized caterer with accurate knowledge and understanding of the business to produce and execute to the nth degree.

Amusement Park Catering

Another option for the caterer pursuing a corporate account is **amusement park catering**. An amusement park may offer more than 100 different eating establishments for the guests who are enjoying the park. Amusement parks cater to corporations and similar businesses that have their annual *day at the park* each summer. These organizations will bring employees and their family members totaling between 50 and 1,500 people. On any given day, multiple corporations will converge on the amusement park's picnic shelters. These organizations need a lunch or dinner for their group. Because of the volume, amusement parks cannot usually handle all of those requests so they will hire an outside caterer.

A caterer must understand the following mechanics before getting involved with an amusement park. First, always begin with the menu. What kind of food does the guest want? Do they want typical picnic foods such as charcoal-grilled hot dogs and hamburgers, or chicken with watermelon and lemonade? Will the caterer supply the decorations, such as red-checkered paper table covers? Will the caterer be responsible for organizing games for the children and adults?

amusement park catering This is a dimension of corporate catering. The management of an amusement park may cater their own functions internally or may outsource the responsibility of providing the food and related service for all on-premise catering events to an independent caterer.

Cost and Profit Relationship

An important consideration for the caterer is the price. The caterer must understand how the amusement park will charge the guest. Usually, the guest will pay a flat price to enter the park. This one price must include the entry fee, use of the park's facilities, and the lunch. Always do the calculations and understand all expenses. If the park charges only a flat price, make sure the caterer's profit is built into this single price. If the caterer's profit is not included, a separate price should be charged by the caterer for each guest served.

A common problem occurs when a caterer agrees to become the primary caterer for an amusement park without fully understanding the true relationship between revenue and expenses. The caterer should never neglect the research needed to ascertain this important relationship. There are two important considerations to evaluating the cost and profit relationship.

1. Make sure the job can be done at the right price. If quoting a price in January for the exclusive right for the summer contract, accurately forecast and predict expenses based on real costs. Some caterers can lose money on these types of arrangements.

2. Make sure the organization is established before pursuing this type of business. Research the event. Explore every detail. This type of an arrangement will require considerable planning.

While working inside the amusement park, park policy may not permit the caterer to engage in any form of advertising. However, they may permit napkins or matches that have the caterer's name or logo on them. It all may depend on what organization is using the facilities. The main reason for not permitting any form of advertising by the primary caterer is the park wants the guest to believe they are providing the food and service themselves.

Social Catering

Social catering is a distinctive field with its own characteristics. Having the event held in a guest's house is one distinguishing facet of social catering. As a social caterer, never promise anything that cannot be done. Clients may ask the caterer for special requests, and at times, clients will be persistent. They may even just tell the caterer, "Research it and do it!" In every situation, a caterer must remain in control and must be comfortable with saying to the client, "We are unable to do that."

A caterer may have friends or clients from a country other than the United States. These visitors may have different food and cultural habits than what a caterer can produce. Weddings are a good example. A caterer may be approached by someone with Asian food and cultural habits. If this happens, the caterer can work with an authentic Asian chef. The Asian chef prepares the Asian cuisine for the bride's family and Asian friends, while the caterer can prepare and serve American-style food. This joint venture between the caterer and Asian chef will provide the specialized knowledge to exceed this customer's needs.

If the caterer is lacking the knowledge, expertise, skill, facilities, equipment, or information to execute a specific function, they should avoid it. If attempting to prepare a specific cuisine without the adequate skills or knowledge base, the caterer, even in his or her goodwill attempt, can create a disaster. This will guarantee the loss of the client as well as any potential future business. *Ingredient for Success 5* sums up this concept: *"Everything must be 100 percent, 100 percent of the time."*

Client's Home

Planning a social function in a client's home can be a challenge. A caterer's role is more than just providing the food, beverages, and related services. A caterer must educate a client. The client must be taught the proper etiquette of being *mine host* when ceremoniously entertaining friends or strangers in one's home. From the time a guest enters the home until he departs, the host is responsible for satisfying their social and physiological needs. In other words, the host is responsible for the guests' complete comfort and happiness. Some truly great caterers orchestrate the entire function. They will educate the client in the etiquette of being a proper host and guide the host step-by-step without the knowledge of the invited guests.

Selecting the Guests. The first and perhaps most important responsibility is to select the appropriate guests. Proper care in consideration of this list begins with the approximate number of guests who can comfortably be serviced in the home. The actual selection of the guests must be based on the mutual compatibility of each guest. Even when the occasion requires a group of strangers to socialize in one's home, it is still important for the group to be harmonious. They must have the ability to be cordial to each other. Next, the budget for the event must be finalized. The budget should reflect the host's style of living. At this step, the caterer can guide the host in making realistic decisions. Making the right decision is based on the constraints dictated by the budget, layout of the home, available kitchen appliances, the number and social status of the invited guests, and finally, the ability of the caterer to provide the right food and service. These factors will influence the final cost.

Individualized Plan. A caterer must strive to individualize each plan to meet the needs of the host. Never blindly apply the same social plan to each client. Promise what can be done well while considering the environment, budget, and available resources at the function. Remember, executing a simple plan of delivering a simple menu that provides the highest quality food and service has the basic ingredients for success. A simple plan can always satisfy the needs of a host. Avoid complex plans that simply sound good and create unrealistic customer expectations. Customer expectations based on unrealistic plans lead to poor food quality, bad service, and dissatisfied clients. Worse, it can lead to an embarrassed host whose reputation becomes damaged.

In the long-lived spirit of hospitality, a caterer's duty is to always follow a simple, well-designed plan based on a host's style of living, guided by a well-defined budget, and tailored to exceed the guests' needs.

Special Care. If catering an event in a client's home, always treat the home with special care. Use the *white glove* approach. Be alert and cognizant of the production and service staff activities, the host, and their guests at all times. Be aware of the flow of service and observe each guest's behavior. If a guest has a glass, make sure it is not set down on a piece of furniture and offer ashtrays to smokers so they do not drop a cigarette on the carpet. These and other similar problems do occur and can happen at any time. Even if someone would not drop a cigarette on a floor, a caterer must have the staff trained to anticipate this type of guest behavior.

As in all catering situations, the caterer must anticipate each guest's needs. If, while catering a stand-up party, a guest has an empty plate, a staff member must be trained to immediately relieve the guest of this soiled plate and fork. If the guest has an empty glass, does it need to be refilled or retrieved? Do the ashtrays need to be replaced with clean ones?

Disadvantages of Social Catering

There are some disadvantages of social catering. One disadvantage may be the caterer's limited capabilities to satisfy the often unrealistic demands of the client. Sometimes, without fault of the caterer, it may be impossible to satisfy a client. Therefore, it is important for the caterer to research and understand the customer's needs before accepting a job. A social caterer must be selective and realistic as to what can be accomplished based on the capabilities of the client's home.

When planning a social event to be held in a client's home, a caterer will need to seek the following information.

1. What is the purpose of the social event? Is the event an intimate dinner for 10–12 people or a cocktail party for 35–40 people?

2. What can be supplied by the caterer or the client?

3. Will the caterer require bartenders and adequate bar supplies? In most situations, the customer must supply their own liquor.

4. Will the caterer's insurance provide adequate protection for the staff as well as the guests? Did the caterer consider the legality of liquor liability? Will the homeowner have special insurance coverage for his or her own party?

5. Has the client made any last minute, out-of-the-ordinary special requests? If so, this is an opportunity for the caterer to generate incremental revenue. Sometimes, as the event approaches, a client, in his or her need to impress the guests, will have last-minute, panic requests to ensure the success of the event.

6. Are the details of the contract specifically spelled out (see Chapter 14)? A common request made by a client is for the celebration to continue beyond the contracted agreement.

What happens when the client requests an additional 2 hours for the event? A caterer must be prepared for these requests by having this spelled out in advance in the language of the contract. A contingency plan must be established so when this request is made, the caterer can implement the request. Basically, if the caterer extends the celebration, overtime charges will be assessed. The client must understand the pricing formula used to calculate the final bill. Overtime charges may also generate additional revenues and hidden profits for the caterer.

A caterer must understand the human nature of the client. The successful caterer should consider studying consumer behavior as it relates to the event and their request of services. Caterers may be bombarded with additional requests during the execution of the event. Make sure the specific details are spelled out and agreed upon by the client and the caterer in the contract. A caterer must refrain from deviating from the contract, especially if this action will incur a loss of revenue. This introduces ***Ingredient for Success 6: "Never confuse being a nice person with being an astute businessperson."***

Summary

The process of selecting a caterer is influenced by multiple factors. A positive reputation may give a competitive advantage in the market. Both referrals and positive word-of-mouth advertising provide excellent opportunities for new business. Working to define the customer based on similar needs helps the caterer develop the market. Researching each job can help to selectively create a preferred customer list that may eliminate undesirable clients.

The professional caterer can work at either an on-premise or off-premise site, in a corporate or social environment. The corporate segment provides financial security, long-lasting relationships, and the challenge of designing creative events. Social catering, primarily held in the client's home, is a distinctive field having its own characteristics. Formulating individualized, simple plans that consider the environment, budget, and available resources are ingredients for success. Building a trusting relationship with the corporate or social client ensures long-term prosperity.

Review Questions

Brief Answers

1. Identify and discuss features that distinguish corporate catering from social catering.
2. Describe some common attributes that a client may use to select a caterer.
3. Discuss why reputation is one of the most important attributes of a successful caterer.
4. Define *referral*.
5. Discuss why *word of mouth* is one of the most powerful advertising techniques for the successful caterer.
6. Identify examples of *unanticipated inconveniences* a caterer may confront.
7. Discuss some types of *hidden costs* the caterer may experience when catering at an off-premise location.
8. Explain how experience will prepare a caterer for the challenges of business.
9. Define a *primary caterer* and *secondary caterer*.
10. What are the advantages of catering in the corporate sector?
11. Discuss how creativity can provide a caterer with a business edge in the corporate sector.
12. Discuss the role a caterer can play in catering for an amusement park.
13. Discuss the distinct characteristics found in catering in the social sector.
14. Discuss the challenges of catering in a client's home.
15. Discuss the Ingredients for Success and explain what these mean to you.

Multiple Choice

Select the single best answer for each question.

1. This form of catering identifies a clientele consisting of business accounts.
   a. corporate catering
   b. social catering
   c. health care catering
   d. independent caterer
   e. primary caterer
2. A caterer who handles approximately 75 percent of a client's business is called:
   a. off-premise caterer
   b. secondary caterer
   c. corporate caterer
   d. social caterer
   e. primary caterer
3. The distinguishing facet of this type of catering is that the event is held in the client's home.
   a. secondary catering
   b. primary catering
   c. corporate catering
   d. social catering
   e. nonprofit catering

True or False

Read each of the following statements and determine if it is true or false.

1. Positive *word-of-mouth* advertising is often considered a very powerful way to promote a caterer.
2. One of the most important considerations a client faces in the decision-making process of selecting a caterer is the caterer's reputation.
3. The distinguishing feature of social catering is that the event is held at the corporate client's place of business.

Putting It All Together

Visit an independent caterer. Discuss the catering manager's responsibilities. Why would a customer select your services as a caterer for their function? What unanticipated inconveniences have you experienced as a caterer and how did you handle them? Write a short report summarizing your visit.

Chapter 3

Establishing the Right Kind of Catering for You

Courtesy Stephen B. Shiring

Objectives

After studying this chapter, you should be able to:

1. Discuss a caterer's market.
2. Explain market segments and relate how a caterer must identify them.
3. Explain the major considerations when carving out a niche.
4. Identify why personal characteristics are a key to success.
5. Discuss mission statements and how they guide the caterer in the decision-making process.
6. Explain a strategic vision.
7. Discuss and identify the elements of the strategic planning tool SWOT analysis (Strengths, Weaknesses, Opportunities, and Threats).
8. Explain primary and secondary caterers.
9. Discuss corporate and social catering.
10. Discuss on-premise and off-premise catering.

KEY TERMS

business growth plan

caterer's market

mission statement

segment

signature menu item

stakeholders

strategic vision

SWOT analysis

Ingredients For Success

7 "Always exceed your customer's expectations."
8 "Create a strategic growth plan"
9 "Build a relationship of trust."

Establishing the right kind of catering to strategically fit a specific market niche is an important decision for a caterer to make. This decision must be made before the first contract is negotiated to execute the first function.

THE CATERING MARKET

caterer's market The group of all actual and potential customers in a caterer's geographic service area who have an unmet need, want, or demand requiring the service of a caterer.

A **caterer's market** is the group of all customers in a geographic service area who have unmet *needs*, *wants*, or *demands* requiring food and beverage service. It is extremely difficult and unreasonable to expect one caterer to service the entire market-range of current and potential customers in need or want of food, beverage, and related services. Remember *Ingredient for Success 2: "We cannot be all things to all people."*

Carving the Market

segment The part or submarket derived from the total of all potential catering customers. Members of these various submarkets have similar, identifiable needs, wants, and demands.

The caterer must carve or **segment** the whole market of customers into smaller pieces or niches. Segmenting the whole market into niches requires the caterer to identify customers with similar needs or wants and group them together. This enables the caterer to decide how to best build the business to satisfy that specific group.

To help the caterer identify the specific niche to pursue, a fundamental exercise would be to invest serious time answering a few key questions (Figure 3.1). By answering these key questions, a caterer will better understand the relationship between their strengths and the market's opportunities.

The purpose of answering these questions is twofold. First, a careful analysis enables the caterer to define who they are today. Second, the answers will provide the caterer with an understanding of what kind of professional development will be needed to provide continuous improvement in operations.

The answers to these questions will also help to establish a *business growth plan*. Remember *Ingredient for Success 2: "We cannot be all things to all people."* Caterers will only be able to effectively communicate their missions to prospective customers and to inaugurate the process of continuous improvement when they are comfortable with their own skills and abilities.

WHO IS THE CATERER?

How caterers define who they are begins with an analysis of their capabilities as a caterer and how they can satisfy customers' needs and wants. This is a starting point to establish the right kind of catering business.

One challenge is to identify the market niche the caterer is most comfortable servicing (Figure 3.2). This niche will determine the customers' wants and needs to be satisfied by the caterer's business. Issues important to the caterer include:

1. Do they specialize only in on-premise catering?
2. Will the caterer specialize in off-premise catering?
3. Will the caterer attempt to position the business as both an on- and off-premise catering operation?
4. Will the caterer be able to compete in the social market?
5. Can the caterer satisfy the needs of a corporate account?
6. Will the caterer try to satisfy the needs of both corporate and social catering customers?

1. What kind of catering can be executed right now?

2. What kind of food and service can be provided right now to meet and exceed the customer's expectations?

3. Is the caterer comfortable with specializing in chicken, steak, roast beef, prime rib, or pasta?

4. What quality standards can be created and maintained in both food and service?

5. What price-range will the caterer charge?

6. How many days will the caterer want to work each week?

7. How many hours each day will the caterer want to work?

8. What kind of food preparation skills does the caterer have now?

9. Will the menu be a specialized, limited-menu or will it be a broad-line menu?

10. What are the caterer's culinary skills and their relationship to menu design?

11. What kind of equipment does the caterer have?

12. What negotiating skills does the caterer have?

13. What is the caterer's knowledge regarding food and service sanitation standards?

14. Who will assist the caterer in these functions?

15. What is the skill level of the staff?

16. What kind of personnel demands will the caterer have to confront?

17. How large or small does the caterer want to be?

18. How fast or slow does the caterer want to grow?

19. How will the caterer evolve after the business has grown in three-to-five years?

20. How will the caterer evolve after the business has grown in ten years?

© Cengage Learning 2014

Figure 3.1 Key questions used to identify a market niche.

MISSION STATEMENT OR PURPOSE

One prerequisite for competitiveness in the marketplace is the ability for a caterer to confidently communicate the mission, or purpose, of the business to potential clients. The company's mission is written in a statement which defines why the caterer is in business. The **mission statement** identifies who the caterer is and communicates what the caterer can do for all potential customers.

This statement of purpose is the foundation of the organization. The mission statement answers the question, "Why am I in business today?" It may also reflect what the caterer plans to become. As a management tool, it guides the caterer's decision-making process. The mission statement permits the business to remain on course while pursuing its market niche by establishing a strategic business plan. It describes the type of business, including current customers, types of catering functions, where the events will be executed, and how to solve the current needs of the present customers. It also positions the caterer in relation to the competition, by defining it as a corporate caterer, social caterer, or an on-premise or off-premise

mission statement A written statement to define why a caterer is currently in business and communicate this purpose to stakeholders in the marketplace. A caterer's guiding light.

Courtesy Stephen B. Shiring

Figure 3.2 Caterers must determine the type of clientele they are most comfortable servicing.

caterer. By addressing these key issues, the caterer will formulate a concept and effectively communicate this concept.

Importance of the Mission Statement

The mission statement is the caterer's guiding light. Every action publicly displayed by the business should evolve from the mission statement. A mission statement helps communicate who and what a caterer is to the **stakeholders**— employees, suppliers, clients, guests, community, neighbors, competitors, government agencies, and others who have a direct relationship with the business. It is important for the caterer to share expectations and long-term plans with the community.

A mission statement is important for a number of reasons. First, the mission statement is important for the internal organization. It reflects the company's culture. A company's culture is a reflection of its core beliefs, values, and history. Employees need to know where the organization is now and where it wants to be in the future. Second, the mission statement positions the business independently from the competition. It separates the caterer selling rotisserie chicken from the local fire hall that is preparing stuffed cabbage and fried chicken. It helps to set the business apart from its competition by communicating how the business is better, different, and more professional.

stakeholders Anyone who has a direct relationship with the catering business, including employees, suppliers, clients, guests, community, neighbors, competitors, or government agencies.

There are many niches in the catering market. The lower priced caterers serve the market niche whose needs may demand macaroni and cheese, cabbage rolls, and chicken for approximately $15 per person. Caterers decide in advance if they want to be part of that segment or a caterer serving specialty foods like steak, ribs, or gourmet foods.

The mission of the operation will validate the caterer's market position, define competitors, identify what they can do, and how they do it. The mission statement will guide the caterer in all decisions, help to exceed the competition, allow the caterer to function more economically, and help provide better service, to become the caterer of choice. A strong mission statement is like the Pied Piper's magic flute. When people know the caterer is responsible for an event, and they hear the caterer's name, it attracts them to the event because of their expectations. This drives **Ingredient for Success 7: "Always exceed your customer's expectations."**

It happened back 70 years ago, so I am not sure how it transformed. One thing that is difficult to do in catering is to operate both a catering facility and an à la carte restaurant out of the same facility. Sometimes there are problems and conflicts, such as duplication of staff. We actually operated that way for many years. However, in the mid-1980s we shut down the à la carte restaurant within the catering facility and concentrated 100 percent on catering. It was one of the best moves we ever made. This helped us focus on what we did best at the time. We did not have the duplication of staff and we had the predictability that leads to a profitable operation. Caterers can predict the operations because they know what is coming in and what parties are booked. When you are an à la carte restaurant, you do not know what is going to come through the door. So it is hard to do both, be a caterer and run the à la carte restaurant. Also, customers get a mixed message. Customers do not know if you are a caterer or if you are a restaurant. When we made that separation, it helped our business tremendously.

Courtesy of Marty Horn, President/CEO of Foodgalaxy.com, Parsippany, NJ

Personal Reasons

A mission statement is more than simply *having a business and making money*. Although a caterer may cite various reasons for creating a business, these reasons are strictly individual and personal in nature, and often reflect their unique catalysts for the business. Start-up businesses can surge from many different directions.

A caterer will start a business for many different reasons including personal passion and individual desires, personal commitments, the belief that it can be done better than someone else, a means to create a respectable living through sufficient profits, and the desire to start a family business. Although personal reasons may drive the motivation to become a caterer, profit resulting from executing catering events will become the focus of a successful business. Good profits will be the desired outcome, but should not be the sole reason for being in business.

GROWING THE BUSINESS

Knowing how to grow a business is an important skill. Growing a business must be strategically planned in advance. Controlled growth requires a caterer to understand successful business concepts and how they relate to their own situation.

Controlling growth is important to the fiscal health of the caterer's business. To formulate a **business growth plan**, a review of the following questions may help.

business growth plan A strategic plan based on the answers to key questions used to identify a caterer's market niche that provides for controllable growth in the appropriate direction as established by the caterer.

1. What is the projected five-year gross sales figure?
2. What techniques will best describe how to satisfy current customers' needs?
3. How will you describe any desire to diversify into a new market niche?
4. How will new customers be attracted?
5. Who will identify these needs, wants, and demands?
6. What is the strategy regarding menu mix and new product development?
7. How will new menu items and specialities be introduced?
8. How will efficient and effective multiple catering events be executed on a daily, weekly, or monthly agenda?
9. How will sustainable trends, rather than short-lived fads, be identified?

Professional Growth

The progressive professional growth of the catering organization must be a well-crafted part of this plan. This takes careful, patient planning. For example, a caterer can only maximize on-premise sales by allowing the facility and staff to efficiently and effectively operate at full capacity. Therefore, the professional caterer must creatively plan financial and personal growth to develop an incrementally better organization every year.

Controlled growth is a management quandary. One dilemma a caterer must prevent is uncontrollable, exponential growth. Growing too fast can financially hurt the caterer. This can happen when a caterer accepts too many functions that need execution in a short period of time without sufficient staff or supplies.

Unfortunately, this dilemma is experienced by many caterers at least once in their career. Without a growth-control plan, every caterer will, at one time or another, experience the dilemma of accepting more responsibility than can be effectively and efficiently controlled. Planning for prosperous growth leads to *Ingredient for Success 8: "Create a strategic growth plan."*

The following illustration describes how a caterer can fall into this type of problem. A caterer may successfully manage $10,000 in gross sales per week. Believing the company can handle an increase to $12,000 per week, additional jobs are taken the following week. However, if the caterer's volume breaking point is in the range of $10,500–11,000, problems emerge. The caterer cannot handle the increase of $2,000 because the facility and personnel have been *stretched* too far, and it does not work out. Instead of generating the expected incremental profit on the additional sales, the caterer will lose money because of uncontrollable circumstances resulting from the lack of an adequate facility and staff.

Strategic Vision

A **strategic vision** is future looking. It is important because it creates a long-term vision for the caterer. This strategy helps the caterer to envision where the business is headed and what kind of demand will exert pressure on the organization. A long-term vision will project growth over the next 10 years. Anticipated concerns include seeking answers to the kind of professional development and special training the caterer needs to reach this proposed concept and what additional internal resources are needed by the caterer to attain this goal.

SWOT Analysis

A technique called **SWOT analysis** is a strategic management tool caterers use to match their business strengths to market opportunities. SWOT is an acronym that stands for identifying internal *strengths* and *weaknesses*, and the external *opportunities* and *threats*. This excellent tool is used to empower the caterer to interpret an overall business position. Using this information, the caterer can best match strengths to a specific niche in the competitive catering market.

SWOT analysis will lead to the identification of competitive strategies the caterer can use. Does the caterer have the internal strengths to pursue a strategy geared to catering on-premise, or only off-premise functions? Does the SWOT analysis reveal the caterer is best suited for social catering? Can the caterer compete successfully in the corporate catering segment?

Strengths

Strengths are identified as internal attributes, skills, characteristics, or assets that a caterer possesses which provide an enviable position of exceptional competitiveness in the market. A strength creates a tactical, defensible, competitive position for the caterer to use as an offensive or defensive weapon. This position makes it difficult for other caterers to compete in the market. Figure 3.3 provides an outline of a caterer's tangible and intangible internal strengths.

Weaknesses

Weaknesses are identified as those internal areas that can limit a caterer's ability to compete successfully in the industry. The strengths listed previously in this chapter could be viewed as weaknesses if a caterer, who does not possess them, competes against one who does.

A caterer can identify internal weaknesses as (1) those tasks they do not execute well or (2) those done deficiently as compared to other caterers in their industry. Weaknesses include lack of physical endurance; lack of culinary, technical, or management skills; and lack of specialized equipment or other tangible or intangible assets.

Lack of physical endurance, or the required effort to complete a job, is one major weakness that can prevent a caterer from becoming successful. The entire staff needs stamina and energy to follow a job from beginning to completion. Planning, implementation, execution, and follow up must be properly managed

signature menu item
Special or unique food
giving the caterer a
distinct recognition as
the sole supplier of
this specialized item.

1. Quality food—Set and maintain high standards for the food and ingredients. In catering, the ability to please diverse palates is a trademark of a successful caterer.

2. Unique food—Is the food different from other caterers? What is the caterer's **signature menu item** or what entree item is the caterer known for (Figure 3.4)?

3. Excellence—There are many average caterers. ***Ingredient for Success 7*** states: ***"Always exceed your customer's expectations."*** Strive to provide better-than-average food and services to guests. Gear strengths to meet and exceed customer satisfaction beyond the food and service. If the function is a social event in someone's home, provide valet parking and entertain the guests. If it is a corporate function, offer to present their awards or prizes for them. If it is a wedding, provide additional related services, such as cake, limousines, tuxedo rental, band or DJ, and bridal supplies. If children are involved, entertain them. If serving a buffet, strive to make it memorable beyond the food and different from the competition.

4. Ambition—The internal drive, intensity, and desire to become the best possible caterer is an intangible strength. Never be happy with mediocrity. Establish performance standards that stretch the organization's capabilities. In the catering field, a work ethic that demands focus is required. A successful caterer cannot be lazy.

5. Passion—The intense emotional drive of excelling as a caterer. Embrace the challenges of working with foods that are created differently, better tasting, more attractively presented, and served more professionally than the competition.

6. Personality—A caterer's good communication skills, the ability to work well with the public, and to understand people contribute to successful catering. A caterer must possess a strong personality, and sell himself, the team, the concept, and the organization.

7. Human Resources—The specialized skill, expertise, or training to work with others. Is the staff prepared to service the guest better than the next caterer? Is the staff competent at carving beef? Does the staff have special skills to execute the event? For example, never ask the dishwasher to put on a clean shirt, then hand him a carving knife and have him positioned to serve—especially if he has never seen a side of beef before. If the staff is extremely loyal to the organization, they will go beyond what is required of them.

8. Commitment to the process of continuous learning—The process of learning is a journey. This journey includes both formal training and self-education. It helps to join local and national organizations; attend seminars; and read books on cooking, management, self-development, and stress release. Always strive to learn something new. Support the process of education by developing an ongoing training program that requires everyone in the organization to learn.

9. Assets—Does a caterer have an incomparable banquet hall or location? Do they have specialized assets, such as their own refrigerated trucks, chafing dishes, or insulated transportation boxes for either hot or cold food and other equipment?

10. Creativity—How is the caterer more creative than others? This business strength is important in the field of catering because there are constant changes in themes based on dissimilar celebrations and needs of the guests (Figure 3.5).

11. Logistics—The ability to successfully work in different off-premise locations is a significant strength for a caterer.

Figure 3.3 Strengths of a caterer.

Courtesy of HLC Inc.

Figure 3.4 Signature items, such as a unique plate, help a caterer distinguish themselves from the competition.

at each stage of the operation. Generally, long, odd hours are required in the catering industry. Working late and doing what it takes to make the event a success is the norm rather than the exception in catering. A typical event may consume 12 or more strenuous hours for a caterer. During this time, numerous demands can weigh upon a caterer. Can the caterer financially do the job? Is the caterer able to endure long hours of relentless stress? How will this stress affect a caterer's overall health? If the caterer cannot manage the event from the formulation through the implementation stages, it may not be a success unless a competent manager is put in place.

Another weakness is when the caterer is expected to fully participate in the event with the freedom of an invited guest. The caterer is separate from the event and cannot comfortably socialize, even though the guest may interpret this lack of participation in a negative way.

Lack of specialized knowledge can be a weakness. Either the lack of management training or culinary techniques can create a potential problem when trying to compete. The lack of competencies in culinary skills can limit a menu as compared to some competitors. This may result in losing potential clients by being unable to satisfy their needs.

Other weaknesses that may prevent a caterer from success include:

1. labor difficulties
2. last minute stock-outs by purveyors of food items that are needed for the event
3. insufficient operating capital
4. unreasonable lease agreements
5. excessive long-term debt
6. excessive payroll

Courtesy of HLC Inc.

Figure 3.5 Understanding a client's needs within the market creates a competitive advantage for a caterer.

7. unrealistic general overhead such as mortgage or rent payments, utilities, equipment payments, repairs, and maintenance

8. insufficient knowledge in the areas of food production, air-conditioning, and refrigeration repairs

9. uncontrollable temper or emotional instability

10. inability to provide leadership, especially in emergency situations

11. poor communication skills

12. lack of attention to details

13. failure to solve problems

14. lack of accounting and financial skills; inability to be cost-efficient and profitable

15. overpromising and underachieving; telling the client what he or she wants to hear to get the job

16. fear of taking risks

Opportunities

Opportunities are identified as those external, controllable, future catering events that best match the caterer's competitive strengths and which enable him or her to meet and exceed guest expectations. Opportunities reveal themselves as potential, profitable-growth zones. A caterer can identify those growth areas and pursue them as part of their overall business plan.

Another precious opportunity caterers have is ***Ingredient for Success 9: "Build a positive reputation."*** Caterers' reputations always precede them in the marketplace. At all costs, every caterer strives to continually build and cultivate a positive reputation. As in other industries, a prerequisite of success is the favorable reputation. At any given event, employees may not perform up to standards or mistakes may be made. If there are delays, explain them. It is the best policy for the caterer to always tell the customer the truth, and never lie about anything.

The caterer has other opportunities including the event itself. A caterer designs each event to the specifications of the client. The caterer controls the design—it is the caterer's creation based on serving the needs of the customer.

The opportunity to work with the newest foods and products in the marketplace is another opportunity the caterer experiences. Often, the caterer is the first to receive a new food item from the purveyor or food broker. The purveyor's distributor sales representative will field test new products through a caterer to determine their popularity.

A caterer will also have the opportunity to work with other caterers and their staffs on certain events. An astute caterer can observe these competitors, glean new ideas, and gain an understanding of their strengths and weaknesses.

Opportunities appear in the market in many different ways. The following illustrate opportunities for a caterer.

1. business location of the facilities
2. potential economic growth
3. physical layout of the facility to support catering functions
4. adequate parking area clearly marked and lighted
5. ownership of the professional food production equipment
6. lack of competition
7. ownership of the facility and equipment
8. hours of operation and days of the week available to cater functions
9. recognition of sustainable trends

As a small business owner, a caterer faces many decisions involving quality that must be made at an early stage of development of the concept. It is well known one can make money by selling a low quality product in mass quantity, or by selling a high quality product in smaller quantities. At North Country Kettle Corn we made the decision to use the best ingredients and offer a very high quality product. We spent an entire year researching and field testing the ingredients for our product line. In addition to the ingredients, to maintain a high quality product, we use only the best equipment. This means proper cleaning, storage, transportation, and replacement when needed. We take great pride in cleanliness. We always follow and exceed the rules and regulations for operating a clean and safe environment. This includes both actual production and service operations including counter space and cooking utensils. After we cook and present our popcorn, we tear down and thoroughly clean everything, including the utensils, so when we get them out to use again, they are clean and sanitized.

As with any small business, a good reputation is pivotal to survival. We bank on high quality products and a clean and up-to-date facility, to ensure our customers leave with a good impression of our business.

Courtesy of Nikko Leitzel

Threats

Threats are identified as those external elements which can cause a potential loss for a caterer. Government regulation and increased changes in the interest rates are uncontrollable threats confronting a caterer. A decrease in the demographics of the area and losses in gross sales, market share, and profitability are major business concerns. Some reasons for these business losses include the entry of new competitors; substitute products; and the relocation, downsizing, or shutdown of corporate customers.

Competition is a major threat to the survival of a successful caterer. Competitive rivalry among caterers is a dynamic function of the business environment. The threat of new businesses entering in a local market is always a concern because of the lack of insurmountable barriers preventing it. The low cost of entering a segment of the catering market means it is relatively inexpensive for someone to start a catering business. There is no type of specialized technology or privileged information barring one from becoming a caterer. However, a positive reputation, a caterer's skills and abilities, client loyalty, and the buying power or economies of scale in a caterer's operation are some barriers new competitors may have to overcome.

Knowing the competition and where it exists will help a caterer develop effective strategies to confront any new competitive threat (Figure 3.6). Conducting frequent surveillance activities to monitor the competition will help a caterer gain strategic information on what others are currently doing.

A caterer's own lack of certain skills and abilities can be a threat. Movement or shutdown of corporations in the caterer's market area is a threat to the business.

Courtesy of HLC Inc.

Figure 3.6 Can a new caterer specializing in Sushi pose a competitive threat to other caterers in the local market?

1. Competition—Caterers must be aware of all competitors, especially those in the same target market. They must monitor and analyze the competition on a continuous basis to understand their strengths and weaknesses. What are their strategies? What do they charge? Where is their location? Do they have any special features? What is their purchasing power? What is their promotional and marketing expertise?

2. Target market or communities—Who are the customers? Are they price sensitive? What are the demographic variables such as age, income, gender, occupation, marital status, and ethnic background?

3. Offering to cater functions for a new market niche without enough analysis—Is the market niche growing? How fast is it growing? What economic and social factors will be influencing the market?

4. Is the client unhappy?—Once the function is running and in place, the happiness of a client is directly correlated to the caterer.

5. Future competition—Will new caterers enter the market? What weakness may be exploited by the competition to steal a share of the market?

6. Human resources—Does a shortage of properly trained, skilled workers exist? Lack of co-operation between members of the service staff and food production employees portrays unprofessionalism.

7. Inadequate equipment—Poor layout and design of production area and a shortage of small wares and equipment are common.

8. Poor management structure—Ineffective scheduling or a lack of planning, organizing, and controlling can result in a poorly executed event.

9. Inappropriate lease—Excessive rent or mortgage payments and/or lack of credit can cripple cash flow and profits.

10. Staff does not care about customer needs.

11. Lack of a plan for sanitation—Poor procedural follow up can cause a food borne outbreak and hospitalize guests.

© Cengage Learning 2014

Figure 3.7 Threats confronting a caterer.

Another threat may be competition in the market niche. When trying to compete in the low-end segment of the catering market, it is very difficult to remain successful and profitable. See Figure 3.7 for a list of potential threats.

Summary

To establish the right kind of catering, an accurate understanding of the caterer's strengths and a precise customer profile based on the identification of unmet needs, wants, and demands is required. To effectively communicate these strengths to the market, a mission statement is created to define the caterer's purpose. Strategically growing the business allows for the proper mix of financial and personal activities correlated to its long-term success. One strategic management tool used to match business strengths to market opportunities is SWOT analysis. SWOT is an acronym for identifying internal strengths and weaknesses, and external opportunities and threats.

Review Questions

Brief Answers

1. Briefly discuss why it is important for a caterer to understand the market.
2. Explain what is meant by a caterer *carving the market*. Provide examples to support your answer.
3. What are the key questions a caterer must answer to determine the market niche most favorable for them to pursue?
4. Why must caterers first understand their capabilities before they can effectively satisfy a customer's needs?
5. Explain the six purposes of a mission statement.
6. Who are stakeholders and why must a caterer respect them?
7. What is a strategic vision? Why is it important for a caterer to create a strategic vision for the business?
8. Describe the management tool SWOT analysis. How can a caterer use this tool to gain a competitive advantage in the market?
9. Give examples of the types of strengths, weaknesses, opportunities, and threats a caterer may have.
10. Discuss the Ingredients for Success and explain what these mean to you.

Multiple Choice

Select the single best answer for each question.

1. Which one of the following reasons explains why a mission statement is important for a caterer?
   a. It guides the decision-making process.
   b. It communicates to the customer the type of business the caterer will become.
   c. It plays a minor role in the creation of a strategic business plan.
   d. It is the first step in understanding who the customers are in the market.
   e. All of the above.
2. The _____ is the group of all customers in a caterer's geographic service area who have an unmet need or want requiring the service of food and beverage.
   a. corporate client
   b. primary client
   c. on-premise client
   d. market
   e. social client
3. The _____ is future looking, creates a long-term direction for the caterer, and helps to answer the type of professional development and special training needed by the caterer.
   a. SWOT analysis
   b. mission statement
   c. strategic vision
   d. primary caterer
   e. secondary caterer

True or False

Read each of the following statements and determine if it is true or false.

1. A strategic vision helps the caterer answer the question, "Where is the business currently going?"

2. SWOT analysis is a catering-industry-specific acronym that means Sweat, Work, and Overtime—something every caterer will do sometime in their career.

3. Threats in the competitive marketplace are identified as those external elements which can cause some business loss for the caterer.

Putting It All Together

Search on the Internet for catering companies. Find if they have a mission statement. Review these mission statements against the criteria discussed in Chapter 3. Does the mission statement describe the catering company? What can you deduce from the mission statement? Would you hire this catering company for your own needs?

Chapter 4

Choosing Your Client

Objectives

After studying this chapter, you should be able to:

1. Explain how a caterer can build a solid customer base using specific prospecting strategies.

2. Explain the details of a catering proposal.

3. Explain why the planned growth of a catering company is achieved through a conscientious building of satisfied customers and the accomplishment of a caterer's financial objectives.

4. Explain why a caterer may refuse to work for a particular client.

5. Define the difference between a client's needs, wants, and demands.

KEY TERMS

customer base

demands

event planners

life cycle of customer events

needs

professional sales staff

proposal

prospecting strategies

relationships

upgrading the event

wants

Ingredients For Success

10 "Customer satisfaction grows your business."

11 "Understand why the customer has selected the caterer—what are the expectations?"

12 "To establish a long-term relationship with a customer and work, as frequently as possible, with each client one-on-one."

13 "Presentations are important— create special, unusual, personable, and impressive competitive proposals."

The creation of a solid **customer base** upon which to draw current and potential clients necessary to support a catering operation now and in the future is one of the most important business tasks a caterer must faithfully perform. This task is a natural extension flowing from the caterer's established mission statement, as discussed in Chapter 3.

CREATING A CUSTOMER BASE

Creating a solid customer base and attracting new customers is a continuous building process for the caterer. There are many good customers available in the market to build a solid base of support; however, caterers must understand their capabilities. They must know the production capacity of the kitchen, understand the current skill level of the employees, and strictly adhere to the financial goals of the organization. They must also be able to accommodate the menu requirements such as providing a low-scale or upscale menu, servicing social or corporate events, and on-premise or off-premise functions.

Prospecting Strategies

A number of considerations must be examined when building a solid customer base. How can the caterer best accomplish the task of building a sustainable customer base? The caterer can begin by formulating a prospecting plan to complement the goals of the organization. Based on this plan (see the business plan, marketing section, in Chapter 6), a caterer can derive assorted **prospecting strategies** to communicate information to potential clients.

The caterer must fully understand how skills are used to meet and exceed customers' expectations. Since building sales depends largely on the number of people who buy the product, the proper place to begin a market analysis is with people. Therefore, a starting point is to understand the needs, wants, and demands of the customer.

Needs, Wants, and Demands

Customer **needs** can be very complex. A human need is a feeling of deprivation of something. Basic human physical needs include food, clothing, and safety. Customers have social needs as well. To fulfill a social need, the client may have an affiliation with an association or a group. The caterer must recognize the client has esteem needs as well. Prestige, recognition, and self-expression are esteem needs a caterer must satisfy.

Clients will package their basic needs into **wants**. A client's wants are always evolving. These wants are defined by the level of sophistication of the client. The caterer's challenge is to understand the difference between what the client *needs* and what the client *wants*. The caterer offers a combination of food and service to solve the client's basic issue.

When clients approach a caterer, they will have unlimited wants, but their budget and limited resources will constrain them. Clients will select the caterer who can provide the most satisfaction based on their budget. Clients' *wants* become clients' **demands** when they are backed by financial resources and buying power.

---

customer base A solid foundation consisting of current and potential clients upon which a caterer continuously builds to support the catering business now and in the future.

prospecting strategies Methodologies used by a caterer to introduce himself or herself to a prospective client with the purpose of building a sustainable customer base.

needs The complex set of human needs that include the need for food, beverage, and related services.

wants A client's basic needs as communicated to the caterer.

demands Derived from the client's needs and wants, demands also include the client's ability to purchase them.

The customer is the most important individual to the organization, as they are providing the funds for the service. Satisfying customers is the basic goal of any caterer. Every satisfied customer will sing the caterer's praise and recommend the services to others. However, this is far from a simple exercise.

Many caterers are very successful because they know how to exceed the explicit and implied needs, wants, and demands of their customers. They understand who the customer is and the characteristics of the target market by completing a market analysis (Figure 4.1).

A caterer often has the opportunity to work with the customer soon after the conception of the customer's idea. The real challenge is to translate their idea—the needs, wants, and demands—into a package. The caterer will bundle a package of complementary tangible products and intangible services to execute based on the client's budget. This introduces *Ingredient for Success 10: "Customer satisfaction grows your business."*

Understanding customer needs, wants, and demands enables the caterer to recommend to each client a winning combination of service and food. Carefully

Understanding the Customer

Demographics: Age, level of income, gender, marital status, family composition, ethnic background, education level

Lifestyle: Family status, extracurricular activities, media preferences, professional and personal organizational affiliations, political affiliation

Geographic Area: Location; urban, suburban, rural, city. Region or neighborhood; residential, business, downtown

Psychographics: Status-seeking, trend-setting, liberal, conservative

Decision Making: Price, quality, brand name, reputation, location, speciality

Sources of Market Data

1. Up-to-date census data
2. Current popularity trends
3. Regional or county planning commissions
4. Banks and newspapers

Sources of New Customer Prospects

1. Customers—direct contact
2. Phone books (local)
3. Employee survey

—preplanned

—regularly scheduled

—conducted often

—short and to the point

—summarized and evaluated by management

© Cengage Learning 2014

Figure 4.1 Market analysis.

listening to the customer is the first step. Listen to hear not only what is being requested by the customer, but what the customer is implying in the request. This is the greatest challenge. Successful caterers listen, listen, and listen.

Translating a customer's message is vital. Adequately composing the right combination of food and service to exceed these needs, wants, and demands is the challenge. To ensure success, the caterer responds by asking the customer clarifying questions. These questions help the caterer translate the customer's requests to produce a synergetic combination of results which exceed the customer's expectations.

Each and every customer has a basic need: they need a caterer. All clients are also in need of good food, good service, professional conduct, and value. Complicating this fact, each customer brings his/her unique wants and desires to the caterer.

It is important to know a client's needs or be able to make suggestions. Each client has an idea as to what the caterer should be able to produce. Often caterers are asked to handle wild and unusual tasks. It is common to get challenging requests from particular ethnic groups, such as a European group who requests half authentic German and half American cuisine at an event.

Jardine's catered a wedding for a couple who requested half authentic Indian and American cuisine. First, we had to convince the couple that half of the wedding party would only eat Indian food and the other half would only eat American food, but the guests would probably eat some of each. Then, we recommended that they bring in an authentic Indian chef to prepare the food, but Jardine's, as the caterer, would serve it. This arrangement worked quite well. We made sure the chef was reliable, dependable, and had the food delivered on time, meeting everyone's expectations and demands. Other times a caterer will run into situations where clients have all kinds of unusual ideas, prompting the following polite response, "Sorry, we cannot produce that in our facility."

Courtesy Bill Jardine

Customer Contact

In providing a general atmosphere conducive to sales of special functions, one important thing to remember is that the prospective buyer must be put in a positive frame of mind. One key is having a professional-looking office with comfortable furniture. This will help to elicit a positive attitude from the prospect. Trying to do business in a hallway or seated at a party table in an empty banquet hall only invites sales resistance. Avoid using the main dining room because constant interruptions and noise are likely to occur in this area. Natalie Dunlap, catering sales manager, The Chestnut Ridge Golf & Resort, has this to say about using a professional-looking office with comfortable furniture: "I have a small conference room which can seat up to six guests that has leather chairs and is beautifully decorated. I use this space to meet with all my potential and existing clients. This room is inviting and warm and makes the sale a lot easier. The client feels at ease and this is when I feel that I can make a personal connection with the client."

Remember to keep the conversation private. A buyer may have special requests and may not be completely at ease if there are people with no direct concern present. This is especially true when discussing financial matters. Common courtesy is to offer a cup of coffee, tea, or soft drink. Keep a refill readily available to avoid a lag in the conversation and to keep the conversation focused on the business at hand.

The total sales atmosphere must be one in which the prospect feels he or she is being helped. The caterer must convey that the decisions being made are in the best interests of the function and the guests. However, the customer may not always be right. Few people fully understand the logistics of planning an event. This is where the professional caterer must make the buyer feel his or her interests are paramount to the success of the event.

Customer Solicitation

The actual solicitation of the function starts with the initial contact between the buyer and the seller. This contact may be initiated by either. The seller (catering manager), using marketing information gathered earlier, may make it a practice to review articles in the local newspaper, seeking out information about prominent people and their families in society columns. These are the prospects (buyers). To keep a record of progress, the catering manager fills out a solicitation form, listing information pertinent to the prospect and to the event which might be scheduled. This includes the name of the individual; address; phone number; the type of occasion; whether or not the person involved has ever used the party facilities before; and when, where, and by whom previous functions were booked. This is all information directly relevant to the solicitation of the sale.

Once the solicitor has determined that the person is a prospective buyer, the prospect is called, offered congratulations on the happy occasion, and invited to make use of the facilities to celebrate the event. It may be a wedding or a retirement party. Any occasion calling for a group celebration provides the catering manager with an opportunity to offer the services of the facility. Oral solicitation may be written out in advance by the manager and the administrative staff asked to do the actual calling, using the outline as a guide. Whoever calls, the basic idea behind the call is to make the initial contact, offer the service, and make an appointment for the prospect to visit the facility to discuss the details.

Reputation

relationship The bond that connects the caterer with a client based on mutual respect for each other.

The best method, of course, is to have the customer approach the caterer. This is when the caterer's reputation becomes most important. Reputation is a great way to attract new customers. This is especially important in corporate catering. Many high-profile companies operate on a limited budget, which is something a caterer must know. **Relationship** and the emergence of trust become important, as the president of one company will often recommend their caterer to others. Trust and reputation imply a level of quality the customer knows the caterer can deliver. Dunlap says, "By building a solid reputation your business will grow. I started working with the corporation Napa Auto Parts, who held a quarterly meeting. These meetings went so well that Napa Auto Parts has referred other sales divisions to have meetings at our facility. We now do business with Napa monthly instead of quarterly."

Current Customers

When a satisfied guest is pleased with the menu, food, and service, this customer becomes a prospect as a future catering customer. These customers enjoy the menu selections and signature items exclusively prepared and served by the caterer at their event. Many small restaurants have grown into catering companies driven by satisfied customers. This is a natural outgrowth of the restaurant.

At one time, Jardine's Catering would cater events at a local steel company's park which had a swimming pool, a picnic area, and an entertainment section. The park was established for use by the families of the steel company employees.

Several years after we catered events at this location, a call came from a company having an employee satisfaction dinner who wanted us to cater a steak dinner for them. At the first meeting with the company's representative responsible for the event we asked, "Why did you contact Jardine's? How did you find out about us?" This information was always requested of our new customers. This is **Ingredient for Success 11: "Understand why the customer has selected the caterer—what are the expectations?"** His reply was, "Our superintendent said to call Jardine's Catering and make sure they could cater this event."

After the event the superintendent came over, introduced himself, and said, "I'm glad that you could do our job. I enjoyed the steak just as much as I did when I was going to college." Our manager's reply was, "Well, how did you taste our steaks when you were going to college?" This superintendent was a lifeguard at the steel company's park and so when we catered there all the park's employees were also fed. Here is an example of a residual effect: Fifteen years later, Jardine's was contacted for a catering event because a lifeguard who was fed remembered how good the food and service were.

Whether to feed the workers is an important consideration when catering an event, especially in an off-premise facility. Jardine's previously catered at a facility rented by the customer. The hall would bring in six to eight of their own people to assist the caterer, including bartenders, cleanup crew, and coat room attendants. Not all caterers feed employees, but our policy was to always feed the workers. To compensate for this, we would always prepare food at an additional 3 percent over the guaranteed number given by the client. We fed the guests, other employees working the event, and then our own staff.

Bill Jardine, Jardine's Farm Restaurant & Catering, Sarver, Pennsylvania

Service Organizations

Membership in many of the community service organizations is a great way to meet people in the community. Becoming a member in community service organizations such as the local Chamber of Commerce, the Lions Club, or Rotary Club provides great networking opportunities. This is another strategy for a caterer to meet potential clients.

Iron Bridge Inn provides service on a local basis for clubs, organizations, and leagues such as golf leagues and women's groups. These specific customers have made special requests, including asking our restaurant to provide them

(continues)

(continued)

with equipment, products, services, and sometimes, employees. We have the facilities and the equipment to service such requests and will cater events generating income from $200–$2000. Catering has built customer appreciation, creates a great public relations opportunity, and is always providing an advertisement for the restaurant. It creates a favorable community response, especially when we provide our services for a charitable event, and helps us in our promotion of the restaurant. Catering is ideal for our research and development process, and in some cases, we first introduce our newer menu items during events. We will use these new products as test samples at catering events to ascertain their popularity through customer response. If we are happy with our results, then we will incorporate them into our restaurant's menu.

The catering menu is created as a result of our guests requesting our basics. People come into the restaurant, look at our hard copy menu and select three items. They may pick a chicken entree, a beef entree, and a pasta dish for their party. If our guests have something special they would like us to make for them, such as traditional picnic foods, then we will package it for them, wrap it all up, and send it out.

We may price catering events differently. We usually have a 60–70 percent markup on the restaurant menu items. As for pricing a catering function, it depends on whether the function is held on- or off-premise. If the event is held off-premise, then the markup percentage is a little lower, set approximately between 30–40 percent. We do this simply because of the labor factor. Once we ship it out of the restaurant, we only have to deliver it to our clients. It is usually sent prepared ready-to-go and our client will set it up, serve it, and clean up after the event. If the event is on-premise, then we use the standard restaurant markup.

We are fortunate enough to have 8–10 golf courses within a 10–15 mile radius around the restaurant. We have catered golf outings in our back room for 40–50 guests. We shut the back room down and have it available only for them. We offer a set menu and give them a set amount of time and it seems to work very well. We do not take reservations at the restaurant, so we tell the golf leagues they can use the room during our slow periods, from 3:00–4:00. But they must be finished by 4:15 p.m. so we can prepare for our dinner service.

One of the best outcomes of our catering services is that they have built for us a loyal customer base who greatly appreciates our extra effort.

Daniel Miller, Manager, Springfield Restaurant Group

Making New Customers

Personal attention and interaction with a prospective client is another positive strategy to build a customer base. At times, the caterer will personally call on clients. If the caterer is interested in catering for a particular client, this is an excellent way to introduce the business to the prospective client and explain how the caterer can best meet the client's needs. Then the caterer can ask for the opportunity to submit a proposal for their banquet and catering events.

A caterer can find new customers by reading the local newspaper. One efficient strategy many caterers have successfully employed for years is to pay careful attention to articles and announcements in the local newspaper. News announcements describing future community events, reunions, and engagements are excellent leads to new business.

When caterers read of an engagement, they send the prospective bride a sincere congratulatory letter. This letter would include an invitation for the couple to visit their catering facility/restaurant for a complimentary dinner or special treat. Upon the presentation of the congratulatory letter, the staff would know they are a newly engaged couple and would serve the couple with great fanfare. The letter might also include an invitation to meet with the caterer's professional staff for a consultation, even if the couple had already selected another caterer, at no obligation or cost.

As a result of successfully implementing these strategies, a caterer can service a **life cycle of customer events**. A client's lifetime may include events such as bridal showers, wedding receptions, anniversaries, birthdays, baby showers, births, baptisms, proms, sports banquets, graduations, college, marriage, and the cycle will repeat. It is even common for loyal customers to request the caterer to prepare the food served at their funerals.

life cycle of customer events The cycle of lifetime celebrations: bridal shower, wedding reception, anniversary, birthday, baby shower, baptism, prom, sporting banquet, college graduation, marriage, and death that requires the services of a caterer. The cycle repeats itself.

Food-Tasting Events

Create an opportunity to speak one-on-one with the customers and potential clients during your slower sales periods. Invite them to attend a customer recognition dinner or a special taste-testing event to sample foods and signature items (Figure 4.2) featured on the catering menu.

For example, a caterer will invite clients and potential customers to a semi-annually featured food feast. At this event, numerous stations are set up offering samples of their speciality and featured signature items. A caterer creates an environment to showcase special food items. An assortment of hors d'oeuvres, dessert items, breads, and beverages are provided.

Customers appreciate and anticipate attending this type of annual event. They are able to sample their favorite foods and are afforded the opportunity to sample new or exotic items being first introduced or field tested for possible inclusion on the menu. Although the purpose of these events is to entertain customers, they may evolve into

Permission of John R. Smith

Figure 4.2 Featuring signature items, such as this gourmet turtle cheesecake, at a taste-testing event helps build new clientele.

a wonderful selling tool and will become very popular with the customers, who appreciate the opportunity to sample foods and interact with other guests. An on-premise caterer can hold these events in his/her facility. An off-premise caterer could rent a facility or negotiate with the owner of a fabulous facility to sponsor the event in its hall.

This introduces *Ingredient for Success 12: "To establish a long-term relationship with a customer and work, as frequently as possible, with each client one-on-one."*

Publicity

Advertising means a caterer will pay to have information placed into the media. *Publicity* is free media exposure. A caterer may exchange catering functions for free air time on the radio or television, or ad space in newspapers and magazines. Donations, special fund-raising activities, and community service may work as a press release to gain free publicity with the appropriate news media.

Planning how to publicize catering services requires considerable forethought by the catering manager. The obvious way to publicize these services is through the menu. Tasteful arrangement of menu selections on durable, yet colorful stock, printed legibly and relating directly to the type of function it is meant to supplement or to the general theme of the event, will do much to influence the decisions of the potential buyer.

Menus should be printed in warm colors. Soft earthy tones, such as browns, oranges, reds, golds, and yellow are relaxing to the eye and important considerations. Complement the ink colors to the paper stock. These are very effective sales tools. However, since it is often difficult to get the menu to the prospective buyer in advance of the personal interview, the caterer must seek additional ways of publicizing the goods and services he or she wants to sell.

A few well-chosen words printed on the regular menus will help to reach a broader market. Some menus may even include a flyer outlining banquet and party offerings. Posters and flyers placed in strategic locations may serve as a communication tool to remind potential clients of additional services that are available.

Publicity can also involve a recently presented event. Follow-up articles on a certain type of event, such as a wedding, published in the newspaper or presented orally as a society news item on a radio broadcast, can be a doubly effective way of getting the attention of those individuals in need of catering.

Advertising

Advertising catering services differs from publicizing them. Advertising requires a considerably larger expenditure of funds and should be budgeted in advance. A caterer should allocate a portion of the operating capital specifically for the purpose of promoting and soliciting business. Obviously, the best exposure is a satisfied customer who had an agreeable dining experience, but even this must be supplemented by an aggressive sales program.

A sales program may consist of a catchy and brilliantly illustrated advertisement placed in the newspaper at designated times. A well-placed advertisement at the entrance to the catering facility, or an effectively worded advertisement on the radio, may entice a prospect to investigate the possibility of holding a future function at the establishment. Since funds are being used to promote this activity, each manager should make every effort to provide some follow-up action, to determine the impact of the program on the prospect, and proven cost-effectiveness.

Closing the Sale

No sales transaction is complete until the sale is closed and the customer has signed the contract (Chapter 14). A mutual agreement between buyer and seller must be consummated. For the protection of both parties, a detailed document signifying this accord must be drawn up and signed by the caterer and the client. Managers should then use a check list to track the preparation of the event (Figure 4.3).

MANAGER'S CHECK LIST
(check when action is completed)

Advance Preparations

_____	Contract and scheduling of meeting
_____	Staffing and scheduling of employees
_____	Special functions sheet filled out
_____	Departmental instruction sheets
_____	Time of meeting
_____	Special setup instructions
_____	Meeting room ready
_____	Setup team ready

Logistics

_____	Tables and seating space
_____	Platform for speakers, tables, and chairs
_____	Visual aids and accessories
_____	Tables for handouts and demonstration
_____	Coffee break schedule
_____	Location and equipment for coffee break
_____	Billing for coffee break
_____	Luncheon arrangements
_____	Billing for luncheon
_____	Pre-registration needs
_____	Cocktail party arrangement
_____	Cocktail party billing
_____	Coat room arrangements
_____	Lighting, heat, and air conditioning
_____	Greeting of guests
_____	Receipt of advance shipping material—storage area
_____	Information for incoming guests

During the Meeting

_____	Employee skills and attitudes
_____	Delegation of tasks
_____	Quality of service

© Cengage Learning 2014

Figure 4.3 Manager's checklist.

Remember, the basic principle behind the scheduling of a special function is the satisfaction of the customer. This includes being satisfied with the costs as well as the production of the event. Before closing a sale, the good catering manager always ensures that the prospect is completely satisfied with the arrangements as outlined. After the event, following up immediately with a letter thanking the client and offering to be of service at future events is good business practice. If the event might be scheduled again, make a note of this fact for future reference.

Business Cards

The use of business cards (Figure 4.4) by the caterer and the staff is another effective prospecting strategy. Employees should be instructed to distribute the organization's business cards to all interested guests attending a function if approved by the client. Remember to use common sense when handing out business cards. This is a very good way to leave a guest with a little reminder of the caterer for future reference. Make a goal to hand out five business cards per day

Portfolio

The use of an attractive, professionally designed and maintained portfolio will communicate a strong visual message. The caterer may make arrangements to offer food and related services to the professional photographer covering the function in return for taking pictures of the food, layout, decorations, and employees. Otherwise, the investment in a quality, digital camera will give the caterer a means to document events for a portfolio. Many potential clients enjoy the opportunity to see previous catering functions executed by the caterer.

professional sales staff Based on need and budgetary requirements, this team's purpose is to represent the caterer in the target market by communicating to potential clients a caterer's skills and capabilities to satisfy customer needs, wants, and demands.

Professional Sales Staff

Planned growth of a catering company is achieved through a conscientious building of satisfied customers and by the accomplishment of a caterer's financial objectives. Implementation of a **professional sales staff** is another method used by a caterer

Figure 4.4 A professional-looking business card communicates the appropriate message to the prospective client.

All Occasion Catering, Inc.

534 Clever Road • McKees Rocks, PA 15136
Tel: (412) 787-5266 • Fax: (412) 787-0766
www.alloccasioncatering.org

Halls available at
Moon Run Fire Hall • Mckees Rocks V.F.W.
St. George Center • Crafton American Legion • Forest Grove Fire Hall

Permission of John R. Smith

Tips from the Trade

The catering sales manager is the organization's communication link to current and prospective clients and the general public. We communicate through advertising, public relations, and sales blitzes. My professional responsibilities here at The Chestnut Ridge Golf Resort & Conference Center are to promote, advertise, and sell the property's catering services. I do this by creating loyal customers. Much of my time is dedicated to giving personalized attention to each client. We strive to exceed our clients' needs, wants, and demands by delivering quality food, beverage, and related services. I am also responsible for prospecting, that is finding new clients. I mine customer inquiries and drill down into our specific target market segments, which include Galas, Fundraisers, Charity Benefits, Proms and Homecomings, Fraternity and Sorority Events, Sports Banquets, Retirement Parties, Reunions, and Bar and Bat Mitzvahs, to create new contacts or to uncover new clients. For me to be successful as the catering sales manager, I need to be a good listener, understand our kitchen and service capabilities, translate customer needs into tangible products and services from our marketing mix, and to be extremely sensitive to the smallest details.

Courtesy of Natalie

to achieve these business objectives. Often, the caterer is so busy with current projects they do not have the necessary time to invest in prospecting for new clients to grow future business.

The inclusion of additional sales staff, primarily working in the field, must be based on need and budgetary requirements. One advantage of this staff is the potential for an immediate and constant presence in the caterer's market niche. Most larger facilities, such as hotel operations, employ professional sales people to increase business.

1. Communicate the caterer's capabilities
2. Provide information
3. Meet with clients one-on-one
4. Give tours of the caterer's operation
5. Design brochures
6. Pursue leads to new business opportunities
7. Design a logo
8. Formulation and implementation of the prospecting plan
9. Plan the marketing budget
10. Elevate developmental signature recipes

© Cengage Learning 2014

Figure 4.5 Professional sales staff functions.

The mission of a professional sales staff is to have a direct connection with the market, to help recognize potential clientele. Specifically, their task is to unlock new business doors. A specialized sales staff can provide a caterer with a dependable commitment to a marketing plan. Elements such as obtaining market-specific research, coordinating a public relations campaign, coordinating promotional tie-ins with suppliers, and composing caterer-generated communication messages are just some of the many responsibilities a caterer can authorize (Figure 4.5).

EVENT PLANNER

event planner A person who directly coordinates for a client the planning, organizing, implementation, and control of their event.

Whether it is a weekend corporate retreat, a class reunion, or a wedding anniversary celebration, **event planners** handle one of the most diverse client bases within the hospitality industry. The caterer will, at some time in their career, work with an event planner. Establishing a professional relationship with event planners is a key to building a sustainable customer base. This following section will explain the role of event planners and their relationship with a caterer.

Roles Event Planners Play for Their Clients

The event planner is one of the most varied roles in the hospitality industry. As the client's most trusted professional contact, the event planner has a relationship that is unique compared to traditional catering or banquet managers. While a traditional catering or banquet manager is often associated with one or two aspects of an event, the event planner's role spans the entire duration of all event planning and execution phases, potentially across multiple venues or different groups of guests. The relationship results in a number of roles that the event planner must play to each client throughout the event planning process.

Regardless of the type of client, the event planning process almost universally begins with a creative vision. The first role of the event planner is to be the creative visionary for their client, to articulate a vision for the event, depicting it in such a way that the client can visualize the event, taste the food, hear the music, and see their guests. These initial conversations are critical to settling client expectations for the overall event and creating a shared vision for the end result.

Tips from the Trade

Prior to your initial meeting with any client, take the opportunity to gather information about the client to help tailor your vision for his or her event. This could include having the client complete an event-specific client information questionnaire prior to arrival or reviewing public Internet sources (e.g., social networking sites, business websites, etc.) to gain a glimpse at their preferences for music, food, and more. This not only adds to your credibility when selling your services, but also expedites the planning process.

Jennifer Currie, Owner Operator, Practically Perfection Events

As the planning process begins, the event planner moves from the visionary role to acting as a knowledgeable liaison for the client. Few clients have any related experience from which to draw on. Without the assistance of a planner, laying the foundation for a successful event is a daunting task. Using their expertise on event components and event flow, event planners must translate their client's needs and vision into event terms and communicate these needs to related catering and other professionals that will be a part of the event.

A strong event planner will be comfortable speaking with a variety of related professionals, including:

- facility management (convention center, property managers)
- audio visual/musical professionals
- catering and banquet management and staff
- photographers and other specialized services (florists, party rental companies)
- corporate business owners or business contacts (for corporate events)

Additionally, throughout the process, the event planner must be able to call attention to potentially overlooked details that could impact the success of the event. The event planner maintains order and organization of all aspects of the event, through all phases of the planning process and event execution. Not only must all pertinent contacts be maintained and readily available, the event planner is also charged with ensuring that all information is disseminated to relevant parties. Determination of event timelines, pre-event follow ups with vendors and venues used in the event, utilization of standardized checklists based upon event type, and review of tickler files by date to ensure key deadlines are met are all examples of typical actions taken by planners throughout the event life cycle to organize the numerous details that must all work in harmony.

In connection with acting as the client's knowledgeable liaison for all things related to the event, the event planner also plays a large role in the fiscal aspects of the process. Planners are essential in negotiating the costs associated with each feature of the event. Using extensive industry experience, the planner must ensure that the client's costs are, at a minimum, in line with industry norms.

Frequently throughout the course of normal business, partnership and referral discounts from complimentary services are acquired by the event planner that often works to the benefit of the client's budget. One example of this would be for an event planner to work in a partnership with a photographer to offer any of the clients a discount if the client books with their photography services for the event.

Tips from the Trade

Partnerships with complementary businesses are a key way to grow your business. In connection with this, gaining exposure during events such as wedding expos or business industry–specific trade shows gains you direct exposure to your client base. During these events do not neglect to interact with other vendors. They can be the source of potential client referrals in the future!

Jennifer Currie, Owner Operator, Practically Perfection Events

The event planner assists in establishing the initial budget and maintains the overall budget for the event. In establishing a budget, the planner must be able to speak knowledgeably about typical costs to ensure that the client's budgetary expectations are reasonable and ultimately met.

Throughout the course of the event planning process the planner may need to revisit the client's budget. Nearly all clients look to do more with less, but at times this might not be feasible. This frequently occurs with food and beverage selection. While a client may envision a lavish carving station or offering a high-end wine, this may not be within their budget, and the event planner is charged with bringing this to the client's attention in a sensitive manner, outlining alternatives, and seamlessly weaving new options into the client's vision.

The culmination of weeks or months of work occurs in mere hours as the event planner shifts into an event execution role. Throughout the entire course of the event, the event planner is the primary contact for all vendors, as well as venue (catering and banquet) managers, and, of course, the client and his or her guests. Of the many responsibilities of the event planner on event day, typically the planner must be ready to:

- address any and all issues that arise
- anticipate complications
- manage established timelines
- multitask and ensure the completion of numerous related and competing tasks
- ensure quality standards
- ensure client and guest satisfaction

At the culmination of the event, the event planner's role shifts from actively managing a specific event to building and maintaining an ongoing relationship with the clients. In the postevent phase, the event planner begins by reviewing the event and addressing any outstanding issues. The aim is to ensure that the final impression of the event planner experience is as positive as possible.

Event planners rely on referrals and repeat business to build their client base. Personalizing future communications with previous clients builds on and maintains the close relationship that is often formed during the event-planning process. The simple act of sending an anniversary card to a client whose wedding you were a part of creates a lasting impression and helps build future business.

Tips from the Trade

Your presence during the event should be as unobtrusive as possible. A properly planned event should flow seamlessly from one portion to the next. Whenever possible, limit your interactions with your client and the client's guests to those that ensure their satisfaction and to communicate timing with them. Remember, your appearance, attire, mannerisms, etc. should all blend in with the venue as well as the guests.

Jennifer Currie, Owner Operator, Practically Perfection Events

Event Planning and the Catering Management Team: Roles and Strategic Partnership

At any event, be it a wedding, birthday party, or business retreat, the entire event is structured around food. People indulge and enjoy for the simple fact that they are in a special event. In our society, food and beverage are associated with nearly every holiday or gathering. Some of the most lasting impressions of any event are connected to the catering we experience there. The catering aspect often receives the most attention from clients and the largest portion of their budgets. For this reason, a strong relationship between the event planner and the caterer is essential to the overall success of an event.

Event Planner's Role in Catering

The planner acts as the central point of communication for the catering team. The planner again acts as a knowledgeable liaison; however, in this instance the information flow shifts from the catering team back to the client, translating the catering industry terms into terms the client appreciates. Acting as this translator allows for both parties to set expectations clearly and to communicate more efficiently.

Once expectations and initial terms are set, the event planner's role in communication evolves to acting as an intermediary between the caterer and the client. Both the planner and the catering team view the event from a business standpoint; therefore, there is less emotion surrounding the event. While both parties have a vested interest in ensuring that the event goes off flawlessly, the production team does not develop the same emotional connections as the client does. The detachment from emotion surrounding the event allows the planner and the catering team to pragmatically address any issues that arise when planning.

Many minor issues may be resolved without the client's involvement, providing a more seamless experience for the client. Frequently issues arise that do need the client's input or approval. In these circumstances, the planner and the catering team have the opportunity to partner and determine options prior to involving the client (see Chapter 16, Conflict Resolution). The planner is charged with going back to the client to explain the issues and the available alternatives. By having viable alternatives immediately available for the client to select, all parties benefit

Tips from the Trade

When addressing all of the issues, keep a focus on the total picture of the event. This is what the client and their guests will remember long after the event's conclusion. Focus your attention on the issues that potentially impact the vision of the event. Delegate when you are able to more easily address minor issues. Your client should never be blindsided when something does not go as planned. Do not be afraid to communicate issues to them and to seek their input when needed.

Jennifer Currie, Owner Operator, Practically Perfection Events

from defusing a potentially emotional situation to one that more productively allows for the planning process to continue.

The planner continues to act as the intermediary and point of contact for issues as the process continues into execution phase. During the course of the event, the planner is the primary contact for the catering team (and the client) to address any issues that arise. To successfully act in this role, the planner must be comfortable with quickly assessing the issue and decisively determining the best course of action.

Event Planners and Independently Owned Businesses Versus National Brands

One of the first decisions made when planning an event is to select the venue. Based upon this decision, the event planner and the client may be presented with the opportunity to select either an independently owned catering business (and other independent businesses, such as audio visual services, photographer, etc.) or move forward working in partnership with the management team of a national brand (such as Hyatt, Marriott, Hilton, or large conference and convention centers).

Independent business owners present event planners with an opportunity to build a mutually beneficial relationship, allowing for ongoing joint business growth and benefits to the clients of each other. Referrals often flow both ways: from the planner to the caterer and vice versa.

The independent nature of both businesses allows for flexibility on product, pricing, and more. A smaller operation may be able to be more responsive to unique client requests as they are not tied to structured corporate guidelines often associated with larger venues or national chain brands. Often, larger national brands have established menus, structured timelines, specific room sets, and so on that are considered their standard and are maintained across the brand for consistency. Deviating from these guidelines may pose a challenge for the planner and the client.

While an independent catering business provides benefits to the event planner and his or her clients, they lack the brand recognition and associated perception of the brand that clients may seek out. For example, a client may value the image of sophistication and elegance associated with having their event hosted at the Ritz Carlton and are willing to pay the premium associated with the brand.

Nearly all larger facilities that have banquet or convention space maintain Banquet Managers on their payroll. These individuals are charged with execution of all events at the venue. They bring with them a wealth of knowledge on the venue and its resources, and direct the hourly banquet staff. Their positions may also create a blurred line of authority for the event planner, as both individuals share a vested interest in the event's overall success. However, the event planner does not have the authority to direct the banquet manager's employees or to arbitrarily make changes to the event (e.g. timing, room layouts) without consultation with the venue's management team.

When working with these managers, the event planner acts as the advocate for the client. The planner has the clearest vision of the client's expectations and throughout the event the planner should work to ensure that this vision is executed as closely as possible. When issues do occur in the course of the event, the planner must work with the management team to reach a solution.

Tips from the Trade

In the week prior to events at a new venue, arrange for a time to meet with the banquet management team. Their familiarity with you and your expectations will help to create a more positive working relationship and allow you greater leverage and involvement in the execution of the event.

Jennifer Currie, Owner Operator, Practically Perfection Events

Creating a positive working relationship with larger national brand venues is vital to an event planner's long-term business success. When an internal catering management team has a positive relationship with a specific event planner, a common bond of goodwill can exist which increases the flexibility of the catering team to the event planners. Flexibility on menu price may result when previously this was not possible. These positive relationships ultimately result in a high level of client satisfaction and potential referrals for future events from both the event venue and the satisfied clients.

Trends and the Future of Event Planning

Many businesses and individuals are feeling the fiscal impact of changes in the economic climate nationwide. Since the early 2000s, many businesses have elected to forgo lavish holidays or annual events in favor of more modest events as fiscal peaks and valleys occur. Event planners must be flexible and responsible to client demands and provide feasible solutions for all budgets.

A planner must also be prepared to integrate and implement societal trends into all events. Some of these trends could include:

- environmentally friendly alternatives (see Chapter 17)
- nontraditional family structures and family roles
- integration/use of social media (see Chapter 5) and other electronic media, both as a resource in event planning and as a part of the event itself

NEVER STOP LEARNING

An informed, educated caterer is prepared to exceed the expanding needs of the consumer in the competitive catering industry. Continuous research of the marketplace provides the caterer with a flow of new information on the rapidly evolving industry. This vigilant attention to the marketplace provides information to help the caterer make decisions regarding emerging market trends, advanced packaging, new products, and updated government regulations in such areas as sanitation and human resources.

There are always new products being introduced by the processors. Twenty-five years ago caterers made all their own hors d'oeuvres, requiring many hours of intense labor. Now, professionally made frozen hors d'oeuvres are available as thaw-and-serve or heat-and-serve items. The major point of this example is to always be aware of the continuous development and introduction of new foods and new ideas.

As trends emerge and create continuous change, the successful caterer must adapt to those changes. A caterer must constantly be looking for trends, such as the emergence of social media technology, its related marketing strategies, and its application to catering (see Chapter 5).

UPGRADING THE EVENT

It is important to understand a customer's needs for many reasons. The caterer wants to plan an event which completely satisfies all of the client's expectations. A caterer can guide the client in their decision-making process by offering professional suggestions, especially by recommending upgraded elements of the total package.

Suggesting upgraded elements when meeting with the client enables the caterer to use experience and expertise to enhance the package and exceed a guest's basic needs. It means the enhancement of food and service by tweaking the plan originally suggested by the client. Upgrading sometimes offers upscaled alternatives for similar prices to create a super value for the customer's budget.

upgrading the event
To enhance the delivery and showmanship of the food and/or service by tweaking elements of the event package to exceed a client's basic needs. These professional suggestions may be based on the caterer's expertise.

Upgrading the event can also mean a caterer suggests specific bridal shops, florists, limousine companies, photographers, and others who can help *professionalize* the event. This reciprocal arrangement can also help a caterer find new customers as these local businesspeople will also send inquiring customers to the caterer.

The client expects the professional caterer to use expertise when discussing the delivery and showmanship of food and service. Professional suggestions are offered to enhance a client's perception of value. Suggestions range from a simple menu addition to the inclusion of additional service personnel. If a client wants to have a champagne toast for the bridal party, the caterer can suggest wine be served to the guests instead. This would be cheaper than serving champagne, tweak the event, and incrementally increase revenue. Suggesting ice cream be served with the wedding cake during the reception may add only a slight cost to the menu, but provides added features to make the event special.

A customer will initiate the first contact with a caterer. The caterer's purpose is to suggest the right combination of food and service at their specific price. However, every contact a caterer has with a potential client does not automatically guarantee a customer. A caterer must be aware of the customer, know the customer, and understand how the customer reacts to suggestions.

HOW THE CATERER PROVIDES PROTECTION

Caterers learn from experience which customers they are not comfortable working with on events. One strategy is for the caterer to ask the potential client for a list of caterers in the past five years with whom they have worked. A caterer can then call these individuals as references.

One great advantage in the catering business is the caterer can be very selective about the client. It is not like a restaurant operation where the doors are open and everyone who enters is your customer. This way, the caterer can build a relationship with clientele the organization is proud to work with and feels comfortable with, and can avoid *undesirables*.

The caterer always has the option of declining work. This is accomplished rather politely, without offending anyone, and without having to say, "Look, I do not want to do work for you." A caterer will say they already have too many events booked during that week or their selected date has already been promised.

In social catering, the caterer must know the income level of the client. Can they afford to have the 15-dollar-per-person event or the 20-dollar-per-person affair? Maybe there's a neighborhood party going on and everyone is contributing to the event. The client decides to have it catered but only wants to spend $10 or $12 a person. At this price, the caterer has a limited budget to include fixed costs, labor costs, and the cost of food. Therefore, it will be very difficult to give the customer much satisfaction for this price.

The caterer must also protect the profit margin. At this point, the caterer must ask, "Is the profit margin adequate to cover all the costs?" "Can the job be done satisfactorily?" "Can the combined expectations of the caterer and the customer be met?" Although there are caterers who will cater events for $15 per person, these events are very difficult to profit from. Look for the next niche up. Research the market. What jobs can the caterer execute that will meet and exceed customer expectations and achieve satisfactory profit returns?

Undesirables

A caterer gets most customers through referrals. These prospective clients know the caterer's reputation but the caterer may not know the client. It is therefore important to complete a background check before accepting a client as a customer, to determine if the prospective client has the ability to meet the financial obligations. Caterers must know if their clients are financially stable.

There may be a number of reasons for a caterer to reject an inquiry from a potential customer or refuse to work with a particular client. The location may be poor or the lack of adequate facilities may be a problem. Some people are very difficult to work with, especially in social catering. Some clients are moaners, complainers, or nitpickers. The more difficult the client, the more difficult it is to satisfy them. These clients are always demanding more than the caterer can afford to provide, or they try to create obligations and expectations the caterer cannot meet.

A group may be historically unruly and a caterer may simply refuse business with this client after the first bad experience.

PROPOSALS

A **proposal** is a communication tool used to effectively inform and educate the prospective client of everything the caterer can do for them during the particular event. The written proposal must communicate how the caterer intends to

proposal A communication tool used to effectively inform and educate the prospective client about everything the caterer can do for them during the particular event.

eliminate the client's concern about the implementation and successful execution of their function. It must realistically communicate how the caterer can exceed their needs.

The proposal is a detailed document. It must list everything the caterer will do. Every detail, from the beginning of the event to its concluding activity, either at the caterer's facility or at an off-premise facility, must be stated. The proposal communicates to the client a first-impression image of the caterer, and information it provides is used by the customer when choosing a caterer.

Length and Complexity

Proposals vary in both length and complexity. The format may be a standard form or can be personally designed and written for each client. However, before creating a proposal to present to the prospective client, the caterer must know the needs, desires, and special requests of the client. It must be clear what the client is looking for and what kind of a budget the client is working with on this project. Is the client offering the caterer $20, $25, or $75? Price is important. The caterer will have to submit a competitive offer which may be compared to other caterers bidding on the event. If a chicken dinner is requested, the caterer cannot propose $175, and if a steak dinner is needed, a $7 proposal is also not feasible.

It is important for the caterer to know which costs are involved in each event. A caterer must have control over operations and know their fixed costs, food costs, and labor costs. Understanding costs is important so the caterer can prepare a competitive proposal that works to everyone's advantage.

Basic Proposal

The basic proposal will spell out in detail everything to be done by the caterer. A proposal is prepared for a variety of reasons. It becomes a planning tool that benefits both the caterer and the client. Each knows precisely what will be done and what is included for the set fee. Nothing is assumed.

A caterer should attempt to create an individual proposal for each client based on their needs. Depending on the type of catering event, a proposal can be very brief—merely listing the things the caterer is going to do. If catering an event for 1,500 people, the proposal would become very detailed and lengthy. All services provided by the caterer should be addressed in the proposal, including:

- Will an attendant park the guest's cars?
- Will the caterer entertain the children?
- Will the caterer provide entertainment?
- Will the caterer provide snacks?

These and similar concerns can be addressed in the proposal.

The proposal will be similar in descriptive detail to the way the final draft of the contract (Chapter 14) is explicitly written. The information in Figure 4.6 will help a caterer prepare a well-written, descriptive proposal.

Proposal

Organization's Name _____ Client's Name _____

Day _____ Date _____ (function's day & date of execution)

DEADLINE OR DUE DATE

Purpose of Function _____ Theme _____

Function _____ (wedding, birthday picnic, family reunion)

Address _____ Direction/Location _____

City _____ State/Zip _____

Phone _____ Fax _____

_____

E-mail _____

Method of Payment _____ (cash, credit card, check, barter, other)

Party making the payment _____ (e.g., wedding—bride/groom's family,

social event—Elizabeth 50% + Samantha 50%, celebration—Stephen 100%)

Uniform Requirements

Wait staff _____ Food Production _____ Beverage Service _____ Other _____

Special Request _____ (e.g. Jammie's birthday, Bill & Joyce's anniversary)

Starting and Ending Time _____ (exact starting and ending time)

Location _____ (exact location of function, directions)

Approximate Number of Guests _____ (best estimate, based on historical data)

Minimum Number Expected _____ (minimum guest count for this event)

*Final guarantee number will be charged unless adjusted prior to 1:00 PM. on _____
(last day for guest to adjust final count without penalty)

Menu Requirements (All menu details as agreed upon with client)

Price Per Guest: $ (_____) (If quote per person, amount specified in this contract)

All food and beverage subject to (_____%) sales tax and (_____%) service charge.

Entree and Sides_____ (exact menu, portion size)

Service Style _____ (explicit description of service responsibilities)

Beverage Service _____ (nonalcoholic and alcoholic beverages and service)

Set up Requirements _____ (any special requests, floor plan, and seating chart)

Chefs—a flat $(_____) labor charge will be assessed for each Chef required for
buffet-line carving stations.

Other Services

Linen and Napkins _____

Skirting Requirements _____

Style of Plateware _____

Style of Silverware _____

Style of Glassware _____

Table Requirements _____

Chair Requirements _____

Tent Requirements _____

Audiovisual _____

Florist _____

Photographer _____

Special Decorations and Service (e.g., ice sculptures, hand-carved centerpieces, individualized flower arrangements, and thematic decorations).

Security _____

Valet Parking _____ Time _____ Guests _____

Entertainment _____

Weather Forecast _____ Update _____

Figure 4.6 Proposal basics.

A famous ethnic orchestra was creating an annual fund-raising event, and Jardine's Catering was invited to submit a proposal. Rather than send a traditional proposal by mail, the catering staff was motivated to create a special and unusual proposal. We wanted to excite the fund-raising committee by demonstrating through the proposal that we were the best caterer for the event. The proposal itself became a formal presentation. We created a sample of foods from the menu being presented to the committee. We packaged the items in a basket which was sent to the committee as part of the proposal. Our creativity and imagination provided a competitive edge other caterers found hard to match.

The catering staff used innovation and expertise to create a professional, personable, and memorable presentation. The baker made a variety of special rolls and breads, baked a miniature apple pie, and carved, in the crust of the pie, the initials of the organization. An American flag suspended on a stick was placed into the pie. The chef prepared a variety of signature sauces and included those in the basket as samples. To complement the food, a bottle of wine and four wine glasses were placed in the basket along with samples of the proposed linens, napkins, plates, and silverware.

To create a sense of urgency and importance, a professional messenger service delivered the basket of food and the traditional written proposal to the committee. Because of this very impressive way the proposal was submitted, Jardine's was awarded the contract. Over the years, we successfully replicated this method many times with success.

Courtesy Bill Jardine

Submitting a Proposal

Creativity and imagination will help deliver a competitive edge when presenting a proposal. To impress the prospective client, a caterer should personally hand deliver the proposal. Remember, other caterers are bidding on this same event. This leads us to *Ingredient for Success 13: "Presentations are important— create special, unusual, personable, and impressive competitive proposals."*

Basket presentations are a unique idea to present a proposal that projects a very powerful image to the customer. Another competitive strategy to secure a contract from a client is to invite the committee to sample the food. At this sampling, provide a variety of the food considered for the event. One final suggestion is the use of a video. Having a professional video available to communicate the mission of the caterer offers an extra addition to any proposal. Remember, the caterer must always create new and exciting methods to stimulate a prospective client because sometimes the caterer gets the job, and sometimes not.

The only limitation to presenting unique proposals is your imagination. Proposals can be done on regular paper without any fancy presentation. They can be done on theme paper with special matching binders or created on CD-ROM with pictures to illustrate what the event would look like. The delivery of the proposal is dependent on the client's needs. If there is a formal presentation, the proposal should reflect this. If the proposal is being sent to the client it can be accompanied by freshly baked cookies, gourmet coffee, or popcorn. Knowing your client's likes and dislikes will give clues to what will impress them. The revenue generated by the event will determine how elaborate the presentation of the proposal should be. Again, your imagination is your only limitation in this area.

Michelle Albright Lennox, Catering/Convention Services Manager, Hyatt
Orlando, Kissimmee, Florida

Summary

The creation of a satisfied, sustainable customer base from which to draw current and potential clients necessary to support a catering operation now and in the future is one of the most important business tasks a caterer must faithfully perform. Creating such a base is accomplished by translating unmet customer needs, wants, and demands into a package of tangible goods and intangible services. Implementing prospecting strategies, such as linking current customers with new prospects, contacting community service organizations, reading local newspaper articles, sponsoring food tasting events, and using advertising methods and publicity will lead to the discovery of new customers.

As long as there are weddings, birthdays, anniversaries, and more, there will be celebrations and events to accompany them. Event planners will have a role in the planning of events provided they are able to be responsive to the changing needs of their clients and adaptable to the shifting trends in society. To effectively inform and educate the prospective client of what the caterer can do during a particular event, a detailed proposal is drafted. The proposal will vary in length and complexity, but it will be similar in descriptive detail to the way the final draft of the contract is explicitly written.

Review Questions

Brief Answers

1. Discuss why creating a solid customer base by attracting new customers is a continuous building process for a caterer.
2. Describe why it is important to understand customer needs before one begins to build a foundation consisting of a solid customer base.
3. Discuss why it is a challenge for a caterer to translate customer needs into a package of tangible products and intangible services the caterer must implement to exceed a customer's desires.
4. Identify five needs all customers have when seeking a caterer.
5. Identify and discuss prospecting strategies a caterer may use to find new clients.
6. Discuss why membership in community organizations is a great way for a caterer to meet prospective customers.
7. Describe what is meant by the term *life cycle of customer events.*
8. Identify and discuss challenges that a caterer might face attracting customers during their slower-sales time of the year. List two prospecting strategies a caterer can use to attract interested clients during this slower-sales period.
9. Identify and explain two strategies a caterer must employ when planning the growth of the catering company.

10. Why is the implementation of a professional sales staff important to the success of a caterer?

11. Discuss the role the event planner plays in a catered event. Why is it important for a caterer and event planner to establish a professional relationship?

12. Discuss the importance of continued education for a caterer and how this helps in the identification of industry trends and changing customer needs.

13. Discuss how a caterer can use a variety of techniques to protect them against undesirable clients.

Multiple Choice

Select the single best answer for each question.

1. This catering tool is used by the caterer to communicate and inform prospective clients what will be provided during an event.
    a. proposal
    b. budget
    c. upgrading the event
    d. contract
    e. prospecting strategies

2. The advantage of a professional sales staff to the caterer is the:
    a. immediate presence in the marketplace.
    b. constant presence in the marketplace as a reminder to potential clients.
    c. identification of potential clients who are in need of service.
    d. communicating information regarding the caterer's abilities.
    e. All of the above are advantages experienced by the caterer.

3. The purpose of a caterer reading the daily local newspaper is to:
    a. keep current with national events.
    b. understand local politics and upcoming elections.
    c. identify local community events and recent engagements.
    d. clip coupons.
    e. None of the above is a valid reason.

True or False

Read each of the following statements and determine if it is true or false.

1. The planned growth of a catering company is achieved only by satisfying customers' needs.

2. An educated, informed caterer is prepared to exceed the always changing needs of the client in the competitive catering industry.

3. One advantage a caterer has over the traditional restauranteur is the ability to select their clients.

Putting It All Together

You are hired as a consultant to assist a local start-up catering company in your area. Your task is to develop and present a detailed prospectus plan for them to use in acquiring new clients for their business. Write a prospecting plan and prepare a sample proposal.

Chapter 5

Social Media Marketing

© drdre/www.Shutterstock.com

Hello QR Code

Objectives

After studying this chapter, you should be able to:

1. Describe social networking.
2. Explain how a caterer can use social networking to build brand awareness.
3. Summarize how social networking is real-time interactive.
4. Identify social media websites.
5. Evaluate social media as a marketing tool.
6. Understand how social media goals can be integrated into measurable business objectives.

KEY TERMS

blogging

micro blogging

photo sharing

social media

social networking

social news

subscribe

video sharing

WHAT IS SOCIAL MEDIA?

The Internet is evolving towards a domain populated with websites generated by user-generated content. The core tenant of this design philosophy is the promotion of user-to-user interactions and experiences. A caterer is probably familiar with websites such as MySpace®, Facebook®, and Twitter®. These websites are **social media**. Other social media sites include Wikipedia®, Shutterfly®, and Yelp®. What makes these websites social media? Social media are media that are socially interactive. Websites that enable a caterer to communicate with and interact with friends, family, customers, and potential clients are social media sites.

How does a caterer interact using a social media site? First, create a Social Media Policy. Use this policy to create communication procedures to guide employee behavior. This policy will allow specific employees permission to access the company's social media site. Second, pursue a strategy to embed yourself into a client's social media communications. Let the satisfied client build the caterer's brand. Positive word-of-mouth testimonials spread over the Internet by a satisfied client creates loyal customer relationships, helps position the caterer's brand, and builds a defensible company image. Conversely, a negative comment is potentially just as damaging.

A caterer can select from many different platforms that comprise the general topic of social media. These social media platforms include:

- photo sharing
- video sharing
- blogging
- micro blogging
- social networking
- social news

Photo Sharing

Photo sharing sites allow users to upload and maintain a library of their personal photos online. Sites permit users to share their library with friends and family. Some other printing services and products are generated from the user's content, such as imprinted items. Popular photo sharing sites include Flickr®, Shutterfly, SmugMug®, and photobucket®.

The Good: These sites are heavily indexed in search engines—for example, Google® Images. Someone searching for a photo of a wedding cake might come across a photo posted by a caterer from a special event.

The Okay: Photos posted to these sites need to be properly tagged. The caterer needs to identify the image, the people, and the brand. Sharing images is a great way for the caterer to visibly remind and reinforce with clients examples of excellent service and quality food provided at the event.

The Bad: Click-through rates for photos are among the lowest. People searching for wedding cake photos are unlikely to browse through to a caterer's website. Furthermore, someone searching for pictures of a wedding cake most likely will not purchase a cake from the caterer, as they are most likely searching for a picture to use in an outside context.

---

social media Websites that enable a caterer to communicate with and interact with friends, family, customers, and potential clients including MySpace, Facebook, and Twitter.

photo sharing Websites that allow users to upload, maintain a library of their personal photos online, and permit users to share their library with friends and family. Popular photo sharing sites include Flickr, shutterfly, SmugMug, and photobucket.

Video Sharing

Similar to photo sharing, **video sharing** allows a caterer to post video to the Internet. Popular video sharing sites include YouTube®, phanfare®, Metacafe®, and Break®. Facebook also provides a video sharing section and a direct link to YouTube-posted videos.

The Good: It quickly engages a caterer's customers. Use videos to entertain, to inform, to differentiate from competitors, and to communicate the caterer's brand to others.

The Okay: Unless a caterer specifically links their videos through another site, people are unlikely to search YouTube for a caterer specifically.

The Bad: An embarrassing mistake becomes a competitor's ace-in-the-hole. With the popularity of cell phones, handheld recording devices are ubiquitous. Remember, not only can a caterer post videos, but others can post videos about the caterer too.

> **video sharing** Allows a caterer to post video to the Internet. Popular video sharing sites include YouTube, phanfare, Metacafe, and Break.

Blogging

A **blog** is similar to a newspaper column; it's typically maintained by an individual with regular entries of commentary, descriptions of events, or other material. Popular blogging sites include: Wordpress®, Blogger®, and Blogspot®.

The Good: A caterer can say anything; their opinion rules. Caterers can use a blog to carefully develop, promote, and communicate their brand, and leave commentary after an event, describing what the caterer does. It is a good way to keep clients and potential clients updated with what the caterer is working on at the time.

The Okay: A caterer needs to optimize their blog by including it on their website and social media sites. If people are unaware of it, they won't read it. Build a subscriber base through current customers and friends.

The Bad: A caterer must be careful of what is written, as blogs sometimes have a negative impact. Have a standard communication policy. Always stay upbeat and positive. Some sites allow subscribers to leave comments on blogs. A caterer cannot control what is being written. Also, the site must be constantly maintained. A site that is not updated every few days will lose people's interest.

> **blogging** Similar to a newspaper column; a blog is typically maintained by an individual with regular entries of commentary, descriptions of events, or other material. Popular blogging sites include: Wordpress, Blogger, and Blogspot.

Micro Blogging

Micro blogging is a blog with messages of 140 characters or less. Typically, people **subscribe** to follow others and receive their messages. Popular micro blogging sites include: Twitter, Pounce®, tumblr®, and Jaiku®.

The Good: The ability to monitor keywords with programs like Hootsuite, Twitjump, or Radian 6 is helpful. Micro blogs offer unique ways to engage customers with instant coupons and specials. A great way to tout successes during or after an event; micro blogging is bragging.

The Okay: The potential can be large, but hard to manage. Micro blogging can offer too much or too little exposure.

The Bad: Anybody can micro blog; the caterer, employees, the customers. The caterer can control what they say, but can't necessarily control what others say about the caterer.

> **micro blogging** Sending blogs with messages of 140 characters or less. Typically, people subscribe to follow others and receive their messages. Popular micro blogging sites include Twitter, Pounce, tumblr, and Jaiku.

> **subscribe** To pledge, such as signing an agreement, a subscription.

Social Networking

Typically, social networking websites are what most people think of as social media. **Social networking** sites provide a hub for communication and interaction. Popular sites include Facebook, Linkedin®, MySpace, and emerging very rapidly is Twitter.

The Good: Social networking sites are a great way to promote the caterer's business. Caterers use these sites to advertise their brand, talk to customers for free, and allow customers to reach the caterer. Use these sites to teach potential clients who the caterer is, to reinforce positive impressions of the caterer, and to show why the client must hire this specific caterer for their event.

The Okay: Overload. Do potential clients read everything that's posted or do they skip important information? A caterer needs to make his or her posts matter by sharing the important information he or she wants customers to see.

The Bad: Not all social networking sites are created equal.

Social News

Social News are websites where people and businesses can share news stories, press releases, links to their websites, and bookmarks to web pages. Similar to social networking, popular social news sites include: digg®, StumbleUpon®, and delicious®.

The Good: Currently attractive and widely read, social news may be the modern day newspaper.

The Okay: These websites are not optimal for customer interaction or brand exposure. Although readers can vote for their favorite news stories, they are not interacting with a caterer specifically.

The Bad: Although these websites can drive traffic, a caterer does have to pay for it. Many times a caterer must pay to get their post to the top of the pile. Does the cost justify the traffic?

WHAT IS SOCIAL MEDIA MARKETING AND WHY USE IT?

Using social media is a way for a caterer to build credibility, generate buzz, and increase revenue. Consider the following factors:

- 49 percent of web users have made a purchase based on a recommendation from a social media site.
- Social media sites are where people are.
- Trust in traditional advertising continues to erode.
- People are already talking about you.
- In some cases, it is free!

Picking a Platform

Take, for example, Facebook. When a caterer creates a Facebook page, the page should be a fan page. Fan pages are public and permit anyone to become a fan. When creating a business presence, make a professional-looking page and have it represent the caterer's brand. Limit the number of administrators to the page. Administrators are people who can post to the page under the caterer's brand name. Fewer administrators keep the message consistent and the brand image accurate.

A caterer can use a Facebook page to:

- Show personality, be fun and engaging.
  - Keep the posts light and fun. Treat your fans like friends.
- Promote events.
  - Participating in a charity event? Help the charity sell tickets by promoting the event.
- Share news and press releases.
  - Won the cook off? Tell the subscribers about the successes. Post specials for the weekend or a new beverage being featured.
- Engage fans and ask questions.
  - Looking to change the menu? Ask the fans what their favorites are.
  - Create contests.
- Share expertise.
  - Is it strawberry season? Post a quick recipe using fresh local ingredients.

Negative comments aren't really bad. Immediately interact with fans and don't delete negative posts. This is the caterer's chance to turn it around and respond to the comment. Make your fans aware that you take care of problems and are focused on customer service. Minimize efficiency and combine accounts. Let Facebook posts automatically upload to the caterer's Twitter page.

Engage Customers

A caterer can drive people to their page by means other than Facebook. Use websites, posters, mailings, and e-mails to gather fans. Always include Facebook information on everything the caterer does. Include the page to business cards, menus, proposals, and advertisements.

Ask customers for feedback: communicating with customers is beneficial; other customers read the comments and learn more about the caterer's business. If customers know you respond to questions, they are more likely to ask questions in return.

Offer Facebook-only coupons and specials. Many consumers are fans of various businesses solely for coupons offered on their Facebook sites. This is a free way for a caterer to promote special offerings. Consider promoting a coupon on Facebook the week before it is advertised to the general public. Remember to include on Facebook advertising that special offers can only be found on Facebook.

Network with other businesses and promote each other on Facebook. Partner with a bridal store, event hall, or photographer. Your business can encourage fans to visit partner sites and they can do the same for you. Add photos to the page showing the ongoing partnering with these other businesses to deliver value in special events.

Paid Facebook Advertising

Facebook offers paid advertising. After a caterer creates his or her fan page, sample ads will begin to appear along the right hand side of it. Facebook offers two different advertising options: Cost Per Click (CPC) or Cost Per Impression (CPM).

CPC offers a caterer the ability to pay each time the ad is clicked. CPM is paid per 1,000 impressions. For each option, you bid on how much money you want to spend and the cost of your advertisement will never exceed the set daily budget. Companies who pay more will see their advertisements before companies that pay less.

HOW DO YOU TELL IF IT'S WORKING?

Business Analytics: Return on Investment

Tie your social media goals to a business objective and measure the effectiveness as it relates to the objective:

- Increase in sales
- Increase in traffic
- Increase in inquires

Social Analytics

A caterer can learn who is talking about them and what they are saying on social sites. Facebook provides page administrators with weekly analytical updates. These updates show the number of people visiting the page, how many fans have joined, how many people have posted to the page, and more. This information confirms if your message is being heard.

Klout.com—the Klout score measures overall online influence. The score ranges from 0 to 100, the higher score representing a wider and stronger sphere of influence. Other websites offer the ability to gauge online success. These websites include: Digg Stats, Collective Intellect, Twitturly, Tweetmeme, and Twitter Counter.

Web Analytics

Web analytics measure customer interactions. Time on site and bounce rate metrics reveal the number of visits and the amount of time people spend on your site. Pass along, comment to post ratio, bookmarks, podcast views, and click-throughs reveal customer interest level.

WAYS TO WEAVE SOCIAL MEDIA INTO CATERING

Promoting a catering business with social media is limited only by one's imagination (Figure 5.1). A Facebook page is a good place to start; Twitter comes next and can link to the Facebook page. Sharing photos and videos of events establishes an online portfolio.

Social media can be used to network with other businesses through Linkedin and Facebook. Customers review your business on social media sites like Yelp. Having a social media marketing plan and being consistent will insure social media success.

Figure 5.1 Caterers are imbedding social media technology into their operations, which help them to reach current and new clients.

Permission of John R. Smith

NEWER SOCIAL NETWORKING OPPORTUNITIES

Foursquare

Foursquare is a social network where friends share their locations and connect with others in close proximity to each other. Foursquare uses digital badges to reward players who "check-in" at different locations. Primarily used in larger metropolitan areas, Foursquare is becoming increasingly popular and focuses largely on retail and food establishments.

Opportunities exist to utilize Foursquare to increase traffic to a specific business location by drawing customers inside where their friends are. Caterers can target clients to attend public events, such as food tastings, festivals, and fundraising activities they are working.

QR Codes

QR or Quick Response codes are 2D bar codes that can be scanned by a smart phone with a QR reader. When scanned these codes link to a website. QR codes give customers the ability to acquire information instantaneously. QR codes are becoming more prevalent. QR codes placed discreetly on menu cards offer customers the opportunity to gather business information without a pen and paper.

Caution!

A caterer needs to think about what he or she is putting out there before it is posted. Once it is posted, it can't be taken back. A caterer's employee's feelings, attitudes,

Tips from the Trade

The application of social media technology into our catering company has certainly changed the way we communicate with our current and prospective clients, as well as how we think, see, and position the business. Approximately 2 years ago I eliminated from the phone book the business contact information for All Occasion Catering and it has not affected our business one bit. We now rely on our company's website, http://www.alloccasioncatering.org/, and social media technology to keep connected with our market. Our website is designed to be completely interactive. Our clients find it easy to navigate through our event pictures, menu items, contract information, and client testimonials. I believe in having our company's policies, pricing, and contract information open for everyone to see. Our website is linked to our Facebook account. We are currently studying how to imbed QR codes into our catering operations to further enhance customer service by enabling our clients the ease of obtaining need to know information, such as nutritional data, from our menu items.

Permission of John R. Smith

and experiences may not reflect those of the caterer. Employees should be familiar with the company's Social Media Policy before creating any social media pages or posting comments concerning the business.

Websites

The Internet is a great way to engage customers. Caterers can use websites in a variety of ways. A website is definitely advertising. It should be professionally created and constantly updated. A standard website for a caterer should contain the following information:

- About—This is a section on the history of the catering business. This section could also contain biographies and photos of the principal business members. This section is a great way for the caterer to connect with customers before meeting.
- Contact information—This section is dedicated to basic information including address, phone number, and e-mail address. If the caterer has a physical location they want to direct customers to, this section should also include a map and directions.
- Menus— Basic menus and pricing are the minimum requirement. Customers may pass over caterers who do not share pricing on their website and not consider them for their events. Past custom menus will also help customers visualize possibilities for their events.
- Photos—The photo section of a caterer's website should include event photos, food photos, and seasonal specials. Keep in mind the saying, "a picture is worth a thousand words." The photos on the web page need to be attractive and appealing. Limit the number of people photos and focus on the food.
- Testimonials—A testimonial section is free word-of-mouth advertising; share with prospective clients the thank you notes past customers wrote.

- Seasonal Specials—Allowing a website to go stale is a big stumbling block. Keep the website up-to-date with seasonal specials. For example, promote the fall season with fall themed colors and foods. Post tips on having the perfect fall event with menu and decorating ideas.

Make sure the website is maintained and current. Forgetting to update your prices on a website when changing a menu will lead to uncomfortable questions from clients. Not removing specials or seasonal products that are no longer offered can also cause problems with customers. Simply creating a website is not enough; an effective website is continually maintained.

Always include links to other social media sites including Facebook pages and Twitter accounts. Websites and social media work together. Links from one site to the other are important. A caterer's web page and social media should present the same message and not conflicting information. Other decisions include options on how to create the website. Do it yourself online or hire a professional. Never have an old website available to customers. If an old website is still up it could damage the caterer's reputation by creating a negative perception of the business. John and Debbie Smith, co-owners of All Occasion Catering, have created an excellent example of an interactive, user friendly, and technologically driven website at http://www.alloccasioncatering.org/.

E-mail Marketing

Collecting e-mail addresses from clients is a very inexpensive way to stay in touch and advertise. Multiple methods can be used to collect addresses, including adding an e-mail line to invoices and orders and asking for e-mail addresses on post event surveys or as part of a website. The e-mail addresses are maintained as part of a database.

E-mails may be sent weekly, monthly, or seasonally to advertise specials, seasonal menus, or to remind customers to book holiday parties. E-mail marketing is also a good way to share coupons with customers. Including eye catching photographs with your e-mail message will also piqué customer's interest.

Cross promotion is easily overlooked. Include a link to your website and your Facebook and Twitter accounts. It's a good idea to create a general business e-mail account to send and to receive e-mail messages. For example, use your business name: abccatering@abccatering.com. Customers are more likely to open an e-mail from a recognizable name than from joe@gmail.com. Make sure to regularly check the e-mail inbox as customers will respond to your advertisement e-mails with questions and orders.

Summary

The Internet is filled with websites allowing users to interact with each other. More and more new sites are established every day. Social media websites are MySpace, Facebook, Twitter, Wikipedia, Shutterfly, and Yelp. Social media websites enable a caterer to communicate and interact in real time with friends, family, customers, and potential clients. Use effective communication strategies to manage your brand. Encourage fans and clients to drive and initiate positive conversation in their social media communications. Positive communication creates loyal customer relationships, helps position the caterer's brand, and builds a defensible company image. Aggressively respond to negative commentary by taking immediate action to offer solutions to correct them.

Promoting a catering business with social media is limited only by one's imagination. Use social media to network with other businesses through both Linkedin and Facebook.

Review Questions

Brief Answers

1. Describe social media.
2. Describe social networking.
3. Explain how a caterer can use social networking to build brand awareness.
4. Explain why social networking is a real-time interactive marketing strategy.
5. List social media websites.
6. Explain how a caterer can use social media as part of their marketing mix.
7. Write a business objective using a social media goal.

Multiple Choice

1. A caterer can select from many different platforms that comprise the general topic of social media. These social media platforms include:
    a. Photo sharing
    b. Video sharing
    c. Blogging
    d. Micro blogging
    e. All of the above
2. A _____is similar to a newspaper column; it's typically maintained by an individual with regular entries of commentary or descriptions of events or other material.
    a. Photo sharing site
    b. Video sharing site
    c. Blog
    d. Twitter page
    e. None of the above
3. Which of the following is not a popular social networking website?
    a. Facebook
    b. Linkedin
    c. MySpace
    d. SpaceBook
    e. All of the above

True or False

1. Social media is a way for a caterer to build credibility, generate buzz, and increase revenue.
2. Websites that enable a caterer to communicate with and interact with friends, family, customers, and potential clients are social media sites.
3. Micro blogging is a blog with messages of 175 characters or less.

Putting It All Together

1. Write a blog post to promote seasonal catering menus. Include information about fresh local ingredients and how they are used in the menu.
2. Respond to the following Facebook post:

   I was so disappointed by your service on Saturday night. When I went through the buffet service there were no mashed potatoes left and the chicken was cold.

Sources

HyderKabani, S. (2010). *The Zen of Social Media Marketing*. Dallas, TX: Benbella.

Qualman, E. (2011). *Socialnomics*. (rev. ed.) Boston, MA: Wiley.

http://www.panorama.com.

http://www.cmo.com.

http://www.blogspot.hubspot.com.

http://www.facebook.com.

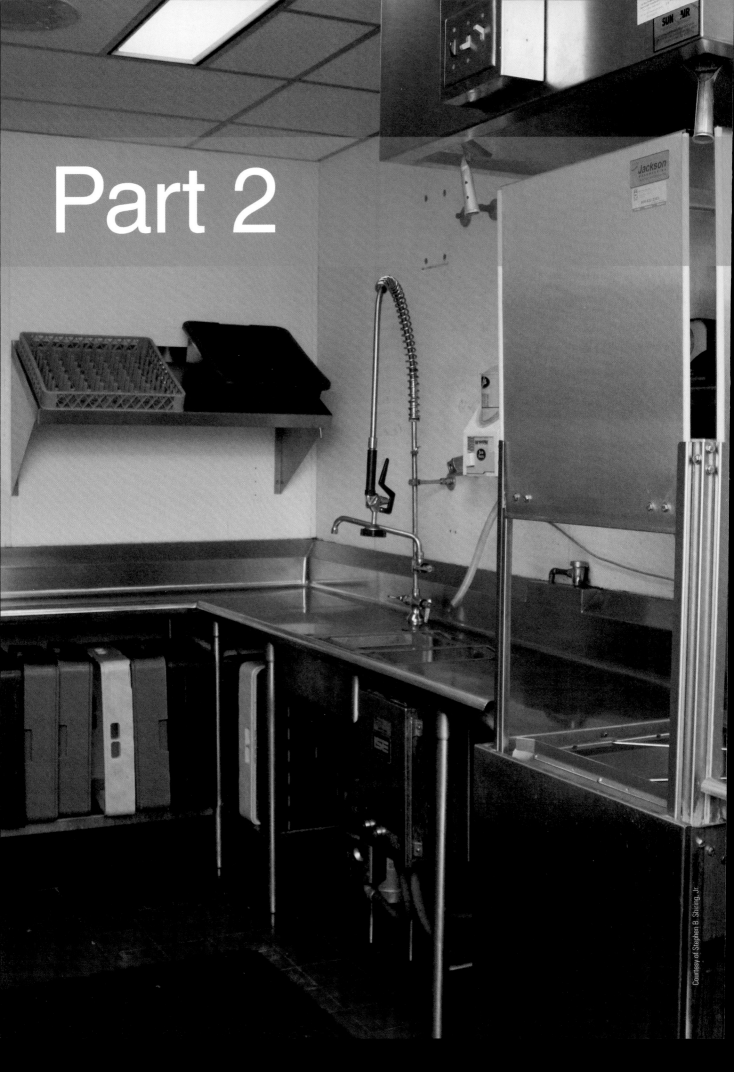

Part 2

The Catering Operation

© Cengage Learning 2014

Chapter 6

The Seven Functions of Catering

Objectives

After studying this chapter, you should be able to:

- Introduce the seven key catering functions.
- Explain why planning is first and influences the other six functions.
- Explain the symbiotic relationship of the seven functions.
- Explain why a caterer must manage resources to exceed customer expectations and meet organizational goals.
- Gain an appreciation for the organizing effort required to execute a catering event.
- Explain why a successful catering effort is the outcome of a strenuous journey demanding a dedicated individual.

KEY TERMS

bundle of tasks

capital resources

controlling

delegate

equipment

execution of tasks

financial resources

formulating

human resources

implementing

legal concerns

objectives

operational task

organizing

prime costs

strategic plan

tactical plan

Ingredients For Success

14 "The closer the caterer gets to the event, the more difficult the event becomes."

15 "Every observable action exhibited by the caterer emulates from the public mission statement."

16 "Accurate forecasting of market trends and changes in food prices are keys to establishing correct pricing and meeting preestablished financial objectives."

17 "Cost control procedures are created for the acquisition of timely information to equip the caterer with the data to scrutinize controllable costs and make appropriate operational decisions."

This chapter provides a brief synopsis of the key components that occur in every catering business.

All caterers, including corporate, social, on-premise, or off-premise, need to have a solid understanding of the following seven fundamental catering functions. The mastery of these seven functions helps to ensure real success. These are the fundamental catering management functions: (1) formulating the tactical plan for the event; (2) executing the operational tasks; (3) organizing resources; (4) matching equipment needs to the requirements of the food and service; (5) implementing the plan; (6) controlling the event by use of financial tools and predetermined standards; and (7) obtaining insurance coverage and ensuring all legal concerns are covered by a contract.

formulating (a plan) To design a specific plan of action to meet the client's needs based on the proposal and contract.

FIRST FUNCTION: PLANNING— THE BASIC CATERING MANAGEMENT FUNCTION

strategic plan Plan established to guide the entire catering organization over the long term, 3 to 5 years into the future.

The first step after the acceptance of the proposal is for a caterer to begin **formulating** a comprehensive plan for the event. After the mutual acceptance of the proposal, the date of its execution may actually vary from a few days to several months. It is reasonable to have events booked 1 to 5 years in advance of the actual date of execution. But whatever the period of time, one fact is true: ***"The closer the caterer gets to the event, the more difficult the event becomes."*** This is ***Ingredient for Success 14.***

Planning is a basic catering-management function. All plans should flow from the caterer's mission statement. Therefore, always remember ***Ingredient for Success 15: "Every observable action exhibited by the caterer evolves from the public mission statement."*** The successful caterer formulates and implements a plan based on competitive strategies deduced from the mission statement (Figure 6.1).

tactical plan Specifically created to provide the caterer precise short-term guidance as required for each catering event. This requires precise detail and precision execution.

Purpose of a Catering Plan

A catering plan serves many purposes. One purpose of a plan is to ensure the caterer's future. A **strategic plan** is established to guide the entire catering operation over the long term, 3–5 years into the future. It attempts to position the organization on a path of success. A second type of plan, a **tactical plan**, is specifically created to guide the caterer in a much shorter time frame. A tactical plan creates a forceful focus on each event. Whereas a strategic plan stretches over a long time frame, a tactical plan is specific to the event. A strategic plan requires modification and rejuvenation as forces in the caterer's market shape and reshape it. Since it is over a longer time period, it is much broader and more general in its design. A tactical plan, on the other hand, has a much shorter life span, requires precise detail, and execution.

Figure 6.1 An effective plan enables the caterer to achieve established objectives.

objectives Framed by the mission statement, they are established to serve as benchmarks against which actual performance can be measured against a predetermined target.

A plan enables the caterer to establish achievable **objectives**. Stated objectives flow directly from the mission statement. Objectives are established to serve as benchmarks to measure progress. A caterer can use these benchmarks to compare the actual performance against a predetermined target. This organizational progress can be specified in its strategic plan, or it can be established for each event as measured against a tactical plan. A caterer may create objectives that are beyond the believable accomplishment of the team to stretch the organization to greater levels.

Common organizational objectives may include the measurement of guest satisfaction, attainment of financial goals, human resource development, greater staff productivity levels, increase in market share, and positive organizational growth. For the specific event, tactical objectives might include guest satisfaction, event preparation, familiarity of location, handling guest count, menu item production, preparing the team, and obtaining the required equipment.

Finally, a plan is a blueprint or map. This powerful tool, when properly used by the caterer, keeps everyone in the organization on the right route. A plan helps to minimize unexpected surprises. It attempts to eliminate uncertainties by creating a supportive organizational environment.

One technique caterers use is known as the *Swiss Cheese Approach*. A caterer will break the master plan into smaller, more manageable segments—Swiss Cheese It! For example, a 1-year-in-advance-event plan can be segmented into the following time lines: a 6-month plan, 90-day, 60-day, 30-day, 2-week, 1-week, 4-day, 2-day, the day before, and right down to the day of the event. Once the plan is created, the staff will execute each element guided by the leadership and management of the caterer.

Time-Line Planning

Formulation of a plan for a catering event must include all principal players responsible for executing the event. These would include the catering manager, the chef or food and beverage manager, the buyer or purchasing agent, and the service manager. These key personnel must meet during the early planning stages to discuss the date, month, day, and time of the activity. Often they will be able to offer advice on management of conflicting events. For the event to become successful and profitable, they must be consulted from the beginning.

The chef or food and beverage manager is responsible for the menu, recipe development, beverages and service, recipe costing, menu pricing, determining production needs, staffing needs, and scheduling of employees. The service manager is responsible for all service staffing needs, table setups, food and beverage service, and scheduling employees. The buyer or purchasing agent is responsible for researching the availability of each menu item and its cost. Following are two examples of a planning time line.

Food Production Planning Time Line

Event Minus 75 Days In planning the menu for the event, it is necessary for the catering manager to fully inform the chef or food manager of the overall theme and objectives. If plans call for the function to become a regular part of the calendar of annual events, food production supervisors must know this in order to recommend compatible menu selections. It will be important to also provide alternative menu selections so that the event will not become prosaic or monotonous to the guests.

The catering manager should, in planning, allow a minimum of 2 or 3 weeks for the back-of-the-house staff to research menu selections, the product market, methods of procurement, and appropriate recipes, and for recipe development.

The chef will, during the planning stage, be concerned primarily with the menu and its development, including the nutritional balance, taste, color, texture, plate coverage, and presentation. The chef will research the relative popularity of the menu items, the availability of ingredients to produce the menu, and know the relationship between the menu and the type of equipment needed for production. Recipes must be selected that will meet the needs and wants of those attending the event. Ingredient costs and production hours are forecasted by the chef based on the event's *budget* (money available for their purchase).

Finally, the chef must decide exactly how many employees are needed to produce the menu. The menu will determine the culinary expertise required of each employee in the food production area. All of these activities must be discussed in detail before a final decision is made to proceed with the event.

The buyer or purchasing agent must have a list of specific items needed to produce the menu. At this time, the purchasing agent will research the product market to ascertain product availability and cost. The purchasing agent will make recommendations on what items must be ordered in advance, their forecasted market price, and which products may not be available. The purchasing expert should suggest comparable substitutes that can be procured to meet production needs.

Event Minus 45 Days At this point, the caterer will have a good idea of what products are available on the market and their relative costs. This is a good time to meet with the chef and finalize the menu. Recipe selections are discussed at this meeting, along with alternatives, especially if the menu is to be repeated or if products discussed at the first meeting are not available.

At this meeting, the chef, using an appropriate staffing guide, should be able to provide the caterer with an accurate description of personnel needed to produce the selected menus. Food costs should also be discussed. A reasonable selling price might be finalized. This selling price must be compatible with the predetermined profit objectives established by the caterer.

It is during this time that the chef or food manager meets, to formulate the production plan, with key production personnel in the kitchen. The chef discusses the function with the production team. Objectives, the menu, and staffing requirements are addressed. In addition to the menu, a production schedule is prepared. This worksheet details the menu items, recipes, special production needs, and preparation procedures. Responsibility and accountability will be delegated and recorded on the production schedule. A copy of this worksheet is posted on a bulletin board in the production area.

The purchasing agent can be present at this meeting to provide information on product availability, suppliers, special handling needs, and the dates and times of expected deliveries. A service supervisor should also be present to coordinate staffing requirements with the food production department.

Event Minus 30 Days One month before the event, the chef or food manager will verify the menu. All required products should be inventoried or readily attainable on short notice. Copies of the finalized menu, individual worksheets, and standardized recipes are distributed to key personnel including production personnel, salad-makers, bakers, and all those directly involved in the production process. Delegation of individual responsibility for each menu item and its production will be verified.

Event Minus 15 Days During this period, the chef or food manager checks with the purchasing agent to ensure inventory is in order. All staffing and work schedules are rechecked. Assurance is made that no positions of responsibility have been overlooked, usually due to illness or employee turnover. A thorough, final verification of all equipment needed to produce and serve the food on the menu is completed. Finally, coordination between the kitchen and other departments who provide support during the implementation of the event is completed.

Event Minus 7 Days One week before the event, the caterer schedules another meeting. All department supervisors must attend. At this meeting, the purchasing agent reports on action taken for the procurement of ingredients and products. The chef or food manager will:

1. advise the attendees of any menu or production changes made since the last meeting.

2. brief the entire team on the production plan.

3. explain the function, its objectives, and the staffing requirements.

4. brief the team on the finalized menu, production techniques, and the finalized production schedule. This worksheet will detail the menu items, recipes, special production requests, preparation procedures, and delegated responsibility.

5. describe the details of plate arrangement for each course, including portion size, garnishes, and extras (appetizers, hot breads, beverages, etc.).

6. explain if the event requires any special arrangements (such as a buffet or salad bar in the dining room). The plan will be outlined at this time and responsibility will be discussed.

Event Minus 1 Day The production schedule (Figure 6.2) outlines the responsibility of the chef or food manager 24 hours in advance of the event.

Early on the day of the function, the chef or food manager should meet with the following kitchen personnel to review details of production: cooks, salad-makers and bakers, food service workers, warewashers, and janitorial (cleanup) workers.

At this meeting, all details of production and kitchen service must be explained and final responsibility delegated. Provision must be made for keeping accurate records (guest counts, scatter sheets, sensitive item inventories, sanitation procedures, customer comments, and production records). During the event, the chef, food manager, or responsible delegate, assumes a position to inspect all food leaving the production area to ensure quality service.

At the conclusion of food production, the chef or food manager should ensure that arrangements have been made for the proper handling and storage of leftovers, once they have been accounted for. A quick check of the garbage can (to see how much and what items have been returned uneaten) and of china and glass breakage during the meal can be effective means of controlling costs and adding profit to future events.

Event Plus One Day This is the time for the caterer to make sure all records for the event are complete. This includes a final report describing the event and recommended changes in menu, production, and service for future events.

Staffing Planning Time Line

At the initial organizational meeting, where the purpose of the function is discussed, some consideration must be given to the staffing needs for the event. Department supervisors should submit preliminary figures on staffing requirements and forecasted labor costs.

Date:

Name:	Hot Entrees:	Cold Entrees:
People: **Time:**		
Type:		
Name:	Hot Entrees:	Cold Entrees:
People: **Time:**		
Type:		
Name:	Hot Entrees:	Cold Entrees:
People: **Time:**		
Type:		
Name:	Hot Entrees:	Cold Entrees:
People: **Time:**		
Type:		

Permission of John R. Smith

Figure 6.2 Kitchen production schedule.

Event Minus 75 Days Staffing requirements should include the food production area, service and/or dining room, bar setup, and cleanup crews. The caterer should also give consideration at this time to any additional people needed for the event, who might not be employees of the operation but are hired on a temporary, one-time basis.

Event Minus 30 Days All staffing needs should be finalized at least 1 month in advance of the function. At this time, managers must give consideration to special training requirements for employees who will assist at the event. Accountability and responsibility for employee training is delegated to the appropriate supervisors at this meeting.

Event Minus 14 Days Two weeks prior to the event, the caterer reviews predetermined staffing requirements. A list of available, substitute employees should be made. This handy reference sheet will be valuable if assigned employees become ill or are otherwise unable to work.

The caterer should review and approve all department work schedules before they are posted. This is done to determine that the right personnel are scheduled (skill-level, regular, part-time, and intermittent). This helps control the cost of labor for the event. Once the schedules have been reviewed and approved by the caterer, they are posted in a visible location in the production area where the employees of the department can see them. Intermittent employees should be contacted by phone or e-mail.

Event Minus 7 Days Seven days before the event, the caterer should be able to answer the following questions.

1. How many employees are scheduled for the event?
2. How many can assist in more than one job?
3. How much training was required?
4. Has training been completed?
5. Who will supervise in each department during the event?
6. Are backup employees and supervisors available?
7. What are the total labor costs by department?

Day of Event At least 1 hour before the function starts, the caterer may require department supervisors to submit a report (orally or in writing) that all staffing requirements have been met and that employees are at their stations ready to assume their duties.

Event Plus One Day One day after the event, all department supervisors submit an after-action report to inform the caterer how staffing requirements were met and how the work progressed during the function. This information, along with total labor costs, will assist the caterer in projecting needs for future events. It will also help to improve the quality of service.

SECOND FUNCTION: OPERATIONS— EXECUTION OF TASKS

operational task(s) A singular, identified activity that must be executed in order to accomplish an objective.

Once the caterer has identified and broken down a customer's needs and wants, it becomes easier to assign specific tasks to exceed their objectives (Figure 6.3). A successful caterer can interpret customer needs and wants but the real challenge is to translate each customer objective into a specific, **operational task**.

The caterer develops the plan with the organizational team. Every detail of the event is written down. Each detail is reviewed and assigned as a task. This

Permission of John R. Smith

Figure 6.3 Thorough planning, control, and flow of operations help produce a desired outcome that exceeds customer objectives.

list of operations, specific to the event, includes both the tasks and steps for executing them. Next, these individual tasks are *bundled* together. By identifying and bundling all similar tasks, the caterer can assign or **delegate** each **bundle of tasks** to the appropriate employee for *execution*. **Execution of tasks** involves the employee carrying out these predetermined goals. All tasks must be identified, bundled, delegated, and executed to exceed customer satisfaction. This procedure enables the caterer to identify and *operationalize* predetermined and intangible customer needs into achievable elements of a plan. Gearing up the catering team to execute these tasks identifies the third fundamental catering function—organizing resources.

THIRD FUNCTION: ORGANIZING THE EVENT

Organizing is the process of formally *structuring* the organization so each assigned task can efficiently and effectively attain the stated objective. A purpose of a formal structure is for the distribution, maximum utilization, monitoring, and control of scarce resources by the caterer. The caterer will organize *human resources*, *capital resources*, and *financial resources* to accomplish stated objectives (Figure 6.4).

Human resources include the skill level, knowledge base, experience level, and maturity level (length of service) of employees. The tasks of recruitment, selection, training, retainment, and advancement of the employees are critical to building a reliable and effective staff.

delegate The assignment of responsibility and authority to an appropriate employee to execute a "bundle of tasks" or a job in the catering operation.

bundle of tasks The catering management procedure to identify and group all similar employee tasks together based on the event's tactile plan. It is used to assign or delegate tasks to the appropriate employee for their execution.

execution of tasks The physical action by an employee to accomplish predetermined goals defined as tasks.

organizing (function) The catering management function of formally creating a structure to support the efficient and effective execution of each delegated task in the accomplishment of stated objectives.

human resources Skill levels, knowledge base, experience level, and maturity (length of service) of the caterer's employees.

Figure 6.4 Controlling inventory through the proper management of ordering, shipping, and receiving procedures is a crucial part of organizing.

capital resources Includes the facility, equipment, land, and inventories of raw materials managed by the caterer to exceed customer expectations.

Capital resources include the facility, equipment, land, and inventories of raw materials (food, beverage, and other supplies) managed by the caterer to exceed customer expectations.

Financial resources deal with the management, distribution, acquisition, control, and investment of money. These resources are managed as they flow through the catering operation. They are used to produce desired financial returns. Financial resources include the caterer's personal financial investment and the ability to secure capital from lending institutions. Monitoring the organization's financial resources is an important management task.

financial resources The management process of procurement, allotment, investment, and control of monetary resources by the caterer to provide a desired financial return with its appropriate investment.

Caterers may have certain financial concerns as illustrated in Figure 6.5. If it is a social client, the caterer may require full payment on the day the contract is signed. If the event is booked 1 year in advance, a 10 percent deposit might be required. At 30 days before, a payment of 50 percent is due, and finally, seven days before the event, full payment is expected, except for any overcharges experienced during the day of the event. *Ingredient for Success 16* explains the importance of being aware of financial concerns: *"Accurate forecasting of market trends and changes in food prices are keys to establishing correct pricing and meeting preestablished financial objectives."*

FOURTH FUNCTION: EQUIPMENT

equipment Caterers determine equipment needs based on the menu, service requirements, type and location of the event, and any special needs of the client.

Equipment needs are based on the menu, service requirements, type and location of the event, and special needs of the client A common first question for the caterer is, "What equipment is needed for this event and how will it be handled?" Figure 6.6 includes some common questions that must be asked to determine the equipment needs for a function.

1. What are the financial estimates for the event?

2. How much is this event actually going to cost?

3. How much money is guaranteed in the deposit? Is it a 50% deposit? If it is a corporate account, will the bill for the deposit be mailed?

4. How and when will the final payment be made?

5. What are the payment terms? Is credit extended? Are the terms 10 days, 15 days or 30 days after the event?

© Cengage Learning 2014

Figure 6.5 Caterers' financial concerns.

1. Will the event be held on-premise or off-premise?

2. If the event is held off-premise, is refrigeration needed?

3. How will the cold and hot food be kept at temperatures required to minimize bacterial growth?

4. How will the hot and cold food be safely transported?

5. What kind of serving equipment is needed for the event?

© Cengage Learning 2014

Figure 6.6 Determining equipment needs.

FIFTH FUNCTION: IMPLEMENTING

Implementing the plan requires direct communication with the team leaders. Communication with the kitchen manager, service or dining room manager, office personnel, and purchasing manager is necessary for the team to know exactly what is required for implementation and execution of the plan.

The kitchen staff must review and bundle each task required to produce each menu item. The service staff needs to review and bundle its tasks relative to the type and style of service. For example, "How and where will the food be served?" "What type of service is required?" "Are linen and china needed?" "Will the food be served using disposables?" "Will the guests be seated and require table service?" "Will buffet style service be used at the event?"

As the event draws closer, the implementation of the plan by the staff becomes increasingly important. Finalizing schedules, identifying staff members accountable for executing each task, and review of procedures prepares the staff for successful implementation of the plan.

implementing (the plan)
The catering management processes of using effective communication skills to launch a plan into action.

Subplan

A caterer will bundle tasks from each subsystem and add these elements together to create a master plan. Each catering function is implemented by its own executable subplan. Therefore, the event's master plan is built by the contribution of each subsystem.

SIXTH FUNCTION: CONTROLLING

controlling One of the most important catering management functions. Ensures the effective and efficient utilization of the caterer's resources in the process of producing food and beverage to accomplish organizational goals.

Controlling the organization's resources is perhaps one of the most important catering management tasks. Control in all facets of the catering operation is needed. The controlling function is built into the master plan through the contribution of each subplan.

The caterer must develop and implement internal and external control procedures into the management of the catering system. Control of food, beverages, and labor costs, including salaries, wages, and employee benefits is an extremely important catering management task.

Labor costs are either classified as direct or indirect costs. Direct labor costs are those employee costs that are directly involved in the production and service of the food. Food production personnel who prepare the food for an event are considered direct costs to that event. Indirect costs are those labor costs required to support the catering business such as administrative expenses.

prime cost(s) The sum of the direct food cost plus the direct labor cost to produce a menu item for a client.

Direct labor costs and food costs are usually bundled and called **prime costs**. *Ingredient for Success 17* explains the major reason why a caterer will create cost control procedures. *"Cost control procedures are created for the acquisition of timely information to equip the caterer with the data to scrutinize controllable costs to make appropriate operational decisions."*

SEVENTH FUNCTION: UNDERSTANDING RISK MANAGEMENT, INSURANCE, AND LEGAL ISSUES

No amount of planning can rectify the damages resulting from insufficient insurance coverage. Caterers must know their legal responsibilities to their patrons, employees, and to protect their own investment. Insurance plans should cover equipment, personnel, and guests at both on-premise and off-premise events.

Ensuring that the basics are covered is an essential step in protecting one's livelihood. But how can caterers protect themselves from unforeseen events? Establishing a crisis team can help address immediate, unforeseen disasters and crises that may occur through no fault of the caterer.

legal concerns All activities and specific obligations the caterer must meet, including adhering to the legality of a contract, charging appropriate sales tax, understanding differences between an employee and independent contractor, and identifying and pursuing legal recourse against a client who fails to pay.

Creating a similar safety management team can help troubleshoot **legal concerns**— particularly at off-premise events that pose their own unique blend of challenges. The team should be responsible for conducting routine safety checks of the staff, equipment, and procedures to ensure proper compliance with HACCP standards.

Above all, the caterer should never perform a function without a well-written, signed contract in place. The contract is the final document for determining liability. A contract should spell out basic stipulations for the event including the number of guests; the date, time, and location of the event; and other agreed-upon specifics to be carried out. It should also include provisions for refunds, cancellations, charges for increases or decreases in the number of guests, and the caterer's level of responsibility in the event of unforeseen occurrences.

Though contracts are officially binding, they offer peace of mind to both the caterer and the client by providing a clear document of exactly what is to be carried out at the given event.

Summary

Seven key fundamental catering functions that occur in every successful catering business are: (1) formulating the strategic plan for the event; (2) executing the operational tasks; (3) organizing resources; (4) matching equipment needs to the requirements of the food and service; (5) implementing the plan; (6) controlling the event by use of financial tools and predetermined standards; and (7) understanding risk management, obtaining insurance coverage, and ensuring all legal concerns are covered by a contract. These functions will be explained in detail in Chapters 7–14.

Review Questions

Brief Answers

1. Identify and define the seven fundamental catering functions.
2. Explain why a caterer's plan must flow from the mission statement.
3. Identify and discuss the three basic purposes of a catering plan.
4. Discuss the difference between a caterer's strategic plan and tactical plan.
5. What is the basic catering management function?
6. Summarize Ingredients for Success 13–16.
7. Describe the process in which a caterer turns plans into operational tasks.
8. Discuss how a caterer would use benchmarks in establishing objectives.
9. In your own words, explain how a caterer's plan is similar to a road map.
10. Discuss how a caterer will bundle tasks.
11. Define *organizing*. What is its primary purpose?
12. List the four resources a caterer will organize to accomplish stated catering objectives.
13. List the prime costs.

Multiple Choice

Select the single best answer for each question.

1. The basic catering management function is:
   a. organizing for the event.
   b. execution of operational tasks.
   c. formulating the plan.
   d. implementation of the plan.
   e. controlling the event.
2. These resources are primarily managed by a caterer to produce a desired financial return and exceed customer expectations.
   a. human resources
   b. capital resources
   c. financial resources
   d. scarce resources
   e. raw materials

3. This procedure enables the caterer to identify and operationalize predetermined, intangible customer needs and wants into achievable elements of a plan.

  a. planning

  b. organizing

  c. controlling

  d. implementation of the plan

  e. execution of operational tasks

True or False

Read each of the following statements and determine if it is true or false.

1. A successful caterer can interpret customer needs and wants but the real challenge is to translate each customer objective into a specific, operational task.

2. Financial resources include the facility, equipment, land, and inventories of raw materials (food, beverage, and nonfood supplies) managed by the caterer to exceed customer expectations.

3. The purpose of a formal structure is for the distribution, maximum utilization, monitoring, and control of scarce resources by the caterer.

Putting It All Together

Discuss how the caterer uses the seven fundamental catering functions when planning a theme-based, sit-down dinner. The fundamental catering management challenge is to explain how each function interacts: (1) formulating the plan for the event; (2) executing the operational tasks; (3) organizing resources; (4) matching equipment needs to the requirements of the food and service; (5) implementing the plan; (6) controlling the event by use of financial tools and predetermined standards; and (7) insurance coverage, a risk management plan, and all legal issues for a Mardi Gras Festival. Be creative and use your imagination. This event will be for 300 people at an on-premise facility. Using the fundamental tasks, offer decorating suggestions, plan a menu to offer a choice of two entrees, a starch, two vegetables, salad, beverage, and dessert.

Chapter 7

Planning—The Basic Catering Management Function

Courtesy Stephen B. Shiring, Sr.

Objectives

After studying this chapter, you should be able to:

- Describe why planning is the first catering management function.
- Explain how a plan provides guidance.
- Explain how a caterer prepares for an event.
- Show the planning sequence all caterers must follow regardless of the event.
- Explain how to formulate a catering plan.
- Describe why a menu is one of the important elements of a catering plan.
- Describe why a catering plan is complex.
- Provide examples of how caterers plan, how they construct a business plan and a hazardous analysis critical control plan.
- Describe how caterers transform objectives into operational tasks.
- Explain how a catering plan is implemented.
- Discuss why catering plans have to be flexible.
- Explain why budgetary constraints guide the formulation of a plan.
- Explain why catering management control features must be built into the plan.
- Explain why training needs of employees must be integrated into the catering plan.
- Explain why barriers may cause catering plans to fail.

Ingredients For Success

18 "Strategies emerge as an outcome of planning."

19 "The longer the length of time between booking the event and its implementation date, the better opportunity a caterer has to create a detailed plan."

20 "To satisfy customer needs, the caterer must over produce to exceed customer expectations."

21 "Outside suppliers are as important as a caterer's own key personnel."

KEY TERMS

benchmarks

blueprint

budget

communication barriers

critical control points (CCPs)

critical limits

customer-satisfaction objectives

financial objectives

formulating

HACCP plan

human resource barriers

master menu

menu

monitoring

objectives

operational barriers

operational tasks

planning

psychographic segmentation

risk

sensitive ingredients

severity

standardized menu(s)

subplan

verification steps

"what if" scenarios

The caterer and the client have agreed to the proposal. A contract has been discussed and signed. Now, the caterer must take the mutually agreed upon data contained in the proposal and make it come to life. This chapter addresses how a caterer builds an event-specific plan based on the client interview, the proposal, and the contract. There will be a discussion of how a caterer begins the planning function; weaves specific details into a plan; and uses the plan to communicate, coordinate, and delegate task responsibilities to team members.

PLANNING—THE BASIC CATERING MANAGEMENT FUNCTION

planning The process of detailing and outlining all tasks required to accomplish an objective. Planning is the first of seven catering management functions.

Planning is the first of the seven catering management functions. **Formulating** a plan is a beginning point to the successful execution of a catering event. Planning can be very hectic at times, but a well-formulated plan will serve the caterer well. A successful caterer is one who is well organized through planning.

formulating (a plan) To design a specific plan of action to meet the client's needs based on the proposal and contract.

Success evolves over time as the caterer becomes more adapted to the planning function. Keeping multiple events organized and straight requires a successful caterer to be well focused and organized. Each event must have an independent **subplan** based on client needs and the caterer's strategic plan. It is a challenge to bundle events due to individual expectations.

subplan Plan developed for each individual catering function derived from the parameters of the caterer's master or strategic plan and the specific needs of the client.

The best caterers are always thinking about their upcoming events. Experienced caterers are concerned with the following questions: What is going to happen? How is it going to happen? Where is it going to happen? When is it going to happen? The most successful caterers make sure it happens—as planned.

blueprint A detailed outline of a plan used to guide organizational behavior.

If organizational skills are not a strength of the caterer, a key team member who possesses exceptional organizational skills is needed. Details are critically important. Even the smallest detail must be discussed and outlined as attention to the minute details is what every customer expects.

objectives Framed by the mission statement, they are established to serve as benchmarks against which actual performance can be measured.

Planning Provides Guidance

First, the plan is a **blueprint**. It becomes the outline for the event. Second, a plan provides guidance; it establishes direction for the catering team. Third, a plan identifies each course of action required to accomplish predetermined **objectives**. An objective is the goal or main purpose of the plan. Fourth, a plan is used to generate strategies to execute the elements of the plan. Strategies enable the caterer to accomplish objectives. *Ingredient for Success 18 states: "Strategies emerge as an outcome of planning."*

"what if" scenarios The caterer's plan should include provisions for unanticipated or unexpected problems. (e.g., "What if" the equipment fails? "What if" the weather conditions don't complement an outside event?) By determining these problems in advance, the caterer will have a backup plan in place should they occur.

The caterer must have an idea of what will be done under any circumstances. **"What if" scenarios** should be added to the plan. For example, what if a client needs to have barbequed steaks prepared over live charcoal and the weather is 10°F below zero? A caterer must compensate for the temperature. How will the cooked steaks be stored until they are served? Likewise, what if the temperature is 95°F hot, and extremely humid? What adjustments must be made to compensate for the heat? The caterer must consider the employees' needs while working over the hot pits. Will the customers enjoy the meal in the sweltering heat at an outside event? One innovative way a caterer solved the heat problem was by hiring a local company that manufactured portable air-conditioning units to install a unit inside a tent. This air-conditioned tent provided a suitable environment for both the guests and the employees.

This innovative idea can create a profitable situation for the caterer if he or she charges an extra 10–15 percent commission on the rental fee for the air-conditioning unit.

Getting Ready to Plan

Once the proposal has been accepted, the caterer begins the creation of an event-specific plan. ***Ingredient for Success 19 states: "The longer the length of time between booking the event and its implementation date, the better opportunity a caterer has to create a detailed plan."***

At this initial meeting, discussion with the key staff members focuses on generating event-specific guidelines or objectives for the event. The objectives are built based on the interpreted customer needs and wants and are then reflected in the *budget*.

What does the customer want? Remember ***Ingredient for Success 2: "We cannot be all things to all people."*** Objectives are also based upon the caterer's financial and professional needs. When a caterer is doing a job for $200 per plate, the amount of planning is certainly different from the planning for the $25- or $35-per-plate event. Obviously, a caterer has more leverage to be creative for the $200-per-plate event.

The plan and its delivery to the customer should reflect the cost of the event. The plan for a client requesting a display of fresh-cut roses, as the table's centerpiece, and linen table clothes is much different from the plan using paper table clothes and plastic utensils. These are factors that affect the catering plan.

All details in the plan flow from the customer's preconceived understanding of what the caterer can do and the caterer's understanding of these expectations. The caterer must write the plan to include when it will be done, how it will be done, how much it will cost, and the potential profit.

Managing the event is a multitask process. Although every caterer develops a personal style for completing the job, all caterers follow a typical planning sequence. Basic planning is almost the same for each job. What is the caterer going to do? How is the caterer going to do it to the best of his or her ability so the client receives the utmost satisfaction for his or her dollar?

Planning Sequence

The planning sequence (Figure 7.1) always includes a review of the mission statement. This important exercise keeps the caterer focused on the stated purpose of the organization. To remain true to the purpose, every action taken by the caterer must mirror and flow from the organization's mission statement. If actions deviate from this statement, it signals that the purpose of the operation has changed, and it is time to reevaluate the mission.

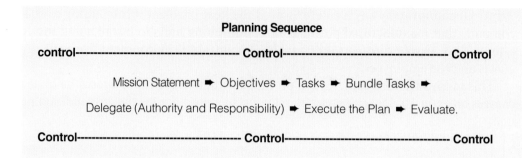

Figure 7.1 Planning sequence.

FORMULATING A CATERING PLAN

Formulating a catering plan requires the knowledge of certain elements before the planning can begin. These elements are the same whether a caterer is planning a small or large event. Five required elements that must be identified before any plan can be created are budget, menu, location, number of guests, and labor requirements. Other concerns include the decorations; floral arrangements; service style; and type of china, silverware, and table cloths.

The caterer transforms the initial catering proposal into a multitude of objectives or **benchmarks** that give life to the proposal as a plan emerges. The main purpose of an objective is to guide the caterer through the process. Every event is different; therefore, each event is driven by its own set of objectives. However, there are two required objectives caterers establish for all events: **financial objectives** and **customer-satisfaction objectives**, based on the client's needs and wants.

Budget

During the initial planning process, financial objectives are important. To create financial objectives for an event, a caterer will start with a budget. The **budget** is a financial plan used to set the parameters for each event. Each event will have its own budget that reflects the needs of the client. It is critical to establish the client's budget early in the process. The client could be looking for a low-end event, an upscale event, or something nestled in between.

A budget is a tactical, single-event, management tool used to explain how resources will be acquired (revenue or gross sales), and how these will be consumed in the operation of the business (expenses) to arrive at a predetermined profit for the specific event. Therefore, a budget also functions as a financial plan. This budget plan will provide answers to help design the blueprint of the catering plan (Figure 7.2) to execute the function.

The budget plan is further broken down into departmental plans. Each event is assigned its own objectives based on the budget plan. The kitchen manager will submit a budget detailing the number of hours consumed in production, transportation, serving, and cleanup tasks. An alternative is for the kitchen manager to establish production standards of hours based on 100 meals. Other budgeted items may include the cost of implementing a marketing plan.

benchmarks A competitor's best practice against which the caterer's own performance is compared and measured against.

financial objectives These are based on the needs of the client and developed from the event budget. They're crucial to the initial planning process and will vary with every event.

customer-satisfaction objectives These objectives are developed by the caterer specific to the client's needs and wants for each individual event. Exceeding these objectives should be the goal.

budget A financial, tactical, single-use plan used to set the parameters for each event.

Event Plan Blueprint

1. What is the profit objective for this event?

2. Will the client be able to pay the caterer? Will the client accept the quoted price that is needed by the caterer to meet the predetermined profit objective?

3. What is the cost of labor?

4. What are the food and production costs?

5. What additional equipment and subsequent rental costs are needed for this event?

6. What transportation is needed for this function? What is the expense?

7. What insurance coverage is required? Is there any additional coverage or expense?

8. What are the indirect, fixed costs, or overhead expenses?

9. Will any additional hidden expenses specific to this event be incurred?

Figure 7.2 Building the blueprint for the event plan: The basic questions.

© Cengage Learning 2014

Caterers' costs are less when they use their own facility because there are no transportation costs. Transportation costs can be excessive based on the distance and amount of time required for travel. Remember, from the employees' departure time until their return, they will be on the payroll.

A well-constructed budget is an important part of the catering management control plan. A budget guides the caterer before the function as a control tool, and after the function as an accountability tool to make comparisons between the budgeted standard and the actual cost incurred in the execution of the event. It is used to evaluate the effective and efficient utilization of organizational resources by the caterer in the execution of the operation.

THE MENU: A TACTICAL PLAN

The **menu** is the single most important factor contained in the overall catering plan. The caterer must create budgetary objectives based on the menu. Caterers construct menus with special attention to satisfying perceived client needs, staff skills, seasonal availability of food, quality and relative cost of food, cost of labor, predetermined profit margins, nutritional needs of the client, presentation and service style, and kitchen production capabilities.

menu This is the most important factor in the catering plan and is built around client needs and wants, availability of products, and the caterer's financial objectives and capabilities.

Menu Format

A caterer will select one of three basic formats when presenting a menu to the client. First, a caterer will construct a new menu based solely on the needs, wants, and demands of the client. After the client has been interviewed, the caterer will build a menu to match the client's tastes and budget. This technique is time consuming because it often requires market research to ascertain product availability and costs. However, greater customer satisfaction is achieved when a caterer creates a menu based on the client's needs, wants, demands, and budget. One important advantage a caterer has when designing a menu for a client is the ability to set the selling price based on the needs, wants, and demands of that client.

A caterer will set the selling price on a customer-by-customer basis (see Chapter 13). A caterer must know how the psychology of the set price affects the customer's perception of value. One customer might believe a menu priced at $25 per person infers poor value and would be much happier to pay the caterer $75 for the same menu. This reflects the *price versus value relationship*. On the other hand, another customer might be more conservative and accept the economical value of $15 with great enthusiasm.

A client, Scott, may be planning a wedding reception. He wishes to spend approximately $65 per plate and wants to serve a stuffed chicken breast as the main entree. During the initial interview, the caterer can *upscale* the event by suggesting Chicken Cordon Bleu. Or the caterer can suggest two entrees, a smaller stuffed chicken breast and a small steak on the side for $15 more per person.

By reducing the cost of the chicken and increasing the cost per plate by $15, the caterer can include the cost of the steak. The customer will perceive this as a much more elegant event. The addition of the steak will help the customer's perception with the guests and increase the caterer's profit margin.

Although this method is an excellent way to increase customer satisfaction, one disadvantage may be an increase of production time in the kitchen. This example illustrates why the caterer must interview the customer. By interviewing the customer, a caterer can determine a client's budget and whether the menu can be upgraded. Always remember that each client has certain desires and tastes. Therefore, even though a caterer is trying to maximize income and build profit structure from the event, customer satisfaction is still the most important consideration.

Standardized Menu

standardized menu
Exact listing of the type of food, beverage and related service offered by the caterer without a client's option to modify, change, or make substitution.

Caterers will create a series of **standardized menus**, offering a variety food, beverages, and service styles. These menus may be presented to each client regardless of the client's specific needs. These may exist as standard menu "A," "B," "C," "D," "E," and "F." The client selects the menu with the best fit to their needs and price range and is not usually permitted to substitute items.

A caterer can use a standard menu format to penetrate the low-end market niche. Using a standard menu format will permit a caterer to deal with a small production facility, lack of available skilled labor, and minimal production equipment to successfully exceed a client's needs. A standardized menu format can offer a choice between only two vegetables, two salads, two potatoes, and a limited variety of simple entrees. However, by offering a lower cost menu, the caterer must generate a higher volume of sales to make sufficient profit margins.

The advantages for the caterer having a standardized menu are simplification of inventory, a limited menu based on the skill level of the staff and the layout of the kitchen, predetermined costs, and contribution to profit margins.

The disadvantages of working with a standardized catering menu include the possible lack of creativity, working on a tight budget, and a predetermined profit margin. When creating individual menus, the caterer has the ability to increase the profit margins much easier than with a standardized menu.

Master Menu

Caterers can also use another method of menu planning. Some caterers provide a **master menu** from which the client can select food and beverage items. This method permits the client to create their own menu based on their budget.

The caterer will present a variety of menu selections from a master menu, similar to an a la carte menu. The highest price the customer begins with may be a selection of the roast beef entree at a base price of $75. Stuffed chicken breast or roast chicken may start at $45 . Then, as the customer selects additional items from the menu, the base price will increase. Add-ons include options for starches, vegetables, salads, beverages, and dessert items.

This type of menu has advantages for the caterer. The caterer has preselected a familiar menu of items his staff can competently produce using the kitchen and production facilities. This can eliminate customers requesting a rare ethnic dish the caterer is not trained to produce.

master menu Standard lists offering a variety of both entrees and side dishes based on the caterer's skill level from which a client selects to create his or her own menu based on individual needs and budgetary requirements.

Complexity of the Plan

The complexity of the plan grows when the size of the event increases. First, the logistics for executing a catering event for 7,000 are different from an event for 100 people. Much more detail is required to ensure the event runs smoothly. When serving an event for 7,000 instead of 100, the menu must be simplified.

PLANNING FOR A CATERING EVENT

To formulate a successful plan, all caterers must identify objectives, which are derived from identified customer needs and wants. The caterer must know what the customers expect by discussing events with them. The customer usually has an idea that the caterer must execute. To do this, a caterer must overproduce— focusing on the little things that can be added within budget to make the event look more elegant and exceed a customer's expectations. *Ingredient for Success 20: "To satisfy customer needs, the caterer must overproduce to exceed customer expectations."*

The caterer is similar to an artist. Every event is a new creation— different and better and exceeding customer expectations. Creativity is a skill resulting from a caterer's experience, and when combined with the skill of interpreting customer needs, it helps a caterer to plan a successful catering event. However, remember *Ingredient for Success 2: "We cannot be all things to all people."* This must apply to each and every potential customer.

A caterer can do little things beyond the customer's expectations to increase the success rate of an event. Simple but effective techniques such as the addition of extra frills and decorative touches on a buffet table can add eye appeal (Figure 7.3).

Figure 7.3 Extra frills and special touches add appeal to an event.

Courtesy Skytop Lodge

A caterer can enhance the attractiveness of a buffet line by serving foods from different height levels. Because customers are accustomed to being served from the same level on a buffet table, new heights create a depth and new field of vision as the eye focuses on the presentation of the food. Varying heights contribute to the overall objective of exceeding a customer's perception of value.

The human eye is in constant motion, scanning items in the environment. Adding floral arrangements, also set at varying heights, is another added feature. A caterer can use different types and styles of vessels to hold food on a buffet table, enhancing the overall artistic presentation of the food.

Colors also attract the eye. Using different colored table cloths coordinated with the color of the food can accent the items. Planned use of different swatches of colored cloth placed beneath certain bowls can highlight the appearance of those items. These accent pieces are used to make the buffet more attractive than a plain buffet.

Planned presentation of the food on the buffet line brings organization to the event. Using a silver bowl instead of a glass bowl can enhance the presentation. A fluted dish instead of a simple round dish can be enough to please a guest. Mirrors placed beneath a certain food will enhance it. All of these simple techniques will help to create an overwhelming degree of satisfaction for the guest.

Objectives Become Operational Tasks

operational task(s) A singular, identified activity that must be executed in order to accomplish an objective.

Objectives are translated into **operational tasks**, which are those singular activities that must be executed to accomplish an objective. Each individual task from turning on the light in the morning to turning it off at the end of the event must be organized and bundled together. All common tasks should be bundled to create a *job*. Since the caterer cannot physically do every task, this step enables the caterer to identify the approximate number of employees required to execute each job for an event. This task facilitates employee scheduling, contributes to identifiable and controllable labor and its related costs, and leads to the creation of a budget for the event.

Delegation

Each bundled task is delegated to a management team member, who then assigns those jobs to employees. This is why successful caterers have good, reliable, trusted people on staff. Appropriate levels of responsibility and authority must be delegated to each team member. Even though each task is delegated to a member of the staff, the caterer must exercise management control techniques to ensure the intricate details of the plan are being implemented and the objectives are being accomplished by the employee. Common catering management control techniques used to produce results are a combination of management team meetings and one-on-one interaction with key people.

If an event is scheduled one year in advance, a caterer will establish a time-line sequence of one year, 90 days, 60 days, 25 days, and so on until the event is completed (see example in Chapter 6). Following this time line, a caterer can implement control techniques to ensure the plan is being implemented by the staff, that everyone accomplishes their own objectives relative to the overall plan, and that every member does their own job.

The caterer may follow up with questions like: Is the team member responsible for the purchasing function doing the job? Has someone received prices from the suppliers on the major food items on the menu? Have the menu plan's food and beverage needs been discussed with suppliers? Have the suppliers of either the tent rentals or china been contacted?

Planning will alert a caterer to the necessity of acquiring rental items in advance. This is especially true when planning for seasonal events. If an event is booked in February for July, a tentative order with the supplier should be placed in February. This permits the caterer to have the flexibility to adjust the order. If a tent is needed to cover an area of 5,000 square feet, only a specialized rental company will most likely handle this type of tent. The caterer must know where to find such a tent and its approximate rental cost. Understanding costs are important so when the caterer meets with the client, reliable prices can be quoted. ***Ingredient for Success 21 states: "Outside suppliers are as important as a caterer's own key personnel."***

A caterer may establish monthly meetings during the first six months before the event. Then, bimonthly meetings can be scheduled from 6 months to 90 days before the event. Weekly team meetings should be established 90 days before the event. This gives the staff a chance to share information. The team member in charge of purchasing food has to know what the wait staff will do. The team member responsible for transporting the food to the off-premise site must know when the food will be ready, what the holding time is, and if equipment is available to keep it cold and hot. The service personnel must be there to disburse the food when it arrives.

Implementation of the Plan

Putting the plan into action, the process of implementing each piece of the plan into the day-to-day activities, becomes the next step for the caterer. This requires a caterer to have all schedules for the event finalized. A key catering management task is the careful coordination of the front-of-the-house and back-of-the-house activities (see Chapter 8).

Postevent Meetings

When the event is over, performance evaluation based on predetermined objectives closes the planning sequence (see Figure 7.1). The management staff must meet and discuss issues focusing on continuous improvement in all phases of the planning cycle and event implementation. Caterers seek answers to such questions as: What could have been done to improve all aspects of the operation? How could the implementation of the event have been made easier? What could have been done more efficiently to help save money, cut costs, or increase customer satisfaction?

In July of 2011, the Atlantic League of Professional Baseball held its yearly All-Star Game in York, Pennsylvania hosted by the York Revolution minor league baseball team. As the exclusive catering company for the York Revolution, Legends Hospitality was asked to arrange the event at the nearby Agricultural and Industrial Museum, which reflected the history and background of York's development. Planning

(continues)

(continued)

for this event took many weeks with multiple rounds of additions, subtractions, and changes. In the end, we implemented one of the most memorable All-Star Game receptions in the league's history. The ability for everyone involved to be both flexible and adaptable is what allowed us to execute this memorable event. This was certainly tested just a few hours before the start of the event. When the weather report called for hot and humid weather, we knew it was going to be just too hot. Immediately, we contacted a local refrigeration company. Within hours, they were able to install a portable air conditioning system to keep the venue cool. This added an unsightly large air condenser to our venue's outdoor reception area. Our florist contacted the nearby floral shops and within an hour had enough large ferns to conceal the newly installed equipment. This whole scenario was quite manageable simply because we had planned ahead for this potential situation. We were monitoring the weather reports in the days prior to the event. We had discussed different scenarios, such as rain and heat, based on understanding July weather patterns. When we saw the weather report forecasting excessively hot and humid weather, we had a back-up option ready for implementation. Creating and relying on a plan without options for unforeseen circumstances is the most direct route to failure. It may sound cliché, but always expect the best outcome, and plan for the worst-case scenario. Managing those potentially event-busting changes with quick and decisive decision making is the key to success.

Adam Baumbach, Catering Manager, Legends—York Revolution, York, Pennsylvania

Flexibility of Plans

Plans must be made so they are flexible. Details laid out in a plan provide guidance and direction, however, flexibility is important because clients often change details before the day of the event. A caterer must anticipate changes and have contingency plans set to respond quickly as the details of the event change.

Jardine's Catering agreed to cater an event for 1,500 people. Six days prior to the event, it blossomed to 6,500 people. Because of the increase, the catering team went into a top-priority mode of immediate plan revision. Team meetings were held twice a day to keep everyone informed. Time constraints were prioritized and plans were revised to provide food and service for 6,500 guests. It also was necessary for the team to build the new infrastructure to support the implementation of the event. Team members were mobilized and sent scrambling to acquire additional equipment and extra staff. Increased communication with the suppliers became another priority. This communication guaranteed the right amount of food, at the best possible price, adhering to specifications, and delivery in time for this event.

Courtesy Bill Jardine

Control Features

During the development of a plan, care must be taken by the caterer to build in control features. Controlling costs using catering management techniques will help achieve predetermined budgetary objectives regarding food, beverages and labor (see Figure 7.4).

A caterer will depend on some type of standard or measurement as a relative point of reference to compare actual costs against a predetermined cost standard. Controls set standards to be used by a caterer in different ways. A standard is used in the selection of approved suppliers who provide the highest quality products at a competitive price. Control of labor and its related costs are also an integral part of achieving budgetary objectives. Proper scheduling and cross-training ensure catering employees are doing their jobs during a catering event.

Staff and Planning

Most caterers work with a relatively small management staff. Many operate with three to five key management personnel, who work together to build a catering plan. They will also lead the employees who are executing the tasks at the event.

Key personnel must be trained so they have an understanding of how the caterer wants the tasks completed. It is important for the caterer to have access to trained personnel. This is especially important in areas where a caterer may experience seasonal variations in business. Often, catering itself is seasonal business. Catering is not usually prevalent in some areas during the winter months. A caterer will place employees on temporary layoff status immediately after the holiday season. Some of these people will seek other, more permanent jobs. When the caterer begins to gear up again in March or April, the staff may need to be replenished. This begins the cycle of continuous training for both new and returning employees. Continuous training for all staff members contributes to a successful organization.

Figure 7.4 A professionally trained chef will help to control food costs.

Employees are the ambassadors of the catering company. Often, a client will interact with a caterer's employees at the actual event. The employee must be professional, look professional, act professional, and be pleasant and personable to all guests. The training and education of each employee is a must. Even the servers must know what type of food is being served so they can be prepared to answer guest questions and to help them navigate through the buffet line.

BARRIERS TO PLANNING

What type of *barriers* must a caterer overcome to create and implement a successful catering plan? There are always barriers that will challenge the caterer, however, there are two basic barriers that will affect all caterers sometime in their career.

Operational Barriers

Barriers which interfere with the tangible elements of production or implementation of the event are called **operational barriers**. These can prevent the successful implementation of a plan.

operational barrier(s) A barrier that disrupts the physical elements of a catering event and may include human error, accidents, time constraints, and Act of God disturbances.

Operational barriers disrupt the physical elements of an event. Human error and accidents are common operational barriers. At an off-premise event, if cooked vegetables fall when being pulled from storage, they cannot be used. How can the caterer handle this? The vegetables are already on the menu. Can the caterer call back to the facility and have more vegetables sent? Or must the caterer spread food out in a different order or format to give the appearance of more food than is present?

Other operational barriers deal with time. In the production of the food, has the caterer adequately planned enough time to get the food prepared? If equipped with electric convection ovens, how will the product get cooked in the event of a power failure? One solution is to have propane or natural gas ovens available. Can the food be prepared at another location and heated on site at the event?

Natural disasters can create barriers to the plan. Storms, lightning, floods, and blizzards will disrupt even the best made plans; however, there is little the caterer can do in many of these situations.

HUMAN RESOURCE OR COMMUNICATION BARRIERS

human resource barrier(s) A type of barrier caused by the staff that disrupts the elements of a catering event. These may include human error, lack of communication, and deviation from standard operating procedures. Also called a communication barrier.

communication barrier(s) A type of barrier (also called a human resource barrier) caused by the staff that disrupts the elements of a catering event. These may include human error, lack of communication, and deviation from standard operating procedures.

The second type of barriers are **human resource** or **communication barriers**. Human error, unfortunately, is the biggest barrier against effective communication. Employees just "forget" elements of a well-thought plan. Usually, employees forget equipment, food, and other staff members, and this list can be endless.

Lack of communication among members of the catering team is always dangerous to the proper formulation and implementation of a plan. Human nature may cause certain employees to add their own procedures to a task, which is potentially dangerous. It must be strictly enforced through policies and rules that all standard operating procedures are followed and not permitted to be changed on a whim of whomever is on the job. As long as the standard operating procedures deliver optimal value to the client, they are to be maintained.

The caterer can create many solutions to these types of barriers by using their own creativity and experience, and knowing where the local convenience store is located relative to the catering site. Convenience stores offer ice, soft drinks, small wares, and other items to satisfy endless needs.

BUSINESS PLAN
(Adapted with permission of Bruce Frankel, virtualrestaurant.com)

A business plan is one of the best types of plans any caterer can formulate. A business plan is a plan of action that serves many purposes. A caterer can use the business plan as a tool to implement the strategic plan and establish short-term organizational goals. It is the central strategy for the development of the business. It will create a focused vision for long-term success.

Virtual Restaurant gives prospective restaurateurs a chance to see probable outcomes of their business assumptions. Through the use of Internet technology, this service is offered easily and inexpensively.

Purposes of a Business Plan

1. The plan provides internal direction for the organization. It sets the direction for the organization.

2. It communicates to stakeholders the intended growth of the company.

3. This plan discloses the organization's financial goals. Financial goals are explained by exhibits of the statement of income, balance sheet, and cash flow statements. These exhibits are extremely important when courting potential investors. Financial analysts will rigorously examine this document to ascertain if the business and associated **risk**, as explained in the plan, is worthy of investment.

4. The plan presents the overall vision for the business. It communicates the concept, business philosophy, and ideas.

> **risk** An estimate of the likely occurrence of a hazard or the chance of loss, damage, or injury.

Writing a business plan will take research, self-examination, and the ability to communicate to all stakeholders. The formulation of the business plan is an exercise to conceptualize the entire catering business. A clear and crisp writing style is recommended. Before writing the details of the plan, select a format or use the outline of a successful business plan.

Front Section of the Business Plan

Each business plan has a front section and a back section. The front section of the plan includes the cover page, executive summary, and table of contents. The back section of the business plan includes the body or the specifics of the catering business and the appendices.

Cover Page

The cover page of the business plan should include the caterer's name, business name, address, phone number, fax number, e-mail address, and the date the report was completed.

Table of Contents

Since most business plans are longer than five pages, accurate identification of the major sections and their appropriate page numbers must be given.

Executive Summary

This executive summary is best written last. It is a recap and summary of the major points from all the other sections. The executive summary can well be the most important section of the plan, since most investors or stakeholders lack the time to read the report in its entirety. It should be no longer than three pages and be written in a clear and convincing style. Refer to the individual sections for reference and use the following format as a guide.

Body of the Business Plan

This section of the report will be the bulk of the business plan. This section may take a significant amount of research, self-reflection, and time to complete.

Writing the Business Plan Company Description Section

Mission Statement

    Nature and philosophy of the business

    Quality, price, service, customer relationships, management style, employee relations

    Corporate style, image

    Social and community image

    Growth and profitability goals

Company Name(s)

    Brand or trade names associated with products

    Subsidiary companies (e.g., a catering division)

Legal Form of the Business

    Corporation? "C" or "S"? In what state(s) is it incorporated?

    Who owns the company? How many shares outstanding? Other major shareholders?

    Partnership? Limited partners? Share amount?

Management

    President, officers, key management, and advisory personnel

Location

    Main place of business, offices or headquarters, branch locations

Stage of Development

    When company was founded

    Milestones reached so far

    Phase of development—idea stage (no product finalized), startup (early stages of operations), expansion, established, reworking

    Where are you within your phase? Has the product been tested, lease signed, suppliers arranged, staff hired, etc.?

Financial and Personnel Status

    Stage of previous and/or present funding

    Present financial state and obligations; past performance if applicable

    Size of work force or anticipated increase

Patents and Licenses

    Trademarks, patents, licenses, copyrights—secured or pending

Company Description

This section includes the name, type of catering business, its location, legal status (business form), startup or continuing, date founded, and menu description. A detailed description of the menu(s) will communicate the level of professionalism, culinary skill level, equipment demands, staffing requirement, and price structure. Include a detailed section explaining how the menus have been developed and tested.

Writing the Business Plan Industry Analysis Section

General Information

Economic Sector—Food Service

The Catering and Restaurant Industry

Size and Growth Rate of the Industry

> Rate of expansion. How it compares with GNP growth

> How your specific sector might be different (corporate catering may be growing while off-premise social catering service is declining)

> Predicted trends and the strategic opportunities they offer (low-fat cooking is becoming more popular)

Sensitivity to Economic Cycles and Seasonality

> How national economic trends (recession, inflation) impact your business

> How local industry (a large company you depend on for business) affects your situation

> How seasonal variations in business affect your cash flow

Regulation

> How local and national regulations affect your business (inspection standards, smoking regulations, wage and tax changes)

Financial Norms and Patterns

> Terms with vendors, customers, the capital market

> Standard markup of products

> Inventory par levels

> Profit expectations, etc.

> (see also Income Statement Showing Industry Averages in the Financial section)

Industry Analysis

This section describes the general catering industry, discusses the economic characteristics of the industry, and assesses the present condition, future potential, and any factors such as trends that may determine them. What are the key success factors that make this industry attractive? What are the factors that make this industry unattractive? Are there any special issues, such as government regulations, or special problems common to this industry?

Key successful factors are those identifiable elements in the catering industry that make an individual caterer successful. These factors may include a specialized culinary skill, the ability to consistently produce quality food using signature recipes at a low cost, a favorable reputation, a convenient and beautiful banquet facility, and access to an appropriate and skilled labor supply. To sustain a competitive advantage against other caterers, a significant level of competence must be attained in these elements.

Writing the Business Plan Food and Service Section

Description of the Products

> General concepts
>
> Specific menu items
>
> Production methods (costs, labor)
>
> How the products (menu) change
>
> Stage of development of the products
>
> How the products compare to competitors
>
> Any special value or aspect about the products (patent, etc.)
>
> Product liability considerations

Description of the Services

> The special services offered (take-out, delivery, meals-for-a-week)
>
> How they help the business and create competitive advantage

Future Plans and Developments

> How the products and services change to meet changing market demands
>
> Are there any products or services planned for future implementation? When?

Products and Related Services

This section describes the menu, food production capabilities, and style of service the caterer will produce. A competitive review of other caterers' food and service is provided. Explain how the caterer will respond to emerging trends and evolving customer needs.

Writing the Business Plan Target Market Section

Who exactly will be buying your food and service?

Demographics

> Age, income range, gender, occupations, marital status, family status, ethnic groups, education, sophistication, home or auto owner, and so forth

Geographics

> Area served—neighborhood, city, region
>
> Density—urban, suburban, rural
>
> Nature of the location—downtown, business, shopping, residential
>
> Transportation—how will they get to the store?

Lifestyle

> Family status, family size, family life cycle
>
> Hobbies, sports, entertainment interests, social events
>
> Television, radio, magazines, and other media preferences
>
> Race
>
> Nationality
>
> Political and other organizational affiliation
>
> Occupation
>
> Education
>
> Religion

Psychographics

    Status-seeking or trend-setting?

    Socially or environmentally conscious?

    Free-spending or conservative?

    Practical or fun-seeking?

Buying Factors and Sensitivity

    Price, quality, brand name, service, reputation

    Special product features, advertising, packaging

    Location, facility design, ambiance, sanitation

    Nature or quantity of other customers

Market Size and Trends

    How big is the target market?

    How fast is it growing?

    Where is the market heading?

    What economic and social factors will be influencing the market?

    How will the market's needs be changing and why?

Strategic Opportunities

    In what ways do you plan to use your understanding of the market to your advantage?

The Target Market

This section describes how the caterer will select the customer based on demographics, geographics, **psychographic segmentation** (lifestyle, social class, and personality characteristics), buying sensitivity, and market size. The target market or the set of all clients who share these identified characteristics will be served by the caterer.

psychographic segmentation The process of segmenting a catering market by variables such as lifestyle, social class, or personality characteristics to identify a target group of customers based on these characteristics.

Writing the Business Plan Marketing Plan Section

Think about What the Customer Wants

    How does the product meet their basic needs?

    How much does price matter?

    How about ease and convenience of purchase?

    How does the product make the customer feel—about themselves and the company?

Marketing Vehicles

What are the ways you will reach potential customers?

    Brochures, flyers, leaflets

    Print media—newspapers, magazines, specialty publications, Yellow Pages

    Broadcast media/electronic—television, radio, computer (Internet), movie theaters

    Specialties—packaging, T-shirts, etc.

    Hotel—In-house publications, video guides, concierge relations, services

    Direct mail, coupons, mailing list, Val-pak

    Promotions, credit card discount programs

Signs—on stores, billboards, trains, cabs, blimps

Trade shows, networking

Point-of-sale devices, promotions, and employee practices

Sampling

Public relations (PR)—as a communication service media solicitor and event planner. PR is free, may create awareness of the caterer by potential clients, and may enhance a caterer's reputation.

Charity events

Marketing Tactics and Strategy

Mix of marketing vehicles you will use, and how they will be coordinated

Will the campaign be divided into different phases? (preopening, opening, etc.)

Creative or unique techniques you will be using

Your marketing goals and methods of monitoring them

Marketing Budget

What is the budget for all phases of the marketing effort?

Sales

Training of employees involved in sales—waitstaff

Catering or special function salesperson

Marketing Plan and Sales Strategy

This section includes how the caterer will promote the company image by sending a message to the potential client. This message that the caterer will convey through all marketing vehicles should be clear and consistent and must reflect the general corporate style and its mission. The image can be conveyed directly (description of products, pricing, services, etc.), or indirectly (suggestive design elements, logos, uniforms). A well-conceived marketing campaign will be used in both a complimentary and appropriate way.

Writing the Business Plan Competition Section

Competitive Advantages and Comparative Evaluation (for the caterer and the direct competitors).

Objective

Price (and hidden costs), credit policies

Location

Quality

Special product features

Image/style/perceived value

Service (and special service features), customer relations, social image

Internal

Financial strength, volume purchasing power

Marketing and promotional program and budget

Operational advantages, strategic partnerships

Company morale—personnel motivation, commitment, productivity

Market Share and Distribution

>How is the market distributed?

>Do any one or two companies dominate the market?

>How will you obtain sufficient market share?

Future Competition

>How and why will new competitors enter the market?

>How long will that take?

>What factors would prevent new competition from market entry? (secret recipes)

Strategic Opportunities

>How can you use your competitive advantages to exploit opportunities in the marketplace?

The Competition

The competition section focuses on the competitors who are aiming at the same target market. Categorize the competition (off-premise, on-premise, corporate, or social caterers). List the competitors in each category.

Writing the Business Plan Operations Section

Facilities

>Location—addresses, parking, floor plans, etc.

>Lease—terms, length, important details

>Improvements—plans, funding, budget

>Key success factors—expansion potential, proximity to market, unique aspects, expertise and adaptation of technology (see Chapter 5), quality customer service, access to financial capital, facility design and location, signature recipes, low-cost production

Production

>Process—how are the products created (stages, flow, efficiency)?

>Labor—kinds and numbers of workers, costs, part-time

>Productivity—how do you increase productivity without reducing quality?

>Suppliers—who are the major vendors?

>Capacity—how much work/volume can the present facilities handle?

>Quality Control—inspections, testing, training, incentive rewards

Cost Controls

>Inventory—forms, systems (computer), practices

>Food and beverage—check systems, management practices, training, periodic inventory

>General—management, inventory

Administrative and Financial Controls

>Bookkeeping systems and policies (payments, billing)

>Accounting systems (report intervals)

>Sales systems (computer)

Customer Service

    Service attitudes and policies

    Complaint process and reconciliation

    Feedback mechanisms

Other Operational Issues

    Safety and health (staff and customers)

    Insurance and legal

    Licenses and permits

Environmental concerns and practices

Operations

This section explains the day-to-day functions of the catering business. Focus on the aspects of the operation that are more important to the overall success and that will provide a competitive edge or innovative advantage.

Writing the Business Plan Management and Organization Section

Compensation and Incentives

How will you motivate and retain key personnel (salary, bonuses, commissions, profit sharing, equity, stock options)?

Board of Directors and Advisory Committee

    For corporations, a board of directors is a legal requirement. An advisory committee is a less formal way of avoiding the cost of a formal board.

    Small caterers don't really need either and instead get advice and information as they need it from various sources.

Consultants, Professionals, and Other Specialists

    Explain how each may contribute to the caterer's short- and long-term development.

    Management, financial, or marketing consultants

    Attorneys, accountants

    Industry specialists

    Architects and design consultants

Key Management to be Added

    If there is a key position that is not yet filled, explain your plans to do so.

    Describe the job and the profile, compensation, and qualifications of the prospects.

Management Structure and Style

    Outline of the lines of authority. Include a flow chart in the appendix.

    Describe the management style. Management style should reflect and support the general corporate style (from the mission statement).

    Include any innovative or unusual aspects of management style that would impact growth or give a competitive advantage.

Management and Organization

This section has a biographical summary of the management team. Carefully written, this may be one of the most important sections of the plan. The educational and professional work experiences will introduce and explain who the most important people are in the catering operation and why. People are the most important resource a catering company will have. A complete narrative of the founder, president, chef, dining room manager, general manager, production manager, and catering manager must include their experience, successes, education, strengths, and weaknesses.

Writing the Business Plan Financial Data and Projections Section

This section of the business plan requires that you:

> Consult your accountant and your attorney
>
> Be conservative and honest
>
> Use standard industry forms and formats

Forms to Include

> Sources of capital and debt service
>
> Use of funding and start-up costs
>
> Menu price and function cost calculations (optional)
>
> Sales calculation
>
> Payroll calculation
>
> Detail of expenses worksheets
>
> Income statement (1–5 years)
>
> Monthly or quarterly cash flow statement (1–3 years)
>
> Amortization and depreciation schedule
>
> Balance sheet

Assumption Sheet

> If you have not clearly stated basic assumptions in the above sheets, make a separate page with information such as sales volume, payroll rates, food costs, and financing costs.

Break-Even Analysis

> How much income must be earned to pay fixed expenses?

Financial Data and Projections

All the decisions from each of the previous sections of the business plan have financial outcomes. Forecasts to best determine accurate numbers must be made. The caterer must gather, sort, and report an accurate financial position. This accurate financial data will determine the present position and current progress of the business, and will unveil probable new decisions about the future. For startup ventures, a reliable set of projected financial statements will offer meaningful information to help make many important decisions. It is perhaps the best (if not the most realistic) way to "see into the future."

Writing the Business Plan Long-Term Development and Exit Plan Section

Goals—What long-term vision is held for the company and the caterer?

    Lifestyle provider—good, stable, reliable income

    Innovator—creative, new, different products and services

    Quality—reputation for excellence

    Expanding and growth—market domination, large company, big bucks

    Niche leader—doing only one thing, but doing it well

    Specifically, where the company will be in the market in terms of sales, units, employees, and so forth, in the next year, 3 years, 5 years, etc.

Strategies—how will the goals be reached?

    Market penetration

    Promotion—increase business by marketing of current products and services

    Expansion—add new products and/or new units

    Other strategies

Milestones—As the company progresses toward the goals, find a way to mark and communicate the progress

List the short-term and long-term goals and the dates they are expected to be accomplished

Short-term goals

    Financing secured, lease signed, catering manager hired

    Catering business opened

    Projected sales level reached

    Second catering unit planned; second catering unit opened

Risk Evaluation—Outlining risks shows the investor that the caterer is not naively optimistic in planning

    Market acceptance, changing demographics

    New competition, new customer tastes

    Management performance, payroll costs

    Regulatory, licensing issues

Exit Plan—How and when will it end?

    Sale—to individuals

    Acquisition—by another company

    Buyout—by stockholders or employees

    Go public—stock traded publicly

Franchise—sell concept, receive royalties

Hand down—to family?

Close

Long-Term Development and Exit Plan

The caterer must describe what the ultimate destination for this business is and how the catering business will look at the different intervals along the way including the short- and long-term goals. What is the long-term vision for the company and the caterer? If the caterer is preparing this business plan to seek investment, then this section should tell investors how much money they can make and when and how they can get it.

Suggested Appendix Items for the Business Plan

Menus

Résumés and financial statements of key people

Lease and other location information (pictures)

Marketing information (logo, dummy ads, packaging)

Supporting media information (newspaper articles, etc.)

Budgets and schedules, and analysis (equipment lists, project charts, flow chart)

Design or construction information (floor plan, renderings)

Contracts, trademarks

Bank loans, financial statements

Market research studies (bibliography)

Appendix

The appendix is the place for supporting documents and information. The items in the appendix should only confirm, reinforce, or elaborate on the major ideas and facts already stated in the main plan. Many people don't even read the appendix, so include all essential items in the plan itself. If the appendix seems too long, put it in a separate binder.

HAZARDOUS ANALYSIS AND CRITICAL CONTROL POINT PLAN

(Adapted from the most recent FDA Model Food Code at time of writing, see http://www.fda.gov)

The most important type of plans a caterer must formulate and implement is a detailed set of action plans designed to keep the food they are serving safe, unadulterated, and wholesome. The single most important guarantee any caterer can imply to a client is the serving of honestly presented food free of bacterial, physical, or chemical contaminants.

Bacterial contaminants cause foodborne illness. These include pathogenic microorganisms such as bacteria, viruses, parasites, fungi, and toxins found especially in fish and plants. Physical contaminants are any foreign material introduced into the food. Metal shavings spewed from a dull blade on a can opener and toothpicks left in food are examples. Accidental spills of cleaning agents into food, pesticides, preservatives, and food additives are examples of possible chemical contaminants.

Monitoring and controlling food as it flows through the catering operation is a key catering management technique in the protection and assurance of serving safe food. Specific monitoring and controlling techniques built into the caterer's food tracking system as it flows through receiving, storage, preparation, cooking, holding, serving, cooling, and reheating is vital.

This monitoring and controlling of food as it moves through the operation is a growing concern for all caterers. The consumer expects safe food and the government demands it. There is absolutely no excuse for anything less than serving food free from bacterial, physical, or chemical contamination.

HACCP (Hazardous Analysis and Critical Control Point) plan A HACCP plan, as defined in the Food Code, means a written document that delineates the formal procedures for following the HACCP principles developed by The National Advisory Committee on Microbiological Criteria for Foods.

critical control point (CCP) As defined in the Food Code, means a point at which loss of control may result in an unacceptable health risk.

monitoring steps The planned sequence of observations, or measurements of critical limits, designed to produce an accurate record and intended to ensure that the critical limit maintains product safety. Continuous monitoring means an uninterrupted record of data.

verification steps Process used to determine if the implemented HACCP plan is working as intended.

critical limit(s) As defined in the Food Code, means the maximum or minimum value to which a physical, biological, or a chemical parameter must be controlled at a critical control point to minimize the risk that the identified food safety hazard may represent.

sensitive ingredient(s) Any ingredient historically associated with a known microbiological hazard that causes or contributes to production of a potentially hazardous food as defined in the Food Code.

To insure food is wholesome, each and every caterer must formulate, implement, and monitor a specific plan of action individually designed to meet their needs. This individualized plan of action is called **Hazard Analysis and Critical Control Point (HACCP) plan.** A HACCP plan is a written document that delineates the formal procedures for following the Hazard Analysis Critical Control Point principles developed by The National Advisory Committee on Microbiological Criteria for Foods.

HACCP is a prevention-based, food safety plan. It is a system that identifies, monitors, and prevents or eliminates specific foodborne hazards—biological, chemical, or physical properties—that can adversely affect the safety of the food. HACCP is designed to prevent the occurrence of potential food safety hazards. It represents an important food protection tool. This hazard analysis serves as the basis for establishing **critical control points (CCPs)**, which identify those points in the process that must be controlled to ensure the safety of the food. **Monitoring** and **verification steps** are included in the system, again, to ensure that potential risks are controlled. The hazard analysis, critical control points, **critical limits**, and monitoring and verification steps are documented in a HACCP plan. Seven principles have been developed to provide guidance on the development of an effective HACCP plan.

A review of the following terms and definitions will help clarify the seven principles:

- *Acceptable level* means the presence of a hazard which does not pose the likelihood of causing an unacceptable health risk.
- *Control point* means any point in a specific food system at which loss of control does not lead to an unacceptable health risk.
- *Critical control point,* as defined in the Food Code, means a point at which loss of control may result in an unacceptable health risk.
- *Critical limit,* as defined in the Food Code, means the maximum or minimum value to which a physical, biological, or chemical parameter must be controlled at a critical control point to minimize the risk that the identified food safety hazard may occur.
- *Deviation* means failure to meet a required critical limit for a critical control point.
- *HACCP plan,* as defined in the Food Code, means a written document that delineates the formal procedures for following the HACCP principles developed by The National Advisory Committee on Microbiological Criteria for Foods.
- *Hazard,* as defined in the Food Code, means a biological, chemical, or physical property that may cause an unacceptable consumer health risk.
- *Monitoring* means a planned sequence of observations or measurements of critical limits designed to produce an accurate record and intended to ensure that the critical limit maintains product safety. Continuous monitoring means an uninterrupted record of data.
- *Preventive measure* means an action to exclude, destroy, eliminate, or reduce a hazard and prevent recontamination through effective means.
- *Risk* means an estimate of the likely occurrence of a hazard.
- *Sensitive ingredient* means any ingredient historically associated with a known microbiological hazard that causes or contributes to production of a potentially hazardous food as defined in the Food Code.
- *Verification* means methods, procedures, and tests used to determine if the HACCP system in use is in compliance with the HACCP plan.

Advantages of HACCP

The Food and Drug Administration is recommending the implementation of HACCP in catering establishments. It is the most effective and efficient way to ensure that food products are safe and wholesome. A properly designed HACCP system will:

1. delegate the caterer as the final party responsible for ensuring the safety of the food they serve.

2. provide continuous self-inspection through the monitoring, controlling, and prevention of food-related problems. Traditional inspection procedures by regulatory agencies are relatively resource-intensive and inefficient.

3. establish critical limits and identify critical control points and monitoring procedures. A critical item, if in a noncompliance, is more likely than other violations to contribute to food contamination, illness, or environmental health hazard. Critical limit means the maximum or minimum value to which a physical, biological, or a chemical parameter must be controlled at a critical control point to minimize the risk that the identified food safety hazard may occur. **Severity** is the degree of seriousness of the consequences of a hazard if it were to become an actuality. Critical control point means the last step, point, or procedure in a specific food system where the caterer can intervene to prevent, control or eliminate an unacceptable health risk.

4. create records that document adherence of operational procedures to rational, scientifically-based data.

5. organize a preventive process rather than a reactive reflex to a periodic regulatory "snapshot" inspection.

6. integrate HACCP-based procedure into daily employee and staff standard operating procedures. Management reinforcements of HACCP techniques and employee training are key factors to successful implementation.

7. make the system self-perpetuating so as not to rely on periodic facility inspections by regulatory agencies.

8. allow the regulatory agency to better determine a caterer's level of compliance by reviewing records and other documentation to verify that the HACCP is working.

severity The degree of seriousness of the consequences of a hazard if it were to become an actuality.

To effectively create a HACCP plan, a safety committee should be assembled to work on formulating this plan. Members of the safety committee working on the HACCP plan may seek information from the catering manager, food production manager, chef, service manager, service and production employees, purveyor's territory manager, supplier and/or equipment representatives, members of the Department of Health and other local regulatory agencies, and the professional pest control operator (see Chapter 14, Safety Committee, to review the guidelines set by the National Labor Relations Act on forming a safety committee). The safety committee should:

1. establish a clear mission and obtainable goals.

2. delegate responsibilities, authority, and assign accountability.

3. be cohesive when challenging each other but congenial when working together.

4. be familiar with the caterer's operation and their customers' needs, wants, and demands.

5. know of the specific production processes and service styles used by the caterer.

6. possess a basic understanding of microbiology.

7. understand how contamination occurs and know appropriate personal hygiene standards.

The implementation of HACCP principles continues to evolve. HACCP principles change as new menu items, recipes, food production, and service procedures are developed within the organization; as they are mandated by the individual state or the Food and Drug Administration; and as hazards and their control measures are more clearly defined by scientists.

To meet the challenges, caterers must keep themselves currently informed of these ongoing developments. Sources of information that can be particularly helpful include trade publications issued by the food industry, professional organizations, the Food and Drug Administration's website (http://www.fda.gov), and continuing education programs. Food safety training sponsored by the National Restaurant Association, and through colleges and universities, is also an excellent resource.

SEVEN PRINCIPLES OF HACCP

The National Advisory Committee on Microbiological Criteria for Foods (NACMCF), which developed HACCP principles, was established in 1988. Its members include officials from several federal agencies including the Food and Drug Administration, Centers for Disease Control and Prevention, Food Safety Inspection Service, Agricultural Research Service, National Marine Fisheries Service, and U.S. Army. The NACMCF also has national experts from academia, state government, consumer groups, and the food industry.

The NACMCF has developed seven widely accepted HACCP principles that explain this process in great detail. To prepare an effective HACCP plan these principles must be followed. Further, a comprehensive review of a HACCP plan must include consideration of these principles:

Principle 1: Hazard analysis

Principle 2: Identify the critical control points (CCP) in food production

Principle 3: Establish critical limits for preventative measures

Principle 4: Establish procedures to monitor CCPs: observations and measurements

Principle 5: Establish the corrective action to be taken when monitoring shows that a critical limit has been exceeded

Principle 6: Establish procedures to verify that the HACCP system is working

Principle 7: Establish effective record keeping systems that document the HACCP system

Summary

This chapter addressed how a caterer builds an event-specific plan based on the client interview, the proposal and the contract. A review of how a caterer begins the planning function; weaves specific details into a plan; and uses the plan to communicate, coordinate, and delegate task responsibilities to team members was discussed.

Tips from the Trade

Over my 38-year career with the Department of Health, in the Food Safety Program, the concept of food safety has evolved. As an inspector, I can tell you that our main focus was really never floors, walls, ceilings, lighting, and ventilation. Our main focus was always the protection of public health and to prevent foodborne illness. We would, in fact, look at the food. We looked at the food, the people, and we were trying to prevent foodborne illness. Today, the leading causes of foodborne illness are a lack of personal hygiene, improper hand washing, and permitting sick employees to work with food. We have had significant outbreaks of the Norovirus. This is caused by a sick employee, who, after using the bathroom, goes back to work with food without washing their hands. Or, after a customer vomits in the bathroom, the caterer sends in an employee to clean, and does so without taking the proper precautions. Again, the employee returns to work in the kitchen without washing their hands. Other causes of foodborne outbreaks include improper cooling of hot foods, and cross contamination between raw and ready-to-eat foods, often caused by not sanitizing cutting boards between uses. Some caterers will use color-coded cutting boards to prevent cross-contamination. Undercooking foods, such as chicken, will cause Salmonella to grow. Also, preparing foods too far in advance, and then holding it at the wrong temperature. According to the Center for Disease Control (CDC), in 2009, chicken was the number one cause of foodborne illness in the United States. According to the California Marketing Institute, people are three times more likely to get sick in catered events than in restaurants. There was an average of 36 illnesses per outbreak that occurred in catered events as opposed to 13 illnesses per outbreak in restaurants.

Of course, we still look at the food, the individuals preparing the food, food safety (floors, walls, ceilings, lighting, and ventilation), and temperature control. Food safety and food temperature control has now evolved to food security. Food security, or food defense and terrorism, goes beyond food safety. Some points to consider when it comes to food defense and terrorism, for any operator, especially a caterer, are to ensure that your supplies and ingredients are safe and secure from the sources you receive them. You do not want to leave anything outside on a loading dock, unattended, for any length of time. Once those products and ingredients come into the facility, keep them safe as they are put away. Food defense also centers on the employees. You need to know who is working in the facility. You want to inspect the perimeter of your place and make sure everything is secure. The caterer should know their employees and who enters their facilities. I am not talking about clients or customers, but the people who enter their facilities from the back of the house. Who has access, who comes in, and who goes out? I think the threat is real, and everyone needs to prepare themselves for those potential problems. Everyone should acquire knowledge about food defense. The Association of Food and Drug Officials publishes a Food Emergency Pocket Guide that speaks specifically about food defense and terrorism.

Permission of Steve Steingart

First, the plan is a blueprint. It becomes the outline for the event. Second, a plan provides guidance; it establishes direction for the catering team. Third, a plan identifies each course of action required to accomplish predetermined objectives. An objective is the goal or main purpose of the plan. Fourth, a plan is used to generate strategies to execute the elements of the plan. Strategies enable the caterer to accomplish objectives. ***Ingredient for Success 18*** states***: "Strategies emerge as an outcome of planning."***

Tips from the Trade

Caterers need to have a basic, applied knowledge of food safety. We measure it in Allegheny County because we require a caterer, food service owner, or operator to have a proficient knowledge of food safety. So how do you get a proficient knowledge of food safety? You have to pass a proficiency exam, which materializes as a food handler's or food manager's certification. This is especially true in a catering operation. Unlike a restaurant, where the same people work every day, a caterer, if they have a big job, will hire temporary employees. These additional employees may lack proper food safety training. Therefore, the caterer is responsible for passing specific food safety knowledge on to them.

The caterer should have an event plan for each function. The plan needs to address proper food handling techniques, such as how and when to restock potentially hazardous foods on a buffet line to minimize time and temperature concerns. Food being replenished on a buffet line must first be stored correctly, second, held on the buffet line, and third, served to all guests at the proper temperatures. The caterer needs to have the right equipment for the job. Every caterer must invest in the correct food warmers, coolers, and related equipment to maintain correct food temperatures in transport, holding, and service. Another critical step is for a caterer to understand the proper cooling practices of food. We require, in Allegheny County, the use of cooling charts. A cooling chart is required so the caterer is able to monitor their food cooling procedure to ensure it is done correctly. They get it to the proper temperature in the proper time frame. In addition, the use of a cooling chart documents the process, and if necessary, can be used in defense, if accused of causing a foodborne outbreak. You can consider the cooling chart as part of the caterer's HACCP Plan. Proper procedures must be followed to reheat food. Finally, today, one of the most important things a caterer needs to understand to ensure food safety is their employee's personal hygiene and health.

Permission of Steve Steingart

The menu is the single most important factor contained in the overall catering plan. The caterer must create budgetary objectives based on the menu. To formulate a successful plan, all caterers must identify objectives, which are derived from identified customer needs and wants. Objectives are translated into operational tasks, which are those singular activities that must be executed to accomplish an objective. Putting the plan into action, the process of implementing each piece of the plan into the day-to-day activities, becomes the next step for the caterer. Plans must be made so they are flexible. Barriers always arise that will challenge the caterer; however, there are two basic barriers that will affect all caterers sometime in their career. Operational barriers disrupt the physical elements of an event. The second type of barriers are human resource or communication barriers.

A business plan is one of the best types of plans any caterer can formulate. A business plan is a plan of action that serves many purposes. A caterer can use the business plan as a tool to implement the strategic plan and establish short-term organizational goals. It is the central strategy for the development of the business. It will create a focused vision for long-term success.

To insure food is wholesome, each and every caterer must formulate, implement, and monitor a specific plan of action individually designed to meet their needs. This individualized plan of action is called the Hazard Analysis and Critical Control Point (HACCP) plan. A HACCP plan is a written document that delineates the formal procedures for following the Hazard Analysis Critical Control

Point principles developed by The National Advisory Committee on Microbiological Criteria for Foods.

Review Questions

Brief Answers

1. Explain why the planning function is the first catering management task.
2. Explain why successful caterers are well focused and organized.
3. Discuss the four basic questions experienced caterers always think about when planning for their future events.
4. Discuss why a budget is a key factor when a caterer is formulating a catering plan.
5. Identify the basic menu formats used by a caterer. Explain the advantages and disadvantages of each format. What factors would influence a caterer's decision to use each format?
6. Discuss why each catering event is driven by its own set of objectives. Identify two common objectives which all caterers must address regardless of the event.
7. Why is a budget considered a financial plan? Explain how a budget guides a caterer when formulating a plan. What information or elements does a budget provide for the caterer?
8. Explain why the catering menu is the single most important factor in the formulation of the overall catering plan.
9. Explain what is meant by the term *overproducing* when discussing customer satisfaction.
10. Define *operational tasks*. Why is it important for a caterer to identify all operational tasks when formulating a plan.
11. Explain why a caterer holds post-event team meetings. Discuss what kind of information a caterer would seek at this meeting.
12. Explain why catering plans must be flexible.
13. Explain the Ingredients for Success and what they mean to you.

Multiple Choice

Select the single best answer for each question.

1. Barriers that interfere with the tangible elements of the implementation of a catering event are called:
   a. communication barriers
   b. human resource barriers
   c. operational barriers
   d. intangible barriers
   e. governmental barriers

2. The first catering management function is _____ .
   a. controlling the budget
   b. creating "what if" scenarios
   c. building an event-specific menu
   d. formulation of a catering plan
   e. implementation of the catering plan

3. Which of the following is an advantage of having a standardized catering menu?

   a. excessive inventory

   b. limited menu selections

   c. complex kitchen layout

   d. uncontrollable costs

   e. lower profit margins

True or False

Read each of the following statements and determine if it is true or false.

1. A catering plan provides direction and identifies each course of action required to accomplish predetermined objectives.

2. The longer the length of time between booking the event and its implementation date, the better opportunity a caterer has to create a detailed plan.

3. The planning sequence will always begin with a review of the caterer's mission statement.

Putting It All Together

You are the owner of the Allegheny Catering Company. The Allegheny Catering Company is located on the beautiful Allegheny Mountain Range situated around the Allegheny River, all nestled in the Allegheny National Forest in Northwestern Pennsylvania.

Your market niche services corporate clientele who seek outdoor adventure activities year-round—activities such as fishing, hunting, horseback riding, boating, and hiking the forest and streams within the Allegheny National Forest.

The Allegheny Catering Company has been contacted by Slugger Computer International Distribution (SCID) to cater an event for twenty-five company personnel. These guests will be attending an adventure-theme management training program. The program will last four days and include adventure-based theme training.

On the evening of the fifth day, a graduation ceremony will be held for the 25 participants. The location of the graduation ceremony and catering site is a plateau off a mountainous trail two miles inside the Allegheny National Forest. The only available natural resource at your disposal is potable spring water. Everything else must be brought to the site by either horseback or all-terrain vehicles.

Your task is to formulate a functional HACCP plan to serve each of the 25 people the following menu:

    a fresh garden salad with choice of three dressings

    one – 1/2 barbeque chicken

    one – 6-ounce New York Strip steak

    one – 60-count baked potatoes

    one – 4-inch ear of sweet corn on the cob

    a sundae ice cream bar offering a minimum of three toppings

    a selection of at least four beverages—two nonalcoholic

The steak and chicken will be the only food prepared at the site. Food will be served at 12:00 p.m. on a Saturday in October. The event is being held in the autumn to take advantage of the colorful leaves prevalent during this time of the year.

Chapter 8

Operations— Execution of Tasks

Courtesy Stephen B. Shiring, Sr.

Objectives

After studying this chapter, you should be able to:

1. Describe a caterer's operation.
2. Explain elements of the front-of-the-house operations.
3. Explain elements of the back-of-the house operations.
4. Describe operational tasks.
5. Explain how to formulate a recipe.
6. Describe how critical the flow of food through the operations is to operations.
7. Describe a standardized recipe.
8. Provide examples of how caterers can create new recipes.
9. Describe how caterers transform customer needs into signature recipes.
10. Explain how a caterer can utilize convenience foods.
11. Discuss why a caterer will use branded foods on the menu.
12. Explain why a catering menu offers several advantages over a standard restaurant menu.
13. Explain why a caterer must build management control features into the plan.
14. Explain the catering management task of scheduling and staffing.

KEY TERMS

back-of-the-house

base recipe

branded menu items

convenience foods

employee work schedule

field testing

financial catering activities

flow of food

front-of-the-house

mechanical catering activities

menu development

operations

physical catering activities

plate presentation

principal

recipe

recipe development

recipe research

scheduling

scratch foods

signature recipe

speed scratch cooking

staffing

standardized recipe

work production schedule

Ingredients For Success

22 "The main outcome of a recipe is to produce a food that will excite the consumer to become a repeat customer."

23 "A caterer must know the holding power of the food."

24 "When developing recipes to complement the menu mix, create them based on the preferred taste of the customer."

25 "The menu is a management tool from which the caterer can control operations."

OPERATIONS

operations A term used by a caterer to describe the task of implementing and executing the daily elements of a catering plan.

A term used to describe the task of implementing and executing the daily elements of a catering plan is called **operations**. The second function of catering represents the transformation of the plan into the mechanical component of the catering business (Figure 8.1). The catering operation involves all activities outlined in the plan which require *front-of-the-house* and *back-of-the-house* execution.

Front-of-the-House

front-of-the-house (operations) Extremely visible, customer-driven service activities designed primarily to please the guest in the dining area, where customer expectations and a caterer's performance intersect.

Front-of-the-house activities are those customer-driven service tasks designed to please the guest primarily in the dining area. These guest service activities are extremely visible to the guest. Guest service is the major focus and receives full attention in the front-of-the-house. The front-of-the-house is where customer expectations and a caterer's performance meet. At this intersection, a customer decides if their total experience, based on the combination of the food and service, meets their expectations. It can occur in the dining room, banquet room, or in the client's own home during an off-premise function.

back-of-the-house (operations) Physical, mechanical, and financial activities performed by a caterer that the customer generally does not get to witness.

The type of service provided depends on the catering event. Common types of service found in catering operations, as discussed in Chapter 12, include American Service, French Service, Russian Service, Self-Service, and Buffet Service.

mechanical catering activities A back-of-the-house catering activity that focuses on the effective and efficient use and maintenance of the equipment.

physical catering activities The back-of-the-house interrelated management activities of purchasing, receiving, storage, preparation, and transportation.

Figure 8.1 Catering team transforms the catering plan into the front-of-the-house and back-of-the-house operational tasks.

Courtesy Stephen B. Shiring, Sr.

Back-of-the-House

Back-of-the-house activities are not generally witnessed by the customer (Figure 8.2). These include the **physical, mechanical,** and **financial catering activities.** The physical activities include hands-on logistical tasks such as handling deliveries; purchasing, storing, preparing, and transporting food; and using proper sanitation procedures. Mechanical activities revolve around the equipment—its efficient and effective use and maintenance (Figure 8.3). Financial activities involve back-of-the-house management techniques which lead to accomplishing predetermined profit objectives by controlling food and labor costs.

Intangible ideas and elements of the plan become reality in the operations stage. This is where a caterer follows the blueprint to satisfy customer needs and event objectives. This is where the job gets done!

Figure 8.2 Back-of-the-house activities, such as following the packing list to gather supplies, is not generally observed by the client.

OPERATIONAL TASKS

Operational tasks are a direct function of the type of catering event being implemented. Operational tasks depend on the customer and the food being prepared. Once the customer has been determined, the caterer begins the first task of operations— developing customer-approved menus.

The term *operation* is a term used to describe many interrelated activities. This

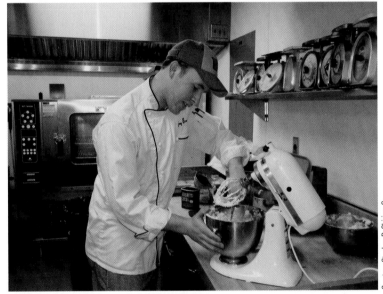

Figure 8.3 Food preparation is usually a back-of-the-house activity.

term is used to simplify the assortment of activities every caterer performs for an event. Operational activities include recipe research, recipe development, scheduling production, defining customer service issues, preparation, transportation, and clean up.

The task of researching recipes follows a common path. A caterer will develop and field test recipes, create signature recipes, decide on either scratch foods or convenience foods, set and control portion size, and use brand name items.

Menu development defines the function of a menu, forecasting, pricing strategies, and item popularity and mix. Production and service are concerned with the type and layout of equipment, scheduling, employee skill level, flow of food, and sanitation. Purchasing tasks are an integral component of operations and will be discussed in Chapter 9.

financial catering activities Back-of-the-house catering activities. Procedures that help to accomplish predetermined profit objectives by controlling operational resources in the daily execution of catering tasks.

menu development The process of defining the function of a menu; forecasting, pricing strategies, and item popularity and mix.

FLOW OF FOOD

Understanding how food moves through the operation is important. This knowledge will help a caterer effectively coordinate many numerous operational tasks that must be performed to create a finished product. The informed caterer can make better operational decisions regarding recipe development, sanitation, scheduling, receiving, storage, preparation, transportation and service of hot and cold prepared foods, storage of leftover food, reheating, and clean up. *Flow of food* as it relates to the organizing function is discussed in Chapter 9.

RECIPES

recipe Specific plan or formula used to describe the preparation of a certain food.

standardized recipe A specific plan. A standard operating procedure that communicates how to use the exact ingredients in the preparation of a specific food. It delivers a consistent quality, exact yield, and portion size each time it is produced. The achievement of financial objectives is supported by ensuring consistency, controlling costs, and preventing foodborne illness.

A **recipe** is a plan or formula used to describe the preparation of a certain food. A **standardized recipe** is a more specific plan that results in a standard operating procedure (SOP). This SOP communicates how a caterer expects to use exact ingredients to prepare a certain food. This food will deliver a consistent quality, exact yield, and portion size each time it is produced. Caterers use standardized recipes to ensure product consistency, control costs, control quality, prevent foodborne illness, and to achieve financial objectives. A standardized recipe implies a fit between the recipe, consumer needs, kitchen layout and equipment, employee skill level, and the caterer's needs.

A standardized recipe provides the flexibility of having the item prepared the same way each time, regardless of who prepares it. A standardized recipe helps deter the desire of kitchen personnel from using their own cooking style and ensures the item will be produced each time to a predetermined standard. An outcome of production is for the efficient and effective utilization of the equipment, by a skilled employee, to prepare quality food, from a standardized recipe. When served, the food must meet these standards every time.

A caterer will strive to become famous for a certain food. Clients request certain speciality foods. These requests are usually based on their preference for the taste, texture, form, temperature, tenderness, and eye appeal of the item. Therefore, the challenge is to make the item the same way each time it is featured at an event.

A standardized recipe communicates standard information. Because even the smallest change will affect the outcome of a recipe, every detail must be included. Providing information such as length of cooking time, type of heat used, and temperature setting will help ensure a consistent product. A recipe should communicate the following standard information: a common recipe name, yield, exact number of portions and their size, exact measurements of ingredients listed in order of use, equipment needed to produce it, specific directions for its preparation, recommended cooking times, critical control points (CCP) for proper handling, and directions for plating, storing, sanitizing, and clean up.

Recipe Development

A caterer is always searching for new recipes used to support unique and different foods. ***"The main outcome of a recipe is to produce a food that will excite the consumer to become a repeat customer." (Ingredient for Success 22).*** Caterers develop recipes in response to changing consumer trends and tastes. **Recipe development** is a continuous task required to support services offered to the customer. Recipes are researched before, during, and after events.

Developing recipes is a direct result of a caterer's love of food, experience, and the basic knowledge of food preparation. **Recipe research** begins by seeking answers to the following questions: What type of event is being planned? What kind of food should be prepared? What are the capabilities of the caterer and staff? What kind of production equipment is available? What are the service requirements? Is service speed required for 1,000 people or is it an elaborate feast for 75 guests? Recipes will vary based on the needs of the client and the guests.

recipe development
Process of creating new recipes in response to changing consumer trends and tastes. Function of a caterer's love of food, experience, and the application of the basic knowledge of food preparation.

recipe research Begins the process of recipe development by seeking to understand the relationship between a client's needs and a caterer's skill level.

> I believe when you are developing a dessert portfolio, you must understand what the menu is, even before you go into desserts. If your menu is more of a home-style, with stick-to-your ribs, full-of-flavor, large portions, then that is how I approach tying in a dessert.
>
> I have worked for many years in fine-dining accounts. This experience has enabled me to develop new dessert recipes. I also read many chef magazines that identify current dessert trends and specific dessert items being served at fine-dining establishments. I am very involved in the chef market so I keep abreast of these developments. A concept called *trickle down* plays an important role in our industry. Trickle-down theory says what happens in fine dining usually ends up in casual dining 3 to 5 years later. So I take my past experience in fine dining and apply it to creating signature desserts. For instance, I enjoy using some of the more exotic fruits, such as passionfruit, in new dessert recipes. I developed an apple-raspberry crisp for a Texas-style steakhouse company and threw passionfruit into the dessert. The customers absolutely loved it. It has become one of their best sellers.
>
> I believe one key to creating a great signature dessert recipe is to marry something that is pretentious with something that isn't. The trick is to create a blend of flavors that you can play around with so it works out well.
>
> *Kenneth P. Darling, Executive Pastry Chef, Heidi's Gourmet Desserts,*
> *Tucker (Atlanta), Georgia*

Recipe Creation

The most effective way to create new recipes is to start with a few items. Work the recipes until they are developed to the satisfaction of the caterer and consumer. New recipes can be found by reading cookbooks and newspapers, searching the Internet, trying new restaurants on vacation, dining in a competitor's restaurant, or even attending a competitor's catered event.

Developing a standardized recipe to complement the existing menu mix requires a certain caution against its immediate use. Sometimes a terrific recipe will not work after it has been increased to serve 100 people. Careful adjustment of seasoning and salt are always a concern.

Experimentation with new food will require it to be adapted to the caterer's menu. Often, changing a seasoning, or adding, or eliminating an ingredient will make it fit. An exceptional caterer will know what products will adapt to the menu mix.

New Recipes

New recipes should be prepared at least six times and field tested before being introduced into the market.

Field testing can be done on friends, customers, family, or employees. Always have the catering employees sample all menu items, but understand, the employees may be biased in their opinion. These individuals may be selected using the following preselection criteria as a guide.

1. Testers must consume a majority of their meals outside of the home.
2. Testers should be comfortable with eating a wide variety of food.
3. The caterer must select a good gender mix.
4. The caterer should identify the preferred age of the customer.

New recipes must be proven to withstand the rigors of catering. ***Ingredient for Success 23*** states: ***"A caterer must know the holding power of the food."*** In other words, will the food be able to withstand storage at 135°F on a steam table, without deteriorating? Will the quality level remain the same after being held for 4 hours, as it was immediately after production? These criteria are used to evaluate new recipes before they can be used in the field. A caterer cannot use a hollandaise sauce that will break down in half an hour for a catering job that requires a 2-hour hold time.

Discovery

Searching for new and different types of food and recipes to expand the catering menu is an active process. Creative food ideas can be discovered while dining in restaurants or attending catered functions.

> While dining in a restaurant while on vacation in California, I asked a waiter to recommend a dessert. The waiter suggested the restaurant's most popular dessert, the Mississippi Mudpie. After sampling this excellent dessert, I asked for the recipe, but was denied. So I returned to the restaurant the next night and only ordered the mudpie. Dissecting and eating it slowly, I identified a mixture of common ingredients and scribbled notes for myself on a napkin. Returning home, I used these notes to create a working mudpie recipe. After a few weeks of experimentation, I tested the dessert and a Mississippi Mudpie recipe was finalized.
>
> That was how Jardine's created our own version of a Mississippi Mudpie. Of course it was based on the original and it was developed so our customers would also enjoy it. The ingredients included an Oreo cookie crust, butter for stabilization, and French vanilla ice cream slightly flavored with coffee. Refrozen, this pie was covered with a fudge topping and toasted almond slices. It was served topped with whipped cream. The Mississippi Mudpie became our second best selling dessert of all time—a true signature menu item frequently requested by customers.
>
> *Courtesy Bill Jardine*

Signature Recipes

A **signature recipe** is a menu item unique to a specific caterer. It may have an added *twist* or *tweak*, such as a certain salad featuring a different taste or a steak, seafood, or a chicken dish made using a unique seasoning or marinade.

Permission of John R. Smith

Figure 8.4 Mississippi Mudpie recipe creates a unique signature dessert for the caterer.

Many caterers began their catering life with a basic menu. A caterer may feature a charcoal-roasted chicken. To differentiate this product from similar products made by other caterers, a basting-sauce recipe of water, vinegar, and oil enhances the flavor, helping the chicken remain moist at a 165°F internal temperature, and leaving it with a golden, sunshine-brown appearance when finished.

Next, a caterer creates a recipe to compliment the chicken. Working from a basic barbeque sauce recipe, a caterer can create his own signature sauce. Many caterers will perfect and develop recipes during their traditionally slower winter months. To create a standardized recipe, it is recommended to keep meticulous notes documenting the following details: ingredients, measurements, ratios and cost, preparation procedures, cooking times and temperatures, storage conditions, shelf life, portion size, and yields.

The result of this effort is a barbeque sauce offering a rich, fresh tomato flavor seasoned with a unique combination of spices and herbs. A caterer will use this first sauce as a **base recipe**, later creating other sauces by adjusting the mix of ingredients. While the first sauce, or base recipe, featured a rich, fresh-tomato flavor, by adding a mix of ingredients, such as apple butter and coffee to the original base sauce, a caterer can create a second sauce with a smoky, hickory-style flavor.

These two examples show the development of a standardized recipe, how a caterer differentiates a basic menu item to produce a customer-requested food that becomes the foundation of the menu mix, the creation of a unique signature flavor to enhance a basic menu item, how a caterer creates a new base recipe which can be featured in multiple menu items, and the meticulous attention to detail required when creating a standardized recipe.

The signature barbeque sauce may permit the caterer to expand the menu mix. A caterer can offer a variety of food selections, including chicken and charcoal-roasted barbeque pork, ribs, and pork loins. Remember one important factor and *Ingredient for Success 24: "When developing recipes to complement the menu mix, create them based on the preferred taste of the customer."*

base recipe A standardized recipe changed by adding additional ingredients to create another menu item to complement the menu mix.

Employee Suggestions

In many instances, staff and employees will offer recipes to the caterer. Be careful to follow the same rigid testing procedures, and adhere to the same established criteria with these recipes. Often, an employee will make a recommendation for a recipe based on preference, believing he or she has developed something unique. Remember, the recipe must meet the taste and needs of the consumer and preferences will vary from location to location throughout the country. Manufacturers of prepared salad dressing, for example, blend different flavors and sell them under the same label in each section of the country because of the taste differences of people in various locations.

Ingredients

When developing recipes, the quality of *ingredients* used in the recipe will affect its outcome. Cheapest is not always the best. Although the purchasing task will be discussed in a later chapter, using the highest quality ingredients will contribute to a quality menu item.

The level of quality is determined by the purpose of the menu item. Knowing the relationship between different foods on the market is important. Always inspect the item for its quality whether it is frozen, fresh, canned, or dehydrated. Since the caterer has the option of selecting from many items in the market, first research how these items fit the menu.

Always purchase the best product at the best possible price for its intended purpose. If 200 7-ounce, boneless, skinless chicken breasts are needed for an upcoming event, a caterer must research the market to find the best product. One purveyor may have a boneless, skinless chicken breast on sale, but they are a random pack. A random pack is packaged without a standard, uniform size. Therefore, the chicken breasts may range from 6 to 7 1/2 ounces. The caterer is confronted with options if he or she orders this item: either accept and try to use the randomly packed chicken breasts or reject the chicken and find another source.

RECIPE ADJUSTMENT

It is often necessary for a caterer to adjust standardized recipes. A standard recipe produces a standard yield designed to produce a specific amount of food. This yield, or standard, is expressed in portion size, volume, or weight. Sometimes, the yield from a standard recipe may need to be adjusted. Yields may need adjustment to fit the capacity of the production or cooking equipment, to alter portion sizes, or to match the number of guests attending an event.

One method a caterer can use to adjust a recipe's yield is the conversion factor method, which uses a conversion factor (CF) to adjust all of the ingredients in a standardized recipe (Figure 8.5). This conversion factor is multiplied by each ingredient in the recipe to calculate the adjusted amount.

Step 1: Begin with the known yield of the standardized recipe. Divide the desired yield by the known yield to obtain the conversion factor. Remember: New yield divided by old yield = conversion factor (CF).

Step 2: Convert ingredients to weight, if possible.

BEEF STROGANOFF

Yield 10 portions, portion size is 6 oz
Adjust yield to 25 portions at 4 oz

Ingredients	Amount
Clarified butter	2 oz
Oil	2 oz
Onions	4 oz
Mushrooms	8 oz
White wine	2 oz
Tomato paste	1 oz
Mustard	2 tsp
Demiglaze	1 1/2 pt
Sour cream	1 1/4 cup
Beef tenderloin tips	2 1/2 lbs EP*

CONVERSION FACTOR

10 portions at 6 oz = 60 oz is old yield
25 portions at 4 oz = 100 oz is new yield
100 oz divided by 60 oz equals 1.67 conversion factor

Ingredients	Amount	Conversion factor = 1.67
Clarified butter	2 oz	3.34 oz
Oil	2 oz	3.34 oz
Onions	4 oz	6.68 oz
Mushrooms	8 oz	13.68 oz
White wine	2 oz	3.34 oz
Tomato paste	1 oz	1.67 oz
Demiglaze	1 1/2 pt (24 fl oz)	40.08 fl oz = 1qt (32 fl oz) + 8.08 fl oz
Sour cream	1 1/4 cup (8 oz, 2 oz)	16.7 oz
Beef tenderloin tips	2 1/2 lbs EP*	4 lb, 10.22 EP oz.

*EP is edible portion. Edible portion is trimmed of all fat, cut into tips, and has a yield of 90%.

Figure 8.5 Standardized recipe: Yield adjustment using a conversion factor.

Step 3: Multiply each ingredient in the original recipe by the conversion factor.

Step 4: Multiply the original total weight of ingredients by the conversion factor (CF).

Use common sense when adjusting a recipe. Spices, salt, garlic, or sugar may not be increased or decreased at the same rate as other ingredients.

CHICKEN BREAST ROMANO

Yield 10 portions
Portion Size is one chicken breast, 4 oz

Ingredients	Amount
Flour	3 oz
Salt	1 tsp
White pepper	1/2 tsp
Eggs	4 ea
Romano cheese	3 oz
Boneless, skinless chicken breasts	10 ea
Butter	4 oz

CONVERSION FACTOR

Yield 10 portions - adjust to 65 portions
Portion Size is one chicken breast, 4 oz

Ingredients	Amount	Conversion factor = 6.5
Flour	3 oz	19.5 oz = 1 lb.3.5 oz
Salt	1 tsp	6.5 tsp = 2 Tbsp, 1 /2 tsp or to taste
White pepper	1/2 tsp	3.25 tsp = 1 Tbsp, 1/4 tsp or to taste
Eggs	4 ea.	26 eggs = 2 dozen + 2 eggs
Parmesan cheese	3 oz	19.5 oz = 1 lb, 3.5 oz
Milk	1 fl. oz	6.5 fl oz
Boneless, skinless chicken breasts	10 ea	65 = 5 dozen + 5 breasts
Butter	4 oz	26 oz = 1 - pt = 16 fl oz, 1 cup = 8 fl oz, 4 tbsp = 2 fl oz

Conversion factor (CF) new yield 65 divided by old yield 10 equals 6.5

Figure 8.6 Standardized recipe: Portion adjustment using a conversion factor.

A standardized recipe's portion size may need to be adjusted, depending on the needs of the client (Figure 8.6). Portion sizes may differ when catering an event for a group of senior citizens, a group of teenagers, or catering the recognition banquet for a senior high school football team.

To change the portion size of a given recipe:

Step 1: Determine total yield of the standardized recipe. Multiply the number of portions by the portion size.
Portions × Portion Size = Total Old Yield

Step 2: Determine the total yield desired. Multiply the desired number of portions by the new portion size.
Desired Portions × Desired Portion Size = Total New Yield

Step 3: Calculate the conversion factor. Divide the new yield by the old yield to get the conversion factor.
Total New Yield divided by Total Old Yield = Conversion Factor

Step 4: Multiply each ingredient by the conversion factor.
Conversion Factor x Old Quantity = New Quantity

CONVENIENCE FOODS

While researching recipes and developing the menu, caterers often complement scratch foods with the use of value-added or convenience foods. **Scratch foods** are the menu items prepared by the staff using standardized recipes. **Convenience foods** are products that are manufactured by a **principal**, or manufacturer, and delivered to the caterer in a *ready-to-eat* or *ready-to-cook* form by a purveyor.

One of the first convenience items accepted by the catering industry was hors d'oeuvres—very small pieces of food usually consumed in one bite. Because of their small size and composition, they require skilled labor to prepare them. Often, they are very expensive to make because ingredients, such as puff pastry or phyllo (very thin sheets of dough), can be difficult to handle.

Caterers have become famous for creating their own scratch, signature hors d'oeuvres. A caterer might fill a certain kind of a mushroom cap with a delicate crab and sausage meat. This item may not be available in a prepared form, so customers may request it. This popular item becomes a competitive advantage for the caterer to offer.

Some popular hors d'oeuvre items can be purchased already prepared and frozen, requiring only a few minutes of roasting time in the oven. For example, take fresh chicken livers, place a water chestnut in the center, and wrap bacon around it. This labor-intense item is now purchased fully prepared and ready to serve.

Many of the world's largest food service companies or principals manufacture a variety of prepared, heat-and-serve, frozen entree items. These products are used by caterers throughout the world. Customers accept these products because of their high and consistent quality. Often, consumers may not realize they are eating a convenience item because of its high quality.

Frozen entrees are widely known and used for their versatility in the catering industry. Caterers, upscale hotels, white table cloth restaurants, and others in the food service segment rely on these items to supplement their menu mix. Many operators will serve the item right from its pan. Other operators may season it with spices or add crumbled bread crumbs to slightly alter its appearance. As a result of these minor alterations, the consumer is led to believe the product is the caterer's own signature scratch menu item. Convenience items provide the caterer with several advantages and disadvantages.

scratch foods Menu items prepared on-premise by the caterer's staff using standardized recipes.

convenience foods Manufactured or processed by a principal and delivered to the caterer in a ready-to-eat or ready-to-cook form.

principal A common term used in the hospitality trade to denote a source who manufactures or processes food.

Advantages of Convenience Foods

1. The quality of the finished product remains consistent each time it is prepared.
2. Precise serving costs, based on exact food costs and portion size per container or case, are easily determined.
3. These foods provide easy expansion of the menu without the added increase of ingredients, storage facilities, cost of control, and employee skill levels to produce.

4. Features include some reductions in handling of bulk ingredients and the elimination of "waste" by overproduction.

5. Convenience items are available immediately, on demand (minus production time) as needed by the caterer.

6. A caterer can reduce the cost of skilled labor by using convenience foods.

Disadvantages of Convenience Foods

1. The cost of the item may be higher than the cost of preparing it from scratch.

2. Nutritional values may be elevated. Many convenience foods have higher levels of sodium and monosodium glutamate than scratch-prepared foods. (Make sure the consumer is not restricted in their diet based on these and other ingredients.)

3. Storage facilities may not be adequate to store these frozen convenience foods.

A caterer can locate convenience foods by asking their distributor's sales representative (DSR) or their local food broker. Caterers should also attend local distributor-sponsored food shows as well as the National Restaurant Association's annual trade show in Chicago, Illinois, each May.

SPEED SCRATCH COOKING

speed scratch cooking Foods that are made from scratch and finished off in the caterer's kitchen with little preparation.

Foods that are made from scratch and are finished off in the caterer's kitchen may be referred to as speed scratch cooking. **Speed scratch cooking** has little preparation, provides excellent quality, and lowers labor costs because less preparation is involved. Speed scratch cooking offers the caterer some of the following strategic advantages.

1. lower inventories
2. less equipment in the kitchen
3. fewer employees
4. less waste
5. less preparation and cleanup
6. better consistency
7. meets and exceeds the customers' expectations

For example, some seafood products, such as shrimp cocktail, can be purchased precooked and individually portioned with just as much flavor and consistency as starting with a raw product and paying somebody to prepare it. Another example is a prime rib. This is a fully cooked, heat-and-serve product that provides the caterer with exact portion costs and extremely high yields.

BRANDED MENU ITEMS

Caterers use brand names to identify certain food items on their menus. One reason is because the consumer recognizes perceived quality levels in certain names. Even though the caterer is not preparing this item homemade (from scratch), the value of using a branded food will satisfy a client's tastes. **Branded menu items** most often used by a caterer include frozen desserts. There are many great frozen cheesecakes in the market. The use of a branded cheesecake on the menu is an excellent example of how a client will recognize and perceive a quality product. Cheesecakes are not difficult, but expensive to prepare, are labor intensive, and lack consistent quality.

branded menu items Food items produced by a principal, backed by its name to guarantee a consistent level of quality.

Caterers may use branded menu items because the principal will pay to have their name placed on the menu. The most popular branded nonalcoholic beverages are carbonated beverages. A caterer would not list just "cola" on the menu, but might add the logo of a particular brand.

Most companies do promotional work. They help caterers by providing glasses, equipment, or supplies. Caterers can use this to their advantage.

Jardine's was once a popular vendor at many county fairs. We would prepare charcoal-roasted, barbeque chicken and serve carbonated *brand X* as the soft drink. The vice president of the carbonated beverage *brand Z* syrup division was having dinner at our place on the fairground. The VP asked: "Why don't you use *brand Z* cola?" We had a very nice conversation and he asked me about the rented tent I was using at the fair. We could seat 120 people under this tent at one time. The VP asked, "Would you be interested in switching products if I provided a tent?" Of course I was interested and we signed a contract right on the spot. Within a week, he had sent me a new tent. This new tent had the same seating capacity as the one we were renting. However, this new tent had a *brand Z* cola banner which encircled the outside of the tent. I switched to *brand Z* and used it for the next few years, mainly because the *brand Z* tent saved our operation quite a bit of money.

Courtesy Bill Jardine

MENUS

Standardized recipes are developed based on the needs of the consumer and the caterer. These recipes are bundled together and marketed by the caterer's menu. *Ingredient for Success 25* states: ***"The menu is a management tool from which the caterer can control operations."***

Advantages of a Catering Menu verses a Restaurant Menu

A catering menu differs from a restaurant menu by providing distinct advantages. Management control is the single greatest advantage offered to the caterer. Unlike a restaurateur, the caterer does not have to forecast future sales. A caterer is not required to make "best guess" customer counts or base food production on menu item popularity trends. Caterers do not have to perform these tasks because each event is planned in advance.

The catering menu is created based on guaranteed customer counts. Once the catering menu is created, the management function of control and execution becomes predictable. Most *unknowns* that challenge the restaurateur are eliminated. This gives a caterer greater control over the production process and the inputs of raw materials and labor.

If a client guarantees 350 guests, the caterer can be operationally prepared for the event. The caterer will know, in advance, the exact number of guests, the menu, what levels of inventory will be carried, the exact portion size per guest, the amount of food to purchase, cost of the food, the production schedule, service requirements, labor costs, and the expected profit based on the negotiated price (Figure 8.6). The client will have paid in advance for this function. This same scenario can be a gamble for a restaurateur. If a restaurateur has forecast and prepared for 350 people on a Saturday night and suddenly, unexpected inclement weather, such as a snow storm or a tornado, hits and only 25 people show up, the night will be a financial disaster.

Mayfair Farms is located in West Orange, New Jersey. My grandfather started it in 1943 as an à la carte restaurant and later added a banquet room. Over the years we built three more banquet rooms on the property. Catering is an extremely profitable operation. A standalone, traditional, à la carte restaurant may have a profit margin at best of 10 percent. The profit margin in catering may be as high as 25 percent. I have a steakhouse where the food cost ranges from 31 to 32 percent. My catering facility has a food cost of 16 percent. Because you sell parties at a higher price than you do in the à la carte restaurant, catering is a tremendously profitable operation when you can hit the critical mass of parties. If you can cater enough parties, you can have a very profitable opportunity.

Courtesy of Marty Horn, President | CEO of Foodgalaxy.com, Parsippany, NJ

A Communication Tool

One basic function of a catering menu is a tool to communicate, in writing, what the caterer can provide in food and service, the value and quality of the food, and service mix based on its price.

How does the caterer plan a menu and who is involved? How does a caterer find the right menu item for each job?

First, a caterer must have certain capabilities. This begins with a properly equipped kitchen capable of producing what the customer wants. The caterer must meet with the customer before the menu is planned. A wedding is the most important day for a potential bride and groom who are planning this wonderful day. A caterer probably would not plan the same menu for a wedding that would also be used for a picnic, although caterers have done picnics for weddings. After meeting with the bride and groom, the caterer would build a menu based on the needs and wants of the customer.

plate presentation The arrangement of good tasting food and its colorful and attractive display on the serving plate.

The caterer must consider the kind of food being prepared, its service presentation, **plate presentation**, and color mix. A plate presentation of mashed potatoes and a roasted, stuffed chicken breast with steamed cauliflower would not appear to be appetizing because of its lack of color. Plate presentation must be attractive and colorful, and the food must taste good.

If planning a buffet menu, it must be attractive and have eye appeal. Eye appeal is important since customers first "eat" with their eyes before they "eat" with their mouth.

A caterer will always be involved with people in need of different types of foods. Because of this, a caterer must always remember, when building a menu, to answer this question: "Does the kitchen staff have the skill level and equipment to produce what the customer wants?" Suppose one day the caterer meets with a bride and groom planning their wedding reception. The next day a meeting is held with the CEO of a manufacturing company who needs lunch served in the board-room during a board of directors meeting. Can the caterer meet the needs of the bride and groom and create what the CEO requests with current staff and kitchen capabilities?

If the caterer is not capable of meeting this CEO's needs, respond by saying, "I am not capable of producing that, but I can prepare this item, which I believe you would be much happier with overall." A caterer must be aware of the customer's needs but the customer must understand the caterer's capabilities. Remember, since the caterer is meeting with the client, he or she has already earned this client's trust.

Flow of Food

Another basic function of the catering menu is to determine production and the **flow of food** through the operation. Production includes budgeting and scheduling, determining what can be produced, understanding how fast it can be produced, requiring the proper equipment, and matching the skill level of the personnel to the menu. A caterer must only offer clients what the production staff can produce.

Production begins with the creation of a labor budget to determine the number of labor hours or labor dollars that will be allocated to the kitchen. This budget includes the predetermined gross income and profit objectives and how the kitchen can help to accomplish them.

flow of food This concept refers to the order in which food will travel through a catering operation, from receiving, to storage, to preparation, to production, and finally to service.

Scheduling

The menu becomes a management tool in production scheduling by answering the following questions:

- How quickly must the food be prepared?
- What ability does the staff have to get the food out?
- How long does it take to prepare each item?
- Who will do the prep work?
- Who will do the finish work?
- Where will the food be held after it is finished?
- What is the capacity of the equipment?
- Can all of the food be cooked at once?
- How will the production be allocated to utilize the equipment?
- Does the food have to be batch cooked and stored?
- Is there any need to precook the food?

- Will anything be cooked the day before the event?
- Will anything need to be cooked two days before the event?
- How will precooked food be stored?
- Will any food be stored in an insulated container?
- After cooking, will the food be frozen or stored in a refrigerator?
- Will the food need to be reheated just minutes or hours before the event?

Staffing

Detailed in the catering plan is each task to be performed to accomplish all predetermined objectives as set for each event. Once these tasks have been identified, they are bundled and delegated to an employee. This catering management task is accomplished through an effective and efficient exercise of staffing and scheduling based on the menu selected by the client.

staffing The catering management task of identifying the correct number of employees needed to execute an event.

scheduling The catering management task to balance a precise number of employees against a given volume of work.

Staffing is the caterer's task of identifying a suitable number of employees required for an event, while **scheduling** balances that number of employees against the given volume of work.

Employee Skill Levels

A caterer can have all types of skill levels in a kitchen. These can range from employing individuals with cognitive delay to do routine jobs, such as salad preparation to certified culinary professionals, such as a chef. A production staff includes pantry, prep, and butcher work, preparing sauces, roasting, and sautéing. Each employee must be continually trained to appropriately contribute to the organization and to avoid the high cost of poor planning, estimating, or food production.

Work Production Schedule

work production schedule A communication tool used to guide the appropriate behavior of the caterer's staff in the execution of tasks.

Scheduling food production begins with the menu. This catering management task helps control food costs. A **work production schedule** is created for a standardized recipe to communicate the following information: recipe number, recipe name, yields, exact number of portions, portion size in exact measurement, and specific handling instructions. Handling instructions will describe the approximate preparation time, where to store the food immediately after it is cooked, if the food needs to be transported, and when and where the food will be served. Special emphasis should be placed on proper handling procedures to ensure against the contamination of foodborne illness.

Employee Work Schedule

employee work schedule The catering management task of assigning tasks to be completed by the employees predicated on the production schedule and event plan.

Scheduling employees is a catering management task that helps control labor costs. A caterer will design an **employee work schedule** based on the amount of work determined by an event's production schedule. When constructing the employee work schedule, careful attention must be paid to the capacity of the equipment and distribution of an equalized work load among the employees throughout the time leading up to the event. Each employee should know their responsibilities and the length of time to complete each task. Explicit instructions describing what everyone will do with the food when they are finished preparing it, how they will get the food to the event, and how it will be served are distributed to each employee.

The first step in scheduling is to identify each recipe and the tasks needed to produce it. Coordinating the menu, equipment, skill level, preparation needs, and production time is critical because tasks will vary depending upon the food category. Successful employee scheduling requires production knowledge of the following categories: appetizers; sandwiches and hors d'oeuvres, sauces, stocks, and soups; salads and salad dressings; fruits and vegetables; red meat; poultry; fish, shellfish; bakeshop (cakes, icing, yeast breads, pies and pastries, quick breads) and desserts; eggs, milk, and cheese; cereals; and beverages.

FOOD PREPARATION

Proper food preparation includes many factors to be considered by a caterer. What type of vegetable will a caterer use? Vegetables are a concern because a caterer must factor the total holding time on the buffet line at 135°F storage in an insulated container. Fresh green peas, for example, may need to be refreshed every 20 minutes. If green peas are prepared and held for two hours, the peas will disintegrate into a mass of dark green mush. A solid vegetable, such as a carrot, green bean, or corn will hold much better over time. A caterer must plan production, preparation, and storage time when considering a vegetable.

Preparation of meat also takes careful planning. For example, when will the roast beef need to be placed in the convection ovens? How long will it need until it is finished? Is there a sauce, au jus or gravy? Will the roast beef be sliced during the function on a buffet line or will it be sliced before the event? Understand the production capacity of the equipment, especially for outdoor events. The caterer may have multiple functions scheduled at the same time. Review of each menu will identify which tasks can be bundled and which items can be produced together. If a salad is a common item found on each menu, salad production is scheduled to produce enough salad for all events. Then it is separated into smaller quantities for each job.

A knowledgeable caterer must make realistic decisions when creating a production schedule. Can a steamer be used during the critical hours right before service? Must the food be prepared before service and held in storage? Because fresh carrots take longer to cook than canned carrots, will it be necessary to precook and finish them right before service? Should the potatoes be baked three-fourths of the way and finished right before service? Can the production facilities handle preparing fresh mashed potatoes? Is a fresh mashed potato, or a frozen mashed potato which requires only a few minutes of preparation, a better choice?

A production schedule and the event menu must be coordinated. Purchasing the right type of food, such as raw carrots verses canned carrots, will affect the production schedule. This includes scheduling the equipment for the entire production line, from planning to final refrigeration. The production schedule must deliver the correct quantity of food at the right time. This happens when the caterer produces tested, standardized recipes. Signature foods are a good example.

Developing a competency and comfort level from the staff, producing the same food, using standard menus, leads to a strong learning and experience curve. Producing a consistent, quality product demanded by the clientele is a strategic advantage for a caterer. Not only will the production personnel learn how to execute their tasks more efficiently, but they will be in a better position to offer suggestions of how to incrementally improve the overall production system.

Innovation and creativity become important factors in food preparation. Employees offering innovative ideas on improving production, redesigning work flow, and streamlining work stations contribute to reducing costs and increasing customer value. Such production tips sometimes present a challenge for the caterer to reward and retain these innovative employees.

Summary

The term used to describe the activity of implementing and executing the daily elements of a catering plan is called *operations*. Elements of operations occur in both the front-of-the-house and back-of-the-house. Front-of-the-house activities are those customer-driven, service tasks designed to please the guest primarily in the dining area. Back-of-the-house activities are not generally witnessed by the customer and include the physical, mechanical, and financial elements. Operational tasks are a direct function of the type of catering event being implemented. These include recipe research, recipe development, menu creation, scheduling production, defining customer service issues, preparation, transportation, and clean up.

Review Questions

Brief Answers

1. Describe what is meant by a caterer's *operation*.
2. Explain the components found in the front-of-the-house operations.
3. Explain the components found in the back-of-the-house operations.
4. Describe a caterer's *operational tasks*.
5. Explain how caterers may formulate recipes.
6. Why is the concept *flow of food* important to a caterer?
7. Describe a standardized recipe.
8. Provide examples of how caterers can create new recipes.
9. Describe how a caterer can transform customer needs into signature recipes.
10. Explain how a caterer can utilize convenience foods.
11. Discuss why a caterer will use branded menu items.
12. Explain the advantages a catering menu provides over a standard restaurant menu.
13. Explain why elements of catering management control features must be built into the plan.
14. Explain the catering management task of scheduling and staffing.
15. Explain what the following Ingredients for Success mean to you.

Multiple Choice

Select the single best answer for each question.

1. Catering management activities include the physical activities and "hands-on" logistical tasks of handling food, preparation of food and the transportation of food. These activities take place in:
   a. the front-of-the-house
   b. the back-of-the-house

   c. an off-premise location

   d. social catering

   e. corporate catering

2. A signature recipe is described as:

   a. a food unique to the caterer

   b. a common food prepared by every caterer

   c. a consistently difficult food to produce

   d. a food requiring "field-testing" before implementation on the menu

   e. a food considered low quality

3. Which of the following is an advantage of using a convenience food item?

   a. excessive inventory

   b. limited menu selections

   c. consistent quality

   d. uncontrollable costs

   e. lower profit margins

True or False

Read each of the following statements and determine if it is true or false.

1. Caterers will use brand names to identify certain food items on their menus.

2. Standardized recipes are developed based on the needs of the consumer and the caterer.

3. The production task begins with the creation of a labor budget to determine the number of labor hours or labor dollars that will be allocated to the kitchen.

Putting It All Together

Visit an independent caterer or the catering department of a hotel, health care facility, college/university, military base, or restaurant known for catering. Ask the catering manager how they use standardized recipes. Ask them to describe their signature foods and how they developed their recipes. Ask how their customers describe their signature menu items. Identify and discuss the mix of menu items and how each one complements the mission of the organization. Write a short report summarizing your visit.

Chapter 9
Organizing the Event

Objectives

After studying this chapter, you should be able to:

1. Describe why organizing is the third catering management function.
2. Explain how organizing helps accomplish the plan.
3. Explain how a caterer organizes for an event.
4. Explain specifications.
5. Explain the main goal of purchasing.
6. Provide examples of common purchasing policies.
7. Describe basic purchasing needs.
8. Explain how to build a caterer and supplier relationship.
9. Explain how a caterer can find a reliable supplier.
10. Discuss why a caterer attends food shows.
11. Describe a food broker, broadline purveyor, and manufacturer's agent.
12. Explain why ordering is important to the purchasing function.
13. Explain standard receiving procedures.

KEY TERMS

broadline distributor

distributor

distributor sales representatives (DSRs)

food broker

formal structure

manufacturer's agents

merchandising associates

ordering

organizing function

receiving

retail grocery store

specialty distributor

specialty wholesaler

specifications

storage

supplier sales representative

territory sales manager

wholesale club

Ingredients For Success

26 "Structure is dependent on the mission of the organization."

27 "Every caterer should have at least two good suppliers, a principal supplier and a backup supplier."

28 "The supplier is only as dependable and responsible as the sales person and the truck driver who delivers the food."

29 "Good receiving and planning provide the caterer with a major economical advantage. Good receiving principles provide control."

ORGANIZING

All caterers, corporate or social, on- or off-premise, need to have a solid grasp of the third catering function: organizing for the event.

The **organizing function** occurs within a supportive organizational structure. Created by the caterer, this formal structure centers on the organization's mission. *Ingredient for Success 26* states: ***"Structure is dependent on the mission of the organization."***

Formal structure refers to the management design of the catering organization, which is designed to help allocate and control resources. A strong, but flexible formal structure must support the implementation of the caterer's evolving strategy, as outlined in the catering plan. It must be responsive to incremental and sudden changes occurring in the internal organization or external marketplace, thus permitting the caterer to adapt to each client's special needs.

When a catering plan is sprung into action, it is the organizing function that bolsters the staff's action to efficiently and effectively execute each task and attain the stated objectives.

Organizing Tasks

Building an organizational structure with the flexibility to support the implementation of multiple-event plans centers on the catering management task of organizing. The core organizing tasks for most caterers include creating the menu, developing recipes, writing specifications, ordering, receiving, issuing, producing, transporting, and service. These major tasks are further divided into individual activities. These individual activities then support each individual catering function plan (Figure 9.1).

Caterers use each of these tasks to implement the event plan, build management control features, and allocate resources. Catering management control techniques are discussed in Chapter 13.

Catering Management Tasks

Menu

The *menu* plays an important role because it is the foundation upon which everything revolves. As discussed in Chapter 8, *Ingredient for Success 25* states: ***"The menu is a management tool from which the caterer can control operations."*** The menu determines the type of food to be prepared, standardized recipe, flow of food, layout and capacity of equipment, size and type of storage facilities, and human resource requirements.

A caterer begins preparation with the menu.

1. What combination of foods has the customer selected for a menu?
2. What needs does the customer have and how can the caterer satisfy them?
3. Does the caterer understand and interpret these needs to procure the appropriate food?
4. How many people are attending the event? This will determine the quantity of raw materials the caterer will need to purchase.
5. What additional resources are needed for this event?

organizing (function)
The catering management function of formally creating a structure to support the efficient and effective execution of each delegated task in the accomplishment of stated objectives.

formal structure Created by the caterer, its purpose is to help allocate and control organizational resources while supporting its evolving strategy as determined by the mission statement and outlined in the catering plan.

Figure 9.1 With careful organizing, a tabletop presentation creates a unique setting for the client.

Courtesy of HLC Inc.

Specifications

After a menu has been selected, the level of quality and service must be determined. Quality is defined by the menu and standardized recipes as outlined in the caterer's mission. An outcome of well-managed production is quality food from a standardized recipe, created by a skilled employee, using the most efficient and effective equipment available.

The customers' perception of quality is exhibited by the menu they have selected. The menu selection will identify the flavor, texture, form, and temperature of the desired food, as well as control the portion size and mix of ingredients (Figure 9.2). By preplanning the menu, the caterer will have already considered eye-appeal; however, the service style will be another variable that influences the customers' perception of value. ***"The main outcome of a recipe is to produce a food that will excite the consumer to become a repeat customer" (Ingredient for Success 22).***

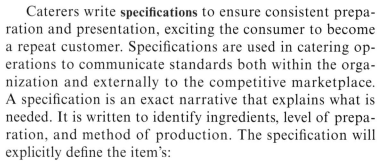

Caterers write **specifications** to ensure consistent preparation and presentation, exciting the consumer to become a repeat customer. Specifications are used in catering operations to communicate standards both within the organization and externally to the competitive marketplace. A specification is an exact narrative that explains what is needed. It is written to identify ingredients, level of preparation, and method of production. The specification will explicitly define the item's:

1. form
2. texture
3. temperature
4. color
5. flavor
6. unit size and its cost
7. portion size
8. purchase size
9. common trade or industry name
10. brand name required
11. federal or trade grade
12. place of origin
13. variety
14. size or count per package

Courtesy of HLC Inc.

Figure 9.2 The menu determines the portion size and mix of ingredients.

15. style of cut or package

16. age or degree of ripeness

17. type of package.

A specification includes all information necessary to produce the exact menu item. A precisely written specification controls quality, reduces costs, and keeps the information clear and concise. The specification establishes the caterer's acceptable standard to guarantee consistency of operations and to keep customers happy. For example, before purchasing a steak, a caterer must write a precise description of that item based on the needs of the client and caterer.

Specifications also are used to guarantee price. First, always purchase from a reputable, trusted purveyor. Most sales representatives in the food industry work on a commission; therefore, some sales representatives may be motivated to over-price items to get a higher commission. Specifications work best when the caterer gives a copy of them to their purveyors. ***Ingredient for Success 27: "Every caterer should have at least two good suppliers, a principal supplier and a backup supplier."***

> **specifications** Concise statements communicated internally and externally, of the exact products needed by a caterer in the operation to maintain standards and exceed a client's needs, wants, and demands.

PURCHASING

The menu has been selected. Specifications have been written for each item. The exact quantity is determined (items required for the function minus inventory). The next task is to purchase the raw materials. The goal of purchasing is to procure the item in agreement with its specification, in the right amount, at the right time, at the right cost, and from the right supplier.

Before executing the actual purchasing task, however, a plan must be formulated. The purchasing plan outlines how the purchasing objective will be accomplished. The plan is written into a purchasing manual to guide organizational members through the purchasing task. The purchasing manual will include policies (general guidelines for employees to follow), procedures, (a description of how the task must be accomplished), and rules (to communicate precise behavior).

Policies, procedures, and rules support the purchasing function by encouraging consistent execution of the purchasing task. Caterers may write policies, procedures, and rules to guide behavior of those directly responsible and accountable for this task. Employees who may be accountable for the purchasing function are the buyer, receiving clerk, production manager, chef, catering manager, and owners. Common policies a caterer can establish to provide guidance may include:

1. accepting gifts

2. making personal purchases

3. accepting free samples

4. setting hours for receiving sales people

5. setting a time range for delivery of food

6. acceptable substitutions of items by the purveyor.

The purchasing manual must include security procedures. Policies and standard operating procedures will describe security concerns such as when to unlock and open the back door, protecting against internal theft, etc. Frequent inspections by the caterer to monitor and reinforce procedures will help control this task.

Right Supplier

The right supplier will meet and exceed a caterer's needs as defined by the customer's needs, wants, and demands. Therefore, variables such as the caterer's mission; the organizational structure; the competitive market; and type, capacity, and layout of the production equipment will influence the supplier's ability to support the caterer.

Basic Purchasing Needs

Almost every caterer has the same basic purchasing needs. These needs exist regardless of individual needs.

Basic Purchasing Needs

1. Does the caterer have an acceptable comfort level with the supplier?
2. Does the supplier have an acceptable reputation?
3. Can the supplier provide the required brand?
4. Does the supplier carry an acceptable product line?
5. Is there an acceptable pricing policy? Will the purveyor negotiate in good faith?
6. Is an acceptable delivery schedule available with professional courtesy?
7. Are orders generally delivered on time?
8. Is the food of an acceptable quality level?
9. Does the supplier have an acceptable merchandise return policy?
10. How often are substitute products sent?
11. Does the supplier have an acceptable, professional support staff?
12. Is the supplier located in a convenient geographical location with a warehouse facility?
13. Is there a minimum dollar amount for the order to be delivered?

Every caterer has variable needs that a supplier must satisfy. If catering a small function, will the supplier deliver a small order? If catering a large function, can the purveyor meet the volume requirements? Is a purveyor's delivery schedule flexible?

It is common for a caterer to execute functions on a weekend, so delivery is sometimes needed on a Saturday or Sunday. It may be necessary to find a purveyor to deliver on a weekend. Some clients may contract for a 2-day event, such as a corporate fund-raising activity or picnic. These events may exceed 10,000 guests each day. If catering this type of function, the caterer should arrange with a purveyor several weeks in advance to schedule weekend deliveries.

Due to the amount of specialty and last minute requests, it is very important that, as a caterer, we have established relationships with suppliers and vendors. The range of suppliers and vendors we deal with on a daily basis is very diverse, from electricians and phone companies to florists and specialty chocolates. At Hyatt we offer our customers our "Preferred List" of vendors. This list covers entertainment, florist, décor rental, audio visual, security, etc. The vendors who appear on this list know that they are always the first to be recommended by our managers; therefore, we expect their quality and service to be consistent, timely, creative, and to always exceed our guests' expectations. These relationships are established through numerous trials of many products and services. At our hotel we have six managers . . . one bad experience with a particular vendor could quite possibly lose the referral of their product or service from our entire catering team.

Dianne Herzog, Catering Manager, Hyatt Orlando, Kissimmee, Florida

Building a Supplier and Caterer Relationship

Building a relationship with a supplier based on trust may be one of the most important considerations for the caterer. Establishing professional relationships with suppliers should be encouraged. Actually, strong relationships between a distributor sales representative and the caterer create a team approach to purchasing by recruiting the sales representative to become a part of the caterer's team. ***Ingredient for Success 28: "The supplier is only as dependable and responsible as the salesperson and the truck driver who delivers the food."***

Professional relationships contribute to a successful purchasing program. The caterer and purveyor jointly build a professional and ethical loyalty toward each other.

When a caterer is looking for a food service purveyor, I recommend they search for someone like us, US Foods. First, being a creative broadline distributor, we offer a caterer both depth and a great variety of product lines. We carry over 12,000 items in our normal inventory. It is a big advantage for a caterer to see the type of variety we have on a regular basis. We do not just have a handful of hors d'oeuvres, we stock between 70 and 80 different ones. We try to find the right items to fit their operation. Caterers are limited by the amount they can charge their clients for food. Each caterer must establish profit objectives and then competitively work within the price points of their selected target market to meet those objectives. We understand this and make it easy for them to find the right product mix, at the best price, to make their business work. Second, quality should be at the top of the list. Quality is what the caterer builds their business on. A caterer can have the best price in the world, but if the product does not work, or if someone eats it and does not like it, they are not coming back. Third, you will want to work with products that stand the test of time. When handling products, especially on the catering end, you will be preparing products that are going to be sent out and not served for maybe an hour or two hours after you deliver them. If that product does not hold as expected, then the customer is not going to get the quality they deserve, and as a result, they are not going to be happy with it, and you will have problems. Finally, the least expensive product is not always the best to buy. It is all about the yield of the product. What is the yield or how much edible portion will you receive from the item is the key.

Permission of Chris Garofalo

Supplier Sales Representatives

distributor sales representative (DSR), supplier sales representative, territory sales manager, merchandising associate Terms used interchangeably to refer to a purveyor's sales representative, the contact between the caterer and the distributor.

Supplier sales representatives are called **distributor sales representatives (DSRs)** or **territory sales managers** or **merchandising associates**. DSRs make a sales call and take the physical order. They are the contact between the caterer and the distributor.

DSRs may have a pager number, telephone number, voice mail number, and an e-mail address. The DSR's job is to match their distributor's resources to the caterer's needs to devise solutions. They will be in the process of menu development, while searching for new recipes or involved in many other stages of preparation. The DSR may offer computer assistance, sponsor continuing education programs, and provide culinary training. They also keep the caterer informed of market changes, new products, market trends, competitive maneuvers, and industry "gossip."

Finding Suppliers

Often, the *supplier* will find the *caterer*. If a new catering business or an established caterer is seeking a supplier, "gossip" or "word" spreads quickly through the catering community. Everyone is alerted to a potentially new customer who has entered the market. Suppliers will quickly send sales representatives to the catering business.

A caterer sometimes actively seeks suppliers by asking for recommendations from other caterers; searching telephone books, trade journals, and magazines; attending seminars and conferences; and seeking advice from local associations. The Internet is also a useful tool.

A caterer can become very popular with a supplier's sales representative, especially if the caterer is a volume buyer. Always be courteous to each sales representative.

MARKET INTERMEDIARIES

distributor (or purveyor) These individuals purchase items directly from the principal (manufacturer or farmer). They set up huge warehouses to handle large volumes of food and supplies for a specific geographic region (see specialty distributor; broadline distributor).

specialty distributor Basic type of market intermediary who specializes in the distribution of one product category, such as produce, cleaning supplies, or chemicals.

specialty wholesaler A specialized market intermediary. This wholesaler furnishes the food service industry with a specialized line of products, such as produce or chemicals.

Purchasing food and supplies is accomplished through interaction with numerous market intermediaries involved in the distribution and delivery of food. The caterer may purchase from a purveyor, otherwise known as a *distributor,* a *wholesale club,* or a *retail grocery store.* The caterer may also interact with a *food broker* and a *manufacturer's agent.*

The caterer will most likely purchase from a purveyor, commonly known in the trade as a distributor. **Distributors** purchase directly from the principal (the manufacturer or the farmer). Distributors set up huge warehouses to handle large volumes of food and supplies, providing service to a predetermined geographical area. There are two basic types of distributors. One is called the specialty distributor and the second is classified as a broadline distributor.

A **specialty distributor** is used when a specific item is required by the caterer. Specialty distributors handle only one product or a limited inventory. They may specialize only in produce or seafood, carry only commercial food service equipment, or handle only detergents and chemical agents.

Bernard Food Industries, Inc., of Evanston, IL, is a **specialty wholesaler** not many caterers' may be familiar with (http://www.bernardfoods.com). This product specialist is a direct sales company that manufactures its own brand name products and packages private label items for the purveyor. They also operate a retail store on the web at http://www.edietshop.com. Bernard Food Industries, Inc. has recognized the needs of their customers who, for medical reasons, must restrict their intake of sugar, sodium, fat, cholesterol, or calories. The products they offer have the same high quality sold to restaurants, cruise ships, spas, and health care facilities nationwide.

These specialized products are offered on the web so that individuals can conveniently maintain their dietary regimen while enjoying delectable foods which might otherwise be prohibited. eDietShop products also appeal to customers who wish to establish healthier eating patterns for their families. All products are labeled with complete nutritional information. Bernard Food Industries, Inc. is the first company to pioneer NutraSweet in cake mixes after it was approved by the Food and Drug Administration.

Bernard Food Industries' primary niche is for long-term care, assisted-living facilities, health care facilities, summer camps, institutional food service, correctional facilities, and school food service. Caterers who service these markets request Bernard's products when they must meet the nutrition requirements of specialized diets because they are customer driven (Figure 9.3).

Broadline Distributors

Broadline distributors are another type of distributor. A **broadline distributor** will stock a large variety of food, nonfood supplies, and equipment. It is common for a broadline distributor to stock in their warehouse between 7,000 and 20,000 different products. A broadline distributor is a speciality distributor and will "bundle" a number of specialized product lines, then warehouse them together (Figure 9.4).

broadline distributor
A market intermediary who bundles a number of specialized product lines, such as food, nonfood, equipment, chemical, and cleaning supplies together.

Food Shows

A food show is an opportunity for a caterer to sample multiple product lines and individual items. These are purveyor or restaurant association sponsored. Most distributors will have a food show at least once a year. The principals' entry or booth fees, paid to the distributor for the right to participate in the food show, pays the expenses.

The reason principals participate in distributor-held food shows are because of the buyers who attend. This captive audience is ready to buy. Each registered participant receives a color-coded badge to indicate the position of the participant. Badges are issued to reveal visitors who do not have purchasing authority, visitors who have recently selected the distributor as their supplier, visitors who are

CUSTOMER-RESPONSIVE POLICIES

1. Break up cases to permit a caterer to mix and match individual products at no additional cost to the buyer.
2. Provide samples of any product.
3. Sponsor product and cooking demonstrations.
4. Provide complete nutrient analysis on each item in a product line.
5. Provide diet cookbooks with complete, standardized recipes.
6. Make direct mail catalog available for individual consumers.

© Cengage Learning 2014

Figure 9.3 Customer-responsive policies.

BROADLINE DISTRIBUTOR BUNDLED PRODUCT LINE

1. produce

2. meats

3. seafood

4. beverages

5. paper products and cleaning supplies

6. equipment

7. branded foods

8. dairy

Figure 9.4 Broadline distributor bundled product line.

© Cengage Learning 2014

deciding if they want to use the supplier, those with purchasing power, and VIPs (Very Important People). The color of the badge helps each principal's representative at the show to quickly identify those visitors who have purchasing authority from those who lack purchasing power.

Distributors have *buying clubs* within their customer groups. These buying clubs may have names like the *Gold Club*, the *Silver Club*, and the *Bronze Club*. To become a member of one of these clubs, an annual payment of a specified dollar amount must be made to the distributor. Membership in some of these clubs denotes special customers who purchase very large volumes of products. These customers benefit from pricing formulas, based on the volume they purchase. The color of the badge worn by these customers will immediately identify a buyer who purchases a large volume of products.

Food shows are local, regional, and national. One of the largest trade shows in the world, the National Restaurant Association Restaurant, Hotel-Motel Show is held each May at Chicago's McCormick Place.

Attending food and trade shows is important because it gives the caterer opportunity to meet the manufacturer's agent who sells to the distributor. They may meet the food service broker, who is the link between the principal and the distributor. Many times, the caterer's DSR, as well as the distributor's entire professional support staff, is available to provide personal attention.

The food show is usually held in a large convention hall or at a conference facility. The food broker will set up booths which display their principal's product lines. The smart caterer will work the show and create networking opportunities by navigating through the maze of booths to:

- sample a variety of new and different foods.
- gather information on new emerging trends, nutrition, and changing lifestyles.
- see new products and technology.
- meet and discuss business in a "low pressure" environment.

Another advantage of attending food shows is the financial incentive granted by the principals. Principals sometimes offer show allowances, which are price discounts that may extend 6 to 8 weeks after the close of the show. The money saved per case may enable the caterer to achieve financial objectives. Caterers can purchase the same item at a reduced price, or a higher-priced, higher-quality item at a discounted price equal to the standard item's cost.

Principals may also offer sales promotions and incentives during the show. For example, a buyer will receive a discounted price per case. The discounted savings are reflected at the time of purchase. The price is automatically adjusted on the invoice when the purveyor ships the product and the caterer takes ownership at delivery.

Food Brokers

A **food broker** serves distinctive functions in the industry. First, the broker will bring the buyer and the seller together in the marketplace. Second, the broker may represent many different noncompeting product lines from noncompeting principals or manufacturers. Third, a food broker understands the attributes of each product line and communicates this information to the caterer. Fourth, the broker provides the principal with a national sales force. The broker is the principal's local sales representative.

Brokers serve a valuable role by understanding the local caterer's needs, wants, and demands and by communicating these to the principal. Brokers monitor trends and try to identify the future direction of the market. Acting as the principal's sales representative, the broker is also assigned as their representative to a distributor. The broker arranges for the distributor to stock and distribute the principal's product line in their assigned geographical area. However, the broker does not take title to the goods sold or set prices for the items they represent.

Brokers maintain an office, but will visit or *call-on* caterers to demonstrate their principal's product line. They will also teach caterers how to prepare the products. A broker may visit a caterer alone or *ride with* or *work with* a DSR from their assigned distributor. A caterer should be notified in advance by the DSR or by the broker to set an appointment.

Brokers conduct training programs to educate caterers about new ideas, products, culinary techniques, and bundling of product lines to build recipes. They also train DSRs. They are the channels used to relay information from the principal to the distributor. The brokerage firm will employ brokers based upon their need, number of principals, and size of geographical service area.

food broker A market intermediary whose fundamental task is to bring the caterer and the principal together in the marketplace to facilitate a sale. Brokers identify trends; conduct training programs; educate caterers to new ideas, products, and culinary techniques; and build recipes by bundling product lines together.

> Catering is a fascinating field. The products that are used by caterers most frequently are what I will call the ***upper grade of products***. Caterers seem to use the rice products we call our long-grain and wild, or long-grain and wild-garden blend, at many weddings or other big feeding events. When people see wild rice on their plate, it gives a perception of "upper class" or upscale dining. The guest's perception is that they are receiving a higher grade of food. These products work very well for a caterer.
>
> The cost of long-grain and wild rice is fairly inexpensive. One advantage our rice delivers for the caterer is that it accents the plate very well when served with a protein. Regardless of whether the protein is beef, seafood, or poultry, our rice product line provides the caterer with many alternatives and allows flexibility when planning a menu for a client.
>
> *Michael P. Simon, Jr., Great Lakes Region Manager, MasterFoodServices,*
> *A Division of Uncle Ben's, Inc., Houston, Texas*

Manufacturer's Agents

manufacturer's agent A market intermediary who is employed by the principal and has direct responsibility for accomplishing sales goals for each product in an assigned geographical sales area. Does not take title to the goods, issue invoices, or set prices.

Caterers will have the opportunity to work with **manufacturers' agents** who are employed directly by the principal to represent their interests in a geographical area. A manufacturer's agent works exclusively for that one principal. This person functions as the account executive for the parent company, very similar to the food broker, but with more responsibility. They have direct responsibility for completing paperwork and accomplishing sales goals for each product with the distributors. They do not take title to the goods sold, nor do they issue invoices or set prices. A manufacturer's agent will meet with a caterer to demonstrate their product lines and help the caterer to achieve success in their business. A manufacturer's agent may also be called a *territory manager*.

There are two types of manufacturers' agents in the marketplace. One is the manufacturer's agent who has direct sales responsibilities. This person operates as an individual in the market and does not share his or her time with anyone else in the promotion and distribution of their company's product. The other type is a manufacturer's agent with broker responsibility, who functions in the same way but has a network of brokers to support the individual's and principal's sales efforts.

Wholesale Clubs

wholesale club A large warehouse stocked with a variety of bulk foods, equipment, clothes, and other items. A membership fee is required for the privilege to purchase at the warehouse location. Caterers may find it advantageous to become a member and purchase food at these clubs.

Wholesale clubs are generally organized as very large warehouses that stock a variety of bulk foods, clothes, and equipment. A caterer can join these clubs for a membership fee, granting the privilege to purchase food and supplies at this warehouse. Wholesale clubs have both advantages and disadvantages (Figure 9.5).

WHOLESALE CLUBS

Advantages

- They offer a competitive price for the purchase of bulk food items, non-food supplies and equipment.
- Many operate seven days a week, twenty-four hours a day.
- No minimum purchase is required.

Disadvantages

- They are "cash and carry" operations. Unless a credit card is used, the wholesale club does not extend credit.
- The caterer must physically shop at the club.
- They must get the items back to the operation using their own transportation.
- A membership fee is charged, usually on an annual basis.
- They lack professional support services, such as menu development, educational services, or computer assistance.

Figure 9.5 Advantages and disadvantages of wholesale clubs.

© Cengage Learning 2014

Retail Grocery Store

Some caterers may use the **retail grocery store** to make purchases. Depending on the production needs and the menu selected, it might be good business to purchase exactly what you need, in the right quantities, at the right price, in the grocery store. Often, the caterer can negotiate a deal with the owner of the grocery store to establish a fixed markup or better pricing formula than a consumer purchase.

ORDERING

Ordering implies the caterer will secure the right amount and kind of raw materials needed to meet production and satisfy the client. Ordering requires an understanding of the menu, number of guaranteed guests, portion size, and standardized recipes. Other factors include the storage capabilities, inventory levels, yield, and production capabilities.

   The ordering task can be further divided by activity. First, determine the correct quantity of raw materials. This is accomplished by identifying each item on the menu. Then, review each standardized recipe's ingredients, expected yield, and portion size. Multiply this information by the guaranteed number of guests. Once the exact amount is determined, subtract this from its inventory level. The difference between what is needed and the inventory level is the amount to order (Figure 9.6). The actual delivery of the order depends on the purveyor's delivery schedule in the area the caterer is located.

retail grocery store Caterers who shop for their goods and services here should be careful to purchase the specific quantity needed. It would also be wise to negotiate a fixed markup or pricing formula rather than pay consumer prices.

ordering The catering management process of communicating the exact needs to a purveyor.

CATERER'S ORDER GUIDE
(Confidential)

Eff. Date:
Run Date:
Order Guide Number   Page:

Purveyor's Name & Address
Territory Manager & Phone Number
Deliver Instructions

Last Purchase Date	Product Number	Units/Each	Description	Line Number	Price

© Cengage Learning 2014

Figure 9.6 Caterer's order guide.

CATERING COMPANY PURCHASE ORDER

Purchase Order Number 00001

Order Date_____

Name of Catering Company_____   Address_____

Purchasing Agent _____ E-mail _____ Voice mail _____ Fax _____

Order Requested By _____ E-mail _____ Voice Mail _____ Fax _____

Authorized by _____ Date _____
(Signature)

SUPPLIER NAME

Address _____ Contact Person_____

E-mail _____ Voice mail_____ Fax _____

Please Ship

Required Delivery Date_____

Terms _____

Freight Charges FOB_____ COD (Amount) $ _____ Pre-paid_____

Special Instructions

Quantity Ordered	Pack Size/ Description	Page No.	Lbs./Quantity Shipped	Unit Price	Extension

TOTAL $ _____

Copies to Purchasing ___, Receiving ___, Accounts Payable ___, Purchase Request ___

Figure 9.7 Catering company purchase order.

Portion Control

One of the most important catering management control tasks is the measurement of ingredients and portions in food production. A caterer will measure ingredients by number, volume, or weight. Standardized recipes are also written with ingredients stated as either weight or measure.

A dipper (scoop) or ladle is primarily used to control the amount of food served, thus helping to control portions. These are excellent tools to standardize each guest's portion size, simplifying the purchasing task. The size of a dipper reflects how many portions one leveled dipper gives per quart. For example, a dipper number 6 delivers six scoops per quart. Ladles range in size, and are used to serve stews, soups, sauces, gravies, or dressings. Some of the most common size ladles range in size from 1 to 8 ounces.

Purchasing the correct amount of food may challenge the caterer when there is a loss because of waste. Unless purchasing a convenience food, which offers a 100 percent yield, food may vary from its *As-Purchased (AP)* form to its *Edible Portion (EP)* form, the amount of food the guest will consume.

The form and amount of food As Purchased (AP) may affect its EP yield. This depends on its storage environment, handling, method of preparation, and consumption form. Meat stored in refrigeration may lose weight as it ages because water will evaporate over an extended period of time. If the caterer cuts steaks from beef tenderloin, some loss of the product is expected because of the handling and processing. Also, cooking the steak will result in a loss of the product as it may shrink due to the loss of moisture and fat during the cooking process.

To purchase correctly, an accurate understanding of the relationship between AP and EP concepts must be comprehended.

1. As-Purchased (AP). This is the amount of raw material purchased. It is in the form as delivered by the purveyor. The As-Purchased amount will always represent the original weight. It is the base, beginning weight; it always represents the total or 100 percent.

2. Edible Portion (EP). The Edible-Portion is the amount of food a caterer will expect the customer to consume. It is always less than the As-Purchased weight.

3. As-Served (AS). The As-Served weight represents the portion size a caterer will serve to the guest. It is always less than the As-Purchased weight.

4. Waste (W). Waste is the amount of product lost during its preparation and storage. Its removal delivers its As-Served or Edible-Portion weight. Waste *will always* be a part of the As-Purchased weight or part of the 100 percent.

5. Waste Percentage (W%). The waste percentage is the amount of waste expressed as a percentage. To calculate the waste percentage, divide the Edible-Portion weight by the As-Purchased weight and multiply by 100.

The following example of the AP/EP comparison using pistachio nuts helps clarify this concept:

A.P.:   One pound (16 ounces) of pistachio nuts in the shell (As-Purchased). Remove the meat from the shell.

E.P.:   One-half pound (8 ounces) of pistachio nuts without the shell.

The caterer must calculate the AP weight to meet the EP needs. First, the caterer will multiply the EP size by the customer count. This amount will be the total EP weight required to serve each guest the correct portion amount. To further illustrate this concept, a caterer is serving 125 guests 4 ounces (EP) beef tenderloin. Therefore, 125 guests multiplied by 4 ounces equals 500 ounces or 31.25 pounds of EP weight. It is extremely important to control portion size. Each guest should be served only 4 ounces. If the guests are served more, the caterer will not have enough beef tenderloin.

The next step is for the caterer to calculate the AP weight. The AP calculation is important because the right amount of raw beef tenderloin must be procured. To calculate this amount, the caterer must know the yield of the beef tenderloin. Each caterer should calculate their own yield information using the same preparation and cooking techniques as stated in the recipe. It is recommended to conduct at least three tests to arrive at the yield. Although accurate records should always be kept by the production staff for reference, the yield can also be approximated using industry standards.

Using the beef tenderloin example, the caterer uses a yield of 90 percent. To calculate the AP amount, divide the EP weight by the yield. Therefore, 31 lbs. divided by 90 percent equals 34 lbs. 7 ounces. The caterer will purchase 35 pounds of beef tenderloin.

If the caterer begins with 35 lbs., and after cooking the beef tenderloin, finds the ending weight is 31 lbs., the waste is 4 lbs. The waste percentage is calculated by dividing the ending weight by the beginning weight. In this case, 31 lbs. divided by 35 lbs. equals 89 percent. For reference and consistency, many caterers use a portion control form (Figure 9.8).

RECEIVING

receiving The catering management task of following specific procedures to inspect, verify, and confirm the delivered item meets the caterer's needs by checking it against a set of written specifications. It includes receiving, storage, and the internal distribution of raw materials to meet production needs.

Receiving is a vital task that requires attention from all personnel. The fundamental task of receiving is to verify all deliveries against specifications and quantity; what has been delivered by a purveyor must match what has been ordered and paid for

PORTION CONTROL FORM								

Production Department Manager/Chef _____

Service Staff Manager _____

Function _____

Day of Function _____ Date of Function _____

Date of Production   _____

Production Schedule Verified _____

Guaranteed Number _____   Percent Overage* _____   Total Portions _____

Menu Item	Recipe No.	Yield	Portion Size	Actual Yield	Portions Served	Difference	Waste	Variance + or -

*Percent overage is an approximate percent based on historical data, forecasting, and the educated guess. It is determined by including the calculation of potential employee mistakes (spilled food, less than 100% food EP yields), food for employee meals, bartender meals, and entertainer meals.

Figure 9.8 Portion control form.

STANDARD RECEIVING PROCEDURES

1. Immediately inspect each item against a copy of its specification and purchase order.

2. Know the quality standard against which all products will be compared.

3. Understand the purveyor's policies regarding a rejected delivery.

4. Understand the purveyor's policy for credit because of an overcharge.

5. Understand the purveyor's policy for issuing a request for credit/pickup.

6. Verify weights, count, and price by comparing the actual delivereditem against the invoice and the specification.

7. Follow first-in, first-out procedures.

8. Write the delivery date and its price directly on the case or item to denote time and value.

9. Schedule deliveries during slower business hours.

10. Schedule enough employees to help put the order away.

11. Sponsor training to prepare receiving personnel in all phases of their job.

12. Keep the receiving area organized, clean, and sanitized.

13. Be prepared to randomly sample items to keep everyone honest.

14. Keep accurate receiving records each day.

© Cengage Learning 2014

Figure 9.9 Standard receiving procedures.

by the caterer. This leads to ***Ingredient for Success 29: "Good receiving and planning provide the caterer with a major economical advantage. Good receiving principles provide control."***

Receiving is the first control point in the flow of food through a caterer's facility. Because it is the first step, careful attention paid to this task can reduce defects that may cause potential problems throughout the entire system. Therefore, it is important to formulate a well-researched receiving plan based on standard operating procedures and guided by policy (Figure 9.9).

The receiving area should be organized as part of the formal management structure. The caterer must implement some form of control and tracking system (Figures 9.10 and 9.11) to verify the actual receiving activities being executed for the benefit of the organization. First, separate all related purchasing and receiving responsibilities. A separate employee should be accountable for the act of buying, receiving, and paying of bills.

Trust is especially important in this activity. Separating these related tasks provides a safeguard against unethical behavior by any one person. Detailed records should be kept of all credit and return requests.

Receiving Fundamentals
(Adapted from the most recent at time of writing FDA Model Food Code)

The receiving area should be well lit. All acceptance of food should be done in an area that is near the delivery door. The storage areas, such as refrigeration, freezer, and dry storage room should also be near the door. The receiving area should be

DAILY RECEIVING REPORT

Date _____

Employee _____

Purveyor	Invoice Number	Item Description	Unit Price	Amount Received	Total Cost	Receiving Temp. (CCP)	Accept/ Reject

Comments:

Figure 9.10 Daily Receiving Reports help track quantities and costs for billing reconciliation.

Day _____   Date _____

Received by _____

Delivered by (Driver's Name) _____

Specification Adherence _____

Critical Control Points _____

Correct Weight _____

Correct Count _____

Correct Prices _____

Comments:

Figure 9.11 Receiving stamps provide vital records and contacts for resolving discrepancies.

equipped with some common tools, which may include a scale, thermometer, can opener, razor knife, and permanent markers.

The thermometer may be the most important universal tool found in a catering operation. It is used by the receiving personnel to inspect items against their specification. The thermometer of choice should have a scale ranging from 0° to 222°F; accurate to +/- 2°F, numerically sealed, bimetallic with a five-inch stem, and having a two-inch sensing area.

The correct thermometer is used to ensure that the food being received by a caterer is at proper temperatures. All refrigerated, potentially hazardous food must be received at a temperature of 41°F (5°C) or below. Upon receipt, all potentially hazardous food should not exhibit any evidence of previous temperature abuse. If a food is labeled frozen and is shipped frozen by a food processing plant, it must be received from a supplier in the frozen state.

Potentially hazardous food that is cooked to a specific temperature and received hot must be at a temperature of 135°F (57°C) or above. Always obtain food from reputable suppliers who comply with local, state, and federal laws.

STORAGE CONTROL

The objective of **storage**, a major component of the purchasing process, is to maintain adequate space for perishable goods, dry goods, beverage, chemicals, and equipment. Organization of the storage area helps reduce clutter and prevents loss of merchandise (Figure 9.12). Frequent cleaning and sanitation eliminate potential insect and rodent infestation. Many establishments fail to recognize the potential loss through spoilage, pilferage, and theft. Spoilage can be prevented by ordering the correct amount, properly rotating stock, and having optimal environmental conditions. Adequate temperature and humidity help to maintain the quality of food. Pilferage is often referred to as inventory shrinkage or skimming. Pilferage is employee theft by stealing. Employees may also eat food without authorization.

If during the process of food production any food or ingredients are removed from their original packages and placed into working containers, always identify the food. Common ingredients such as cooking oils, flour, herbs, spices, and sugar are often transferred into appropriate storage containers. Always identify the food in their new containers with its common name. The date may be also added to the container. When the food or ingredient is easily and unmistakably recognized by an employee, such as with dry pasta or dry noodles, the common name of the food may not need to be identified on the container.

storage The correct placement of all items on-premise in the storeroom, refrigerators, and freezers. Providing protections from spoilage, pilferage, and theft are some key tasks of the storage function.

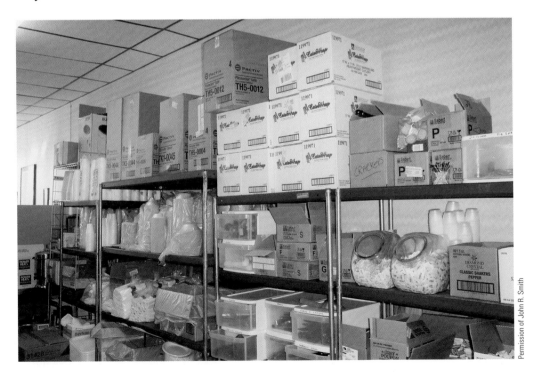

Figure 9.12 An organized storage area reduces clutter and pilferage.

Always be on guard to prevent cross contamination. This can be accomplished by separating raw animal foods during storage, preparation, holding, and display.

Storage or Display of Food in Contact with Water or Ice

The caterer should not store packaged food in direct contact with ice or water if the food is subject to deterioration if the water enters its packaging or container.

Unpackaged food must not be stored in direct contact with undrained ice. However, whole, raw fruits or vegetables; cut, raw vegetables such as celery, carrot sticks, or cut potatoes; and tofu may be immersed in ice or water. Raw chicken and fish that are received immersed in ice in shipping containers may remain in that condition temporarily while awaiting preparation, display, service, or sale.

In-Use Utensils, Between-Use Storage

During any break in the food production process, all food preparation and dispensing utensils should be stored in a proper manner (Figure 9.13). Always use common sense when storing food and ingredients (Figures 9.14 and 9.15).

INVENTORY MANAGEMENT

Inventory management is the key to protecting the physical assets for all events. Inventory control is the task of managing the amount of merchandise in the storage areas. Each caterer will need to maintain a minimum level of inventory, depending

---

UTENSIL STORAGE DURING PRODUCTION AND SERVICE

Food utensils should be stored:

1. in food with their handles above the top of the food and the container.
2. in food that is not potentially hazardous with their handles above the top of the food within containers or equipment that can be closed, such as bins of sugar, flour, or cinnamon.
3. on a clean portion of the food preparation table or cooking equipment only if the in-use utensil and the food-contact surface are cleaned and sanitized at the acceptable frequency.
4. in running water of sufficient velocity to flush particles down the drain, especially when used with moist food such as ice cream or mashed potatoes.
5. in a clean, protected location if the utensils, such as ice scoops, are used only with a food that is not potentially hazardous.
6. in a water container if the water is maintained at a temperature of at least 135°F (57°C) and the container is cleaned frequently.

© Cengage Learning 2014

Figure 9.13 Proper storage of food utensils during production and service. (Adapted from the most recent at time of writing FDA Model Food Code.)

FOOD STORAGE PRINCIPLES

Food shall be protected from contamination by proper storage:

1. in a clean, dry location.

2. where it is not exposed to splash, dust, or other contamination.

3. at least 6 inches (15 cm) above the floor.
   a. Food in packages and working containers may be stored less than 6 inches (15 cm) above the floor on case lot handling equipment.
   b. Pressurized beverage containers, cased food in waterproof containers such as bottles or cans, and milk containers in plastic crates may be stored on a floor that is clean and not exposed to floor moisture.

© Cengage Learning 2014

Figure 9.14 Food storage principles. (Adapted from the most recent at time of writing FDA Model Food Code.)

on the type of caterer. Proper management of inventory keeps the right amount in storage and prevents the over purchase of items, which may lead to problems such as spoilage, quality deterioration, theft, and pilferage.

Inventory is a financial investment for the caterer. Each item in the inventory should be marked with the date and its unit price when it is received. Pricing each item individually or by the pack, package, or case will alert every employee to the value (real cost) of the item. This is one method some caterers use to communicate the value of inventory.

The caterer will want to balance the investment of the inventory, or its stock levels against how fast it can be consumed in the operations. It does not make good business sense to tie up money into a large inventory. This is why inventory must be coordinated with production and forecasted against future functions. This will

PROHIBITED AREAS FOR FOOD STORAGE

Food may not be stored:

1. in locker rooms.

2. in toilet rooms.

3. in dressing rooms.

4. in garbage rooms.

5. in mechanical rooms.

6. under sewer lines that are not shielded to intercept potential drips.

7. under leaking water lines, including leaking automatic fire sprinkler heads, or under lines on which water has condensed.

8. under open stairwells.

9. under other sources of contamination.

© Cengage Learning 2014

Figure 9.15 Food storage prohibited areas. (Adapted from the most recent at time of writing FDA Model Food Code.)

establish individual par levels, or the amount maintained in storage to be sufficient to meet the production needs without excessive money invested. A challenge of managing this inventory is to avoid stock-outs. A *stock-out* occurs when an item is depleted before the next order is delivered. Frequent stock-outs cause break downs in the production system by creating pauses in production. When a stock-out occurs, the caterer will have to send an employee to the store to purchase this item.

Inventory management also determines the amount of inventory consumed for each function or for a particular accounting period. This is accomplished by tracking all purchases. First, the dollar value of the beginning storeroom inventory is calculated. All purchases transferred to the storeroom are added (less any items that have been issued). The total should equal closing inventory. *Issues* represent items requisitioned from the store room. Direct issues are items sent immediately upon receipt by the caterer into the production system.

Another task of inventory management is the physical counting of each item to find out what is in storage. Physical inventories may be taken at the end of a function, end of a weekly accounting period, or at the end of the month. Appropriate inventory control alerts the caterer to shortages or other discrepancies that may occur in the catering system. One method to calculate the cost of sales is illustrated in Figure 9.16.

Inventory control affects the entire operation. The cost of food sold will emerge on the income statement (see Chapter 13). This figure represents everything that was consumed in the production process, lost through waste or pilferage, and consumed by employees when unauthorized. The challenge for the caterer is to interpret this cost of goods sold by determining if the value is higher or lower than the established standard.

Product and stock rotation are also vital. The process of rotating inventory should always be a main concern for a caterer. Organization of storage areas insures proper sanitation and distribution of all products from their designated areas. Properly placed inventory also provides accurate accounting of products for effective reordering techniques.

The inventory turnover rate is calculated to find how quickly the entire stock level is being consumed or to determine how each individual item or category is being sold and replaced in storage. This rate will signal how effectively the caterer is

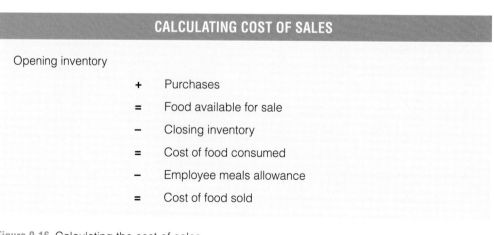

Figure 9.16 Calculating the cost of sales.

managing the inventory. An inventory turnover rate is calculated using the cost of food sold and the average inventory rate. The average inventory rate is determined by adding the opening and closing inventories for the period and dividing by two. To calculate an inventory turnover rate, take the cost of food sold divided by average inventory cost.

Summary

The organizing function helps to accomplish the catering plan. Created by the caterer, this formal structure is designed to help allocate and control resources. A strong, but flexible, formal structure must support the implementation of the caterer's evolving strategy, as outlined in the catering plan. The core organizing tasks for most caterers include creating the menu, developing recipes, writing specifications, ordering, receiving, issuing, producing, transporting, and service.

Review Questions

Brief Answers

1. Describe why organizing is the third catering management function.
2. Explain how organizing helps accomplish the plan.
3. Explain how a caterer organizes an event.
4. Explain specifications.
5. Explain the main goal of purchasing.
6. Provide examples of common purchasing policies.
7. Describe how to build a caterer and supplier relationship.
8. Explain how a caterer can find a reliable supplier.
9. Discuss why a caterer attends food shows.
10. Describe the role of a food broker, broadline purveyor, and manufacturer's agent.
11. Explain why ordering is important to the purchasing function.
12. Explain standard receiving procedures.
13. Explain what the Ingredients for Success mean to you.

Multiple Choice

Select the single best answer for each question.

1. A(n) _____ refers to the management design of a catering operation.
    a. informal structure
    b. formal structure
    c. invisible structure
    d. intangible structure
    e. covert structure

2. Specifications are used in the catering operation to:
    a. confuse competition
    b. create "what if" scenarios
    c. communicate standards
    d. design a catering plan
    e. implement a catering plan

3. Which of the following is an advantage of attending a food show?
   a. sample a variety of different kinds of foods
   b. see new products and emerging technology
   c. network with other caterers
   d. secure financial incentives from manufacturer's agent
   e. all of the above are considered advantages

True or False

Read each of the following statements and determine if it is true or false.

1. A manufacturer's agent is employed directly by the principal to represent their interests in a geographical area.
2. The primary purpose of a food broker is to bring a buyer and a seller together in the marketplace.
3. All caterers have basic purchasing needs, regardless of the specific needs unique to their own operation.

Putting It All Together

Contact some representatives from the food distribution channel—a broadline purveyor, a specialty purveyor, a food broker, and a manufacturer's agent. Seek information to describe what their roles are in the distribution channel. Ask for information regarding the services they provide a caterer.

Chapter 10

Equipment

Courtesy of Stephen B. Shiring, Jr.

Objectives

After studying this chapter, you should be able to:

1. Describe equipment and design considerations.

2. Explain how a caterer selects the type of utility to use as the energy source.

3. Explain why the menu is a powerful tool used to determine the design and layout of workstations.

4. Explain individual workstations, such as preparation, hot and cold food production, and final preparation needs.

5. Explain the appropriate methods and techniques a caterer must implement to prevent occurrences of foodborne illness.

KEY TERMS

commercial food safety kitchen

multitasking equipment

retherm

workstation

Ingredients For Success

30 "The menu is the single most important tool used to determine precise equipment needs based on the type of food being prepared."

31 "Minimize utility costs through manageable conservation of natural resources by planning for the current and future selection of energy-efficient equipment."

32 "Needless steps and unnecessary movement cause worker fatigue, which leads to reduced productivity and increased labor costs, and contributes to preventable accidents that escalate workman's compensation claims."

33 "Insulated carriers will not only carry food but will also carry bacteria."

34 "Be sure that all hotel pans and small equipment units can be transported properly."

EQUIPMENT AND DESIGN CONSIDERATIONS

In the catering operation, the challenge is for a caterer to efficiently and effectively design and equip the food production facility by maximizing spatial relationships and functionality, while minimizing capital investment through the selection of **multitasking equipment**. *"The menu is the single most important tool used to determine precise equipment needs based on the type of food being prepared." (Ingredient for Success 30)*.

The fourth catering function involves identifying what furniture, fixtures, and equipment are needed to equip the facility. The answers to the following questions will help to identify the type of equipment needed:

1. What kind of menu will be produced? What type of equipment is required to produce the food, hold it, **retherm** it, transport it, serve it, and clean it?

2. Who is the target customer? Remember *Ingredient for Success 2: "We cannot be all things to all people."* If the focus is to cater breakfast functions, the type of equipment may be different from that required to prepare complete meals for dinner functions.

3. What are the current and emerging consumer and industry trends?

A caterer must first determine the mission of the organization and then set a strategic direction as the first step toward creating an effective menu. To adequately prepare the food production area, the caterer must understand the relationship between several key factors that shape, build, and can lead to the success of the catering business. These factors are always exerting either covert or overt pressure on the catering business. They demand attention, requiring the caterer to constantly monitor their business environment. The following factors will influence the caterer's ability to adequately equip a food production system:

1. performance and functionality of design—simple to take apart and reassemble

2. maintenance, reliability, and warranty of equipment; availability and cost of replacement parts

3. employee skill level and relationship to the production needs of the menu

4. current and future equipment requirements based on customer needs, wants, and demands

5. application and development of new technology

6. government regulations, including HACCP procedures and safety features

7. competitors' adaptation of technology to reduce labor and utility costs

8. innovations in product design, aesthetics, components, and/or construction features

9. food, labor, and energy costs

10. maximization and utilization of the available space

11. versatility of equipment to reduce capital outlay

12. spatial relationships and good fit

13. proper flow of people and product through the system

multitasking equipment Food production equipment that offers the ability to be used for multiple procedures or processes in the preparation of food. For example, a tilting braising pan can perform multiple cooking duties such as braising, frying, roasting, thawing, and hot or cold holding.

rethermalization (retherm) The process of taking a prepared product, either prepared from scratch or purchased in a prepared state, that was either chilled or frozen, and applying heat to bring it to a desired serving temperature. Depending on the item, final rethermalization temperature is based on HACCP-recommended procedures for reheating prepared foods. For example, a temperature of 165°F is required to retherm a poultry product before serving it.

14. energy management in gas, electric, water, and HVAC (Heating, Ventilation, and Air Conditioning

15. voluntary conformity with sustainable business practices such as with Leadership in Energy and Environmental Design (LEED) and Energy Star compliant equipment.

UTILITIES

The decision to use either natural gas, electric, or sustainable sources such as solar power or wind turbines or a combination of these as the energy sources to drive the equipment in the production area, is another factor that affects the purchase of equipment (Figure 10.1). While there are advantages and disadvantages for each kind of utility, the decision to use one or another may simply be a personal preference of the caterer or may be limited to availability at the facility.

Regarding the various utility options mentioned, gas is the best alternative for a caterer's commercial food safety kitchen. The reason is that gas produces a higher BTU (British Thermal Units). Ranges vary in their BTU per hour (BTU/hr) capacity. The wrong range, for example, will not only produce too high of a BTU/hr output but it will consume more energy than needed, thus increasing utility costs and wasting energy.

Figure 10.1 This wind turbine, attached to the Eat'n Park Restaurant near Pittsburgh, Pennsylvania, is designed to generate 2,000 kilowatt hours a year.

THE MENU

The menu is a powerful tool used to determine the design, layout, and equipment for the production and service area and each individual **workstation** created within the production area. As the menu designates the design of a kitchen, do not mistakenly believe the design is set in stone. An astute caterer reinvents the menu to remain current with trends, seasonality of food, and customer demands. Therefore, menus change. Select flexible and versatile equipment to accommodate incremental changes in the menu. Otherwise, as the menu evolves, the caterer may need to change the kitchen and update or install new equipment.

When planning an off-premise event, the food will have to move cold or hot from the kitchen in transportation containers to the site. The menu will determine what kinds of transportation containers are needed and the type of portable kitchen equipment needed at the site.

workstation Areas in the production kitchen influenced in design by three basic dimensions: method of preparation, type of cooking method utilized, and volume of food produced. Common workstations include preparation, hot food, cold food, final preparation, warewashing, and transportation.

When Jardine's first opened, electric power was the only utility available at their location so there was no decision to be made. All of the production equipment purchased was powered by electricity. Because electricity is rather expensive when compared to natural gas, we were vigilant in creating a structured production schedule to minimize energy use and its cost. This production schedule

(continues)

(continued)

eventually evolved into a bigger program which featured *energy conservation awareness training* for the employees.

Later, when natural gas became available, a decision was made to switch the equipment from electricity to natural gas because gas is less expensive. Using natural gas significantly reduced the operation's monthly utility costs.

This illustrates *Ingredient for Success 31:"Minimize utility costs through manageable conservation of natural resources by planning for the current and future selection of energy-efficient equipment."*

Courtesy Bill Jardine

Caterer's Commercial Food Safety Kitchen

commercial food safety kitchen A food production kitchen meeting the minimal structural design requirements with appropriate commercial equipment, refrigeration, and utensils, in compliance with the National Sanitation Foundation (NSF) standards or their equivalent, and Food Safety Regulations.

The efficient design of a caterer's **commercial food safety kitchen** requires knowledge in layout and design, sanitation and safety, engineering and electrical drawings, plumbing schematics, HVAC (Heating, Ventilation, and Air Conditioning) and refrigeration requirements, equipment specifications, interior design, budgeting and bidding procedures, construction and installation, cost analysis, and professional hands-on catering experience (Figure 10.2). David Curran, of Curran-Taylor, Inc., Food Service Equipment, Supplies, and Design of Canonsburg, Pennsylvania, and Naples, Florida, says the decisions made in the design phase of the commercial food safety kitchen will affect its long-term operational success. The catering industry presents the owner/operator with difficult challenges, any one contributing greatly to the success or failure of the operation. For example, caterers confront ever increasing food, labor, and energy costs. Space is becoming harder to obtain. Competition is getting better and is always challenging.

Figure 10.2 Commercial food safety kitchen.

Courtesy of Stephen B. Shiring, Jr.

Curran offers the following advice to those considering the installation of a commercial food safety kitchen in one's home or in an empty building: "You have to look at your building with a skeptical eye. Keep the design simple but effective, easy to maintain, to sanitize and keep clean. Be aware unexpected costs can become a major factor." He says every commercial food safety kitchen needs two things: floor drains and an exhaust system. When considering floor drains, water drainage is a significant need since water does not run uphill. An existing building may have no floor drains. The installation of equipment, such as a three-bay sink, steam-jacket kettle, steam table, or warewashing machine will require a water line. If this is the case, a common requirement when working with an existing building is the entire floor must be jack-hammered up, incurring unexpected costs. Second, the installation of an exhaust hood and ventilation system must be solved. Where will the exhaust hood be placed and to where will it be vented? Steam lines, ventilation ducts, and water lines cannot be routed through a dry storage area. Curran emphasizes the need to work with experienced professional equipment and design specialists to ensure an efficient, effective design and installation of a caterer's commercial food safety kitchen.

WORKSTATIONS

Common workstations designated in a caterer's production facility are created by the menu with emphasis on time and motion studies. Understanding the flow of food and production tasks leads to carefully laid-out workstations. Carefully laid-out workstations minimize movement and needless steps (Figure 10.3).

Ingredient for Success 32: "Needless steps and unnecessary movement cause worker fatigue, which leads to reduced productivity and increased labor costs, and contributes to preventable accidents that escalate workman's compensation claims."

Tips from the Trade

Catering is done in so many different ways. Many people are still catering small jobs out of their homes. I think that is just pushing the envelope a little bit too much. I am a big proponent of food safety. Home equipment is just not designed to handle all of the food safety parameters, such adhering to proper temperatures in storage, preparation, cooking, transportation, and final service to the customer. Your home refrigerator is not designed to cool food down to 41°F or to store it at the proper temperature. Unsafe cooler and freezer temperatures create unsafe foods (Chapter 7, HACCP). I am very leery of someone catering from his or her home and strongly against it. Now, if you are catering out of your home, that does not mean you cannot install commercial equipment in your garage or remodel the home. My word of advice is to be very, very cautious. I would say from a catering aspect, if you work your entire life to build your business, it can only take one outbreak of a foodborne illness to destroy it. If I can stress one thing, it is absolute food safety. Learn food safety, learn the correct temperatures, enroll in the National Restaurant Educational Foundation ServSafe® program, and become certified.

David Curran, Curran-Taylor, Inc., Food Service Equipment, Supplies, and Design, Canonsburg, Pennsylvania, and Naples, Florida

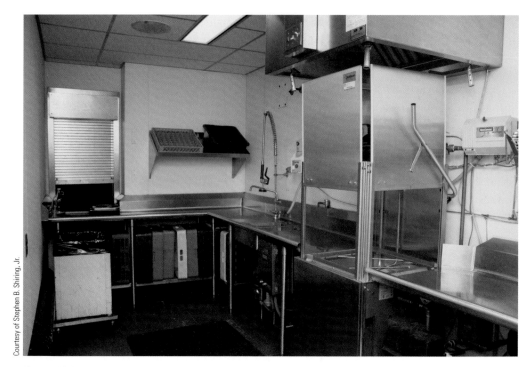

Courtesy of Stephen B. Shiring, Jr.

Figure 10.3 Workstations should be designed to minimize needless steps.

Workstations are created using three basic dimensions: method of preparation, type of cooking method, and volume of food. These three dimensions determine the equipment and corresponding spatial requirements of a workstation.

Complexity of the menu, ranging from simple preparation skills to more complex culinary techniques requiring professionally trained chefs, will affect workstation design. The menu mix, including the use of convenience and scratch foods and the number of similar or different kinds of food, affects equipment needs and the menu complexity.

Workstations are usually organized by similar task. The designer must know how much baking the caterer will be doing, how much roasting space will be needed, and what size range top is required based on the volume of food being produced at any one time.

By analyzing the menu, workstations can be planned. Common workstations in a typical catering operation are generally organized into one of the following categories based on the flow of food through the system and similar production tasks: receiving and loading dock, storage areas, preparation, hot food production, cold food production, final preparation, warewashing, and transportation, and cleaning and sanitizing. Care should be taken to ensure that the caterer does not have to waste time hauling refuse long distances to waste disposal sites. Such sites include dumpster, recycling bins, and composting areas.

Receiving

The receiving area is located in a convenient location to accept deliveries. Some common types of equipment located in the receiving area are scales, thermometers, handcarts, trucks, and containers. Hand tools including a hammer and wire cutters are recommended. Markers and labels needed to date the deliveries are a must.

A major function of the receiving task is to inspect each delivery. Accurately verify what is delivered by the purveyor is exactly what was ordered by the caterer. It is highly recommended for all caterers to follow the Hazardous Analysis Critical Control Point (HACCP) system, as discussed in Chapter 7. The receiving area is the caterer's first control point and the first line of defense to ensure the food being received is at the proper temperature, free of biological, physical, and chemical hazards. The National Restaurant Association Educational Foundation's International Food Safety Council recommends all caterers to have a written plan to address food safety.

Storage

Since a majority of a caterer's business volume fluctuates depending on the time of the year, type of event, and number of events per day, a critical need to balance storage capacity against business volume becomes a vital planning consideration. Proper storage procedures include dating all items and following First-in, First-out (FIFO) to ensure inventory rotation.

There are three major types of storage. These are dry storage, refrigerated storage, and freezer storage. Separate storage areas for chemicals, cleaning supplies, linens and napery, paper products, service equipment, props, and dishes are commonly found in a caterer's commercial food safety kitchen (Figure 10.4). Remember if chemicals and cleaning supplies are in the kitchen, a separate dry storage area must be designated for them. Never store chemicals near food preparation areas.

Figure 10.4 Separate locked storage area for chemicals and cleaning supplies.

Courtesy of Stephen B. Shiring, Jr.

Dry Storage

A dry storage area should adequately ventilated and maintained at an appropriate temperature of between 50°–70°F and a relative humidity of 50 percent to 60 percent. It must be free of pests and rodents. Food must be stored at least 6 inches off the ground on preferably metal racks.

Refrigerated Storage

Refrigerated storage is critical in keeping food below the proper cold storage temperature of 41°F and out of the food danger zone. Refrigeration equipment in a caterer's commercial food safety kitchen includes a walk-in refrigeration unit and a reach-in refrigeration unit. Refrigerated storage is the hardest. It is important to follow proper sanitation procedures and keep raw meats, poultry, and seafood in the proper way. Ideal refrigeration storage allows each food group to be stored separately. This operational step prevents cross-contamination, one of the leading causes of foodborne outbreaks.

Freezer storage is designed to receive and keep food frozen at 0°F. Freezers should be maintained at –10°F. Capacity utilizes both walk-in and reach-in units.

Courtesy of Stephen B. Shiring, Jr.

Figure 10.5 Preparation area food mixer.

Courtesy of Stephen B. Shiring, Jr.

Figure 10.6 Separate hand washing sink for the employees.

Preparation Area

The preparation area should be located near the storage areas. Some common types of equipment located in the preparation area include reach-in refrigerators and freezers, work-top refrigerators and freezers, food mixers and attachments (flat beater, wire whip, dough arm, pastry knife), food slicers, food choppers, ovens, ranges, tilting braising pan, sinks, garbage disposal units, measuring tools (scales, ladles, scoops, volume measures), hand tools (serving spoons, hand whips, food turners, spatulas, tongs), kitchen cutlery, pots and pans, and refrigeration and freezer units (Figure 10.5). It is recommended to install in a convenient location a separate hand washing sink for the employees in the food preparation area (Figure 10.6).

Each workstation should be equipped with the latest in thermometer technology to accurately verify and log food temperatures. Using thermometers will assist in adhering to the requirements of a caterer's HACCP verification and monitoring plan. During the food production phase it is important to limit the exposure of potential hazardous food in the temperature danger zone between 41°F and 135°F.

Employee cleanliness and proper hygiene are most important in ensuring the preparation and service of food free from harmful bacteria. While preparing food, production employees should keep their fingernails trimmed, neatly filed, and maintained so the edges and surfaces are cleanable. When working with food, fingernail polish or artificial fingernails should never be worn. A simple plain ring, such as a wedding band, is the only permissible piece of jewelry to be worn while preparing food. Medical information jewelry is not permitted to be worn on the hand or arm.

When handling the food, all employees must follow appropriate food handling procedures. Always minimize the contact of raw food with bare hands. Never touch exposed, ready-to-eat foods with bare hands, except when washing fruits and vegetables, or if it will be an ingredient in an item needing further cooking. Use common sense when handling food. Use suitable clean and sanitized utensils such as deli tissue, spatulas, tongs, single-use gloves (Figure 10.7), and dispensing equipment.

Every employee must be taught to wash his or her hands before engaging in food preparation and before handling clean equipment, utensils, or unwrapped single-serve and single-use articles. Only an approved hand-washing sink should be used, never a sink used for food preparation or a service sink used for the disposal of mop water.

Hygienic practices must also be followed to avoid cross-contamination from eating, drinking, or using tobacco products. An employee should only eat, drink, or use any form of tobacco in approved, designated areas to prevent contamination of exposed food, clean equipment, utensils, and linens.

Figure 10.7 Gloves should be worn whenever handling exposed, ready-to-eat foods.

All food production personnel must wear hair restraints. These include hats, hair coverings or nets, beard constraints, and clothing that covers body hair.

Use of Gloves

An effective technique to prevent foodborne illness is for employees to follow good personal hygiene procedures including proper and frequent washing of their hands. Proper handwashing, combined with appropriate use of gloves, will create an effective barrier against foodborne illness (Figure 10.8). Gloves should not be worn in lieu of washing hands. It is important to have the correct size of gloves for each employee.

APPROPRIATE USES OF GLOVES BY THE FOODHANDLER

1. Single-use gloves should be used for only one task, such as working with ready-to-eat food or with raw animal food, and for no other purpose. They should be discarded when damaged or soiled, or when interruptions occur in the operation.

2. Slash-resistant gloves that are used to protect the hands during operations requiring cutting should be used only in direct contact with food that is subsequently cooked, such as frozen food or a primal cut of meat.

3. Slash-resistant gloves that have a smooth, durable, and nonabsorbent outer surface, or covered by single-use gloves, should be used with ready-to-eat food that will not subsequently be cooked.

4. Cloth gloves may not be used in direct contact with food unless the food is subsequently cooked, such as frozen food or a primal cut of meat.

Figure 10.8 Appropriate uses of gloves by the food handler. (Adapted from the most recent at time of writing FDA Model Food Code.)

204   **Part 2** The Catering Operation

Courtesy of Stephen B. Shiring, Jr.

Figure 10.9 The hot food production area contains a variety of ovens so care must be used when handling food or equipment in this area.

Gloves should fit properly. A glove that is too large will not stay on the hand and one too small will rip easily. Gloves should be changed regularly before starting another task, if ripped, if it has become soiled, after handling raw products, or after 4 hours.

Hot Food Production

The hot food production area (Figure 10.9) may contain some of the following types of equipment: range, range oven, microwave oven, convection oven, combination convection oven/steamer otherwise known as a "combi oven" (which is extremely convenient and very popular, but expensive) fryers, broilers, griddles, tilting braising pan, steam-jacketed kettle, low or high pressure steamers, and refrigeration and freezer units. It is important to establish procedures to ensure final cooking temperatures are achieved (Figure 10.10).

The Importance of Equipment to Your Business

As stated in the Chapter 11, Obtaining Equipment, it is important to acquire the right equipment. Equipment ranges can be, but are not limited to, the following: combination ovens, convection ovens, steam-jacketed kettles, tilt skillets, ranges, flat top, grill, deep fat fryer, coolers, freezers, slicers, buffalo choppers, meat grinders, holding boxes, and mixers. It is important to purchase the right size of equipment. The wrong piece of equipment at the right price is still the wrong piece of equipment. It is vital to have the appropriate equipment to fit the needs of your chef's and menus. The food is the major backbone of the business, and to keep the business running successfully and profitably, the right equipment is a prerequisite to execute the menu your chef has created.

FINAL COOKING TEMPERATURES FOR SELECTED FOODS

1. Fruits and vegetables that are cooked for hot holding should be cooked to a temperature of 135°F (57°C).

2. Cooked and refrigerated food that is prepared for immediate service in response to an individual consumer order, such as a roast beef sandwich au jus, may be served at any temperature.

3. Potentially hazardous food that is cooked, cooled, and reheated for hot holding shall be reheated so that all parts of the food reach a temperature of at least 165°F (74°C) for 15 seconds within two hours.

4. Potentially hazardous food, reheated in a microwave oven for hot holding, shall be reheated so that all parts of the food reach a temperature of at least 165°F (74°C). The food should be rotated or stirred, covered, and allowed to stand covered for 2 minutes after reheating.

5. Ready-to-eat food taken from a commercially processed, hermetically sealed container, or an intact package from a food processing plant that is inspected by the food regulatory authority with jurisdiction over the plant, should be heated to a temperature of at least 135°F (57°C) for hot holding.

© Cengage Learning 2014

Figure 10.10 Final cooking temperatures for selected foods. (Adapted from the most recent at time of writing FDA Model Food Code.)

Cold Food Production

Cold food production is called a *pantry* or *garde manger*. It is also known as the *pantry chef*. This includes the production of all cold foods such as appetizers, salads and salad dressings, cold appetizers, and some desserts. The important aspect of the garde manger station is to make sure cold foods are served cold, with a temperature range at or below 41°F (5°C).

As a professional caterer, the need for adequate plate service is most important. Most common preparation techniques include chilling of the china and

Tips from the Trade

Consult with your chef when designing a kitchen. Why? Simple: the chef will cook the food. The chef holds the key to a caterer's success. If a client is served bad food, the catering business will not survive very long. An astute caterer will always consult with the chef before purchasing equipment. Chefs use equipment in kitchen environments and do know the difference between good and bad equipment. The chef will be responsible for creating, writing, and changing the catering menu. Set the chef up with what he or she really needs to ensure a successful catering kitchen. All too often a chef inherits a kitchen and must "make due" with what is available. To ensure success, consult with the chef early and invite him or her to be an integral part of the catering kitchen from the very beginning.

Courtesy of Chef Bryan Groton

Figure 10.11 Consult with the chef when designing a kitchen.

refrigeration of raw materials, foods in process, and prepared foods. Common pieces of equipment found in cold food production are glass racks, chilled plates, ice machines, and refrigeration and freezer units. Transporting cold foods should be done as close to service as possible. A mistake professional caterers can make when planning an event is to misjudge the amount of refrigeration and storage required for an event. For this reason, caterers should prepare themselves by providing some form of refrigeration or cooling techniques for each event. A common refrigeration technique is the rental or leasing of large refrigeration units that will be placed close to the event.

Raw fruits and vegetables handled in the cold food production area must always be thoroughly washed in water to remove soil and other contaminants. They must be washed before being cut, combined with other ingredients, cooked, served, or offered for human consumption in ready-to-eat form.

Final Preparation Area

The final preparation area should be located near the service area (on-premise location) or near the loading area to assemble for off-premise events. Transportation of most catered foods is accomplished by the use of insulated carriers that accommodate both hot and cold foods. A professional caterer should be aware of both the handling and storage capacities of the many available insulated carriers on the market today.

An important aspect in maintaining proper sanitation with insulated carriers is careful maintenance in relationship to cleanliness. The insulated carriers should be

Tips from the Trade

What we have found over the last few years in working with local restaurant chains and caterers is the product you are getting from your food source is not necessarily always clean or free of bacteria. We actually did a test with a local client. We took samples of their supposedly bagged, prewashed, precut and ready-to-eat lettuce and tested it for bacteria. The results were eye-opening! It was disgusting. We were both shocked, pretty mortified. When we purchase ready-to-eat food, such as lettuce, we are assured it is already cleaned. Our results showed the ready-to-eat product was no better or worse than lettuce dug right-out of the ground. Do not just assume what you are receiving from your source is bacteria-free food. The client came to us and asked what we could do to make this product safer to eat. Well, there are different technologies offering solutions to this kind of problem. For example, many companies are using a chemical sanitizer (Quaternary Ammonium Chloride) to clean the lettuce. This solution leaves residue on the lettuce and restocking the chemical is an ongoing expense for the user.

We offered them a new solution. There is a new process available, it is not a new technology, but its application to food service is new, and that is ozone. Ozone is just three molecules of oxygen put together. Two molecules of oxygen are stable, three are not stable. When the ozone is applied to the produce, being unstable, the three molecules separate, and in the process, energy is released. The energy released during the application kills the bacteria. The equipment resembles a little jet pack. This jet pack unit is mounted on the wall above the preparation sink and plugged into a 115 volt outlet. The process is very user friendly. The employee sprays down the lettuce, fruits and vegetables with the ozonated water. The jet pack lasts approximately 3–5 years until the cell inside the unit needs replaced. Therefore, it is inexpensive, effective, and safer than traditional systems of cleaning produce.

David Curran, Curran-Taylor, Inc., Food Service Equipment, Supplies, and Design, Canonsburg, Pennsylvania, and Naples, Florida

washed and sanitized before and after each event. A helpful reminder is ***Ingredient for Success 33: "Insulated carriers will not only carry food but will also carry bacteria."***

Food Transportation Equipment

Each caterer needs to be diligent in the balance between preparation, cooking, holding, transport, display, and the service phase of potentially hazardous food and to strive to eliminate and minimize unnecessary delay from each subsequent phase. As far as equipment for transporting food is considered, a caterer needs to use equipment that is specifically designed to keep cold food cold and hot food hot. Hot food must be kept above 135°F.

There are different types of equipment available to transport hot food. Food transportation equipment can be classified as either having its own internal heat source within the storage cabinet or not. Food can be transported in a heated holding cabinet that can be plugged into an outlet. Most caterers use a Cambro (http://www.cambro.com) or similar type of insulated carrier. An insulated carrier does not have its own heat source. A Cambro Camcarrier, for example, features an airtight removable gasket and is designed to keep either food cold or hot at a safe temperature for hours. They are designed to be easily carried and handled, married or stacked on top of each other at the event site, in storage, or during transportation. One problem is once the food is placed inside an insulated carrier, it will begin to lose its temperature. As a result, the caterer needs to monitor the temperature of the food. If a caterer is not using a carrier with its own heat source to actually keep the food hot, then limit the amount of time between preparation, transportation, and service.

Heated banquet cabinets and the Cambro Camcarrier are designed to hold food not to cook food. All food should must be cooked to the proper temperature and documented before putting it into the "hot boxes." Once in the storage equipment, the food needs to be constantly monitored. Remember, "hot boxes" are great products to hold hot food hot. It is a mistake to use a heated banquet cabinet, a chafing dish, or a steam table to cook or "reheat" food.

Sterno

Sterno is a heating source that you put beneath a chafing dish (Figure 10.12). A chafing dish is most commonly used to hold hot foot above 135°F on a buffet. Components of a chafing dish are a dome cover, a pan for the food, and a pan for water. These components assemble together and are held together in place by a frame or rack having a fuel holder.

The caterer assembles the chafing dish by the following technique: place the Sterno into the fuel holder on the frame. Place a pan holding water into the frame. It is recommended to put hot water into the pan to quicken the time it takes to bring it to the proper holding temperature. Light the Sterno. The Sterno will keep the water hot and produce steam. It is recommended to light the Sterno at least 20 minutes prior to inserting the hot food into the chafing dish to ensure the water reaches 212°F. Bring the water to a boil. Make sure you place the dome cover over the water pan to retain the heat. After the water has reached the proper temperature, insert the pan of hot food into the chafing dish above the water pan. Keep the food covered to ensure proper heat retention to keep the food above 135°F.

Tips from the Trade

A common cause of foodborne illness is the failure to keep hot food hot. A question I field most frequently is, "How to safely display hot food during service? A commonly used term by everyone in the industry to describe chafing fuel, portable fire, and/or a hot flame is Sterno. Sterno is actually a brand name. Knowing how to apply the correct amount of heat to maintain proper serving temperatures is critically important in every event. A caterer can track temperatures and Sterno fuel usage either by a trial and error method or by recording the food temperature in a logbook during the

event. There are different techniques used to control the amount of fuel consumed, depending if the Sterno must last 4 or 6 hours. In compliance with sanitation regulations, food cannot be held longer than four hours, either in a hot box or in the chafing dish. It is important to remember a caterer must keep the hot food above 135°F and cannot afford to make a mistake with time and temperature.

David Curran, Curran-Taylor, Inc., Food Service Equipment, Supplies, and Design, Canonsburg, Pennsylvania, and Naples, Florida

Cold Holding

One concern Curran sees in the catering industry is how caterers may not put as much of an emphasis on holding cold food, such as salads, at proper temperatures as they do on keeping hot food hot. Maintaining proper cold food temperatures is as important as ensuring proper hot food temperatures. According to the FDA food temperature danger zone, cold foods must be kept at 41°F or below. Curran recommends the use of prefrozen protective solutions to keep food cold. Both Cambro and Carlise offer protective solutions built right into the holding or serving unit.

Figure 10.12 Sterno fuel.

Food Production Procedures

Proper food handling procedures during the preparation process helps ensure the quality of the food. It is every employee's responsibility to handle all food in a safe manner. Figure 10.13 lists proper thawing and cooling procedures for handling potentially hazardous food and details the appropriate cooling methods.

STYLE OF SERVICE

The menu determines the design, layout, and equipment for the service area. Style of service may include buffet service, banquet service, French service, Russian service, or family style service (see Chapter 12). Skill requirements of the production staff, number of personnel, and their cost of labor are determined by the desired style of service.

The intended service style will dictate how the caterer organizes the efficient and effective progression of raw materials as they flow through the production area. This includes easy access of all raw materials based on time and motion utilization needed to prepare the menu items.

Capacity needs of the production equipment are based on the menu items and subsequent volume of food produced to satisfy the number of guests.

The physical sizes of the storage areas are influenced by the menu, projected number of guests, and the volume of food needed to be produced. Refrigeration

Tips from the Trade

One equipment catering trend in hospitals and nursing homes is the elimination of Sterno as a fuel source. Sterno is being phased out and replaced with electric chafing dishes. I do not foresee the catering industry at large replacing Sterno as a fuel source because it would be just too much of an inconvenience and all the time the rules are balanced between convenience and proper heat retention.

David Curran, Curran-Taylor, Inc., Food Service Equipment, Supplies, and Design, Canonsburg, Pennsylvania, and Naples, Florida

THAWING POTENTIALLY HAZARDOUS FOODS

Thawing Procedures

1. Potentially hazardous frozen food that is slacked to moderate the temperature should be held under refrigeration that maintains the food temperature at 41°F (5°C) or less.

2. Potentially hazardous food should be thawed under refrigeration that maintains the food temperature at 41°F (5°C) or less.

3. Foods completely submerged under running water should be thawed:

   • at a water temperature of 70°F (21°C) or below.

   • with sufficient water velocity to agitate and float off loose particles in an overflow.

   • for a period of time that does not allow thawed portions of ready-to-eat food to rise above 41°F (5°C).

   • for a period of time that does not allow thawed portions of a raw animal food requiring cooking as specified or to be above 41°F (5°C) for more than 4 hours including:

      (a) the time the food is exposed to the running water and the time needed for preparation for cooking, or

      (b) the time it takes under refrigeration to lower the food temperature to 41°F (5°C).

4. Frozen food being thawed as part of a cooking process must be:

   • cooked as specified following proper temperature guides.

   • thawed in a microwave oven and immediately transferred to conventional cooking equipment, with no interruption in the process.

   • thawed and prepared for immediate service in response to an individual consumer's order.

Cooling Procedures

1. Potentially hazardous cooked food should be cooled:

   • within 2 hours, from 140°F (60°C) to 70°F (21°C).

   • within 4 hours, from 70°F (21°C) to 41°F (5°C) to less.

2. Potentially hazardous food shall be cooled within 4 hours to 41°F (5°C) or less if prepared from ingredients at ambient temperature, such as reconstituted foods and canned tuna.

3. Except as specified, a potentially hazardous food, received in compliance with laws allowing a temperature above 41°F (5°C) during shipment from the supplier, shall be cooled within 4 hours to 41°F (5°C) or less, except for shell eggs if placed immediately upon their receipt in refrigerated equipment that is capable of maintaining food at 41°F (5°C) or less.

Cooling Methods

Cooling shall be accomplished in accordance with the time and temperature criteria specified by using one or more of the following methods, based on the type of food being cooled.

1. Place the food in shallow pans.

2. Separate the food into smaller or thinner portions.

3. Use rapid cooling equipment.

4. Stir the food in a container placed in an ice water bath.

Figure 10.13 Proper thawing and cooling procedures and appropriate cooling methods for handling potentially hazardous food. (Adapted from the most recent at time of writing FDA Model Food Code.)

and freezer storage are two areas a caterer must consider. Depending on the style of service, reach-in or walk-in refrigerators or freezers may be needed.

The Hazardous Analysis Critical Control Point Plan (see Chapter 7) will be developed based on the requested style, menu, equipment, and storage facilities.

Holstein Manufacturing is a family run business with deep roots in Iowa. Our first grills and rotisseries were made to help promote Iowa's pork industry. Over the last 20 years, we have expanded our line of catering and food preparation equipment while adding many specialty products. At Holstein Manufacturing, it's our goal to continue meeting our customers' needs and expand the line of products we offer.

Catering is a growing business! Caterers who purchase our equipment service anywhere from 100 to 2,000 people at one time. They need bigger equipment to be able to cater the function and make it profitable for them. Efficiency and labor costs are the two big concerns for a caterer. With our bigger equipment, we can help the caterer cut labor costs and make production more efficient.

For those large cookouts, a 240 lb. live weight hog or seven 20 lb. roasts will be cooked and ready to eat in 7 hours or less! In addition, the chicken rotisserie with skewers will roast 72 whole birds in less than 2 hours. If the baskets are used, 64 chicken quarters and larger cuts of beef, pork, and fish can be roasted.

Our backyard barbeque equipment for patios is also a growing business. Leisure time has to be spent some way, and cooking good food is the way to use some of that time.

Courtesy of Holstein Manufacturing Inc.

Off-Premise Equipment Safety

How will the caterer transport the food? How will the food be kept hot enough to prevent it from becoming unappetizing? How will the caterer keep it hot enough to prevent an outbreak of foodborne illness? How will the caterer keep the food cold?

A major task for the off-premise caterer is keeping the food at the proper temperatures to avoid the growth of harmful bacteria and to make sure the food is either hot or cold for the customer. Every caterer needs to structure the event plan with detailed *HACCP procedures* (see Chapter 7), including directions detailing precise instructions on the selection and use of the right equipment.

Basic Large Equipment

The traditional pieces of reliable production equipment have been the standard workhorses of any kitchen. A range top is one such piece of equipment, while a stove will provide for both cooking and/or sautéing. A deep fryer is another important piece of equipment available for preparation of many prefabricated products. Some food service companies today provide complete lines of prepared and frozen foods that are designed to be deep fried and transported immediately.

Another large piece of equipment is a pressureless steamer, which serves two purposes. The use of steam provides the caterer with the opportunity to not only cook, but to reheat foods prior to service. Other equipment includes convection ovens, which are ideal for banquet service as the oven capacity permits multiple professional sheet pans (17-3/4" × 25-3/4") at one time. Steam-jacketed kettles are important to make stocks, soups, and sauces. When planning the workstation production schedule for an event, calculate and forecast what a typical party size will be. If a typical event will average 50 guests, install a 20-gallon capacity steam-jacketed kettle. If an average event will host 500 guests, a 100 gallon kettle will be more feasible. As the size of the kettle increases, the utility cost to use the kettle will also increase.

Basic Small Equipment

Small equipment can make or break the service at any event. Necessary pieces of small equipment include knives, spatulas, sheet trays, and cookware. A variety of pots, frying pans, and hotel pans are major pieces used in all production kitchens. In addition, the caterer must be aware of the size and shape of all insulated transport carriers. *Ingredient for Success 34* states: ***"Be sure that all hotel pans and small equipment units can be transported properly."***

Cleaning and Sanitizing

Regularly scheduled cleaning and sanitizing is an integral part of a well designed HACCP plan. Talk with your professional equipment supplier to determine which warewashing system is most appropriate for the volume of your business. Work with a professional pest control representative to eliminate and prevent rat, mice, and cockroach infestation. Seek information on effective cleaning and sanitizing solutions from a chemical sales representative. Seek a customized plan to satisfy your unique operational and client needs. For example, will linens, table clothes, towels, aprons, and other laundry be served in-house? What type of washing machine and detergents will be most cost effective? What kind of flooring needs to be cleaned in the kitchen (ceramic tile), dining areas (carpeting), or foyer (linoleum)?

Imbed a regularly scheduled cleaning and sanitizing routine for each workstation into daily operating procedures. Assign each workstation employee specific cleaning and sanitizing tasks and hold them accountable for their completion. Clean and sanitize as you go. Verify these daily tasks using a manager's report or log.

Proper cleaning and sanitizing of all food equipment, utensils, and storage areas are required, especially if their surfaces come into contact with food. Wash using potable (i.e., drinking quality) water and a detergent, rinse to clean; sanitize to reduce, remove, or eliminate any harmful levels of bacteria, then air dry.

The benefits of cleaning and sanitizing must be emphasized to employees at all times. There are a number of acceptable procedures to do the job depending on what is being cleaned and sanitized.

STORAGE OF EQUIPMENT

The maintenance of adequate storage facilities for all equipment and utensils is a critical consideration. Cleaned and sanitized equipment and laundered linens, as well as any single-service and single-use articles, must always be stored at least 6 inches above the floor and away from a wall. This equipment should be either covered or inverted. Single-service and single-use articles should be stored in their original protective package. If not, make sure the storage provides protection from contamination. The equipment storage area must be clean, sanitary, dry, and well lighted. There are areas in a catering establishment that are not appropriate for the storage of equipment and utensils (Figure 10.14).

NON-APPROPRIATE EQUIPMENT STORAGE AREAS

1. employee locker rooms (located in a designated room or area where contamination of food, equipment, utensils, linens, and single-service and single-use articles can not occur)

2. bathrooms

3. garbage-storage rooms

4. mechanical rooms

5. under sewer lines that are not shielded to intercept potential drips

6. under leaking water lines, including leaking automatic fire sprinkler heads, or under lines on which water has condensed

7. under open stairwells

8. under other sources of potential contamination

© Cengage Learning 2014

Figure 10.14 Nonappropriate equipment storage areas. (Adapted from the most recent at time of writing FDA Model Food Code.)

Summary

The fourth catering function involves the ability of a caterer to efficiently and effectively design and equip the food production facility. It must always be remembered that *"The menu is the single most important tool used to determine precise equipment needs based on the type of food being prepared." (Ingredient for Success 30)*. Factors that affect the selection of equipment include performance and functionality of design; the maintenance, reliability, and warranty of equipment; availability and cost of replacement parts; employee skill level and relationship to the production needs of the menu; current and future equipment requirements based on customer needs, wants, and demands; the application and development of new technology; government regulations, including HACCP procedures and safety features; competitors' adaptation of technology to reduce labor and utility costs; and innovations in product design, aesthetics, components, and/or construction features, all influence the selection of equipment for a food production system. Careful analysis of the preparation areas, the hot and cold food production areas and the type of utilities are other concerns for the caterer. Both basic large and small traditional pieces of equipment will require the caterer to research their capabilities and fit them into the food production system. Finally, adherence to the Model Food Code must be maintained to ensure implementation of HACCP standards.

Review Questions

Brief Answers

1. Describe common equipment and production design considerations.
2. Explain how a caterer may select the type of utility to use as the energy source.
3. Explain why the menu is a powerful tool used to determine the design and layout of workstations.

4. Explain the type of equipment normally found in each of the following individual workstations: preparation, hot and cold food production, and final preparation.

5. Explain what the Ingredients for Success mean to you.

Multiple Choice

Select the single best answer for each question.

1. Multitasking equipment provides which of the following advantages?
    a. maximizes spatial relationships
    b. maximizes capital investment
    c. decreases the functionality of the equipment
    d. increases movement and worker fatigue
    e. all of the above

2. The organization of workstations is affected by:
    a. bundling similar tasks
    b. complexity of the menu
    c. employee skill level
    d. type of cooking method
    e. All of the above.

3. Which of the following is not considered a factor that influences the caterer's ability to adequately equip a food production system?
    a. employee skill level
    b. future equipment needs
    c. networking with other caterers
    d. government regulations
    e. competitive maneuvering

True or False

Read each of the following statements and determine if it is true or false.

1. The menu is a powerful tool used to determine the design, layout, and equipment of the food production area.

2. Common workstation design in a caterer's production area focuses on time and motion studies.

3. The menu determines the design, layout, and equipment for the service area.

Putting It All Together

Ingredient for Success 30 states: *"The menu is the single most important tool used to determine precise equipment needs based on the type of food being prepared."* Search the Internet and locate a caterer's menu. Using this menu, brainstorm a list of the commercial food preparation equipment and common workstations you would expect to find in this kitchen. What factors influence the caterer's ability to adequately equip a food production system?

Chapter 11
Procuring Equipment

Courtesy of HLC Inc.

Objectives

After studying this chapter, you should be able to:

1. Explain how a caterer acquires equipment.
2. Evaluate the different sources a caterer can use to purchase equipment.
3. Define a commercial caterer's food safety kitchen.
4. Describe the distinct advantages of purchasing equipment from a professional equipment supplier.
5. Compare and contrast the advantages and disadvantages of renting or buying equipment.
6. Define tableware.
7. Write and appraise the five step structured buying model.
8. Construct a flowchart listing each step a plate physically moves through in a catering operation.
9. List three evaluative criteria used in the decision making process to select a catering plate.
10. Select the appropriate china based upon its composition and a caterer's need.

KEY TERMS

architects

bone china

cash and carry businesses

ceramic plates

consultants

earthenware

equipment auctions

flowchart

melamine

open stock

professionally trained full-service equipment supplier

stoneware

tableware

vitreous china

consultants Experts who work with the caterer to determine equipment needs, including writing equipment specifications based on need, request for bid to equipment dealers, and installation.

architects Architects work with the caterer to determine equipment needs, including writing equipment specifications based on need, request for bid to equipment dealers, and installation.

equipment auctions Sites that offer used food service equipment for purchase based on a bidding process.

(This chapter is based on a personal interview with David Curran, president of Curran-Taylor, Inc., conducted on Monday, August 22, 2011 at the Curran-Taylor Corporate Headquarters, in Canonsburg, Pennsylvania. Curran is a founding member, board of directors, and treasurer of PRIDE Marketing and Procurement Group. He's also a founding member and on the management committee of the online equipment site, Food Service Equipment Warehouse. This chapter is also based on a June 2011 interview with John Marino, specialty sales manager, and Michael Tkach, director of ceramic engineering, The Homer Laughlin China Co., Newell, West Virginia.)

OBTAINING EQUIPMENT

A caterer has a choice of purchasing or renting equipment. David Curran, president of Curran-Taylor, explains, caterers have options when procuring equipment. These procurement options include the professionally trained full-service equipment supplier, hiring **consultants** and **architects**, shopping at cash and carry businesses, surfing Internet sites, and attending **equipment auctions**. Curran offers a summary of each procurement method.

Tips from the Trade

For the most part, when people tell me they want to start a catering business, they usually know, more or less, their menu because they begin with, "Okay, this is what I do well and this is what I want to offer." Or they have already been cooking for their neighbors or family. This makes it a little bit easier to recommend what kinds of equipment they will need. My next inquiry is to ask them what kind of operation are they going to need? Are they going to put the catering business in their garage or are they going to secure a separate building and install a full food safety commercial catering kitchen? Are they going to cater from the local social club or church kitchen? A lot of planning goes into it. Most people are going to start small. We advise them to purchase very basic equipment such as a convection oven (Figure 11.1) and a range top. Those two would be the biggies because you can still do pretty much anything you want on them. With a range-top you can still cook your soup, pan fry, and prepare a wide range of menu items. A convection oven will give you a lot

more uniformity in the oven cavity without worry of experiencing either hot or cold spots because hot air is forced through fans which circulate around the food. You will have to be very diligent as to how you are going to hold the temperature when the food comes out of the oven, especially if you are transporting the food. If someone really gets into catering full-time, then I would recommend the purchase of a combi oven (Figure 11.2). A combi oven is probably the greatest piece of equipment available today. Combi ovens control the amount of steam and moisture within the cavity of a regular oven. You can control both the steam and moisture two different ways, by putting more in or getting rid of it all. Another option a combi oven provides is the ability to hold the cooked food at the proper safe temperature before it is served. You can do anything in a combi oven, from French fries to pies.

David Curran, Curran-Taylor, Inc., Food Service Equipment, Supplies, and Design, Canonsburg, Pennsylvania, and Naples, Florida.

Courtesy of Stephen B. Shiring, Jr.

Figure 11.1 Range top with conventional oven.

Courtesy of Stephen B. Shiring, Jr.

Figure 11.2 Combi oven.

Professional Equipment Supplier

Of all of the buying options, Curran strongly recommends working one-on-one with a **professionally trained full-service equipment supplier** like Curran-Taylor. Curran-Taylor is a fully integrated food service design and build consultation firm featuring a professionally trained staff able to provide turn-key operations. Whether someone needs to purchase a single piece of equipment or is seeking information to help resolve system problems in the operational workstation areas, such as storage and receiving, food preparation, food production, holding, transport, and service,

professionally trained full-service equipment supplier A fully integrated food service design and build consultation firm featuring a professionally trained staff able to provide turn-key operations, from concept to opening.

Curran-Taylor is a one-stop shop location. It combines the expert services of a consultant and architect to provide layout and design of a commercial food safety catering kitchen. A full-service equipment supplier serves the complete equipment needs of a caterer. This process can begin with an individual's idea to create a catering business (see Chapter 6, Business Plan) and continue through each successive phase to its grand opening.

Curran-Taylor is a founding member of PRIDE Marketing and Procurement group. PRIDE is an alliance of approximately 125 food service equipment dealers located across the US. Membership in PRIDE enables these dealers to combine their collective buying strength. This permits them to leverage their negotiating power against the manufacturer, enabling them to purchase at the lowest cost. According to Curran, the competitive strength of the group's collective buying power represents a marketable percentage of the manufacturer's total business. When this happens, it creates significant negotiating power. Since each member individually can exert significant influence in the marketplace, the manufacturer cannot afford to lose them. The strength of this negotiating power and influence by the buying group is then inherently transferred to the buyer who purchases equipment from the local equipment supplier.

For example, True® Manufacturing is the largest manufacturer of refrigeration equipment (http://www.truemfg.com) in the market. Each individual buying group member may, on average, purchase between $200,000 and $400,000 in refrigeration equipment from True Manufacturing. However, when the individual sales are considered as part of a composite of the buying group, its annual sales exceed $35 million. Subsequently, this provides each buying member significant influence when dealing with True Manufacturing.

One distinct advantage of purchasing from a local supplier, according to Curran, occurs if the user experiences a problem with the piece of equipment. What the manufacturer really looks at is, "How did the user purchase this piece of equipment?" If the user purchased the equipment from a source other than a direct relationship with a local equipment supplier, the manufacturer might say, "Okay, the caterer might get mad at us and may never by our fryer again. So what? There are thousands of users who need fryers, and losing one customer is no big problem. Or if the fryer has a broken part one month past the warranty, and if this part has been a continuing problem, and if this same part was replaced during the warranty phase, and now the equipment is out of warranty, and the same part is going bad, well, that tells us there is an underlying problem that the service agent did not catch. When it comes down to it, the manufacturer is more concerned whether I am happy and if I am standing up for the caterer, which, of course, we do all of the time. Now, since I am buying hundreds of thousands of dollars from that manufacturer every year, they do not want me to get angry."

When purchasing from a local equipment supplier, imbedded in the purchase price is a guarantee of serving the buyer's needs. The job of the local equipment supplier is to be the middleman, representing the buyer in all discussions with the manufacturer. The local equipment supplier, for example, cannot help the caterer if the manufacturer knows the equipment was purchased through either a bidding process, determined by the consultant, or purchased from an Internet site. Another advantage to the caterer, when purchasing equipment from their local equipment supplier, is help from the manufacturer's service agent. Curran says the manufacturer's service agent is a local person working on behalf of the equipment manufacturer in that geographical area who calls on the equipment supplier. Since the manufacturer's service agent will receive credit for the sale of that piece of equipment, when purchased from the local equipment supplier, they will also have a vested interest to ensure the buyer is satisfied with the product. If the manufacturer's service agent did not receive sales credit for the equipment, then most likely, they will be of little service in resolving user problems.

Curran summarizes the distinct advantages when purchasing equipment from a professional equipment supplier:

1. Gain significant influence in the market channel by the professional equipment representative to obtain competitive pricing from the manufacturer.
2. Exert pressure on the manufacturer on behalf of the buyer to resolve equipment problems.
3. Simplify the warranty process between buyer and manufacturer.
4. Provide hands-on reliable service to repair equipment malfunctions.
5. Obtain professional guidance in the installation of the equipment.
6. Ensure manufacturer's rebates and other discounts are credited to the buyer's account.
7. Coordinate training sessions on proper use of the equipment between the manufacturer's representative and the buyer's staff.
8. Be an advocate for and represent the buyer when dealing with the manufacturer.
9. Be a reliable source of information to resolve system problems in the operational workstations.
10. Keep caterers current to new and emerging trends, technologies, and equipment.

Consultants and Architects

The second equipment procurement strategy is to hire a consultant or architect. The consultant/architect will work with the caterer to determine the best solutions to their equipment needs. As a result, the consultant/architect will write equipment specifications based on need. The consultant/architect will send the equipment specifications to various equipment dealers requesting a bid on the specification. Equipment suppliers receiving the bid will "just put numbers to it" without any further professional input and submit these bids on the project back to the consultant/architect. The consultant/architect will award the equipment to the lowest bidder. One advantage of this method is the caterer delegates the equipment specification process and related purchase to the consultant or architect, thus freeing the caterer to concentrate on the catering business. One disadvantage Curran has personally experienced with the bid request method is an angry end user. He explains, after winning the bid and installing the equipment, the end user became angry over the equipment. Even though the equipment installed by Curran was specified according to the bid, after its installation, the user complained it was not what he wanted and blamed Curran. Because the buyer was unhappy, somehow it now became Curran's responsibility to correct the problem. In this case, the unhappy user had no recourse with the equipment supplier to rectify the problem since the equipment was specified by a third party. Today, Curran-Taylor will not bid on equipment specified by a third party.

Cash and Carry Business

The third method of procuring food service equipment is to purchase it from a **cash and carry business**. For example, to serve this segment of the market, Curran-Taylor has opened a cash and carry business called Liberty Mart. There are four Liberty Mart locations. These locations are found in Pittsburgh, Canonsburg, and Altoona, Pennsylvania, and Naples, Florida. Curran-Taylor uses their purchasing strength to leverage bulk purchases of popular equipment brands and makes a caterer or restaurateur would normally use in their operation, such as ranges and refrigerators. These items are then stocked at their Liberty Mart locations. Buyers are invited to visit these cash and carry locations and if a decision to make a purchase occurs, they can go on their way with product in hand.

Internet Sites

The fourth method of procuring food service equipment is to shop online. The ability to quickly search many sites enables a caterer to locate equipment based solely on the lowest price. According to Curran, the Internet is becoming a viable option for caterers to buy equipment for the following reasons:

1. Twenty-four hour access to a worldwide equipment market.
2. The ability to access and print hard copies of technical data and equipment specifications.
3. Capacity to review the layout and design features of professional commercial catering food safety kitchens.
4. Pictures of the equipment are shown.

As a result of these advantages to the buyer, Curran has created an Internet site called Food Service Equipment Warehouse to service this emerging market (http://www.foodservicequipmentwarehouse.com).

A major motivator to shop online is the lure of obtaining equipment at lower prices. The ability to quickly search many sites enables a caterer to locate equipment based solely on the lowest price. However, Curran advises against using an Internet site for purchasing equipment for the following reasons:

1. A lack of the personal touch, no personal customer service (see the advantages for purchasing from a professional equipment supplier earlier in the chapter).
2. When the buyer has an equipment problem, his or her only remedy is to go back to the Internet site.
3. The Internet site is more interested in the money business than the food service business, only interested in moving equipment and maintaining turnover.

Curran says no one wants to pay more than they have to for a piece of equipment. His advice: "Do your homework and research the equipment. Once it is determined that it best solves your needs, then sit down with the local equipment dealer. Whether it is us or someone else that you know and trust, work it out with them. Negotiate in good faith to where you are both happy. Remember your local equipment dealer is your most valuable resource. You can always work out the money. Believe me; no one ever wants to turn away from a sale. The guy you are buying from has to stay in business too, and there can be a symbiotic relationship there."

When purchasing either new or used equipment, a caterer should work with a reputable equipment dealer who will guarantee the equipment and with manufacturers who offer special discounts or sales. A caterer can also attend food or trade shows and negotiate with the manufacturer's representatives who are displaying equipment at the show and purchase these "show models," usually at a discounted price.

Rental Services

A caterer may opt to rent equipment. Professional rental services exist that will provide everything from a napkin to a refrigerated truck. Many caterers will supplement their equipment inventory with rented equipment. Some caterers decide to build an inventory of equipment based on frequency of use (Figure 11.3). If the equipment is a required element of every catering function, such as a chafing dish, the caterer will most likely invest in the item. In addition, a caterer may purchase equipment if they plan on catering a large annual function for the next 5 years. The caterer can then reduce the equipment expense by depreciating it over that time.

Figure 11.3 Storage and inventory control of equipment versus renting as needed.

The decision to purchase or rent will be determined by the individual caterer's situation and location. Often, a caterer will purchase equipment needed to support the infrastructure of the business, such as ovens, refrigeration units, and other back-of-the-house equipment.

Advantages of Rental Equipment

1. No storage area is required for the equipment.
2. No maintenance of the equipment is needed.
3. Handling of the equipment is minimized—rental company may deliver and retrieve equipment.
4. Rental company may wash, sanitize, and repackage items.
5. Special equipment needs and their costs may be charged to the client.
6. No investment or capital expense is required for the equipment.
7. Security and inventory control may be tighter, as each item must be accounted for.
8. The caterer can "field-test" a variety of equipment before making a long-term investment by purchasing it.
9. The caterer has access to a variety of equipment available from storage inventories held by different rental companies.

Disadvantages of Rental Equipment

1. The equipment may not be maintained as well as the caterer would like it to be.
2. In the event of last minute requests, or the caterer forgetting to reserve the equipment, the rental company may be out of stock.
3. If a caterer loses a piece of rented equipment, a replacement charge will be incurred.
4. A caterer can build a reputation on having custom designed and elegant pieces of equipment. A caterer may have an inventory of specially designed plates, special roasting ovens, and so on.
5. Many caterers help each other during the catering season. Friends may lend equipment to each other. Therefore, owning the equipment gives the opportunity to lend it to friends or rent it to competitors.
6. Having to secure equipment from another source can be inconvenient.

Equipment Auctions

Equipment can be purchased at auctions. Used food service equipment is always readily available. Why? First, corporate accounts follow a new equipment replacement strategy to take advantage of tax incentives and depreciation. Second, restaurants and catering businesses fail.

Curran says price is the sole advantage of buying used equipment. The disadvantages are:

1. Probably won't get a warranty.
2. History or service record on the equipment is usually not available.
3. Purchase someone else's problem.
4. Incur additional expenses, such as disconnecting it, transporting it, and reinstalling it .

Tips from the Trade

Renting china and linens rather than owning them is an option a caterer can consider. We do not own china or linens. We are just handling the service side of the event. Therefore, we do not have either the investment and/or the associated storage costs from owning it. If our client wants either china or linens, we refer them to reliable rental companies. We have developed a strong relationship with these rental companies over the past 10 years.

There are really high quality linens and chair covers in the market. Some of it can be expensive. There can be as much as a $20 per tablecloth difference depending on the quality of the linen. We pass those associated rental expenses right on to the client. This way the client can make decisions based on their needs and budget restrictions.

Permission of John R. Smith

5. Make a mistake of buying something not exactly wanted, then having no recourse to change or modify it.

6. Usable life span may be shorter.

7. May not be energy-efficient, lack replacement parts for repair, or contain a banned refrigerant.

8. Won't qualify for energy rebates offered by utility companies (must be Energy Star certified).

9. Older technology and design.

Whereas deals can be found by buying used equipment, buyers beware. Take the time to educate yourself beforehand and be cautious. Just because an item is up for auction does not mean the pricing is low. Do your homework prior to looking at a used piece of equipment. First, know exactly what a comparable new piece of equipment will cost and then only be willing to pay pennies on the dollar for the used equipment. Second, educate yourself on the exact item being sold. The used piece of equipment, for example, may no longer have parts available if it needs to be repaired, or it houses a refrigeration unit that contains a refrigerant now banned from use.

(This section is gleaned from a personal interview June 2011 with John Marino, specialty sales manager, and Michael Tkach, director of ceramic engineering, The Homer Laughlin China Co.)

tableware Dinnerware (i.e., dishes), glassware, and flatware used in setting a table for a meal.

TABLEWARE

Tableware is the dinnerware (i.e., dishes), glassware, and flatware used in setting a table for a meal (Figure 11.4). A critical management decision that impacts guest satisfaction and the financial resources of the operation is the procurement of appropriate dinnerware for a catering operation. Many factors determine which plate will be appropriate for a caterer to use. Caterers define their identity beginning with an analysis of their capabilities and how they can satisfy customers' needs and wants. A review of Chapter 2 will help to identify the core mission of your business and is also a beginning step in selecting the right plate for your needs.

A common mistake is to delegate research to an outsider, such as a salesperson. Rather than follow a prescribed step-by-step buying process, many leap to the final purchase decision. Often, a buyer only relies on an outside source to make the final decision for him or her. Unfortunately, such decisions are usually hastily made, influenced primarily by the purchase price, resulting in a mistake. It is important, however, to rely on professional equipment sales representatives to provide all of the information to assist you in making the correct buying decision. Michael Tkach and John Marino of The Homer Laughlin China Company (Figure 11.5), offer a proven structured buying model to guide a caterer in making the right decision—every time!

Courtesy of HLC Inc.

Figure 11.4 Tableware.

Figure 11.5 Employee entrance to the Homer Laughlin China Company, Newell, West Virginia.

The Structured Buying Model

In a caterer's busy world, it is understandable, when faced with tremendous pressures of day-to-day operational decisions, to delegate special needs to a consultant or other hospitality professionals. However, it is important to understand that obtaining accurate and timely information is a priority when selecting the correct dinnerware. Tkach and Marino recommend the following five-step buying model for caterers to follow when searching for the appropriate plate: (1) need recognition, (2) information search, (3) evaluation of alternatives, (4) purchase decision, and (5) postpurchase evaluation.

Step 1: Need Recognition

Caterers need plates. The social life of a caterer manifests itself during the process of delivering guest services. It is this interaction with a guest that defines the caterer publicly regardless of the event—be it simple, elaborate, ceremonious, religious, or joyous—the one common facet for each caterer is the guest's experience at the dining table. Caterers need plates to help deliver consistent customer satisfaction.

open stock plates held by the manufacturer or equipment supplier for immediate delivery.

You can purchase **open stock** (plates held by the manufacturer or equipment supplier for immediate delivery) or have dinnerware custom designed to reflect your own personality. Most are manufactured offshore; Homer Laughlin China is "Made in America."

Step 2: Information Search

Obtaining timely and appropriate information is necessary for a caterer to make the correct purchase decision. The effort and need to search for information is influenced by your experience, knowledge of dinnerware, the style and composition of the china, the target customer, available market information, government regulations, and emerging trends.

Sources of Information. Information required to make an intelligent final decision is obtained from both internal and external sources.

Internal Sources of Information. First, the caterer needs to look inside the business. The appropriate plate complements the tableware and is reflective of the type of catering done. The decision of an appropriate plate must be taken into collective consideration with the appropriate flatware, glassware, and accompanying linens.

John Marino says, "I do not think entrepreneurs go into catering or opening a new restaurant thinking about the practice of the fundamentals of actually moving that plate around—cleaning it, getting it off the table, racking it, stacking it, and other similar fundamental operational tasks."

His recommendation is for the caterer to physically analyze the work being done in the operation. You analyze the work by designing a **flowchart** to show a plate physically moving through the operation. At each subsequent fundamental operational step, describe the work being performed. Careful analysis from this exercise will provide excellent information from which you can begin your external search. He provides the following checklist of operational steps (questions) to include on your flowchart:

flowchart Shows how a plate physically moves through the catering operation. Describes the work being done at each subsequent fundamental operational step.

1. Where and how is the plate stored?
2. Will the plate be packed for transportation? How will the plate be packed for transit?
3. What kind of food will be served on the plate?
4. Will the plate's physical appearance, on the table, be important?
5. Who and how will the plate be handled during food preparation?
6. What is the service method? Will the guest handle the plate (buffet) or will it be served?
7. Sample a meal from the plate.
8. How will the plate be removed from the table?
9. Will a bussing cart or tub be used to carry the soiled plates from the table to the cleaning station?
10. Will the soiled plate be hand-carried to the cleaning station?
11. Will the plate be stacked?
12. What are the cleaning procedures?
13. Will the plate be racked for dish tank operation?
14. Who will pack the plate for transportation?
15. Who will load the plates on the van/truck for transport?
16. Who will unload the soiled dishes from the van/truck for cleaning?
17. What are the physical characteristics of the plate that are needed (Figure 11.6)?
18. Will the plate be decorated or undecorated?
19. What flatware will be used with the plate? Will the flatware affect the glaze on the plate?
20. Do you need the entire body or surface area for the food?
21. What size rim?
22. What is the impact of your replacement program (for broken plates) on the bottom line?
23. Will the dinnerware fit appropriately on the table?
    Example: Oversized plate on a 36" table

Figure 11.6 Mike Tkach, HLC chief ceramic engineer, testing the composition of the coloring agent used in Fiestaware.

Courtesy of HLC Inc.

melamine A plastic, a durable synthetic polymer used in the manufacture of plates.

ceramic plates Plates are classified according to their body type: a flint body, an alpha alumina body, or as bone china. Ceramic plates are bone china, stoneware, earthenware, and vitreous china (e.g., porcelain).

bone china A hard-paste porcelain containing bone ash, making it easier to manufacture, stronger, not chipping easily, and with an ivory-white color that lends itself to decoration.

stoneware A hard pottery made from siliceous paste, fired at high temperature to vitrify (i.e., make glassy), the body is heavier and more opaque than porcelain and differs from terracotta in being nonporous and nonabsorbent.

Example: 10 seats around a 72" banquet table, customer wants a 12" plate, it doesn't fit

24. What type of dish machine cleaning process is being used, chemical or high temperature?

Example: Precious metal cannot be used in chemical dish machines

External Sources of Information. Several reliable external sources can be referenced to obtain product specifications and market information on plates. These external sources include:

1. Other caterers
2. Professional associations, such as the National Association of Catering Executives (NACE)
3. Equipment sales representative, such as Curran-Taylor
4. Manufacturer representatives, such as from Homer Laughlin China Company
5. Food and equipment shows, such as the National Restaurant Association Hotel & Motel Show
6. Internet sources
7. Industry-specific books, journals, and magazines, such as *Foodservice Equipment Report*, and Internet sites (http://www.fermag.com, http://www.foodservicewarehouse.com, and http://www.catersource.com).

Step 3: Evaluation of Alternatives

What type of plate to purchase is the first consideration. Tkach recommends evaluating each plate alternative against the following three criteria: (1) composition, (2) aesthetics, and (3) performance, before making the final purchase decision (Figure 11.7).

Dinnerware Composition. Dinnerware differs (Figure 11.8) (Figure 11.9) (Figure 11.10). Differences in dinnerware include composition, quality, durability, color, style, and shape. Durability affects replacement costs. Plates are either decorated or undecorated. The body of the plate can be porcelain, clay and/or other ceramic materials, durable plastics such as **melamine**, metal, wood, or glass, or it's classified as disposable or a single use item. Melamine, a plastic, is a durable synthetic polymer. **Ceramic plates** are classified according to their body type: a flint body, an alpha alumina body, or as bone china. Ceramic plates are **bone china, stoneware, earthenware,** and **vitreous china** (e.g., porcelain).

Ceramic Composition. Bone china is a hard-paste porcelain containing bone ash. The addition of bone ash to china stone and china clay (i.e., hard china) make bone china easier to manufacture; it is stronger, does not chip easily, and has an ivory-white color that lends itself to decoration. Stoneware is a hard pottery made from siliceous paste

Courtesy of HLC Inc.

Figure 11.7 HLC Gothic offers an elegant curvilinear shape accented by intricate white-on-white lattice sculpting and a detailed pointed-arch pattern on the rim.

Figure 11.8 The Ameriwhite Collection, an alpha alumina body, The Pristine in The Marquis Collection, the Parliament provides enhanced chip/impact resistance and superior heat retention.

Figure 11.9 Unique design or style of a plate. HLC Pesto/ Indigo Times Square bowl and plate offer rich hues and innovative glaze treatments, ensuring that no two pieces are exactly the same.

and fired at high temperature to vitrify (i.e., make glassy); the body is heavier and more opaque than porcelain and differs from terracotta in being nonporous and nonabsorbent. The usual color of fired stoneware tends toward gray, though there may be a wide range of color, depending on the clay. Earthenware is less strong, easily chips, and is more porous than stoneware, but its low cost compensates for these deficiencies. Due to its higher porosity, earthenware must usually be glazed to be watertight.

Tkach offers the following illustration. "A caterer may have a Mediterranean themed event, for example, where earthenware would be very appropriate to the event's theme; however, it will not be very durable. So what do you want? Do you

earthenware Less strong, easily chipped, and more porous than stoneware, but its low cost compensates for these deficiencies. Due to its higher porosity, earthenware must usually be glazed to be watertight.

vitreous china (e.g., porcelain) "Vitreous" means the material has an extremely low permeability to liquids, is nonporous, therefore there is no absorption.

Figure 11.10 Unique design or style of a plate. HLC oversized RE platter 18 3/8" and Colonial ramekins.

Figure 11.11 Color of a plate. HLC Fiestaware. Fourteen bold colors complement each other beautifully and can be mixed and matched with other shapes, most notably rolled edge and narrow rim, making Fiesta the quintessential enduring statement of retro American style.

want authenticity or do you want some extended life in the china? You have to make that decision."

Stoneware has a rustic appeal, is fairly durable, but is limited to grayish glazes. Fine china, like vitrified china ("vitreous" means the material has an extremely low permeability to liquids) is nonporous, therefore there is no absorption. Earthenware lacks strength and durability and will absorb water into the body of the plate, an undesirable trait. When compared to vitrified china, stoneware, or bone china, earthenware is fairly weak. Bone china is expensive and is a very high end product.

Most equipment and purveyor sales representatives will stock and provide to a caterer a selection of china. Each plate and manufacturer offers their own plates having unique characteristics and related costs.

Aesthetics and Performance. Next consider the following details: design or style, color, and the shape of the plate's rim or edge. Plates feature a narrow rim or a rolled edge (Figure 11.11) (Figure 11.12).

The shape of the plate's edge will affect its ability to withstand chippage from repeated sharp blows against it. A very blunt, rounded-over edge delivers maximum strength to the plate's rim or edge. For example, The Homer Laughlin's Diplomat

Figure 11.12 Example of a narrow rim plate, HLC Alexa elegantly thin and light, yet ruggedly chip resistant and durable.

Figure 11.13 The Homer Laughlin Diplomat China Group. Its roll on back, wide rim, and heavy gauge durability are the hallmarks of this timeless line.

Figure 11.14 Diplomat/Cavalier product profile sheet.

1187 plate designed specifically for catering functions features a durable body complemented with a rolled-edge that is practically resistant and indestructible to chippage (Figure 11.13) (Figure 11.14). However, this plate, with the rounded-over edge, may not appear aesthetically pleasing, but there is no chippage.

Plate chippage increases as the aesthetic design and style of rim also increases (Figure 11.15). Therefore, a trade-off exists between the aesthetics and the performance criterion of a plate. The final key point is to consider the size of the plate.

Figure 11.15 Impact tester pendulum type for ceramic tableware. Conducting an impact resistance test of HLC ceramic tableware in the Quality Control Lab, at The Homer Laughlin China Company.

THE HOMER LAUGHLIN CHINA COMPANY
CHINA USES AND QUANTITY RECOMMENDATIONS

All installations vary, but the recommendations below will help you select the right pieces and quantities. TO GET QUANTITY OF EACH PIECE, MULTIPLY NUMBER OF SEATS TIMES THE ORDERING FACTOR SHOWN FOR EACH TYPE OF DINING; THEN ORDER CLOSEST DOZEN QUANTITY.

Piece	Suggested Use	Fine Dining	Family Theme Dining	Cafeteria	Banquet	Institutional
5" to 6" Plates	Bread & Butter - Salad - Bowl or Bouillon Underliner - Beverage Underliner	2		6	1¼	3
6¼" to 6¾" Plates	Bread & Butter - Salad - Dessert -Underliner for Bouillon	1½	3	3		3
7" to 7½" Plates	Salad - Sandwich - Desserts - Underliner for Grapefruit, Appetizer or Large Bowl	1½	2		2½	
8" to 9" Plates	Entree - Sandwich Luncheon - Large Salad - Underliner for Salad	1½	2½	2		2
9½ to 9¾" Plates	Dinner - Large Luncheon - Underliner for Salad - Breakfast - Open-face Sandwich	1½	2½	2	1¼	
10¼" to 12¼" Plates	Entree - Steak - Prime Rib - Chops - Service Plate - Large Underliner	2	2		1½	
7" to 7½" Platters	Baked Potato - Asparagus - Salad - Cold Seafood	1	1½			
9" to 9½" Platters	Luncheon Plate - Fish Plate - Specialty Items - Salad	1	1½	½		
11" to 13" Platters	Steak - Fish - Lobster - Prime Rib - Surf 'n Turf	1	1	½		
Mug	Hot or Cold Beverage		3	2½		2½
Tea Cup	Beverages	3	3	2	1½	1½
Saucer	Cup or Bouillon Underliner	2½	3	2	1½	1½
Bouillon Cup	Bouillon - Soup - Gelatin - Custard - Sugar Bowl - Crackers	1	2	1½	1½	1½
Fruit Dish (Monkey Dish)	Vegetables - Salad - Cobbler - Pudding - Butter Dish	2	3	6	2½	3
Grapefruit	Soup - Cereal - Fruit - Small Salad - Stew	1	1	1½		1½
Oatmeal Bowl	Soup - Cereal - Stew		1	1		1
Rim Deep Soup	a la carte Soup and a la carte Salad - Chili - Pasta	½	½			
Pitcher/Creamer	Cream for Beverage, Syrup	½	½		½	
Sugar Bowl/Packets	Crackers - Sugar	½	½		½	
Sauceboats	Au jus - Salad Dressing	½			½	
Service Plate/ Insert Plate	Tabletop Decoration - Underliner for Appetizer	1½ / 1½	1½ / 1½			
A.D. Cup	Demitasse Coffee	1	1			
A.D. Saucer	Underliner for A.D. Cup	1	1			
Bud Vase	Tabletop Decoration	1½	1½			
Salt & Pepper	Salt & Pepper	½	⅓			
Beverage Server	Tea, Coffee, Hot Beverage	⅓	⅓			
Accessory Items Ash Tray. 4–7/16"	Ashes, Soap, Mints	½		½		
Celery Tray, 9½"	Relishes, Hot & Cold Hors d'oeuvres	¼		¼		

Figure 11.16 China uses and quantity recommendations.

Tips from the Trade

(Personal interview with Michael Tkach and John Marino, The Homer Laughlin China Co., Newell, West Virginia, a discussion with the experts on handling china.)

John

The purchase of china is an investment. Proper handling of the china is the key. China does not have a limited shelf life. Using it three turns a day in a restaurant, or use it once or twice a week in catering, should get, on average, at least 10 years of usage from our china, a great return on your initial investment.

Mike

You are going to throw it away because you dropped it and it broke. Breakage is out of our control. You are going to chip it, which we have some control over, and lastly, you are going to wear the glaze off due to the abrasive mishandling of the plate's surface. In addition, metal markings caused by the flatware or mishandling during the cleaning process also will affect the aesthetics of the plate.

John

Breakage, we do not get breakage. Shipping and transporting china from one location to another is how breakage occurs. I had a call from a customer about a strange crack that appeared exactly in the same spot on all of their plates. The crack appeared after using the plates after a few months. Well, the trucker dropped the box of plates as he was delivering it. The drop caused a stress fracture that was not immediately apparent. The impact of the fall compromised the integrity of the china. As far as just breakage, we really do not have much breakage. It all comes back down to proper handling. If the china is handled properly, if your equipment is properly set up to handle the pieces you have, and if you have enough china in your inventory, then you can expect a long life of good use from it. Many times a cause of excessive abrasions or chipping is directly correlated to not having enough china on hand. The caterer or restaurateur did not start with an adequate inventory of china for the volume of business. Recycling the

china too fast, that is, not giving it time to rest, just using it too often, causes problems.

Mike

I would like to make a statement for the china to rest. You need an adequate inventory of china to prevent it from constantly moving from the table to the dishwasher and back out to the table again. Using china without a rest creates an accelerated wear (Figure 11.16). The china does not see a normal wear that we recommend. To ensure a normal usage rate, we recommend a par level or number of pieces of dinnerware based on the expected size of a catering or restaurant operation.

John

Ninety percent of the china returned to us as a customer quality complaint is directly attributed to the product being mishandled by the user. I do approximately two or three replacement orders each week. One of our customers, for example, will return a platter and say 'I have six chipped platters.' Well, at this point, I would provide our lab with a write up about the location from my fact finding questions, so that we can determine the cause of the problem. Typically the cause is misuse but providing additional product doesn't really solve the problem. What we do is give **GIFTS**

> **G**o to the Individual
>
> **I**dentify a Resolution
>
> **F**ix it, Plus One (that is the Key)
>
> **T**ransfer Genuine Concern
>
> **S**et Up a Return Visit

The worst thing you can do is just throw good product at a bad situations. If a customer continues having problems with product they will eventually get tired of dealing with the same problems and go elsewhere with their business. What we do is actually solve the problem, typically by actually going to the location and working with the crew on the information listed above. The Homer Laughlin China Company's 5-year limited warranty guarantees the replacement of our product against normal use, but even if the user is the root cause of the issue,

(continues)

(continued)

we will replace the damaged product but only after the cause of the issue has been fixed.

Chippage is usually caused by improper handling procedures, such as using the wrong size (dish) racks; using metal racks; sloppy bussing procedures and techniques (stacking plates too high, overloading the bussing tub); and not following proper ware washing procedures. I often tell caterers, "You incur a tremendous expense to set up a new catering commissary, you buy good china, and then the person paid the least in your business is handling the china and is the one that costs you the most money." If the plate is not handled correctly in the dish room, if it is not rinsed properly or if the wrong dish rack is used in the dishwasher, that investment of china is going to be compromised. Ten percent of our returns might be a quality problem, a minor flaw in a custom piece, such as a crooked decal, for example. Or the buyer did not fully understand their needs and purchased the wrong china. It is interesting. We analyze the returned china in accordance to our standard quality control procedures. Sometimes the cause of the problem is really obvious. I analyze the chip using my magnifying glass. Immediately, I can tell whether there is a problem with lamination. I can tell if there is a problem with the glaze. I do this just by looking at the chip on the plate. If I can't tell, I will send the plate to the lab for additional quality control testing. Mike will conduct a chip test to make absolutely certain that piece of china was manufactured according to our specifications. When the plate has been determined to have been manufactured according to our strict quality control standards, and the plate has been chipped, we still replace it. The Homer Laughlin China Company has a chip warranty. We always honor our warranty and replace the china.

We implement a total quality management replacement plan. Our policy, when replacing this china, is for our sales representative to explain the chipping was caused by a user handling error and not a quality control problem in the manufacturing process. We offer to visit their operation and conduct a ware handling study to identify and solve this chipping problem. We want to prevent it from happening again.

Our salesperson will visit the account and conduct a ware handling study. It does us no good, whatsoever, to keep on replacing china if we do not know the root cause of the problem. Sometimes, our sales representative can immediately identify the problem. The dish racks are metal as opposed to coated wire. The plates do not properly fit in the rack. When a person buys a cup, they call us and they get the dimension of the cup, and then the dimension of the cup with the handle. The dish racks are actually built to accommodate that specific piece of china. Using the right equipment and proper handling techniques are important. Using the right rack prevents the cup from jiggling around in the dish tank. We watch how the tables are cleaned, we watch the bussing procedures, and we observe the plates being handled in the kitchen. We say to the account, "We have identified the following operational procedures as the root cause of the chippage." Once identified, we offer solutions to correct these problems. We help our account implement these solutions.

John

There are some things that affect china that is totally out of our control. For example, metal markings on china. China is returned to us with what is called "metal markings."

Mike

Metal markings are metal deposits left behind on a plate's surface. Mishandling china will cause scratches in the glaze. Mishandling occurs when plates are stacked too high, when an employee uses a scrapping implement with a metal edge, or uses an abrasive cleaner. Abrasive handling causes scratches in the glaze on the plate's surface. These scratches are sharp. As a guest is eating from the plate, the scratch in the glaze actually catches or snags metal as the stainless steel knife or fork or spoon is leveled off against the surface of the scratch. The metal is deposited into the scratch. Ceramic engineers have tried to make softer glazes or harder glazes to protect the china's surface. The type of stainless steel flatware you are using, such as 18-8 (chrome-nickel steel), will have an impact on how much metal is going to get caught on the scratch. Metal markings affect the aesthetics of the plate.

Preventing abrasive handling is the single best way to avoid metal markings on the surface. A chemical cleaner is used to remove metal markings by soaking the china in this solution. If using a chemical cleaner, follow the instructions carefully. Beware, the chemical soaks remove metal markings on a plate, but it will also remove any decorative metals on the plate as well. You cannot use chemical soaks on china decorated with precious metals, such as gold, platinum, or palladium. It will eat the precious metals off the plate as well. This chemical cleaner is strictly designed for undecorated colored ware, such as Fiesta colors.

John

If purchasing high end china, avoid buying flatware based only on its aesthetics. You want to buy flatware that is a better grade. Less expensive flatware will be made with a softer metal. Harder glazes on these plates will easily catch the metal and cause metal markings on the china. The salesperson will lay out the china and a sample of flatware and will say, "Doesn't this pattern look beautiful" with emphasis on the various price points. But it is like everything else, you get what you pay for. The quality of the flatware directly impacts the glaze on the china.

The better educated students of catering are more likely to know what questions to ask. They will most likely interact with a food service dealer. Many times this is a full service dealer who represents heavy equipment and food, but also carries china. You really need to be very well educated when you go into this sale. The sales representative is going to sell you what he is going to get commission on, or what he knows about, and the same thing with the flatware. He may sell you all of your dishwashing products, but he may not be aware, until you ask or remind him, if there is a particular dishwashing product that is better for gold-decorated plates. He is basically an equipment salesman and the subject might not come up. If you know there is a better detergent for gold-decorated china, it helps you make the best buy for your needs.

In our training seminars, I explain to my dealers they are the one person who must integrate with everybody else. They must integrate all of the other products in the kitchen. For example, a salesperson will sell the operator the dish racks and the tubs for bussing. These items directly affect your china. Most likely, you are probably not tied into that sale. So you will have to go into that kitchen and educate the operator. This plate can

go in the broiler; this is the correct busing tub and these are the proper ware handling procedures. Here are the appropriate cleaning products. If you have a problem with any one of these other things in the kitchen, it directly affects your china.

Here is an illustration. We had a complaint because an account was experiencing plates chipping. We replaced the plates. The salesman went in to visit the account. Later, the equipment representative stopped at the account. Unfortunately, we could not identify the problem. Now, sometimes, especially when you have kids' dishwashing or kids' bussing and waiting, it's like the principal walked into the room and suddenly everybody is on their best behavior. Our representatives came in and out several times to see if they could catch the situation as it really was happening. The employees were not doing anything wrong. They had proper ware handling techniques. The bussing, scraping, ware washing and other handling procedures were fine. Eventually, we discovered the shelving on which the plates were being stored were not wide enough for their 12-inch plates. Sure enough, we observed when the china was being placed on the shelving, the edge of the plate slid against the wall behind which the shelving unit was braced. This storage procedure was impacting the china and chipping it. In theory, the operator should have created a flowchart, moved the plate through the operation, and identified this before the purchase of the china was made. The salesperson should have also looked at each step in the ware handling process, including this storage area. They should not have had their new shelving sized or made until they made a decision on the size of the china they were going to store on it.

You cannot separate one task from the other. The bus pans are our worst enemy. The big plastic tubs are a problem. Many of our upscale, finer caterers and restaurateurs instruct their waitstaff to hand carry the china from kitchen to table and from the table back into the kitchen. This is one of the first things we ask when we conduct a ware handling analysis for our client. "What kind of tubs do you use to bus the table? How do you place a plate in the tub? How do you stack the plates in the tub? How many plates do you stack on top of each other in the tub? Do you place the edge of a plate against another plate's edge? How do you stack the cups? Do you stack or nest the cups together in the tub? How heavy is the tub to carry?"

(continues)

(continued)

One of our representatives tells a story about a problem his account was having with a beautiful, custom designed, gold-edged plate they had been using. The gold began to display little pits on its surface against the body of the plate.

Mike

Microwaves are either absorbed or reflected. Microwaves are absorbed by fats, carbohydrates, water, and proteins. Microwaves are not absorbed by metals and are reflected. When you place a nonmicrowave-safe gold-trimmed plate into a microwave, the microwaves will be reflected from the gold metal and in the process will "arc." The arcing of a microwave, as it is reflected off against the gold metal, will leave a distinguished pit in the metal. This pit is a tale-tale mark on the metal that the plate had been put in a microwave. The mark looks like a worm had crawled across the gold decorated plate. If you look at this mark under a 6x or 10x magnifying glass, it reveals a very distinguishable mark. There is no other cause for this distinguished mark. We are frequently told, "Oh, no it's not the microwave." Our response is, "Yes it is." We instruct our account to use a magnifying glass and look at the mark. We know what the mark looks like. We have replicated that activity in our research lab. We have reproduced that mark on gold-decorated plates. We usually find the owner or manager of the account did not know his employees were using the gold-decorated china for their own personal use. For example, this is a common scenario to this kind of problem. A company watchperson, guard, or staff member takes a cup of coffee with them to the guard house or back to their office. At this location, someone happens to have a microwave oven available. They are unaware the very nice, expensive, custom designed china is not microwave safe. Their coffee gets cold, and they put the cup of coffee into the microwave to reheat it. If the person repeatedly takes a cup of coffee with them to their office or guard house, usually it's not the same cup, so, after awhile, all of the cups have those little marks on them. We are told, "It's not our fault." That one you cannot lie about. The mark is unique and only caused by a microwave. They are not seeing it because they need to look at the mark using either a magnifying glass or a microscope. The solution to that problem is either to lock down your custom gold-decorated china or use microwave-safe gold on your custom china.

Summary

A caterer has a choice of purchasing or renting equipment. These procurement options include using a professionally trained full-service equipment supplier, hiring consultants and architects, shopping at cash and carry businesses, surfing Internet sites, and attending equipment auctions. The caterer must weigh the benefits and costs associated with each choice prior to procuring the piece of equipment.

Tableware is the dinnerware (i.e., dishes), glassware, and flatware used in setting a table for a meal. A critical management decision that impacts guest satisfaction and the financial resources of the operation is the procurement of appropriate dinnerware for a catering operation. Many factors determine which plate will be appropriate for a caterer to use. In a caterer's busy world, it is understandable, when faced with tremendous pressures of day-to-day operational decisions, to delegate special needs to a consultant or other hospitality professionals. However, it is important to understand that obtaining accurate and timely information is a priority when selecting the correct dinnerware. The following five-step buying model is offered for caterers to follow when searching for the appropriate plate: (1) need recognition, (2) information search, (3) evaluation of alternatives, (4) purchase decision, and (5) postpurchase evaluation.

Review Questions

Brief Answers

1. Explain how the caterer acquires equipment.
2. Evaluate the different sources a caterer can use to purchase equipment.
3. Define a commercial caterer's food safety kitchen.
4. Describe the distinct advantages of purchasing equipment from a professional equipment supplier.
5. Compare and contrast the advantages and disadvantages of renting or buying equipment.
6. Define tableware.
7. Write and appraise the five-step structured buying model.
8. Construct a flowchart listing each step a plate physically moves through a catering operation.
9. List three evaluative criteria used in the decision making process to select a catering plate.
10. Describe ceramic plates, bone china, stoneware, earthenware, and vitreous china (e.g., porcelain).
11. Describe common equipment and production design considerations.

Multiple Choice

Select the single best answer for each question.

1. Which of the following is recommended by David Curran as the single best source for a caterer to purchase their equipment?
   a. professional equipment supplier
   b. consultants and architects
   c. cash and carry businesses
   d. Internet sites
   e. equipment auctions

2. Which of the following is not considered as a distinct advantage to a caterer when purchasing equipment from a professional equipment supplier?
   a. obtain competitive pricing from the manufacturer
   b. exert pressure on the manufacturer on behalf of the buyer to resolve equipment problems
   c. simplify the warranty process between buyer and manufacturer
   d. provide hands-on reliable service to repair equipment malfunctions
   e. ensure manufacturer's rebates and other discounts are credited to the equipment sales account.

3. A caterer may opt to rent equipment. Which of the following is not considered an advantage of using rental equipment?
   a. Storage area is not required for the equipment.
   b. Maintenance of the equipment is not needed.
   c. Special equipment needs and their costs may be charged to the client.

d. Having to secure equipment from another source can be inconvenient.

e. No investment or capital expense is required for the equipment.

True or False

Read each of the following statements and determine if it is true or false.

1. A critical management decision that impacts guest satisfaction and the financial resources of the operation is the procurement of appropriate dinnerware for a catering operation.

2. Plate chippage increases as the aesthetic design and style of rim also increases

3. Ceramic plates are classified according to their body type: a flint body, an alpha alumina body, or as bone china.

Putting It All Together

Visit Curran-Taylor Equipment, Supplies & Facility Designer at http://www.curran-taylor.com. Outline the main features, services, and distinct competence of Curran-Taylor. What type of services do they offer? What products do they represent? Describe their key departments: Facilities Design, Equipment and Furnishings, Supplies and Small Wares, Projects Research and Development. Would you use this equipment supplier—why or why not?

Visit The Homer Laughlin China Company (HLC) at http://www.hlc.com. Outline the main features, services, and distinct competence of HLC. What distinct product lines do they feature? Review and summarize each product line. How are they different? What services does HLC provide for a caterer interested in purchasing china? Would you purchase china from HLC? Why or why not? If you were touring HLC, what question would you ask these company representatives: research and design staff member, salesperson, member of the art department, ceramic engineer, or the president of the company?

Chapter 12

Implementing

Courtesy Skytop Lodge

Objectives

After studying this chapter, you should be able to:

1. Explain what service means to a caterer.

2. Review the front-of-the-house service activities.

3. Describe how the caterer can build a reputation based on service.

4. Explain how caterers can build a professional service staff.

5. Explain how caterers can use standards to define service. Provide examples of how a caterer can develop service standards to mirror the organization's mission statement.

6. Describe an informal organizational structure and explain how it can affect employee morale.

7. Explain and provide examples of what appropriate personnel means to the catering organization.

8. List the attributes of appropriate service personnel.

9. Explain the differences between informal and formal service styles used by caterers.

10. Describe the defining characteristics of each service style.

11. Explain how a tabletop is set.

12. Explain how to purchase linen.

KEY TERMS

American service

appropriate personnel

buffet service

cover

family-style service

French service

informal structure

overlay (napperon)

Russian service

service

service standards

sit-down dinner

small wares

tabletop

teamwork

undercloth (silencer, silence cloth)

Ingredients For Success

35 "The end result of the job relies on the entire staff working together— teamwork."

36 "Construct detailed diagrams of every buffet in advance."

37 "The more service given, and the better care taken of the customer through exceptional attention to detail, the happier the client will be and the more repeat business will be generated from that event."

38 "Consider every job a major production."

39 "A caterer's performance is a reflection of the business."

This chapter covers the importance of building a team-oriented service staff. An explanation of the common types of service approaches used by caterers will be discussed. Delivering consistent customer service geared to exceed a customer's needs is perhaps one of the most important missions of a catering business. Unfortunately, however, it is often the most lacking skill found in the catering industry. Although a formal description will be given to specifically define each type of service, most caterers will borrow and incorporate techniques from each style. These techniques are married together for the efficient and effective service of food and beverages required to exceed a guest's expectations.

SERVICE

service Caterers define service as it applies to their mission statement. Their reputation is built on delivery of service so developing hiring and recruiting strategies should complement a caterer's service objectives.

The delivery of **service** to the guest is a catering management task that is very important to the effective and efficient execution of an event. Because a caterer's reputation can be built on service, it is necessary to develop an effective recruiting and hiring strategy to complement service objectives.

To ensure consistent delivery of service, a caterer must define *service* as it applies to the mission of the operation. Remember **Ingredient for Success 2: "We cannot be all things to all people."** Even though a caterer cannot satisfy every need in the marketplace, setting a clear direction through the mission statement begins the ongoing process of maintaining a professional service staff. The maintenance and continuation of that staff is established by planning and setting service objectives.

What is *service* to the caterer, organization, employees, and client? A caterer has built and refined the back-of-the-house tasks—now the front-of-the-house needs definition so each employee understands his or her role in service delivery. For example, a guest was attending one of the many corporate-sponsored receptions during the National Restaurant Association's annual trade show. The reception was held in the grand ballroom of a fine service-oriented hotel in Chicago. Approximately 1,500 guests were in attendance. Having a carbonated beverage, appetizer plate, fork, and napkin in hand was a bit overwhelming. A little shuffling and the fork fell to the carpet. Before it could be retrieved, a member of the service team quickly responded. She not only picked up the fork, but smiling, simultaneously handed a clean one in its place. This is service!

service standards Predetermined levels based on the organization's mission established to gauge an employee's performance.

A caterer needs to create obtainable, observable, and trainable **service standards** so each employee understands his or her role. To build a strong reputation, a caterer must have highly trained employees. This is one factor often lacking in the catering industry. To maintain highly trained employees, a key component of the catering mission plan should be continual training programs. Regardless of whether it is a small caterer with 4 or 5 employees, or a large employer with 175 employees, a caterer must plan to train for the effective and efficient delivery of service.

When planning the details of each event, the caterer must include specific training needs in each plan. Either a review or a new *training goal* needs to be implemented with the plan. This is true regardless of the style of service requested by the client.

teamwork A collective staff working together to implement the catering plan. A necessity to executing any event successfully.

Building Professional Service

Ingredient for Success 35 states: *"The end result of the job relies on the entire staff working together—teamwork."* **Teamwork** is an absolute requirement for the efficient and effective execution of any catering event. Implementation of the catering plan through teamwork happens successfully when the caterer has created and nurtured the *informal structure* of the organization.

The **informal structure** of a caterer's organization represents the relationships among the caterer's employees. Employee relationships occur regardless of the formal structure bound by policies, procedures, and rules, and are extremely important to the positive morale of the organization. The guest can observe or "feel" the positive or negative health emitting from the service staff during an event.

Since employees spend many hours together preparing and executing the event, the importance of a positive atmosphere, created through team building to accomplish organizational goals, cannot be overemphasized.

To build a positive informal organization, a fundamental step is hiring **appropriate personnel**. A caterer can define what *appropriate personnel* means to the organization by creating personnel standards. This human resource standard will clearly define the type of personnel needed to accomplish the tasks identified by the caterer and the organization's mission.

A caterer must take tremendous care and time to recruit and hire the appropriate person to execute the right tasks. Characteristics of appropriate personnel include:

1. a positive, energetic attitude
2. a spirit for teamwork
3. a professional demeanor
4. enthusiasm
5. a sincere concern for the guests and their needs
6. acceptance of responsibility
7. acceptance of positive feedback on performance
8. a commitment toward delivering consistent service
9. a kind, friendly, courteous, trustworthy, and loyal personality
10. an "ownership attitude"
11. nonstop smiling
12. an ability for listening to understand
13. respect for guests and their opinions—never arguing with a guest
14. respectful speech including use of "Sir" and "Madam"
15. an understanding that the guest is the most important person at the event.

informal structure
The interpersonal relationships that emerge as a result of employees working together to accomplish a common goal.

appropriate personnel
The human resource standard as defined by the caterer to describe the required individual needed to accomplish the specific task.

CREATING AN EMPLOYEE-SUPPORTIVE CULTURE

The ability to attract and retain appropriate human resources is a great challenge to all catering professionals as well as to the entire hospitality industry. Scarcity of labor and the challenge of recruiting and retaining appropriate staff have been a concern to the hospitality industry since 1900. It was because of the need for a professionally trained employee, specifically a steward, that the movement began to create a training school in the United States. The idea of an academic program offering professional development and industry experience was one reason why the movement to establish a more formal educational system began.

The subsequent establishment of specific hotel and restaurant management programs later merged with many existing institutional management programs at America's colleges and universities. Whereas these offer some relief to the need for qualified personnel, the evolution and continued growth of the industry have kept appropriate employees in high demand.

The catering profession is one that requires long and difficult hours. Caterers usually work hard while others are enjoying the function. Holidays, weekends, summer festivals, and late nights may lead to displeased employees.

A challenge to the successful caterer is to attract employees who want to work these hours. Caterers need to find dedicated individuals who seek full-time or part-time work and must offer wages to complement their life styles. Parents of school-age children are often attracted to this schedule because they can work while their children are attending school. Other employees can be found at colleges, universities, and vocational-technical schools. Caterers find this pool of potential employees favorable.

College students seek the income and can work around their school schedules. Work experience, especially for students enrolled in departments of hospitality, business, or culinary arts, is extremely valuable. These programs often require work-related experience as part of their graduation requirement and some require internship experience.

Vocational-technical schools grant students a flexible schedule. They are encouraged to seek employment and are permitted to leave school to work. Innovative training partnerships can be created between the educational facility and a caterer to benefit both the student and the caterer.

One way a caterer can build a great team is to formally structure the organization to be receptive of new ideas. This encourages employee participation. It must begin at the top, with the owner/caterer, and be a crucial component of the organization's mission.

One important component is to create an environment so all management personnel can accept this mission. Proper training of management and employees is critical. Basic training established to meet precise organizational goals must be part of the plan. Training techniques that arouse passion can help this process. Building an internal culture that rewards creativity and innovation; seeking employees who display courtesy, respect, and efficiency; and clearly defining each role in relationship to the entire operation contribute to an employee-supportive culture. Management's acceptance of employees' ideas will help create this culture. The organization must always strive for continued incremental improvement in all activities.

Long hours and demanding work are just one element of the catering adventure. One distinct advantage a catering operation does have over other traditional food service operations is the need for incessant creativity and innovation. This characteristic is a required element of the profession since consumers' needs are always evolving. Prospective clients challenge a caterer to create new and exciting themes, menus, and reasons for events. Unexpected situations challenge the caterer to instantaneously implement creative solutions. These challenges provide an opportunity for active employee participation in decision making. What better ways to encourage employee creativity and motivation? Listening to the employees and supporting active employee participation during the planning and execution of an event will energize the staff. This aura of excitement will definitely be felt by the guests. Internal excitement becomes a magnet used to attract other innovative and creative personnel. Eventually, instead of the caterer trying to *find* an employee, innovative and creative personnel will gravitate toward the organization.

Job specifications and descriptions for the creative and innovative needs of the company should be written. Current employees should be encouraged to recommend friends and family who fit the needs of the company. Many caterers reward employees with incentives for recommending appropriate personnel.

UNIFORMS

The caterer can further enhance a guest's perception of the professional service delivered through the use of a standardized uniform and dress code for the staff. A uniform should be designed to:

1. complement the mission of the organization
2. complement the type of service being performed
3. identify the employee as a member of the catering staff
4. communicate to the guest what job task is being performed.

Uniforms can range from a black tuxedo to a clearly-defined, standard-style outfit unique to the caterer. A uniform standard will carefully define each component, from the hair style to polished shoes including some or all of the following:

1. Shirt—explain style, color, long or short sleeve, and material composition
2. Pants—explain style, color, and material composition
3. Belt—describe color and style
4. Shoes—describe the acceptable color, style, and cleanliness (clean and polished)
5. Tie—describe style and color
6. Hair and facial hair standards—describe acceptable length, style, grooming, and hygiene
7. Jewelry, makeup, and appropriate scented perfumes or cologne regulations— describe appropriate makeup, only a simple wedding band, and small earrings
8. Hygiene standards, bathing requirements, cleanliness of the uniform
9. Socks—describe style and color
10. Hat requirements

TYPES OF SERVICE STYLES

There are several formal and informal styles of service. These service styles may be used in combination with each other, depending on the needs of the client and the type of event. Common types of events include private family functions; business or corporate functions; and community, group, and association functions. These include banquets, receptions, meetings, picnics, baptisms, bar mitzvahs, anniversaries, office parties, holiday parties, charitable events, and weddings.

It is best to maintain a written description of the various service methods the caterer is competent to handle. This list may include the type of function, the type of equipment needed to execute this event, and the various kinds of service provided in conjunction with each. This list can then become a handy reference when the caterer is meeting with the prospective client.

All catering operations have certain attributes commonly requested by customers. There will always be a great demand to use a facility for wedding receptions, dining-in functions, retirements, promotion dinners, and other events with similar needs. Each of these functions demands a special setting and a special menu. Other events may require several alternative settings and menus. An effective way for the catering manager to break down the list of functions is to base it on a common menu and staffing requirements.

A typical list, using this method, might look like this:

TYPE OF EVENT	SERVICE
Formal dinner	Formal table service
Informal dinner	American type service
Buffet dinner (smorgasbord)	Modified table service
Regular luncheon	American table service
Buffet luncheon	Modified table service
Brunch-style buffet	Minimal table service
Modified standup luncheon or tea	Buffet service
Pool-side or patio party	Bar and set-up service
Barbecue or cookout	Bar and set-up and clean-up service
Nationality (dinner or luncheon)	Formal American or buffet service

© Cengage Learning 2014

Once the type of function and service is decided upon with the prospective client, the caterer is in a position to offer a number of menu suggestions. These menu suggestions can be prepared and served in a manner most suitable to the client's needs and at the same time to best meet the caterer's profit objectives.

Formal styles of service include French and Russian service. The most common types of service used by caterers are the informal styles, which include buffet, American, and family-style service.

French Service

French service is one of the most elaborate styles a caterer can perform for the guest. Preparing the food at tableside using *a gueridon* (a small table with wheels) and a *rechaud* (a pan set over a heating element) is the distinguishing characteristic of French service. This style of service is often reserved for the most intimate, smaller

French service An elaborate style of service where food is prepared at table-side using a gueridon (a small table with wheels) and a re-chaud (a pan set over a heating element).

functions. French service requires expert specialization in handling the equipment, excellent culinary skills in preparing or finishing the food at tableside, and superior service skills when presenting the finished food to the guest. Many caterers would not execute this style of service because of its difficulty.

Although the traditional, classical French style of service requires an exceptionally trained, skilled staff and efficient coordination to use, many caterers adapted a modern approach to this style of service. For example, a major department store manager invited VIPs to a private recognition luncheon, held in their facility, as their way of saying thank you. These important guests were primarily elderly women who had spent a large amount of money each business quarter at the department store. The luncheon included a tremendous amount of personal attention from the department store employees and the women were given the first view of the newest clothing fashions received by the department store.

Because of the small, intimate size of the group, the caterer adopted the French service style of tableside cooking to provide each guest with more personalized attention. Based on the staff's capabilities, the caterer developed a service to fit the needs of the client and to completely satisfy their guests. It was a huge success. The menus were kept simple and elegant by using the caterer's signature recipes. Most of the food was prepared in advance at the caterer's facility and was finished tableside in front of the seated guests. The guests were most impressed with the quality of food and the exceptional attention they received from the staff.

Classical French service, similar to this, would be very difficult for banquets serving large numbers of people because of the increased staff and equipment that would be required.

Russian Service

Russian service is a very formal and elegant type of service. The distinguishing characteristic of Russian service is the unique presentation of food to the guest. Its elegance is derived from the use of silver serving platters, the skillful handling of the serving utensils, and the arrangement and presentation of the food.

Russian service requires the food to be arranged artistically in the kitchen on silver platters. The server carries this platter into the dining area and presents the food display for the guest's visual excitement. First, a hot plate is served. Next, the food is individually presented to each guest.

An advantage of this type of service is its beauty and speed. A waiter can quickly serve many guests while providing the perception of personalized attention. Using this type of service, a skilled waiter, trained in the service procedures, can easily maneuver around tables and through the dining room. However, this form of service does require skilled employees. Mastering the skill of handling the multiple, repetitive tasks involved in this serving style requires practice and time. Since the use of silver platters and fine serving utensils is required, this can be an expensive investment for a caterer. Once the silver serving utensils are purchased, a caterer must protect their investment. Caterers' may lose this equipment by theft. Unethical employees will steal it and unethical guests may take it home with them. Equipment

Russian service This formal and elegant style of service distinguishes the use of silver serving platters, the skillful handling of the serving utensils, and the arrangement and presentation of the food.

is also lost when it is forgotten at off-premise locations or left in the back of rented trucks and other vehicles. The caterer should plan to count each piece at the conclusion of every event.

Buffet

buffet service A common style of service used to serve food. The distinguishing characteristic of buffet service is that customers actively participate in supplying part of the service by serving themselves from an organized table offering a variety of food.

Most caterers will offer buffet service. **Buffet service** is perhaps the most common type of service a caterer will execute both on- and off-premise. A distinguishing characteristic of buffet service is the customer's active participation in the service. The consumer supplements a caterer's service.

The guest is invited to the buffet table at a predetermined time and sequence based on the number of guests to be served. They will leave their seat and enter a line leading past an organized table of serving plates and a variety of food, garnishes, and artistic displays The main difference between buffet and banquet style service is the customer's active participation in the service at a buffet. At a banquet, on the other hand, the guest remains seated and the serving staff serves everyone together at a predetermined starting time.

Buffet service requires a caterer and the staff to be very well organized. When serving buffet style, a key attribute of the service style is artistic creativity. It is important, whether it is the owner, spouse, cook, or member of the waitstaff, to have someone on staff with artistic ability.

Since "consumers eat with their eyes as well as their stomachs," an attractive buffet, with artistic flare, is very important. A caterer should ask, "Does the buffet offer an appetizing appeal? Is the buffet well organized?" A caterer should always review the competitor's buffet when attending these functions.

Building a buffet to create an appetizing appeal begins with the menu. Menus can offer a variety of food. Based on a price scale, the menu can be built around a simple lower-cost option or a more elaborate, higher-cost option. It will depend on the customer's needs and budget. Is chicken, pasta, or beef requested by the guest or will prime rib and lobster Newburgh be served? What salads and side dishes will complete the menu? The final menu should include a variety of colors, textures, shapes, tastes, and an appealing appearance based on the approved budget.

Building a Buffet

Depending on the type of event, most buffets begin with selecting a plate. The size and type of plate will influence the amount of food a guest can select. At the buffet, it is most important to have all of the guests move in the same direction.

To help maintain and control its cost, temperature, and palatability, food on a buffet should be offered in the following sequence: salads and other cold foods; the lowest food-cost items on the menu; the side dishes, including breads and vegetables; then entrees from least expensive to most expensive. This is known as the *flow of food* concept in which the cold foods are set out first and the hot foods are placed toward the end of the buffet. This helps keep the hot food hotter, especially when the dining area is air conditioned and the plates are cool in temperature. If a large volume of guests is expected, the buffet line should be accessible from both sides. A separate table for both the dessert and beverage station should be used.

Important Accents

The element of display is an important attribute for a buffet. A variety of different colors should be included. Multiple green salads should never be placed together. Foods with bland colors, such as a mashed potato and an au gratin potato, should not be placed side-by-side. It is best to use foods that are visually appealing. Each item on the buffet should be complemented. Where will the item be placed on the buffet? What type of dish or bowl will the food be served from? Will the food be served from a chafing dish? What height-level will the food be served from? Making a diagram can help to answer these questions and create an attractive buffet. ***Ingredient for Success 36: "Construct detailed diagrams of every buffet in advance."***

Food at a buffet should be served from different heights. Common props, such as empty milk crates, dish racks, and cardboard boxes, can be integrated into a buffet.

A mixture of mirrors and lighting enhances buffets. White lights can be placed beneath the buffet table. Colored flood lights are often used beneath the skirting on a buffet. Small lights can be strung around the under edge of the buffet table to highlight the skirting and make it appear more attractive.

The use of greens, ferns, flowers, edible flowers, and fresh herbs helps to make the buffet more attractive. Different size dishes and dollies also add to its appeal. If serving shrimp from the buffet, serve it using a bowl that looks like a huge scallop or use silver trays. Creativity and color enhance the buffet and make it more appealing.

The caterer must be organized. Since there are aspects common to all buffets, standard operating procedures (SOPs) to guide both the management staff and employees with the task of building the buffet can be created. See Figure 12.1 for SOP guidelines.

STANDARD BUFFET OPERATING PROCEDURES

1. Themes—selection is based on numerous factors
   A. Nationality
   B. Country
      1. Regional
      2. District
   C. Sport
   D. Holiday
   E. Occasion
      1. Wedding
      2. Baby shower
   F. Seasonal
   G. Seafood

(continues)

Figure 12.1 Standard buffet operating procedures.

© Cengage Learning 2014

(continued)

2. The Buffet Plan
   A. Menu creation
   B. Number of covers
   C. Price of covers
   D. Time of serving
   E. Location where the buffet tables are to be displayed
   F. Menu zoning arrangement—diagram the buffet in advance. Describe how to set it up.
   G. Number of serving lines. These are based on the number of covers and zones, recommended 100 guests per zone.
   H. Number, size, and shape of tables
      1. Banquet table
         a. 6 feet × 30 inches
         b. 6 feet × 36 inches
         c. 8 feet × 30 inches
         d. 8 feet × 36 inches
      2. Round table
         a. 60 inches in diameter
         b. 72 inches in diameter
         c. 84 inches in diameter
      3. Half-round table is 60 inches in diameter
      4. Quarter-round table is 30 inches in diameter
      5. Serpentine
      6. Trapezoid has 30-inch sides and is 60-inches across
   I. Type and color of table cloths. Skirt the tables and add the lights or props.
   J. Set the buffet with empty chafing dishes and empty bowls to help visualize the completed buffet.
   K. Label each bowl and chafing dish using a note card with the name of the food item as it will appear on the buffet. This review will eliminate any potential confusion once the staff is ready to set the food. Light heat fuel one-half hour before service.
   L. Nonedible pieces
      1. Ice carving
      2. Tallow
      3. Flower arrangement
      4. Fountain
   M. Other concerns that might need to be added to enhance the theme or atmosphere.
      1. Buffet table shapes
         a. Factors that determine shape
            1. Number of serving lines
            2. Size and shape of the room
            3. Seating arrangement
            4. Preference of the guests
            5. Occasion

2. Calculation of the buffet table size
    a. Skirting
        1. Straight skirt—allow one foot of material per foot of table.
        2. Pleated skirt—allow one yard of material per foot of table
3. Zoning—to expedite service never exceed 100 covers per zone.
    a. Basic zone arrangement
        1. Appetizers
        2. Fish
        3. Poultry
        4. Meat—beef, game, and pork
        5. Salads
        6. Hot foods
    b. Plates indicate where zone starts
    c. Pastry and beverages should be on separate tables
4. Food serving trays
    a. Types
        1. Silver
        2. Mirrors
        3. Plastic trays
        4. Cut crystal—bowls and trays
5. Equipment and supplies needed
    a. Banquet tables
    b. Chafing dishes
    c. Heating fuel
    d. Extension cords
    e. Stands for plates and trays
    f. Salad bowls
    g. Utensils for serving food
    h. Heat lamps
6. Service Preparation Procedures
    a. Count clean and sanitized china, silverware, glassware, silverware for the buffet.
    b. Check all china and glassware for chips, cracks, and foreign material (food spots, lip stick).
    c. Check all silverware for spots, food particles, and tarnish.
    d. Handle with care and follow proper sanitation handling techniques. Only touch flatware by the handles and glassware by the stem.
    e. Inspect all linen and napkins for cleanliness, stains, and holes.
    f. Clean, sanitize and fill all sugar/artificial sweetener holders.

A buffet will vary, even if using standardized menus, since customers have their own needs. Based on these needs, clients may select different foods from the menu. A customer may select two starches from a group of six, and two entrees from a group of eight. Then, the customer may select two salads to complement those entrees from a group of 10. This makes each buffet a little different.

When planning a buffet, make sure to determine the staffing requirements, employee scheduling and food-quantity requirements. The challenge is to have enough food on hand. A rule of the thumb suggests that the last guest must have the same opportunity to select from the same variety of food as the first guest. The serving dishes may not be as full, but an adequate supply and variety should be on hand. There is nothing more disappointing to a customer than when they approach a buffet and it is empty or low on food. This is one clue the caterer is not well organized.

Key tasks of planning a buffet are determining portion size and calculating the approximate amount of food each customer will eat. Researching the most popular foods in an area will help a caterer determine how much each person may eat. If roast beef is the favorite, a caterer must plan to have more roast beef than chicken on the buffet, but if chicken is the favorite, more chicken should be prepared. Remember to attractively place the inexpensive foods first on the buffet line.

Plan accordingly, and study the diagrams. Review the diagrams with the staff. Have beautiful serving utensils and attractive dishes. Organize the buffet and make it an artistic piece the customers will rave about.

Salads on a Buffet

When using a salad on a buffet, the choice of salad dressing can be limited. If a tossed salad is set on the buffet line, blue cheese dressing, French dressing, signature dressing, and a low-fat Italian are too many choices. Each guest may spend between 35 and 45 seconds to decide which dressing to use. If there are 150 people and each person takes one-half minute to decide on a choice of dressing, the caterer must calculate 75 minutes on the service line consumed by the guest just making a decision on the type of salad dressing. To save time at the buffet, the caterer might encourage the client to have a preset salad for each guest on the table.

Food Handling Tips

Although buffet service may be handled by a smaller staff of employees, without effective methods of portion control, food waste may negate savings in reduced payroll expense. Concern is on serving hot foods hot and cold foods cold. Key food handling tips include:

1. Keep all food out of the temperature danger zone, 41°–140°F (5°–60°C). Use only food service equipment that will keep this food out of the danger zone.

2. Assign responsibility to monitor the temperature of the food, using an appropriate thermometer, at 2-hour intervals.

3. Discard all food that has been held on a buffet line for a maximum period of four hours.

4. Always use appropriate serving utensils and have the handles facing the guests.

5. Use only hot holding equipment, such as chafing dishes, to hold hot food. Never use hot holding equipment to cook or reheat food. This is a violation of the Model Food Code, since it will permit the food to remain in the temperature danger zone too long.

6. Never add fresh food to prepared foods being held on the buffet line.

7. Never add raw foods to already cooked foods.

8. Assign the responsibility to an employee to keep the buffet line stocked with food, trays, china, silverware. Advise staff to keep the area clean and appealing for the duration of the service. Keep all the kitchen personnel advised as to the number of guests remaining in line, especially when replenishing food items.

9. A half-full container looks unappealing. Toward the end of the serving period, transfer food from large containers to smaller bowls to make the food more appealing.

10. If serving very expensive food items, assign an employee to serve these items.

11. Place emphasis on providing exceptional table service (coffee, tea, water, beverages, and personal attention) at all times.

12. Always protect the food on the buffet line by keeping it covered, or using sneeze guards or other similarly styled food shields.

13. Always provide clean plates and silverware for guests at the buffet line. Assist the guest by providing an employee stationed at the buffet line to monitor clean plate usage.

American Service

American service, often displayed as a **sit-down dinner**, can be a very elegant event. The caterer must be well organized and start with a good plan based on the menu decisions. What is the entree? Will the entree be served in courses? Is the staff trained so they know how they are going to serve it? What utensils do they need to serve the food? How many courses are planned? What time will the service begin? How much time will it take between courses? Is the table set the way the customer anticipates it to be done? The distinguishing characteristic of a sit-down dinner is that the food is arranged artistically on the plate before it is brought out.

The sit-down dinner is as important as the buffet. One advantage of the sit-down dinner is lower food costs than a buffet because the caterer will not have to overprepare. Remember, when offering a buffet, the caterer prepares enough food so the first and last guest have enough to eat.

Another advantage of planning a sit-down event is the caterer knows exactly how many guests will be served. This allows the caterer to calculate the exact portion-per-guest and the total amount of as-served food required for the event. A rule of thumb when calculating a sit-down dinner is to prepare 2 percent to 3 percent more

American service Food is preplated and brought out to the guests. Sit-down dinners are considered American service where portion control is maintained, keeping food costs low.

sit-down dinner A very elegant event where the caterer must be well organized and have a good plan. Typically, the food costs are lower than with a buffet dinner because the caterer prepares a set portion per guest with a slight (2 percent to 3 percent) overage.

than is required for the guaranteed number of guests. Once the food is purchased, production is set with the 2 or 3 percent overrun. The food is prepared, plated, and served to the guest. The guest will not come back for seconds or thirds as will happen on a buffet.

Again, building the menu for the guests begins with their needs. After the menu has been selected, the caterer must consider the entree. If the caterer is serving a stuffed chicken breast, chicken cordon bleu, a strip steak, or prime rib, complementary accompanying dishes must be selected.

When building a menu, color and variety are important. A chicken breast should not be served with mashed or scalloped potatoes and a steamed cauliflower. The lack of color will definitely affect the guests' opinion of the food. When serving something light, such as a stuffed chicken breast, it is recommended to add a medley of vegetables, a glazed carrot, or a fresh green bean in a mushroom sauce, or perhaps an au gratin or a red skinned potato. These combinations add color and make the plate of food attractive.

Caterers use garnishes to enhance the plate appearance. The use of an edible flower on the plate is an excellent example of a garnish. When plates are set down in front of the customers, they should look at the plates in awe. Imagine using the plate as the painter uses the canvas. The center of the plate is framed by its outside rim. Blending the right flavors, textures, colors, temperatures, and visual appeal can create a special art work. The goal is to excite the guests, have them talk about the artistic presentation, and appreciate the quality, flavor, and overall appeal of the food.

Tabletop

The social life of a caterer manifests itself during the process of delivering guest services. It is this interaction with a guest that publicly defines the caterer. Regardless of the event—be it simple, elaborate, ceremonious, religious, or joyous—the one common facet for each caterer is the guest's experience at the dining table.

How a caterer will be defined—that is, builds his or her reputation—will revolve around a guest's experience at the table. The flawless execution of the appropriate table service and the subsequent delivery of quality food are most important when building a caterer's reputation. Regardless of the professional care in the back-of-the-house during the food preparation and handling stage, nothing will compensate for poor arrangement and service experiences in the dining room. Therefore, from the service, each detail builds to the standard against which the performance will be gauged (Figure 12.2).

A caterer must always make the tabletop attractive and the food must always have eye appeal to please the guests. Strong factors making the table arrangement elegant and attractive are well-laundered tablecloths, and napkins that are neatly organized and properly sanitized, as well as spotless tableware.

tabletop This includes any items placed on the table that are needed by guests for their dining experience.

The **tabletop** includes any items placed on the table that are needed by guests for their dining experience (Figure 12.3). Items include tablecloths and napkins, otherwise known as napery; plateware or china, such as the service plate, dinner plate, salad plate, bread and butter plate, and soup bowls; flatware or "silverware," such as forks, spoons, and knives; and water and wine glasses, collectively called glassware (Figure 12.4).

Figure 12.2 The tabletop delivers an unforgettable dining experience.

Courtesy of HLC Inc.

Figure 12.3 Tabletop design and analysis.

THE HOMER LAUGHLIN CHINA CO.

1-800-452-4462   Newell.W.·Va.26050   Fax 304-387-0593

TABLETOP DESIGN ANALYSIS

Account: _____ Date: _____

_____ Chain: _____ Units: _____

_____ Phone: _____

Key Decision Makers:_____

Designer/Decorator:_____

Contractors: Kitchen: _____ Furniture: _____

Opening Date: _____

Market Segment:

_____ Fine Dining   _____ Banquet   _____ Retirement

_____ Theme   _____ Cafeteria   _____ Catering

_____ Family   _____ Hospital   _____ Other

Seats: _____ Coffee Shop   _____ Regular Dining

_____ Banquet   _____ Lounge

Decor: _____ Traditional

_____ Contemporary

Courtesy of HLC Inc.

(continues)

(continued)

_____ Theme

_____ Period

Colors: _____ Carpet

_____ Upholstery

_____ Walls

_____ Tabletop /Tray

_____ Linen /Placemat

_____ Napkins

Lighting:_____

Other Significant Dining Room Features: (plants, metal, etc.)

_____

Atmosphere: _____ Formal   _____ Casual

Menu, Features:

Appetizer _____

Soup _____

Salad _____

Entree _____

Dessert _____

TABLETOP DESIGN
ANALYSIS

Check Average:

Breakfast _____   Lunch _____   Dinner _____

China Budget: _____

Type of Seating: Tables _____   Booths _____   Counters _____

Table Sizes: _____   _____

Table Turns at Peak: _____ Tables   Booths _____   _____Counters

Banquet Covers: _____   _____   _____

Lowerator Items: _____   _____

China Storage Facilities: Minimal   _____ Adequate

Previously Used Pattern/Mfg._____

Competition: Pattern/Mfg._____

Other Pertinent Information:

ANALYSIS CONDUCTED BY:_____

A caterer can create *signature* plateware using a unique logo or their own trademark. This can help to distinguish the reputation of a caterer and customize the type of china used. Of course, the type of tabletop equipment will depend on the needs of the customer and the mission of the caterer (Figure 12.5 and Figure 12.6).

Regardless of a caterer's mission, a concern is the maintenance of the tabletop accessories. One common problem is breakage or *chipping* of the glassware and plateware. This is always a concern when transporting equipment to off-premise catering sites. Proper packaging for safe transportation and handling not only protects the plateware and glassware, but will also protect the guests and employees.

Broken or chipped accessories can cause serious injury to guests. Improper lifting and

Figure 12.4 A complete place setting for one guest at the start of a meal.

handling of bulky items can lead to an employee injury. Broken glass and plates can seriously lacerate an employee's hands. When an accident happens, the employees' immediate response is to quickly clean the area. This sometimes happens without thought of personal safety, especially if the employee feels responsible for this

Figure 12.5 The Homer Laughlin custom design Coon Creek Club.

Figure 12.6 The Homer Laughlin custom design Fish Plate Artistry in Action.

action. Checking tabletop accessories before each event can help avoid this type of accident.

Linen. When setting a table, clean, stainless, and pressed tablecloths without holes should always be used. The type of tablecloth will depend on the client's needs. It can be linen, cotton, polyester, cotton and polyester blend, plastic, or paper. The location of the function, indoors or out, on- or off-premise; its purpose; and a customer's budget will affect this selection.

If table linen or cotton is being used, it is recommended to purchase or rent the highest quality a caterer can afford. If just beginning, it will be necessary to rent the tablecloths and napkins. Prices are usually affixed per napkin and per tablecloth. If renting napery, always request its specifications from the rental company. By knowing the specifications, a competent decision can be made as to whether it will meet a caterer's needs. Napery composed of linen, 100 percent combed cottons, polyester and cotton blends, or 100 percent polyester is available. Each one has its own distinct characteristics, strengths, and weaknesses.

Purchasing wisely is most important when deciding on napery. The caterer must understand a few common facts before ordering.

1. What is the purpose and how will the napery fit the mission of the organization? This is a strong consideration.

2. What are the needs of the caterer in relationship to the type of clientele and type of functions that will be catered?

3. What material or blend of material will be selected? Based on the type of material, what is the expected life of its service? How durable is it?

4. Will the napery be laundered in a commercial laundry or will it be handled on-premise by the caterer? If the linen is handled on-premise, the caterer may launder the napery in-house, requiring additional handling, such as folding and ironing.

5. What is the most appropriate color and style?

6. Are personalized or crested table linens necessary?

7. What is the cost of the tablecloth?

8. What is the correct size needed?

9. What size tablecloth is required to fit a round table?

10. What is the inventory requirement?

Chris Gowdy, director of marketing at Mount Vernon Mills, Inc., Riegel Consumer Products Division, in Johnston, South Carolina, reminds the caterer that the accurate measurement of the table is necessary to correctly specify the corresponding tablecloth size. This measurement is one of the most important specifications required, he says. To help his customers, Gowdy designed a very useful guide, the *Riegel Sales Reference Guide*. This guide provides step-by-step instructions explaining how to properly measure a table and match this measurement to the appropriate size tablecloth (Figure 12-7).

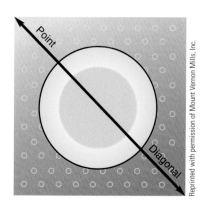

Figure 12.7 Measuring tables for tablecloths.

Setting the Table

The needs of the client will direct a caterer's plan to deliver the maximum benefit in regard to the accessories required to set an appropriate table. Although standard rules guide a caterer in the proper etiquette of table setting and service, the needs of a client will customize the package for them. An informative review of basic guidelines and rules of etiquette on setting tables can be found at the website of Learn 2 Set a Table at http://www.tutorials.com, and at the Milliken Table Linen website at http://www.millikentablelinens.com. These two sites will contain information on standard place setting guidelines, formal place setting guidelines, napkin variations, and folding guides, as well as guides to purchasing napery.

Creativity and artistic expression, communicated to a guest the moment they arrive at the table, help to create little details that make a lasting memory. The artistic expression derived from a flawless table is a powerful form of nonverbal communication. A guest's impression of the layout and design of the tabletop is part of the complete package that will help grow the reputation of a caterer.

The first step is to diagram, on paper, a precise cover or setting in advance of a function. Diagraming the table setting in advance allows time to conduct ample research, plan, and create a standard for all service employees. The standard shows the exact placement of each required dish, china, and small ware.

Small wares refers to sugar holders, salt and pepper shakers, ashtrays, pitchers, creamers, ice buckets, and compote dishes. A diagram allows for the careful matching of colors, table decorations, and napkins, and the coordination of center pieces with the menu and theme.

small wares The additional service items placed on the table including sugar holders, salt and pepper shakers, ashtrays, pitchers, creamers, ice buckets, and compote dishes.

Careful planning creates a coordinated, synchronized, synergetic effect, tying together all of the individual components of an event, such as the tabletop accessories, menu, service, and decor. It causes a guest to focus attention toward a common point, the dining table, and more specifically, the center of the plate.

Everything must be neat, clean, and well organized before the task of setting a table begins. The first assignment is to cover the table using the correct size **undercloth, silencer**, or **silence cloth** as it is sometimes called. Depending on the material composition and its design, a silence cloth may have elastic corners that permit it to hug or attach to the table. It may be made of flannel or plastic. If the undercloth does not have elastic corners, it should extend approximately 5 inches over each side of the table.

undercloth (silencer, silence cloth) A cloth placed beneath the tablecloth to prevent it from sliding. It also protects the table surface, provides cushioning for the tablecloth, reduces the noise of placing or moving china and glassware, and brings out patterns on the tablecloth.

The use of a silence cloth serves many purposes.

1. It helps to prevent the tablecloth from sliding on the table.

2. It helps to protect the tablecloth from excessive wear and tear, extending its usable life.

3. It helps to protect the table surface from heat or dampness.

4. It makes the tablecloth feel softer as it provides a cushion effect.

5. It helps to silence noise caused by setting down china or glassware and the movement of other tabletop implements.

6. It gives the tablecloth a heavier look and brings out any pattern on the cloth.

When this thick silence cloth, or undercloth, is smoothly in place, the tablecloth is spread over it. The crease in the middle of the cloth should fit exactly in the middle of the table, with the crease of the cross-fold meeting precisely at the center. The correct size tablecloth will hang evenly over the edges of the table. It should never touch the floor. When serving a dinner event, the overhang should drop between 12 and 15 inches. When catering a luncheon event, the overhang should drop between 8 and 12 inches. The chairs should be set away from the table in such a way as to prevent the bottom edge of the tablecloth from touching a chair. Skirting may also be used to wrap the table, eliminating the overhang of a tablecloth.

overlay (napperon) A small tablecloth placed over the larger one to help protect it and accent it with additional color.

A feature some caterers use to accent or protect the tablecloth is called an **overlay** or **napperon**. The overlay or napperon is a small tablecloth that covers the larger one. Overlays are used to accent the tablecloth by using a different color combination. The overlay provides the caterer with another decorative feature or creative option. Its functional purpose is to protect the tablecloth from stains, spills, and crumbs.

Next, the plates are put into position on the table. When possible, the distance between plates should be at least 20 inches. The standard *cover*, or individual guest space or position, is 24 inches wide with a depth measuring 15 inches. This distance is measured by a caterer from the center of one plate to the center of the plate set parallel, or beside it. The plate is set one inch from the edge of the table. However, plates can be set as far away as 2 inches from the edge of the table.

It is very important for a caterer to position the plates precisely on a table. The position of the plate sets a mark or reference point for placement of the silverware. The bottom rim of the plate will be parallel and in precise alignment with the lower tips of the utensils' handles, and the lower edge of the napkin. Correct placement of the plates leads to a symmetrical and artistic tabletop.

cover The complete place setting for one guest at the start of the meal including the service plate, flatware, napkin, and water glass.

A **cover** is the complete place setting for one guest at the start of a meal. This includes all the accessories required by one guest to dine. A complete place setting includes a service plate, flatware, napkin, and water glass. The name of this service plate has changed over the years. A service plate has been otherwise known as a *place plate*, *cover plate*, *show plate*, *base plate*, or *lay plate*.

A service plate is much more decorative than a dinner plate. It is slightly larger, approximately ten to eleven inches, or about one inch larger than a standard dinner plate. Its main purpose is for decoration. During formal service, the service plate is placed in advance of the meal and set in the center of each cover. It is set down approximately one or two inches from the edge of the table with the pattern facing the guest. This ornate plate is used as the foundation on which the plates of the first course are placed. No food is ever set directly on a service plate. The service plate is removed and replaced by a caterer immediately before the first hot course or right after the soup is consumed.

Table Ornaments. Once care has been used to position the plates on a table, the center ornament should be set. A caterer may use center ornaments to complement the theme of an event. For example, a carousel horse set at each table can magnify a circus theme. At another event, the use of wildflowers in a simple but powerful arrangement communicate an atmosphere of an old-fashioned farm gathering.

Center ornaments are unlimited by a caterer's artistic expression and imagination. However, these are certainly limited by a client's budget. The most effective table ornaments are those created by the imagination of a caterer that are simple but unusual. Where other caterers may feature ice carvings as the main table ornament, signature ornaments may feature unusual and exotic flowers in appropriate arrangements. These may include an arrangement of flowers portraying a professional football player kicking a football. Unique table ornaments can be created using a combination of different items. Flowers, candles, and antique artifacts, such as tools, books, farming implements, post cards, pictures, and clothing may be used to provide an unforgettable experience.

The table decorations should always fit or complement the purpose of the event. This is why successful caterers create their own complete package based on the client's individual needs. It is another facet of the complete service mix that will differentiate a caterer from the competition.

The table ornament should always be married to the theme. It is best to keep it simple and not overdecorated. The caterer should not pile things together merely to cover space. Open space is an important component of the complete thematic package. The purpose should be understood and the ornament matched to the event. Is the event a formal function? Is it a ceremonious event? The facility, food, tablecloth, napkins, and color schemes must be coordinated. The concept of height should be applied to the table ornament. Various heights can be used, but the view of the guests should not be obstructed. These guidelines must be reviewed often while formulating the plan of the event.

Flatware, Napery, and Glassware. After setting the table ornament, the flatware or silverware is set. The menu will determine the amount and kind of silverware required on the table. Is a cocktail fork, a salad fork, or an entree fork needed? Is a butter knife required? Is an entree knife needed? Perhaps a steak knife is required, especially if something needs to be cut, such as roast beef. Spoons will be placed next to the knife. Will a dessert spoon be needed? Maybe a spoon for iced tea or a soup spoon is needed as well.

To ensure an easy arrangement, it is important to imagine a grid or an imaginary template set on the table. This grid or template will guide the proper placement of flatware and accessories on the table and will create a symmetrical appearance. By following imaginary lines stretching out across the entire table, the caterer can achieve a well balanced tabletop (Figure 12.8).

Forks are placed to the immediate left of the service plate, on the grid so they are parallel with the plate. The tines of the forks are up. Knives are placed to the right of the plate with the cutting edge facing toward the plate. The knives must be parallel to each other and in alignment with the forks. The arrangement of the forks and knife is easy to remember. While eating, a guest will use the fork in the left hand and a knife in the right hand. The silverware will thus be parallel and in alignment.

Spoons are placed to the right of the knives, parallel, with the bowl facing up. If an oyster fork is needed, place this to the immediate right and parallel to the spoons. This small fork may also be placed on the oyster plate.

The amount of silverware is determined by the menu. Each menu item must either have its appropriate piece of silver placed at the cover or be brought in before the service of the course. The silverware should be set according to the sequence of its use. The first pieces to be used are placed farthest from the plate and the guest will work in toward the plate.

It is recommended to only place three forks. Two or three knives may be placed at a cover. This number does not include the butter knife or the oyster fork, if required. When dessert requires silverware, it can be set at the cover, immediately

Figure 12.8 Proper table setting placement.

before service of the dessert, or be brought in on the dessert plate. If the dessert silverware is set at the cover, the spoon is placed above the fork.

The napkin can be set to the caterer's preference. If set to the left of the forks, its edge is kept parallel to the silverware, using the imaginary tabletop grid. If folded in a simple square, the napkin's open corner is placed in the lower position nearest the plate. Napkin selection should be based on the theme and budget of the event.

Will a paper napkin be sufficient, or must it be linen? Will the napkin be folded? If yes, what kind of fold will complement the event? What color napkin will be used? If white, what color tablecloths will be used? Does the napkin match the color of the tablecloth?

A subtle way to incrementally increase the profit of a function is to suggest colored linen and/or napkins to the client. Most linen companies will charge the same price for either white or colored linen. The caterer can possibly charge the client an incremental fee per person for the use of colored linen.

Table settings need glassware. Is water and/or wine being served with the meal? Will one or two glasses be needed? Is a white wine glass or a red wine glass needed? Is a glass for champagne needed? If serving coffee or tea, will a cup and/or saucer be needed? These are needs which must be determined in advance and a plan prearranged to satisfy them.

Placement of the bread and butter plate is above the tips of the forks. It is laid on the grid so the plate sits on a line parallel to the water glass. The bread and butter knife is set on the plate, parallel to the edge of the table, with the cutting edge facing the guest, and the handle extending to the right. The knife can be placed on the right edge of the plate, blade facing left. It can be placed toward the area just inside of the plate, with the handle running parallel to the plate's right-outside edge. A caterer will set the water glass one inch above the tip of the knife, closest to the service plate. When the cover is set, the grid will create a symmetrical arrangement on the tabletop.

Small Wares. The classical table setting requires a placement of salt and pepper dispensers between every two covers. If the table is set with eight or more guests, individual salt and pepper dispensers can be set at each corner of the table. If set at a small table, individual dispensers can be placed at the two corners. Following the guidelines of classical table service, the bread and butter plates and the salt and pepper dispensers are removed immediately after the salad course.

When a caterer uses a place card to assign a cover to a specific guest, these are placed above the service plate or at the top center of the cover. All covers should be set on the grid so they face directly opposite of each other.

Compote dishes are set at the tabletop to balance the table setting and hold either mints, nuts, or an assortment of both. They are usually set toward the end of a table and should range between two or four in number.

Candles are used by a caterer to create an ambiance, complement the theme, or balance the tabletop. Candlesticks or a candelabra can be used to enhance the table decorations. The height of the candle should correspond to the height of the holder. Tall candles should be used in a low holder and smaller candles in a tall holder. Etiquette requires the use of tall candles in formal functions. The candles are lit before the guests enter the dining room. They will remain lighted until the guests have departed, even if the candles have burned down to their sockets. When using candles, the caterer should check with the facility, in advance, to make sure there is no *open-flame* policy.

Service

Diagrams of table settings will help the service staff. After diagraming the table settings, caterers meet with the waitstaff and explain the details of the plan. To execute the plan, the service personnel must know specific details of the service.

1. What time will the food be ready for service?
2. Will runners bring the food out on trays?
3. Will tray jacks be used?
4. Will the service staff be responsible for retrieving the food from the distribution area without the runners and serve it themselves?

These service concerns hinge on the type of catering function. Service and customer care provide the groundwork for ***Ingredient for Success 37: "The more service given, and the better care taken of the customer through exceptional attention to detail, the happier the client will be, and the more repeat business will be generated from that event."***

A caterer always wants to exceed the customer's expectations. Remember, if catering an event for 350 people, make sure enough waitstaff is scheduled to properly serve 350 guests. Customer service is just as important on a small job. If organizing an event for 35, 40, or 50 people, a caterer must overwhelm the customer with service.

If the waitstaff is responsible for pouring beverages, such as water, coffee, or iced tea, standard operating procedures should be established based on the catering objectives and the function plan. If the consumer's glass is half-full, always refill it during the first half of the meal. Then, during the last half of the meal, ask the customer if they would prefer to have his or her glass refilled. This will standardize procedures and create continuity in the delivery of service.

Standard operating procedures will also help the caterer to prevent waste and breakage, and reduce beverage costs. It will help to reduce labor time spent clearing soiled cups from the tabletop. This overall savings is compounded over time when one considers how much time is lost while hassling with excessive beverages remaining in cups on the tabletop. It will also help to reduce beverage costs. Establish procedures to help the service staff with the little things such as ice, creamers, rolls, and butter. These are the individual decisions each caterer makes to differentiate them from the competition.

When serving cold beverages, it is important to have ice in all pitchers. Customers do not like warm "iced" tea or warm "ice" water. When serving coffee, serve it hot! Offer a choice between decaffeinated and regular. Creamers must also be served using pitchers or portion-control creamers. A 6-month, unrefrigerated, shelf-stable, portion-control creamer is available that can eliminate the worry of serving spoiled cream. These portion-controlled creamers can be served from an attractive bowl placed directly on each table or served individually with the coffee.

Similar decisions are made when serving bread, rolls, and butter. The caterer can purchase foil-wrapped butter pats that look very elegant, or individual butter pats that are covered with a small piece of paper can be used. Little touches include serving the butter at room temperature. There is nothing more aggravating to a customer than placing butter on a nice, fresh roll or piece of bread and finding that the butter, having just been pulled from the refrigerator or freezer, is as hard as a rock and will not spread.

These are some examples of the little things taken into consideration in advance by a caterer to promote good customer service. The caterer must think, prepare, make notes, have charts, build checklists, and train the staff because each job is important and every job requires exceptional attention to even the smallest of details. ***Ingredient for Success 38: "Consider every job a major production."*** A caterer wants to project a proud, competent image either as the owner or as an employee of the organization. ***Ingredient for Success 39: "A caterer's performance is a reflection of the business."*** When the job is finished, the caterer wants to have rave reviews from the customers. A caterer should think of each job as the most important job they will ever do.

Preset Tableware

If tableware is preset, care must be taken to prevent its contamination. Recommended techniques include wrapping it, keeping it covered, or inverting it on the tabletop. Any unused exposed place settings will be removed when a consumer is seated. If it is not removed, it must be cleaned and sanitized before further use.

Clean Linens

All linens should be free from food residues and other soiling matter. Linens that do not come in direct contact with food should be laundered between events if they become wet, sticky, or visibly soiled. Linens and napkins that are used on the tabletop will be laundered between each use. Wet wiping cloths will be laundered daily. Dry wiping cloths will be laundered as necessary to prevent contamination of both food and serving utensils.

Soiled linens should be kept in clean, nonabsorbent containers. Clean, washable laundry bags are also acceptable as a storage container. Always handle soiled linen separately to prevent the cross-contamination of food, clean equipment, clean utensils, and single-service and single-use articles.

Linens and napkins may not be used in contact with food. However, they can be used as a liner in a container for the service of foods, such as breads, if they are replaced each time the container is refilled for a new consumer.

Laundry facilities on the premises of a catering establishment should be used only for the washing and drying of items used in the operation of the establishment. However, separate laundry facilities located on the premises for the purpose of general laundering, such as for institutions providing boarding and lodging, may also be used for laundering food establishment items.

Improper Use of Tableware

Caution must always be exercised when handling soiled tableware, either at their removal during a function or when cleaning after its completion. Proper techniques and an appropriate level of service staff must be used, and the cross-contamination of clean and sanitized pieces always avoided.

Soiled tableware cannot be reused by a consumer. This includes single-service articles, or tableware to provide second portions or refills. Consumers are not permitted to use their soiled tableware to obtain *seconds* from a buffet line or other food display area. A clean plate or utensil should always be used. Exceptions include the refilling of a consumer's drinking cup or container, which includes personal take-out beverage containers, such as thermally insulated bottles, nonspill coffee cups, and promotional beverage glasses. These can either be refilled by an employee or the consumer at a self-serve area. They must be refilled in such a manner as to prevent contact between the pouring utensil and the lip-contact area of the container.

A caterer cannot permit a take-home food container returned by the consumer to the caterer to be refilled with a potentially hazardous food.

Family-Style Service

Another form of service is called **family-style service**, where the food is delivered to the table in serving dishes or platters with enough quantity for each guest seated at the table. Family-style is considered self-service. As the food is passed around the table, the guests help themselves.

Guests can be seated by 4, 6, 8, or 10 per table. Usually, at a family-style event, there are standard-set tables. It is very important to know how many people are seated at each table. If serving two entrees, such as breaded pork chops and oven-baked chicken to eight guests, 10 pork chops are placed on a serving plate and 10 pieces of chicken are placed on another serving plate, along with enough salad in a serving bowl and enough vegetables in their own bowls to serve eight people.

The serving dishes, platters, and bowls are placed directly on the table. No food is served by the waitstaff to any guest. Customers like this form of service because they are overwhelmed with the thought, "I can have all that I want to eat." In reality, a caterer will use just slightly more food than if preplating the food as in the American style, for each guest.

The salad is delivered first, followed by the rolls, assorted breads, butter, and side dishes. Finally the main entree is delivered. The guests' beverages are kept filled with water, coffee, or wine. If the bottle of wine is left on the table and the guests are serving each other, empty bottles should be promptly removed. Remember, even with family-style, the more service a caterer can offer, the more impressive it is for the customer.

family-style service In this self-service type of catering, food is delivered to the table on platters or large serving dishes with enough for everyone seated. The guests pass the platters and help themselves.

Family-style service offers some advantages for the caterer. Since the food is presented informally to the guests at the table on platters, the waitstaff does not have to be highly trained in service techniques. Also, the speed of service is very fast. The food is neatly arranged per platter and delivered as is instead of requiring each portion to be individually placed on a plate for each guest. One concern with family-style service is the menu. Depending on the number of items being served, a careful determination of table space is necessary to make sure there is enough room.

Regardless of the type of service—buffet, sit-down, or family style—the staff must be aware of the needs of the guest. Careful attention and anticipation of the guests' needs is required. Especially important is the removal of the soiled plates and dishes. If serving multiple courses, the soiled dishes are removed as the new courses are served. The soup dish is removed when the salad is served, and the salad is removed when the entree is served. When finished with the entree, the entire table is cleared except for the coffee cup or beverage glass. Then the dessert is served. After dessert, everything is completely removed from the table.

The serving staff should always be alert to bussing opportunities. Since the entree, bread and butter, and salads are served in bowls and platters, extra dirty dishes will always appear on the table. These empty serving bowls and platters should be removed so the customers do not have any dirty dishes in front of them. There is nothing more unappealing for the customer than to be sitting at the table looking at dirty dishes for 10 to 15 minutes after finishing their meal.

SERVICE GUIDELINES

Any unused, potentially hazardous food, returned by a consumer after it has been in their possession, may not be re-served or offered again by the caterer as food for human consumption.

However, a container of potentially nondangerous food may be re-served from one consumer to another if the food is dispensed so that it is protected from contamination, and the container is closed between uses, such as a narrow neck bottle containing ketchup, steak sauce, or wine. If the food remains in an unopened original package and is maintained in sound condition, such as crackers, salt, or pepper, it can be re-served to a consumer.

ROOM ARRANGEMENT

The arrangement of tables is an important factor contributing to the success of the function. A caterer may use any number of arrangements, but it is important to create an environment suitable for the *purpose* of the function. Some common functions may include a business meeting, a wedding, and a social event. When planning the arrangement of a room, a caterer should research the following room layout considerations:

1. size or square footage of the room area
2. aisle space required for service personnel to navigate while serving the food
3. service area or wait stations, including soiled dish area
4. placement of the beverage stations, coffee stations, and portable bar

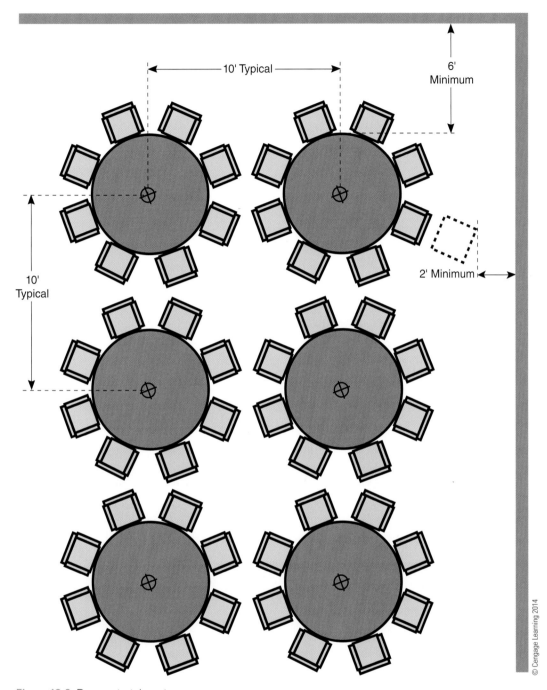

Figure 12.9 Banquet-style setup.

5. number of seats at each table
6. shape and size of a table
7. total number of guests
8. activity and flow of the guests
9. fire and safety codes in relation to the capacity of the room and the emergency exits

Many caterers, to help decide on the arrangement of the room, will create standard operating procedures designed to *standardize* each type of function. The term *banquet style* (Figure 12.9) is generally used to describe room setups for meal functions.

1. Use round tables (generally 66–72 inches round).
2. Sit 8 to 10 guests per table.
3. Tables are usually 10 feet apart from center to center.
4. Place chairs a minimum of 2 feet from side walls.

Figures 12.9, 12.10, and 12.11 illustrate some of the most common meeting and dinner table arrangements.

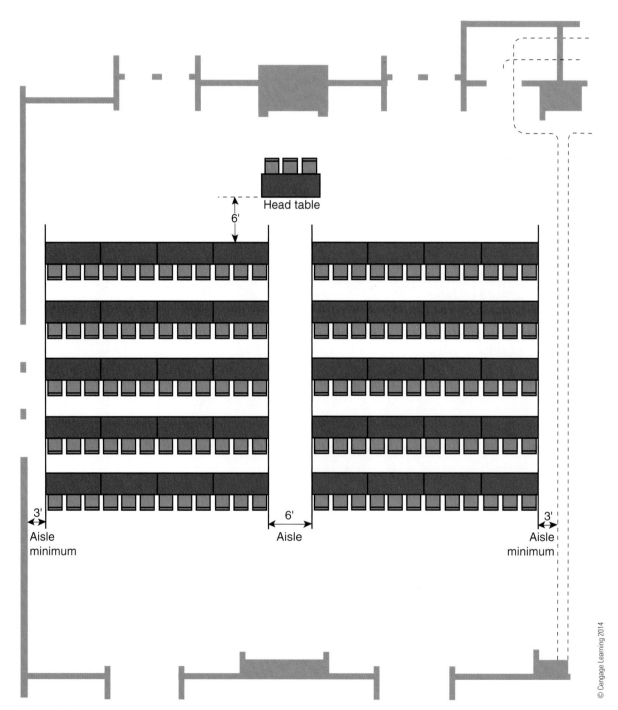

Figure 12.10 Schoolroom/classroom setup.

© Cengage Learning 2014

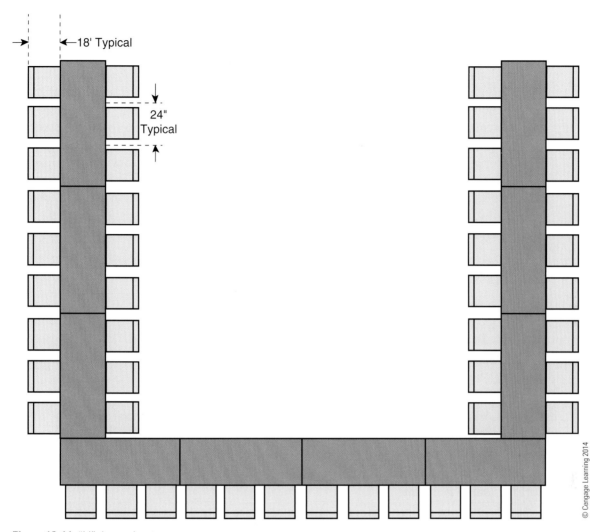

18' Typical

24"
Typical

© Cengage Learning 2014

Figure 12.11 "U"shaped setup.

Summary

Delivering consistent customer service, geared to exceed a customer's needs, is perhaps the most important mission of a catering business. Successful caterers will define service based on their mission statement as to what it means to the catering operation. Service occurs in both the front-of-the-house and back-of-the-house activities. Many caterers will build their reputation by providing service to meet and exceed the needs of their clients. Understanding service leads to implementing an exceptional training program, to educate and build skills necessary to create a professional service staff comprised of appropriate personnel.

There are several formal and informal styles of service. These service styles may be used in combination with each other, depending on the needs of the client and the type of event. Common types of events include private family functions, business or corporate functions, and community, group, and association functions. These include banquets, receptions, meetings, picnics, baptisms, bar mitzvahs, anniversaries, office parties, holiday parties, charitable events, and weddings.

It is best to maintain a written description of the various service methods the caterer is competent to handle. This list may include the type of function, the type of equipment needed to execute this event, and the various kinds of service provided in conjunction with each. Formal styles of service include *French* and *Russian* service. The most common types of service used by caterers are the informal styles which include *buffet, American,* and *family-style service.* The needs of the client will direct a caterer's plan to deliver the maximum benefit in regard to the accessories required to set an appropriate table. Although standard rules guide a caterer in the proper etiquette of table setting and service, the needs of a client will customize the package. An informative review of basic guidelines and rules of etiquette to setting tables must be completed before the execution of each event. A review of information on standard place setting guidelines, formal place setting guidelines, napkin variations, and folding guides should be completed based on the event itself.

Review Questions

Brief Answers

1. Define the term *service* as it relates to catering management.
2. Discuss how service plays an important role in satisfying customers' needs at the front-of-the-house.
3. Explain how a customer is directly involved in the service activities of the caterer.
4. Explain how a caterer can build a reputation based on service.
5. Explain how a caterer can build a professional service staff.
6. Explain how caterers can use standards to define service. Provide examples of how a caterer can develop service standards to mirror the organization's mission statement.
7. Describe an informal organizational structure and explain how it can affect employee morale?
8. Explain and provide examples of what appropriate personnel means to the catering organization.
9. List some of the common attributes of appropriate service personnel.
10. Explain the differences between informal and formal service styles used by caterers.
11. Describe the defining characteristics of each service style.
12. Describe how teamwork plays an important role in satisfying customer objectives.
13. Explain what the Ingredients for Success mean to you.

Multiple Choice

Select the single best answer for each question.

1. This style of service is characterized by the use of table-side cooking using two pieces of equipment called a *rechaud* and a *gueridon.*
   a. Russian service
   b. American service
   c. buffet service
   d. French service
   e. family-style service

2. A distinguishing characteristic of _____ service is that the customer actively participates in supplying part of the service. The consumer supplements a caterer's service.

   a. Russian
   b. American
   c. buffet
   d. French
   e. family-style

3. _____ service has the food delivered to the table in serving dishes or platters with enough quantity for the number of guests seated at each table. The food is passed around the table with each guest serving themselves.

   a. Russian
   b. American
   c. buffet
   d. French
   e. family-style

True or False

Read each of the following statements and determine if it is true or false.

1. To ensure a consistent delivery of service, a caterer must define *service* as it applies to the mission of their operation.

2. Caterers can further enhance a guest's perception of the professional service delivered through the use of a standardized uniform for the staff.

3. It is disappointing to a customer to approach a buffet and find the caterer has run short of food and/or it is empty.

Putting It All Together

Interview local caterers. Ask them to describe the service styles they have used to serve their guests. What special training needs, requirements, or pieces of equipment did they need to obtain before executing the event? Ask them to describe how the service style satisfied the needs of the client. Is there any style of service which they would never use? Why? Detail your findings.

Diemo Video Picture

Chapter 13

Controlling

Objectives

After studying this chapter, you should be able to:

1. Describe the catering management function of control and explain why it is needed.
2. Describe why the control of an organization's resources is an important catering management task.
3. Describe the process of control.
4. Explain why the caterer must develop and implement both internal and external control features into the catering management system.
5. Explain why the easiest task for most caterers to neglect, without an immediate penalty, is the control function.
6. Explain why elements of control begin when the caterer designs specific internal techniques to direct an employee's behavior in accomplishing predetermined objectives
7. Explain why controlling has multiple meanings and serves multiple purposes.
8. Explain why a caterer needs timely and relevant information to ensure appropriate business decisions.
9. Explain why a caterer must be concerned with protecting the uninterrupted flow of cash into the organization.
10. Define a formal payment policy and list its advantages.
11. Describe how a caterer arrives at a final price to charge the client for an event.
12. Explain the relationship between financial goals and predetermined profit objectives.
13. Explain why, if an event has experienced a financial loss, the caterer must very carefully study and review the circumstances that have contributed to this failure.
14. Explain why it is important for a caterer to always be on the alert for unexpected price changes and hidden costs.
15. Provide an example of how a caterer might misjudge, misquote, or inaccurately speculate on an event.
16. Explain why the caterer must implement internal controls to protect the company's assets.
17. Describe creative methods for earning revenue other than from food and beverage sales.
18. Explain how membership in an appropriate organization or association benefits a caterer.
19. Describe the balance sheet and the income statement.

KEY TERMS

balance sheet

cash flow

client-based pricing method

code of ethics

competitive-based pricing method

controlling

cost-based pricing method

formal payment policy

income statement

market-penetration pricing strategy

market-skimming pricing strategy

overhead

prime costs

Ingredients For Success

40 "A caterer's business success depends on enforceable controls. Creative acquisition, storage, preparation, and service of food and beverage will minimize labor requirements. Strong budgetary objectives derived from accounting systems will provide analysis of financial information."

This chapter addresses the sixth catering management function—*controlling*. Catering managers establish control techniques to protect the financial interests of the organization. Comprehensive control techniques are accomplished by an astute caterer who knows that the most effective way to earn a profit is to first understand how and why a caterer may lose money. If a caterer understands how money may be drained from the organization, effective controls can be used to tighten operations.

This sixth catering management function must be an integral component of the whole organizational plan. The objective of building control techniques is for the survival of the business and the attainment of the organization's mission. This includes a detailed strategy of how the control techniques will be implemented into each event plan.

CONTROL

Controlling the organization's resources is an important management task required to ensure the financial health of the business. Caterers create control techniques using financial tools and predetermined standards to accomplish the other catering management functions.

Control techniques must become a key component integrated into each of the other catering management functions to have a successful organization. Whether formulating or implementing the event plan, executing the operational tasks, or organizing resources, the ability to integrate fundamental catering management controls ensures the capability of comparing actual performance against planned objectives.

Both internal and external control features must be developed for the catering management system. Control of food (Figure 13.1), beverages, and labor costs—including salaries, wages, and employee benefits—are examples of internal costs. Internal costs such as direct food and labor costs associated with producing the food are usually bundled and called **prime costs**.

prime costs The sum of the direct food cost plus the direct labor cost to produce a menu item for a client.

Ingredient for Success 17, first introduced in Chapter 6, explains why a caterer needs to create cost control procedures. *"Cost control procedures are created for the acquisition of timely information to equip the caterer with data to scrutinize controllable costs and make appropriate operational decisions."*

According to *Ingredient for Success 40*, *"A caterer's business success depends on enforceable controls. Creative acquisition, storage, preparation, and service of food and beverage will minimize labor requirements. Strong budgetary objectives derived from accounting systems will provide analysis of financial information."*

Permission of John R. Smith

Figure 13.1 Caterers must manage portion control based on the guaranteed number of guests and food costs.

Lack of Control

Using effective catering management controls enables the caterer to evaluate key objectives regarding each event. Often, small catering businesses lack long-term sustained success because of neglecting to effectively execute the control function.

The caterer must assume the jack-of-all-trades approach and cannot always rely on a professionally trained management staff for input of specialized knowledge into the decision-making process. As a result, the caterer must personally execute each catering function. Since each catering function requires a commitment of time, certain elements may lack appropriate monitoring. Unfortunately, the easiest task for most caterers to neglect, without an immediate penalty, is the control function because control is, by nature, a task simultaneously done while every other element is in progress. But neglecting to enforce control procedures when executing operational tasks sends a negative message to the employees that could result in lost revenue.

Elements of Control

Elements of control begin when the caterer designs specific internal techniques to direct an employee's behavior in accomplishing predetermined objectives (Figure 13.2). Since the caterer bundles common tasks together and delegates these to an employee for execution, control techniques are required to guide the employee in the appropriate direction. Effective control techniques provide guidance without direct supervision.

Tips from the Trade

More than anything else, I value my postevent staff meetings. After every single event my team and I meet somewhere quiet to review the successes and challenges we faced during the previous event. I find these meetings to be incredibly helpful. It is important to balance positive reinforcement with making corrective observations. These types of meetings should not be used to single anyone out or berate someone for making a mistake; they should be used as a forum for discussion on what worked and what did not work during the event. I find that some of the best ideas for improving service or controlling costs come from these staff meetings. Five or 10 minutes is all you need to effectively conduct a postevent

wrap-up, a preview of the next day's activities and expectations, and a quick question-and-answer that includes praise and corrective steps to take. I have found that they have really helped me gain a better understanding of my staff and a greater sense of ownership since I actively include my staff in decision-making aspects of our service. My staff leaves every day knowing exactly what is expected of them and I gain a better understanding of what makes my staff tick. It's a win-win situation for everyone and fosters a positive work environment.

Courtesy Adam Baumbach, Legends Hospitality Management.

Figure 13.2 The catering manager directs an employee's behavior in accomplishing a predetermined service objective.

Multiple Meanings

The sixth catering management function, **controlling**, has multiple meanings and serves multiple purposes. First, control means to establish standard operating procedures to ensure employees' proper execution of their tasks. These standard operating procedures set an appropriate amount of time to execute the task. Second, controlling means the establishment and timely implementation of predetermined objectives, derived from the mission of the organization. Third, control is a process used to integrate each independent catering management function into an achievable event plan. Fourth, control helps to protect a caterer's assets, including money, food, beverages, and equipment. Protection of a caterer's assets must be every employee's responsibility. Finally, control creates the efficient utilization of the caterer's assets to produce a product at a profitable price.

controlling One of the most important catering management functions. Ensures the effective and efficient utilization of the caterer's resources in the process of producing food and beverage to accomplish organizational goals.

Process of Control

The process of control is the focus of *Ingredient for Success 17: "Cost control procedures are created for the acquisition of timely information to equip the caterer with data to scrutinize controllable costs and make appropriate operational decisions."* First, the caterer must have timely and relevant information to make appropriate decisions. These decisions must benefit the business and the client. Appropriate market information is critical when researching menus and establishing a fair market price to charge the client.

Second, the benefit of timely and relevant information helps to create achievable standards and operating procedures. For example, designing appropriate standard operating procedures, to implement a hazardous analysis critical control plan for an event, must be based on appropriate information.

Third, the caterer must monitor each event, comparing actual performance against predetermined objectives. Appropriate financial information to set and

Tips from the Trade

Most of the factors for controlling a catering event should be considered during the planning process. We hold weekly department meetings and everyone who is involved in the event attends. Every Friday morning we have a department managers' meeting, especially before a busy weekend. At this meeting, we review each event's timeline and the specific details. We always confirm the delivery of any speciality item that was ordered for an event, such as a special beer, wine, or an ice sculpture. We create layouts and floor plans showing the function room set up, including the guests' tables and food stations. We plan the flow of the room to ensure all guests are served in a timely manner, and we try to eliminate bottlenecks and crowding. Floor plans help the staff to correctly set the room as specified. Some events may require you to "flip" a room in a short amount of time, and having a floor plan ready speeds up this process and saves time. The department managers have the opportunity to ask questions, and the coordinators are able to make the appropriate changes.

As the coordinator, I always meet with the chef a few hours before the start of the event. Together, we walk through the event from start to finish, noting any changes to the menu, the timing, or the guest count. Together we check the spelling of names, and print the finalized menus that are placed on each table. I always create a detailed checklist for each event, on which I include the required tasks to execute the event and the customized details specifically designed for it. This keeps me organized, on time, and ensures even the smallest details are not missed. A timeline will let you know exactly what should be happening at that particular moment.

Here is an example of what one of my timelines looks like on a typical Saturday night from 4:00 P.M. to 8:00 P.M., implementing two weddings and a rehearsal dinner (Figure 13.3).

Jennifer Babaz, Assistant Coordinator, Skytop Lodge "Courtesy Jennifer Babaz", Skytop Lodgev

accomplish financial objectives is crucial to the immediate and sustained success of the catering operation. The only effective way to immediately correct defects in the system is to quickly eliminate problems by using appropriate information.

CASH FLOW

cash flow The uninterrupted series of cash installments by the client to the caterer for executing the catering function.

formal payment policy The explanation and guidelines created by the caterer to describe for the client how payment is made. Creates a positive cash flow into the organization.

A caterer must protect the uninterrupted flow of cash into the organization. **Cash flow** includes a client's series of payments made to the caterer for services. **A formal payment policy** is used to monitor the cash flow into the organization. A formal payment policy explains how the client will pay the caterer for the food and services rendered. Of special concern, however, is the caterer's need for a steady cash flow and to ensure that prompt payment is faithfully made.

Payment Policies

Forty years ago, it was common practice to invoice the client for the food and services rendered between 2 and 4 weeks after the event. As corporate catering grew, many caterers' payment policies evolved to accommodate corporate clients' financial payment policies. These policies often pay a caterer within 60 days after an event. Social clients soon began to adopt similar policies. They began to disburse

Time	Name	Event	Location	Weather Back-up	Special Notes
4:00–4:30	Wedding #1	Ceremony	Formal Garden	South Porch or Library	2 outside buses arriving at 3:30 and 3:45
4:30–5:30	Wedding #1	Cocktail Hour	South Porch	Library	
5:30–9:30	Wedding #1	Reception	Laurel Ballroom		Bar closed first and last ½ hour of reception
5:30–6:00	Wedding #2	Ceremony	Evergreen Garden	Hemlock Ballroom	Bride always late
6:00–7:00	Wedding #2	Cocktail hour	Evergreen Porch	Garden View Lobby	Ice Sculpture – Martini Luge
6:00–6:30	Rehearsal #1	Rehearsal	South Porch/ Formal Garden	Library	
6:30–7:00	Rehearsal #1	Hayride	Leaving from North Porch	Canceled if inclement weather	Will need 2-3 trips – also have handicapped shuttle ready
7:00–10:00	Rehearsal #1	Picnic	Streamside Lodge		Bar with Beer and Wine Only
7:00–11:00	Wedding #2	Reception	Evergreen Ballroom		4 hours open bar
8:30–10:00	Rehearsal #1	Campfire	Streamside Lodge	Canceled if inclement weather	Dining Room to provide S'mores

Figure 13.3 An example of a timeline planning tool for a typical Saturday night from 4:00 P.M. to 8:00 P.M., implementing two weddings and a rehearsal dinner.

their final payment between 45 and 90 days after the event. Unfortunately this type of payment policy can limit cash flow.

One control to ensure a prompt payment by the client is for a caterer to write a formal payment policy based on the financial needs and the mission of the catering operation. One example is the structured client payment policy, requiring the client to pay one-third of the total bill when the contract is signed. Payment of the next one-third is due immediately before or on the day of the event. The final one-third of the bill is due within 30 days after the event. This type of payment schedule is flexible and could be adapted depending upon the type of function and the client.

In today's market, successful caterers must create very structured payment policies to protect themselves against clients defaulting on their obligation to pay their bills. A caterer incurs certain pre-event expenses such as purchasing and preparing food, hiring and training the staff, and acquiring or renting equipment. These and other expenses negatively affect the caterer's financial position.

Payment policies can be written to cover these pre-event costs. At the signing of the contract, the caterer receives one-third of the money owed. Another one-third of the bill must be paid 45 to 30 days before the event. Finally, the last payment is made 2 weeks before the event. Written into the contract and spelled out in detail is a statement notifying the client that if the caterer incurs any additional costs, the client will be invoiced separately for them. This type of payment schedule is highly recommended as it:

1. ensures the caterer will receive prompt payment for services rendered.
2. guarantees a positive, steadier cash flow.
3. eliminates any unnecessary stress from the caterer worrying about when payment will be made.
4. helps to ensure the business's success.

More and more caterers are becoming successful because they have implemented a structured payment schedule that delivers a consistent, positive cash flow. This steady cash flow helps to eliminate financial worry and stress. An added bonus to a structured payment policy is that the customer must agree to it before hiring the caterer, and the caterer can make sure to get some money up front.

> Hyatt has established corporate policies that dictate proper billing and collection procedures. We do have some flexibility when writing contracts depending on the amount of estimated charges. For instance, if the estimated amount is less than $1,000, I will require the estimated charges as a nonrefundable deposit. All invoices that will be paid by check, cash, or credit card must be prepaid 10 days prior to the actual function date. We do provide direct billing for accounts which will exceed $2,000 total. A direct bill application must be submitted 30 days in advance and is subject to the hotel's approval.
>
> *Dianne Herzog, Catering Manager, Hyatt Orlando, Kissimmee, Florida*

PRICING THE EVENT

How does a caterer determine the final price to charge the client for an event? There is no universal method used to derive a final price per event because caterers use different procedures to calculate costs. A caterer can charge each client a different price for the same menu based on the package, quality of food, and level of service. Each caterer calculates pricing formulas based on specific needs.

A caterer may decide to offer a one-price *total package* to the client. This package will include an option of selecting from a variety of menus that differ in price, according to the type of entree and style of service.

There are three basic methods to arrive at the price for any function. The first method is called the cost-based pricing method, the second is the client-based pricing method, and the third is competitive-based pricing. Two additional pricing strategies are called market-skimming pricing and market-penetration pricing.

cost-based pricing method Adding a standard markup to the direct labor and food cost to determine the client's final cost for a function.

If using the **cost-based pricing method**, the caterer will calculate the actual cost to produce the function and then add a predetermined markup to arrive at the client's cost.

The actual expense per event will vary depending on the menu, type of service, competition, market demands, special requests, and the time of year (e.g., Christmas, New Year's Eve, or Mother's Day). A caterer must first calculate the total cost of executing an event, set an achievable, fair profit objective, and then verify that the client is capable of making the structured payment schedule.

Establishing the expenses for a function will determine how much the caterer must charge the client in order to meet the predetermined profit objective and exceed the guest's expectations. The actual mechanics of *crunching* the expense numbers for a final price may vary. There are different mathematical formulas a caterer can use to total the expenses, and arrive at a price to charge the client.

One important consideration in setting a price is to include overhead. **Overhead** is the cost of operating the catering business regardless of the type or number of functions executed. Overhead is a term used to describe indirect labor, utilities, indirect material cost, insurance, taxes, depreciation, and repairs and maintenance of equipment. These costs are indirectly related to the cost of executing a catering function. Remember that prime costs are direct labor and food costs incurred in executing a catering function.

A caterer must calculate or budget a total overhead cost for an operating period. Once determined, budgeted overhead costs can be allocated directly to each function. A dollar amount, or a percentage factor, used to allocate a partial cost of overhead, may be added to the direct cost of the event to determine the client's price.

The second basic pricing method is called the **client-based pricing method**, which uses the client's perception of the function's value as the foundation for setting the client's price. The caterer's costs may not directly influence final price. Rather than basing the client's cost on the direct food and labor cost, the caterer may use other perceived services from the complete package, such as valet parking or special linen requests, to adjust the price to the client's perception of value. Theoretically, the caterer can therefore charge every client a different price. Price is based on the client's perception of the value of food and related services, and their ability to pay.

The third method of pricing a function is the **competitive-based pricing method**. This method bases client cost on the comparative price as charged by the other caterers in the market. This price is not determined by direct costs or a client's perceived value. Rather, it is set by the market conditions and competitive *jockeying*.

The two additional pricing strategies are called market-skimming pricing and market-penetration pricing. A caterer implements a **market-skimming pricing strategy** by setting a very high price to skim *off* the profits from the market. This may happen if there is only one type of specialized caterer in a market to service specialized needs. One disadvantage is that the large profits may attract competition into the market.

A caterer may use a **market-penetration pricing strategy** to gain a large market share by penetrating a new niche or market. Prices are initially set low, but must be compensated by high volume. Again, low price may attract competitors into the market.

Menu

Establishing the cost for the event begins with the menu. If the menu features one-half chicken, the caterer will realize a much different profit structure than if featuring a filet. The caterer will also have a much different profit structure if doing a breakfast event than if catering a sit-down dinner. Standardized recipe cost sheets (Figure 13.4) help establish menu costs.

overhead The cost of operating the catering business regardless of the type or number of functions executed. It describes indirect labor, utilities, indirect material costs, insurance, taxes, depreciation, and the repair and maintenance of equipment.

client-based pricing method This pricing method bases the cost of a function on the client's perceived value rather than the direct food and labor costs to produce the event.

competitive-based pricing method This pricing method bases the cost charged to a client for a function on the relative cost charged by competitors in the market, rather than on direct food and labor costs or demands.

market-skimming pricing strategy This pricing strategy sets a rather high initial price to skim profit from the market.

market-penetration pricing strategy This pricing strategy sets a low initial price to penetrate a new segment or to gain an overall market share.

STANDARDIZED RECIPE COST SHEET

Event _____

Date of Event _____ Time of Event _____

Week Number of Operation _____

Date Recipe Costed _____

Adjusted Date Recipe Costed _____

Date Approved _____

Catering Manager _____

Production Manager _____

INGREDIENTS	INGREDIENT COST		
Item	Amount	Unit Cost	Total Cost

Recipe Yield _____

Portion Size _____

Portion Cost _____

Total Recipe Cost _____

Recipe: Prepared by _____

HACCP Instructions Reviewed _____

Critical Control Points _____

Suggestions for Improvement _____

Production Process Defects _____

Recipe Number _____

© Cengage Learning 2014

Figure 13.4 Standardized Recipe Cost Sheets help establish menu pricing.

Expenses

The caterer must understand what expenses will be incurred from executing the event. If the caterer is doing a breakfast for 35 people at an off-premise site located 5 miles away, calculating total costs for the event must include the cost of transportation and the cost of labor to get the food to the location.

One method used to determine the cost and price structure is to quote a flat price for the entire event (Figure 13.5). A flat price must cover all expenses including labor, preparation, and transportation of the food. Will the caterer drop off the food at the location and leave? Can the caterer leave the equipment safely overnight and retrieve it the next morning? If not, will the crew be required to return immediately after the event to retrieve the equipment? Or will the crew be required

EVENT COST-PRICING WORKSHEET

Do Not Hang on the Bulletin Board!

Name of Event _____ Date of Event _____

Prepared By _____ Date Prepared _____

Contact Person _____ Number _____

E-mail _____

Time of Service _____ Service Duration _____ Location of Event _____

Guest Count _____ Price Per Person $ _____ Date Price Quoted _____ Initials _____

Revised Price and Reason for Revision:

$ _____ / _____ Date _____ Initials _____

	MENU ITEM	PORTION SIZE	PORTION COST*
Appetizer	_____	_____	$ _____
Entree I	_____	_____	$ _____
Entree II	_____	_____	$ _____
Starch	_____	_____	$ _____
Vegetable	_____	_____	$ _____
Salad	_____	_____	$ _____
Dressing(s)	_____	_____	$ _____
Bread	_____	_____	$ _____
Butter/Spread	_____	_____	$ _____
Dessert	_____	_____	$ _____
Beverages(s)	_____	_____	$ _____
Condiments	_____	_____	$ _____
Other	_____	_____	$ _____
Total Raw Food Cost			$ _____
Extra Production Costs, Etc.			$ _____
Total Cost Per Person			$ _____

$ _____ divided by _____ % equals $ _____
Total Cost Per Person   Desired Food Cost Percent   =   Selling Price Per Person
                         Standard Markup Percent

*See Figure 13.4 for each individual recipe item.

Figure 13.5 An Event Cost-Pricing Worksheet helps a caterer determine how much to charge a client for an event.

to stay at the event? If staying, will the crew provide services and clean the facility at the conclusion of the event? Or will the client provide any services themselves, such as delivering the food, serving the guests, or cleaning up? All of these activities have an impact on the cost structure of an Although the cost of the food would definitely be much higher for the luncheon than for the breakfast, the caterer would have the same expense of labor, transportation, and overall fixed expense for catering this event. These are some variables a caterer must think carefully about when calculating the price to charge a client for a catering function.

Each event must be reviewed on an individual basis. Menu prices will be based on different factors. A banquet menu is often priced according to the choice of an entree. If the entree selection offers a choice of stuffed pork chops or chicken breasts, the cost might be $25 per person. If the entree options include steak or prime rib, the cost per person might be $45. An option of either shrimp or a lobster would most likely be an even higher price.

Other Factors

There are other factors to consider that are not covered in the selling price (Figure 13.6). What are the number of hours required to execute the event? What is the cost of serving an appetizer? A different pricing formula is required when figuring the expense of serving an appetizer because the caterer must determine the type of appetizer and how many will be served to each person. Will soup be served? Will it be served with a salad? These details must be considered when setting the client's price.

I think all of us who have been in the catering business for a number of years have received, sometime during our career, a severe education in pricing an event. It is not good business to merely ask the questions, "Can I really afford to do that? Well, I want the job, am I willing to sacrifice?" That kind of reasoning does not pay the bills. You must always look at the financial structure of each event. A caterer should not do a job unless he can make money.

In addition, when bidding on a job against a caterer who offers lower quality work, always maintain a fair and reasonable price that includes the profit structure needed to successfully operate your business.

If you are ever bidding on an event, make sure you are comparing apples to apples, or oranges to oranges. If two or three caterers are bidding on the same event, make sure each is submitting a similar menu. When I bid on an event, I ask for specifics. Are we going to do a 14-ounce boneless New York strip steak with a one inch tail, graded USDA choice? What size baked potato are we using? Are we serving both butter and sour cream? If we are serving a tossed salad, what type of salad dressing are we using? The menu must be spelled out exactly so our quote is basically in the same ballpark with the other caterers. If I am purchasing higher quality ingredients than the other caterers, my costs might be higher, but at least we are pricing apples to apples and not apples to oranges.

Bill Jardine, Jardine's Farm Restaurant & Catering, Sarver, Pennsylvania

Each caterer establishes the selling price per event based on a per-person cost basis. To do this, the caterer must know exactly what the total costs for the event are including fixed costs, transportation costs, labor costs, and food costs.

Financial Goals

To attain the profit objectives set for the business, the caterer must set financial goals for each event. These goals may be different for each event, depending on the function. The caterer must understand the financial aspects of catering in order to make a profit.

SERVICE OR EQUIPMENT NOT COVERED IN "SELLING PRICE"

ITEM	TOTAL COST	PER PERSON COST
1. Table Top:		
(a) Special Linens and Napkins	$ _____	$ _____
(b) Centerpieces (candles, etc.)	$ _____	$ _____
(c) China, Flatware, Glassware	$ _____	$ _____
(d) Other	$ _____	$ _____
2. Tables, Chairs	$ _____	$ _____
3. Silver Trays, Chafing Dishes, etc.	$ _____	$ _____
4. Special Bar Equipment	$ _____	$ _____
5. Truck Rental	$ _____	$ _____
6. Miscellaneous Equipment	$ _____	$ _____
7. Facility Rental	$ _____	$ _____
8. Tent(s)	$ _____	$ _____
9. Cake(s), Pie(s), Cookie(s)	$ _____	$ _____
10. Truck Rental	$ _____	$ _____
11. Extra Personnel or Hours	$ _____	$ _____
(a) Server _____ hrs x $ _____* =	$ _____	$ _____
(b) Back-of-the-House _____ hrs x $ _____* =	$ _____	$ _____
(c) Truck Driver/Other Labor _____ hrs x $ _____ =	$ _____	$ _____
(d) Employee Meals _____ x RFC _____ =	$ _____	$ _____
12. Other _____	$ _____	$ _____
13. Allocated Fixed Cost Factor or Amount	$ _____	$ _____
Sub Total	$ _____	$ _____
14. Add ____ % of Sub Total for Admin. Cost	$ _____	$ _____
15. Bring forward Selling Price Per Person from the bottom of Figure 13.5.	$ _____	
Total Selling Price Per Person	$ _____	

*Present Amount

Figure 13.6 Worksheet to calculate service and equipment not covered in the "selling price".

We participated in an event called "The Taste of Honolulu." Many cities have these events to feature local cuisine. Attendees pay script and the idea is for the caterers and vendors to get their money back while featuring their signature foods.

Our booth was so popular that, by the end of the first day, we were nearly sold out of all our food. We prepared our food based on the promoter's forecast of what we would sell. After having spent the entire day working this event, we had to return to our facility, clean and sanitize everything, and begin production again. We produced one and one-half times more of what we had originally made because we sold it so quickly. We produced food almost the entire night to be ready for the next day. After working most of the night, we returned to the event with a four hour rest to start all over again.

I think the promoter had given us an accurate number as far as the number of people who came to the event. But the estimated number who would actually come to us and purchase our food was too low. There were actually three categories of vendors: those who did not have much of a line, those who had a long line because they were slow, and those who had a fairly long line but kept it moving. We were one of the vendors who had a constant line. We had so many workers that we were able to put the food out very quickly. In one respect, that was great. We were able to keep people moving through the line. But, in another respect, it was not so good because we sold all our food in the first day. When people see long lines, they often think, "Oh, that must be a good place because everyone is going there to eat." That might not necessarily be the case. It might really mean that it has slow service. Our booth had both good food and fast service. Unfortunately, that worked against us in one respect.

Henry Holthaus, Certified Executive Chef/Instructor, Culinary Institute of the Pacific, Honolulu, Hawaii

Once the caterer becomes established and builds a clientele who knows the menus are priced fairly, the customer will return as long as the caterer continues to exceed their needs and provide good food and service. It takes a caterer time to build a reputation based on honesty, integrity, and a sense of customer loyalty. This kind of positive reputation is built on a foundation of mutual trust. Customers know that they will not be excessively charged or underserved.

I had a first time event. Circumstances happened which were totally unforeseen. I was the prime vendor at a charitable event that lasted for a week. The organizers misjudged the amount of people they believed would be attending the event and, likewise, the amount of food that would be consumed. We lost a considerable amount of money because we purchased additional equipment to handle the event, thinking it would be a high-volume event. Our plan was to spread our costs over 3 years to make money on it. Well, in a week's time, I lost $10,000. This is a considerable amount of money for a caterer. You have to work a long time to make up that amount. These are the types of events that educate caterers very quickly. The ironic thing about this example was that about five years later, I was asking another caterer to describe some of his worst experiences. He started to tell me about this event they catered and lost "megabucks" on it. They lost between $8,000–$10,000 5 years after I had done the same event. He apparently went into the event with the same plans as I had. Maybe if we both had been a little smarter, we would have researched it much better, talked with the caterer who had done the previous job, or had a little communication with other caterers, and made a decision not to do it.

Bill Jardine, Jardine's Farm Restaurant & Catering, Sarver, Pennsylvania

Extraneous Factors

A caterer must also be aware that at times, based on extraneous factors, the anticipated profits do not materialize. If an event has experienced a financial loss, the caterer must very carefully study and analyze it. What are the factors or the circumstances that led to this failure? How can they be avoided in the future?

What if the caterer quotes a menu price to a client who is negotiating the contract nine months in advance? Say the client wants a steak dinner for a corporate picnic. If the caterer is researching the price of a boneless strip loin in October, remember that the market price can change. The caterer must base the cost of the future event on the market price of the boneless strip loin in October. What happens if, in July, the meat market experiences a change in price? Instantly, the expense of a boneless strip loin increases by $2 per pound above the quoted price. If the expense has increased by $2, how can the caterer protect himself?

Contract Protection

One technique used to protect the caterer against unexpected price changes in the market and unforeseen circumstances, when negotiating with a client at least 6 months in advance, is the use of a contract. It is common to include a statement in the contract to protect the caterer and the client against this kind of change. Something similar to the following statement can be included: This is an approximate price. The finalized price will be given (15 or 30) days before the event. The caterer can then be assured of receiving a fair market price for the services rendered. If the price suddenly decreases, then savings can be passed on to the customer as well. Giving the customer a savings on the original price will definitely communicate the caterer's dedication to building a solid reputation based on honesty, integrity, and a sense of loyalty built on mutual trust.

Underlying Causes of Lost Revenue

When executing a catering event, one should always be on the alert for hidden costs that may suddenly reveal themselves and severely dilute the anticipated profit objectives. A caterer's insurance costs or expense of labor may have increased. Sometimes the caterer may just misjudge, misquote, or unsuccessfully speculate on an event.

I owned a barbeque restaurant on the island of Oahu. I bid on a job to be the exclusive caterer for the Sandy Beach Pro Am Surf Tour. This five-day event was a surfing tournament held on the island of Oahu, in Hawaii. The promoters told me this event would attract at least 2,000 people each day for five days. Therefore, I based the bid on 10,000 people. I came out with an original number that I believed was very fair to begin with. I projected approximately $2 per person per day collected from each participant. I was going to be the exclusive caterer at the site. No other vendor was permitted to set up. I thought a soda was going to be at least 75 cents and most people would be drinking soda.

After the tournament, the revenue from catering this event was 50 cents per person total throughout the five days. It was partially because the attendees were kids who did not have much money and complained about the prices (even

(continued)

though I sold nothing for more than $3). Also, across the street from this event, outside of the jurisdiction of the promoters, were lunch wagons, taking some sales away from me. This is an example of a caterer losing revenue because of a promoter who exaggerated the number and type of people expected at an event. Caterers must research each event to understand who their market is going to be. If the market represents a clientele 25 years of age and younger, calculate a very high cost per person.

These outdoor types of catering events offer special challenges to the caterer. You usually have to leave all of your equipment at the site. In this illustration, we left everything out on the beach. We camped right there to guard the equipment. We had people attempting to steal our food during the night. We had a crew member stand guard throughout the night, then get up early the next morning, take a cold shower out on the beach, and start all over again. I was up with the sun at 5:30 A.M. and working until the event was over at 6:00 P.M. Then we would clean up, get everything together, feed the crew, and before I knew it, the time was 9:30 or 10:00 P.M.

Better research may have revealed some of the hidden costs incurred at this event, allowing me to provide a more accurate bid.

Henry Holthaus, Certified Executive Chef/Instructor, Culinary Institute of the Pacific, Honolulu, Hawaii

PROFESSIONAL SERVICE COMPANIES

The caterer needs to build a relationship with professional service companies such as photographers, florists, and rental companies. Professional service companies will return a set percentage of the client's cost to the caterer for just the referral. A caterer making a referral for a tent rental costing $4,000 may receive 10 percent to 15 percent. Commissions are a positive addition to the caterer's profit structure. If catering a wedding, negotiate with a cake baker for a percentage of each referral. Other service companies will include entertainment, a photographer, limousine service, or any of a number of services offered to a bride, including wedding gowns and tuxedos (Figure 13.7).

All of these incidentals add to the function's profit structure. These are great ways to earn additional revenue to complement the food and beverage service.

Depending on the purpose for renting a limousine, you may need the assistance of a caterer. For special events, such as a birthday, a wedding, travel, business meetings, or even a winery tour, the customer may request food to be provided. As the caterer, it is recommended to offer the client a simple menu providing delicious food due to the constraints of having limited storage space within the vehicle. One of the first constraints is the kind and type of storage space available inside the vehicle. This will determine if portable coolers or hot boxes are needed. Next, a guaranteed head count is required to know the amount of food to prepare for the event. The type and kind of food that could be served on a limousine ride are finger sandwiches, a fruit and vegetable platter, or cheese and cracker platters, especially if going on a wine tour. In addition to the food, the necessary utensils, plates, napkins, beverages, and other client special-need requests will need to be provided. Just like catering for a large event in a banquet hall, both time and planning goes into catering for a single limousine ride because the caterer still must exceed the customer's expectations when it comes to dining on the road.

Ben Cavallaro, Unique Limousine, Harrisburg, Pennsylvania

Unethical Purchasing Behavior

One of the most important catering management tasks is the purchasing function. The caterer strives to build a positive relationship based on mutual trust with the suppliers.

Mutual trust means the distributor sales representative (DSR) will satisfy the caterer's needs. The DSR may reward the caterer's loyalty by giving bottom line pricing on all products. It is important, however, to establish a primary and a secondary supplier, or a backup distributor to keep everyone honest. DSRs work on a commission and may get a little complacent. The caterer should always check distributor invoices for accurate pricing because a DSR may inflate prices to increase their commission.

Figure 13.7 Caterers build positive relationships with professional service companies such as Unique Limousine.

The caterer must use internal controls to protect the company's assets. A trusted, ethical, and intelligent member of the team must be responsible for the purchasing function. The buyer has been formally granted a significant amount of position power in the organization and can legally bind the organization with suppliers through contracts. Some buyers may have the ability to spend a significant amount of the organization's money. Imagine the operating budget of a large caterer for food, beverage, equipment, and supplies.

Controls are important to help prevent or eliminate the opportunity for unethical behavior. A buyer can enter into an illegal arrangement with a supplier. This is called collusion. A kickback occurs whenever the buyer receives money for an illegal activity. A supplier may agree to reward a buyer with a personal kickback each time the buyer uses the supplier. Maybe a rental company agrees to pay the caterer 15 percent of each rental contract referred by this caterer to the supplier. In this case, maybe the catering company receives 10 percent and the individual buyer gets 5 percent. Caterers should avoid this type of unethical behavior by hiring buyers who can be trusted and who work to protect the company's assets.

A company approached me after I had one of my employees terminated. The representative from a meat company informed me how this employee had planned to make a deal for the summer catering season. The representative informed me that the individual wanted to cut a deal where the buyer would guarantee all of Jardine's business for a couple of beef items in exchange for a personal kickback of 50 cents per pound. I was thoroughly disgusted with the distributor for coming to me after the fact. I asked why he did not approach me when the employee first suggested the deal. I told the distributor I did not think it was fair that he kept this knowledge to himself without informing me.

Although this practice was prevalent in the past, I do not think it is as common today because more distributors refuse to engage in that kind of dishonest practice. But there is always that one person, so each caterer must be vigilant by creating and enforcing good, internal control techniques.

Bill Jardine, Jardine's Farm Restaurant & Catering, Sarver, Pennsylvania

Code of Ethics

code of ethics A formal statement used to describe the caterer's philosophy regarding an employee's professional conduct and behavior.

Each caterer must write and live by a **code of ethics**, which is a formal statement written and communicated to each employee and each stakeholder. Stakeholders are the owner, employee, customer, supplier, competitor, and the community.

The purpose of the written code of ethics is to guide individual behavior. A written code of ethics will define acceptable behavior for everyone in an organization. Each person may have a different religious or philosophical view of everyday life, but a written code of ethics will help prevent any misunderstanding of professional conduct that may lead to personal gain. The caterer and the employee may be confronted each day with questions regarding their conduct and behavior. A written code of ethics may prevent harm done to others and help an employee to make the best behavioral decisions.

The code of ethics can be introduced during the recruitment and hiring stages. A written code of ethics may be integrated into every employee training program and should become part of each employee's job for it to work.

Just as a written code of ethics will guide individual conduct, it will also guide the entire organization. The caterer must communicate a standard of moral conduct. This standard will guide the entire organization in its decision-making process to accomplish its mission. The ethical standard will help to create an ethical environment.

Professional Associations

The "Tips from the Trade" in this text are situations that are experienced by real caterers. Because caterers often experience similar situations, memberships in professional organizations are recommended. Membership in a local catering organization, the National Association of Catering Executives, the National Restaurant Association, or the American Culinary Federation is important for networking with other professionals. They meet and discuss experiences: issues with clientele, problems they confront in their market, and creative solutions they have used to contribute to their success.

THE FINANCIAL COMPONENT

The crucial financial concern of every caterer involves making decisions to acquire and employ resources to maximize the efficient and effective administration of the operation. Every caterer must forecast his or her short-term and long-term financial needs. The acquisition of funds from external sources to finance these business activities is one task of financial management. Monitoring and controlling those funds as they flow through the catering operation is another.

The fundamental purpose of financial management is to maximize shareholder or owner wealth—that is, wealth being measured by the current market price of the firm's common stock, or value of the operation. The goal is to create a healthy balance between risk and profitability. This balance teeters between achieving an optimal return on the owner's investment while averting unwarranted risk.

Financial management is a key concern of every catering operation. Key financial management activities include raising capital, building relationships with the suppliers of this capital, establishing a credit policy and installing an accounting and budgeting system.

The primary financial responsibility of a caterer is to secure funds and to allocate those funds to selected purposes within the operation. Where can the funds be obtained? What mix of funding is the most advantageous for the caterer? How will the funds be repaid? These are some basic questions that must be addressed by a caterer.

The caterer can secure external funds from financial markets. Two segments of the financial market are the money market and the capital market. If the maturity of the financial instrument matures in less than one year, it represents the money market. If the maturity of the financial instrument is more than one year, it represents the capital market.

The caterer will need to obtain external funding to build inventories, purchase new equipment, pursue projects, engage in new product development (signature items), and to assist in the management of the cash flow cycle.

The caterer can secure external funding in the form of financial assets of cash, stock, and debt. This is accomplished through what is commonly referred to as *equity* or *debt financing*. Equity financing is accomplished by raising funds through the issuance of stock, retained earnings, or funds generated from depreciation. Debt financing is the use of a borrowed amount that is owed within a definite payment schedule and/or due date.

Stock refers to common stock or ownership in an organization. Retained earnings are the profits generated by the firm that are reinvested in the organization. Depreciation is the process of amortizing or allocating the cost of an asset to the accounting period in which it is used to generate earnings for the caterer. Depreciation is an expense that is deducted from the generated revenue during the accounting period. It is not a cash payout by the caterer to an external source, but rather it is placed back into the operation for internal use.

Debt represents a promise to pay a specified amount plus interest to a creditor at an agreed upon future date. Government securities, corporate issues, and international instruments are other financial instruments that can be used to raise funds. Cash is issued by the US Treasury as coins and paper currency.

Accounting Function

The role of the accounting function is to provide timely and accurate information enabling the caterer to make effective business decisions. The ability to analyze and interpret key financial reports is a technical skill of utmost importance. Effective business decisions made in a timely manner will better enable the caterer to improve the organization's financial position.

The purpose of an accounting system is to summarize and provide an accurate and complete report of all business transactions incurred by the caterer in the daily operation of the organization. This is accomplished using bookkeeping procedures. Bookkeeping leads to the function of an accountant. The function of an accountant is the evaluation and analysis of the data to create accurate and complete reports summarizing the business transactions.

These reports serve many different purposes. First, these financial reports are required by government agencies for tax reporting purposes. Second, these financial reports communicate the financial vitality of the operation to creditors and suppliers. If a caterer needs to obtain funding for a special project, or an advance of working capital to restart the business after a seasonal shutdown, the success of securing a short-term or long-term loan will be determined by these financial reports. If taking on a rather large function, the acquisition of food and supplies may necessitate a short-term loan or a line of credit from a bank to cover the initial cost. These reports provide the information a bank needs to approve a loan. Third, these financial reports are used to inform investors if and how the business has maximized their wealth, as measured by the current return on their investment or by the current value of the market share of common stock. Fourth, they provide an accurate and precise financial picture of the operation used by the caterer to make appropriate day-to-day operational business decisions and to enhance the success of the operation.

Accurate and complete reporting of all business transactions enables any owner to track the financial success of day-to-day business operations. Ownership of a catering operation may take one of the following basic forms: a sole proprietorship, partnership, or corporation. Depending on the form of ownership, the principal owners may not be actively involved in the day-to-day operational management decisions. The owner(s) or a board of directors may be established to represent the financial interests of the *silent owners*. This board will create a structure and delegate the day-to-day operation of the catering organization to a management team. While the management team will have the authority and responsibility to operate the catering firm, accurate and complete accounting reports will keep the absentee owners in touch. These reports will provide valuable information so the owners can assess the effectiveness and efficiency of the management team in accomplishing all financial and operational objectives.

Financial Statements

The two key financial reports prepared from the accounting system to summarize and provide an accurate and complete report of the caterer's operation are called the balance sheet and the income statement. The **balance sheet** is a financial picture of what the organization is worth on a specific date, at the end of the month, or at a specific time during the year. The **income statement** reveals how well the operation is performing financially over a specific period of time.

balance sheet The statement of financial position that shows the accounting equation: total assets = liabilities + owner's equity.

income statement The statement of revenues, expenses, gains, and losses for the accounting period.

Balance Sheet

The balance sheet is a picture of the financial condition of the business at a specific moment in time. The financial condition of a catering business will depend on:

1. amount of personal investment incurred by the owners.
2. the ability to obtain credit or borrowed capital.
3. the ability of the caterer to enter and compete in the market.
4. the location of the catering business and the local economic conditions.

Every balance sheet will have three main categories: the value of what the business owns (assets), how much the catering company owes its creditors (liabilities), and how much the caterer or owner is worth at a specific reference point in time (owner's equity). Owner's equity, or capital, is the amount of money or the investment made by the caterer to start the business.

Assets, liabilities, and owner's equity are listed by category according to their similarity. Assets include cash, accounts receivable, inventory, land, building, and equipment. Assets are further classified as either current assets or fixed assets. Current assets are cash, accounts receivable, inventory, and prepaid expenses. Assets are considered current when they can be consumed during a normal operating period, such as one fiscal year, although it can be any time period. One fiscal year is usually segmented by every three months, or quarter, of the year.

Current assets may be easily and quickly converted into cash. Accounts receivable represent accounts whose money will be collected in the near future. They are considered a current asset because a caterer can sell this account, called *factoring*, to a collection agency in return for cash. Inventory, or the raw materials a caterer uses to create a finished food item from a recipe, will be sold to a client in exchange for cash. Cash is then used to purchase the raw material to restock inventory. Prepaid expenses represent advanced payment made by a caterer for such needs as insurance premiums. Insurance coverage is needed during the current fiscal operating period or quarter.

Fixed assets are those that a caterer uses in the business over a longer period of time than one year. They are also called *plant assets*. These assets are used in the catering operation to produce food and assist in the delivery of service. Fixed assets include land, buildings, furniture, fixtures and equipment. Workstations designed with specific equipment, such as ovens, mixers, and slicers are considered fixed assets. These major fixed assets help the caterer to operate the business.

Caterers can increase the assets of the business by investing their own money into the business. Assets can be increased by securing a loan or receiving an extension of credit, such as when a purveyor delivers an order of food and extends the caterer fifteen days to pay the invoice. Loans can be secured from lending institutions or other investors, such as family members. Assets are increased when a caterer renders a service to a client in exchange for cash.

Liabilities and owner's equity form the *equities* side of a balance sheet. When the catering business receives cash, secures a loan, or an infusion of money from the caterer himself, these transactions increase the owner's equity. An owner can be either a sole proprietor, which means a single owner; a partnership, which means it is jointly owned by two or more individuals; incorporated, which basically means the catering business exists separately from its owners as granted by a charter issued by one of the 50 US states. The owner's equity in a corporation is called stockholders' equity.

Liabilities, like assets, are also classified by a time frame. Liabilities are either short or long term. Current liabilities are those that will be extinguished or paid during the normal operating period, usually one year. Current liabilities are usually incurred by a caterer securing current assets to be used in the execution of a catering event. If a caterer purchases food for an event having 1,500 guests, the cost of the food is classified as a current liability. It is expected that the caterer will pay the current liability or accounts payable from the revenue received from the client. Other current liabilities include utility bills, payroll taxes, and local property taxes.

Working capital is the excess of current assets minus current liabilities. Working capital is required for the caterer to execute the daily operations. Potential uses of working capital include:

1. purchasing and securing opening inventories.
2. paying for the startup costs at the beginning of a new catering season.
3. paying the caterer's first and last month's rent and utilities.
4. covering expenses during the time required for a new business to generate enough revenue to support full operation.

Long-term liabilities are those whose due date is longer than one year from the date of the balance sheet report. One such example is a mortgage incurred on the building, which may have a 30-year due date.

The balance sheet will help identify the assets and liabilities at a given time (Figure 13.8). The balance sheet is best understood by the following accounting formula:

$$\text{assets} - \text{liabilities} = \text{the amount of owner's equity}$$

This balance sheet formula must meet the standard rules of mathematics, where each of the items found positioned on either side of the equal sign must balance.

The standard accounting formula is the format for the operating layout of the balanced sheet:

$$\text{assets} = \text{liabilities} + \text{owner's equity}$$

Notice in Figure 13.9 how both sides of the equation balance. Review the accounting equation using the numbers from the balance sheet to see how the equation balances. The balance sheet reveals valuable information about assets and equity (Figure 13.10).

Income Statement

The income statement (Figure 13.11) is a financial report that reveals how well a company is performing financially during a specific period of time. It summarizes the inward flow of operating revenue (sales) against the outward or potential flow of costs and expenses.

The format of an income statement will vary depending on the needs of the caterer. The basic formula of the income statement is the same:

$$\text{operating revenue} - \text{operating expenses} = \text{net income or loss}$$

Operating revenues, or net sales, result from a caterer receiving payment from a client for food and service provided. A caterer will incur expenses in the execution of a catering event that are usually grouped by similarity. *Cost of goods sold* represents the expense of the actual food and beverages used by a caterer to serve a client. Subtracting the operating revenue (generated from the sale of goods and their cost) from the net sales gives a *gross margin*. Operating expenses are those costs incurred by a caterer to operate the business. Controlled operating expenses are those directly influenced by the caterer. These include wages and salaries. Direct operating expenses are those expenses that are incurred by servicing the client. These may include laundry, napery, glassware, china, silverware, and licenses.

THE CATERING COMPANY (NAME OF COMPANY)
BALANCE SHEET (TITLE OF REPORT)
DECEMBER 31, 2014 (DATE OR PERIOD OF REPORT)

ASSETS

Current Assets

Cash	$ 13,000
Accounts Receivable	1,000
Inventory	2,000
Prepaid Expenses	1,000
Total Current Assets	17,000

Fixed Assets

Land	10,000
Building	25,000
Less: Accumulated Depreciation*	25,000
Total Fixed Assets	30,000

TOTAL ASSETS	**$47,000**

LIABILITIES AND CAPITAL

Liabilities

Current Liabilities	
Accounts Payable	3,000
Notes Payable	2,000
Accrued Liabilities	1,000
Total Current Liabilities	6,000
Long-Term Liabilities	10,000
Total Liabilities	16,000

Capital

Billy Caterer	31,000
TOTAL LIABILITIES AND CAPITAL	**$ 47,000**

*Depreciation expense is the cost of the normal, physical wear and tear of a fixed asset over its limited and useful life. This cost is allocated to the various fiscal periods as depreciation expense.

Figure 13.8 The balance sheet identifies the caterer's assets and liabilities at a given time.

ACCOUNTING EQUATION

Assets	minus	Liabilities	equals	Owner's equity
$47,000	−	$ 16,000	=	$31,000

Figure 13.9 Both sides of an accounting equation must be equal or "balanced".

INFORMATION DERIVED FROM A BALANCE SHEET

On the asset side, a balance sheet will reveal the:

- amount of operating cash.
- amount of cash tied up in food inventory.
- investment in land and building.
- cash for any down payment on land and building.
- cost of furniture, fixtures, equipment, and utensils.
- cost of parking lots, driveways, lighting, and other improvements to the property.

The equities side of the balance sheet will show the:

- necessary short-term funds that must be borrowed.
- amount of payables.
- amount of long-term mortgages on building and land.
- type of business ownership—a proprietorship, partnership, or corporation.

© Cengage Learning 2014

Figure 13.10 The balance sheet reveals valuable information regarding assets and equity.

THE CATERING COMPANY (NAME OF COMPANY)
INCOME STATEMENT (TITLE OF REPORT)
FIGURE SKATING BANQUET (EVENT)
APRIL 30, 2014 (DATE OR PERIOD OF REPORT)

Revenue (net sales)*	Dollars	Percentage	
Food	$ 2,000	66.67	$2,000/3,000
Beverage	1,000	33.33	$1,000/3,000
Total Revenue	$ 3,000	100.0	
Cost of Goods Sold			
Food	$399	19.95	$ 399/2,000
Beverage	150	15.0	$ 150/1,000
Total Cost of Goods Sold	$ 1,140	38.0	$1,140/3,000
Gross Margin	$ 1,860	62.0	$1,860/3,000
Controllable Operating Expenses			
Payroll	$1050	35.0	$ 1050/3,000
Direct Operating Expenses	300	10.0	$ 300/3,000
Total Operating Expenses	$ 1350	45.0	$ 1350/3,000
Rent and Other Occupation Costs	$ 300	10.0	$ 300/3,000
Net Income	$ 210	7.0	$ 210/3,000

*Revenue or net sales in this example are generated by charging 200 guests $10.00 each for food and $5.00 each for beverages.

© Cengage Learning 2014

Figure 13.11 Sample income statements are available for both public and competitive review analysis.

One very useful method for interpreting the income statement is to have each item listed by category, calculated as a percentage of sales. It is much easier to evaluate the financial status of the business by using percentages. A raw number by itself is meaningless. Figure 13.11 shows that the food cost for the Figure Skating Banquet is 19.95 percent. Is this a good percentage? Is it a bad percentage? How can it be interpreted?

The real value of a financial statement is the information derived from it by the caterer. Using percentages, a caterer can compare different events and time periods, as well as their own expenses against different caterers. Comparisons can also be made against industry standards. Financial organizations annually survey caterers to ascertain information regarding their operations and publish this information for public review. A caterer may compare their financial picture against these industry-average ratios.

A caterer must formulate a financial plan based on the mission statement that best suits their needs. The plan will guide the caterer in establishing the necessary financial objectives to meet financial and strategic goals.

The caterer must determine the cost of food and beverages used in the execution of each catering event. This is easily accomplished by keeping careful records of what items were actually consumed. It is necessary to take a physical inventory of every item stored in the business during the regular accounting period.

Summary

This chapter discussed controlling, the sixth catering management function. Catering managers establish control techniques to protect the financial interests of the organization. Comprehensive control techniques are implemented by an astute caterer who knows that the most effective way to earn a profit is to first understand how and why a catering business may lose money. If a caterer understands how money may be drained from the organization, effective controls can be used to tighten operations.

This sixth catering management function must be an integral component of the whole organizational plan. The objective of building control techniques is for the survival of the business and attainment of the organization's mission. This includes a detailed strategy of how the control techniques will be implemented into each event plan. Caterers create control techniques using financial tools and predetermined standards. Whether formulating or implementing the event plan, executing the operational tasks, or organizing resources, the ability to integrate fundamental catering management controls ensures the capability of comparing actual performance against planned objectives.

The elements of a plan of control will include the acquisition of timely and relevant information, securing an uninterrupted flow of cash, defining a formal payment policy, establishment of financial goals and predetermined profit objectives, and the knowledge that control functions are the easiest task for many caterers to neglect.

Review Questions

Brief Answers

1. Explain what *controlling* means to a caterer.
2. Describe why controlling the organization's resources is an important catering management task.
3. Explain why each catering function will require elements of managerial control.
4. Describe the process of control.
5. Explain why the caterer must develop and implement both internal and external control features into the catering management system.
6. Explain why the easiest task for most caterers to neglect, without an immediate penalty, is the control function.
7. Explain why elements of control begin when the caterer designs specific internal techniques to direct an employee's behavior in accomplishing predetermined objectives.
8. Explain why controlling has multiple meanings and serves multiple purposes.
9. Explain why a caterer needs timely and relevant information to make good business decisions.
10. Explain why a caterer must be concerned with protecting the uninterrupted flow of cash into the organization.
11. Define the formal payment policy and list several advantages.
12. Describe how a caterer arrives at a final price to charge the client for an event.
13. Explain the relationship between financial goals and predetermined profit objectives.
14. Explain why if an event has experienced a financial loss, the caterer must very carefully study and review the circumstances which contributed to this failure.
15. Explain how a caterer can protect himself against unexpected price changes in the market.
16. Explain why it is important for a caterer to always be on the alert for hidden costs.
17. Explain how the caterer might misjudge, misquote, or inaccurately speculate on an event.
18. Explain why the caterer must implement internal controls to protect the company's assets.
19. Describe three creative ways for the caterer to earn additional revenue other than from the traditional sale of food and beverages.
20. Describe how membership in an appropriate organization or association benefits a caterer.
21. Explain the Ingredient for Success and what it means to you.

Multiple Choice

Select the single best answer for each question.

1. The cost per catering event will vary depending on:
   a. menu
   b. type of service
   c. customer being served
   d. style of service
   e. all of the above

2. In today's market, _____ protects the caterer against clients defaulting on their obligation to pay their bills.
   a. budget control
   b. appropriate information
   c. structured payment policy
   d. membership in associations
   e. reputation

3. Which of the following best describes *controlling*?
   a. Controlling means to establish standard operating procedures to ensure an employee's proper execution of daily tasks while consuming an appropriate amount of time.
   b. Controlling means the establishment of predetermined objectives derived from the mission of the organization.
   c. Controlling is a process used to regulate and integrate each independent catering management function into an achievable event plan.
   d. Controlling refers to the efficient utilization of the caterer's assets to produce a need-satisfying product at a predetermined, profitable price.
   e. All of the above.

True or False

Read each of the following statements and determine if it is true or false.

1. Food and labor costs are usually bundled and are called prime costs.
2. The creation and implementation of control techniques by the use of financial tools and predetermined standards are the heart of this sixth catering management function.
3. Elements of control are completed when the caterer designs specific internal techniques to direct an employee's behavior in accomplishing predetermined objectives.

Putting It All Together

You are the owner of the Allegheny Catering Company, located on the beautiful Allegheny Mountain Range, near the Allegheny River, nestled in the Allegheny National Forest in northwestern Pennsylvania. Your market niche services a corporate clientele who seek year-round outdoor adventure activities such as hunting, horseback riding, and hiking in the forest. Other activities include fishing and boating on the streams near the Allegheny National Forest.

The Allegheny Catering Company has been contacted by Slugger Chemical International Distribution (SCID) to cater an event for 25 company personnel. These guests will be attending an adventure-theme management training program that will last 4 days and include adventure-based theme training.

On the evening of the fifth day, a graduation ceremony will be held for the 25 participants. The location of the graduation ceremony and catering site is a plateau off a mountainous trail 2 miles inside the Allegheny National Forest. The only available natural resource at your disposal is potable spring water. Everything else must be brought to the site by either horseback or all-terrain vehicles.

Your task is to formulate a functional HACCP plan to serve each of the 25 people the following menu:

a fresh garden salad with choice of three dressings
one – 1/2 barbeque chicken
one – 6-ounce New York Strip steak
one – 60-count baked potato
one – 4-inch ear of sweet corn on the cob
a sundae ice cream bar offering a minimum of three toppings
a selection of at least four beverages—two nonalcoholic

All food must be prepared at the site. Food will be served at 12:00 P.M. on a Saturday in October. The event is being held in the autumn to take advantage of the colorful leaves prevalent during this time of the year. Good luck!

Chapter 14

Understanding Risk Management, Insurance, and Legal Issues

Courtesy of Stephen B. Shiring, Jr.

Objectives

After studying this chapter, you should be able to:

1. Describe why insurance and legal concerns are important to the caterer.
2. Explain intrinsic and extrinsic rewards.
3. Explain why the caterer must develop and implement the right insurance and legal program.
4. Explain how a caterer can avoid, transfer, or reduce risk.
5. Explain the purpose of a crisis management team.
6. Explain the purpose of a safety management team.
7. Explain why a caterer needs to conduct frequent safety surveys.
8. Explain the basic insurance coverage for property, liability, and workers compensation.
9. Explain personal and advertising coverage, fire damage liability, medical expense coverage, and automobile coverage.
10. Explain why a caterer must create a contract that covers the basics.

Ingredients For Success

41 "The creation and maintenance of the right insurance and legal package, based on the mission of the organization, will protect the caterer against any unpredictable crisis."

KEY TERMS

automobile insurance

avoid risk

banquet event order (BEO)

contract

crisis management team

employment practice liability

engager

extrinsic rewards

fire damage liability

informed consumer

insurance program

Insurance Services Office (ISO)

intrinsic rewards

liability insurance

medical expense coverage

personal and advertising injury liability

producers

property insurance

reduce risk

risk management

safety management team

throw-ins

transfer risk

There are definitely more challenges to managing a catering operation than the visible, concrete tasks of preparing food, serving the guests, and exceeding the visible and covert needs of the client. The ownership and management of a catering business will challenge and continuously test the caterer. Each subsequent success will create the feeling of great accomplishment and reward. Successful caterers experience a plethora of intrinsic and extrinsic rewards.

REWARDS

intrinsic rewards The internal satisfaction or feelings of achievement a caterer experiences as a result of executing a successful catering event.

extrinsic rewards The tangible rewards gained from executing a successful catering event, such as earning a competitive salary.

Intrinsic rewards are those that the caterer experiences as a result of the successful implementation and execution of an event. A powerful feeling of achievement is created when the client, guests, and everyone involved *demand* to see the caterer and sing praise of how the Herculean tasks had just been accomplished. The positive reputation of a caterer is an intrinsic reward.

Extrinsic rewards are those that the caterer experiences outside of the event itself. The financial reward of executing a catering event is one example. When the event has been properly managed, a caterer can earn a comfortable salary and employ a staff which benefits the local community.

To protect the caterer's intrinsic and extrinsic rewards of a successful business, catering management decisions regarding insurance and legal issues must be made. *Ingredient for Success 41* states: ***"The creation and maintenance of the right insurance and legal package, based on the mission of the organization, will protect the caterer against any unpredictable crisis."*** Some basic information will be provided to assist the caterer in choosing the right risk management and insurance program for the organization and its mission.

RISK MANAGEMENT

risk management A complete analysis of the potential causes of loss inherent in a caterer's business and the appropriate defense to provide protection or to avoid, reduce, or transfer the risk.

Any business is a risky venture and catering is no different. Some of the daily risks a caterer confronts are obvious, while others are very subtle and may go unforeseen until it is too late. Some events can literally cripple and destroy a catering business. Suppose, for example, a caterer purchased and installed new deck convection ovens. Installed by the manufacturer, the lower-oven malfunctioned during the first week of its operation. Both ovens were destroyed and the entire building was seriously threatened. In this specific case, the manufacturer paid for all damages and replaced the ovens.

Here is another tragic scenario: A fire roars throughout the night, destroying much of the caterer's building, equipment, and inventory. These assets, having been the accumulation of one's life work, vanish in the night. Compound this scenario with the addition of a wedding scheduled for the next day. Consider the potential loss in terms of a caterer's assets, staff, reputation, as well as the client's decorations and belongings, placed in the building.

What can a caterer do, especially if the building, equipment, inventory, and other assets were destroyed? Imagine the enormity of the crisis as the potential profit and future earnings based on upcoming guaranteed events have suddenly disappeared. **Risk management** is the task of identifying these potential hazards and creating a safety and health program to prevent their occurrence.

SAFETY AND HEALTH FOR THE CATERING PROFESSION

Accident prevention for employees in the catering industry is not dissimilar from other professions. Many hazards associated with food preparation and serving are common to other industries and professions. Working with sharp objects, as well as the potential for burns and skin dermatitis, are common problems among professions in the food and beverage industry, as well as many others in hospitality. Slips, trips, and falls are the cause of many accidents at work, and they are certainly a concern for those in the catering industry. Finally, since catering typically involves delivering products to event locations external to the normal work environment, employees in the catering industry are exposed to hazards associated with driving vehicles, sometimes larger delivery trucks, on the highway. What makes safety and health in the catering industry unique and challenging is the wide and diverse variety of hazards and potential causes of accidents and injury. During the course of their work, catering employees can be exposed to these and many other potential hazards. In addition, perhaps one of the more difficult aspects of workplace safety in catering is the fact that the caterer often works in a different and unpredictable environment every day. Finally, the caterer must be cognizant of the risks of fires, water damage, or liability as a result of their employee's actions. It has been compared to being a ringmaster of a traveling circus, which while exhilarating, can also be fraught with risk and potential for tragedy.

This section is not likely to provide an exhaustive accident prevention program for those in the catering industry. It is assumed that the one entering the profession, particularly if it is larger than a one-person operation, will have, through experience and training, a general understanding of the safety hazards and conditions that can be encountered when catering. Also, people in the profession would be wise to take the basic information here and spend some time conducting additional research to more comprehensively protect themselves and their employees on the job. However, it will provide a basic understanding of the multitude of issues facing anyone in catering, and will provide a foundation for ensuring the safety of those working in the field.

Safety and Health Program

Regardless of the industry or profession, providing for employee safety and health at work requires management commitment. Just as management is responsible for providing the tools and equipment for the job, for training employees in their work tasks, for complying with employment laws, and for compensating them, they are responsible for providing a work environment that is free of safety hazards. The Occupational Safety and Health Act of 1970 requires employers to furnish employees employment and a place of employment which are free from recognized hazards that are causing or are likely to cause death or serious physical harm to the employees. This general duty clause, as it is called, applies to all employers, regardless of size and industry. In addition to the federal OSHA act, many states have their own safety requirements, in addition to laws regarding compensating employees injured on the job.

Complying with these laws requires management to identify hazards in the workplace, to develop safeguards to prevent or to minimize them, and to train their employees in how to perform their jobs safely. The Occupational Safety and Health Administration (OSHA) identifies five elements of an effective safety and health program. They are management leadership and employee participation, workplace analysis, hazard prevention and control, safety and health training and education, and program evaluation. These elements are essential for effective safety and health in all workplaces, but are critical for a small and diverse business like catering.

Management leadership is demonstrated in a number of ways. One is by communicating safety formally through a safety and health policy, and informally through day-to-day interaction with employees. Particularly in a small business like catering, management is often working side-by-side with employees. Setting an example by following all safety rules, pointing out safety hazards, and listening to employee concerns is an excellent way to set an example for safety. Providing training, particularly for new employees in how to perform their jobs safely, is another responsibility that demonstrates effective management leadership.

One of the key aspects of management leadership is actively identifying potential hazards in the workplace. This is difficult enough in a static, controlled work environment. Once identified, they can be either eliminated or controlled. Dynamic work environments like those encountered in the catering business provide additional challenges. Hence training employees in how to recognize and control hazards is particularly important in the catering industry. Hazards in catering can be categorized by those that occur in food preparation, those that are a concern while transporting and setting up at the catered location, and those that need to be prepared for and mitigated at the location.

Hazards

Sharp Objects. Knives and other sharp utensils are a common cause of injuries in the food preparation business. Injuries range from relatively minor cuts to the loss of fingers. Beyond ensuring that they are sharp and are the proper tool for the job, injury prevention is primarily attained by using proper handling guidelines and exercising caution. A cutting board or other flat surface should always be used when cutting with a knife. Food preparers should never hold objects in the palm of their hand when cutting or slicing. Knives should be held securely with the strongest hand and fingers curled over the object to be cut when slicing (Figure 14.1). When deboning, cutting or trimming, users should cut away from their body. Following these general principles should prevent common cuts and punctures when preparing food.

Machinery and Equipment. The use of slicers, mixers, food processors, and other mechanical equipment can pose a number of hazards. Equipment must be inspected before each use to ensure that guards are in place to protect against cuts, burns, or injuries from moving objects (Figure 14.2). Electrical equipment can pose shock hazards, particularly in

Figure 14.1 Proper cutting techniques prevent serious injury.

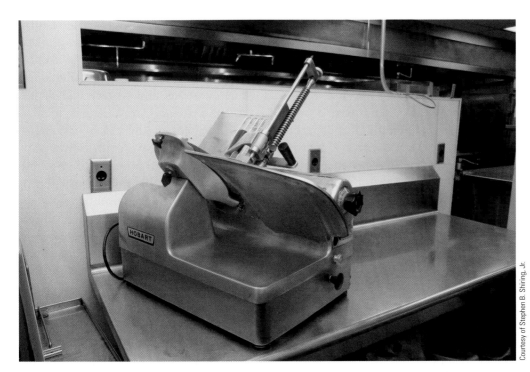

Courtesy of Stephen B. Shiring, Jr.

Figure 14.2 Always inspect the equipment prior to its use to ensure guards are in place to prevent injury.

the wet environment of a kitchen. It should be inspected before each use for frayed cords, exposed wiring, damaged or cracked cases, or defective plugs. In addition, outlets in food preparation areas must be installed with an effective ground and ground fault circuit interruption (GFCI) protection. Grounded outlets must be used to provide a path to ground when using grounded equipment. However, in addition to a proper ground, electrical equipment used in wet areas must have GFCIs. A GFCI detects whenever electrical current is unbalanced in an electrical device and opens the breaker to prevent electric shock.

When cleaning electrical equipment, it must be shut down and disconnected from the electrical source. To prevent accidental startup, hardwired equipment without a detachable plug must be shut down, the circuit breaker opened or fuse removed, and a lockout/tagout device attached.

Slips, Trips, and Falls. Slip, trips, and falls are a common cause of injuries in all work environments. They are frequently caused by unsafe conditions in the workplace, such as wet or slippery surfaces, tripping hazards, or unguarded holes and floor openings. Work areas should be inspected each day before beginning work. Liquid or grease spills should be cleaned up immediately. Until they can be cleaned, warning signs should be posted so that workers can exercise caution. Nonslip mats can be used in areas that are prone to slippery surfaces. General litter and clutter should be cleaned up throughout the day to avoid tripping hazards and to maintain a clean work area. Stairs are a frequent cause of falls and should be inspected regularly for hazards. Particularly in work establishments, materials may be left on stairs, steps can be uneven or in poor condition, handrails can be missing or insufficient for the stairway, and lighting insufficient. These areas should be inspected frequently for these hazards and employees should be reminded when carrying objects or materials on stairs to keep their view unobstructed and hold railings. Falls from a different level frequently occur when using ladders or step stools to access storage shelves, cabinets, and other areas on a different level. When used they should be inspected regularly to ensure that they have slip resistant bases, are not damaged or defective, and are the proper size and rating for the job. Employees must also be trained in the proper use of ladders on the job. Resources are readily available for free or little charge from ladder vendors, trade associations, and sources such as the National Safety Council (http://www.NSC.org).

Mechanical Equipment. Food preparation often involves the use of mechanical equipment such as mixers, slicers, food processors, and so forth. Setting up, conducting and taking down equipment at events may require the use of portable power equipment as well. Employees working in catering should follow basic safety guidelines to ensure their safety when working with or around mechanical equipment. As always, equipment should be checked regularly to ensure guards are in place and it is in overall good condition. (Please see section on electrical equipment for electrical safety precautions.) Many accidents occur from guards being removed or not used, exposing hands and fingers to moving parts and blades. Manufacturer's instructions should be reviewed for safe and proper use.

Hot Surfaces and Liquids. The potential for burns is an ever present hazard in food preparation that is compounded for caterers by the need to provide heat sources at events and locations where food is served. As always, the first precaution is to ensure that equipment such as pots and pans, deep fryers, portable heaters, sterno heaters, and so forth are in proper condition. Basic precautions should then be followed such as using the proper oven mitts when handling hot objects, ensuring handles on pots and pans do not protrude from counters or stoves, and using caution when lifting lids by opening them away from the body to allow steam to escape. Hot oil can pose a particularly dangerous burn hazard, so care should be taken to dry food items and lower them and utensils slowly into hot oil. There is a potential for burns to servers and patrons as well from portable heating devices or transporting and transferring hot food in serving trays during events. Tables used to support buffet tables must be stable and secure, particularly when used on uneven surfaces outdoors. Linens used on tables should be secured, particularly at outdoor events with the potential for wind, to ensure they do not come in contact with portable heating devices.

Chemicals. Burns or irritation to the skin and eyes or long-term disease from chemical exposure are a common hazard in nearly all jobs, and catering is no exception. Chemicals used in food preparation, and in particularly cleaning and sanitation, must be used, stored, and disposed of properly. Chemical safety starts with ensuring that users have the necessary information to use them properly. Every chemical used in the workplace must have a material safety data sheet (MSDS) available for reference (Figure 14.3). The MSDS is prepared by the chemical manufacturer and must contain information such as chemical ingredients, potential hazards, required personal protective equipment, proper storage, and what to do in an emergency. In an effective safety and health program, MSDSs are maintained for all chemicals and employees receive training in how to safely use them. A good resource for chemical safety is the OSHA website (http://www.osha.gov). Some chemicals require the use of

Courtesy of Stephen B. Shiring, Jr.

Figure 14.3 Material safety data sheets (MSDSs) are a must to ensure an effective and safe work environment.

latex gloves for personal protective equipment, and these are also often used to ensure sanitary conditions in food preparation and serving. Caterers should be aware, however, that some individuals have or can develop allergic reactions to latex and natural rubber. While some substitute materials are available, in food preparation and service practicing good sanitation and hygiene should eliminate or minimize the use of latex gloves.

Overexertion and Muscular Skeletal Hazards. All workers are exposed to hazards to the musculoskeletal system on the job. Anyone who is lifting, carrying, and moving objects has the potential for strain, sprain, and overexertion. Because of the often unpredictable nature of their work and work environment, caterers need to pay particular attention to these exposures. Therefore, the best way to avoid this type of injury is to train all employees in proper lifting techniques, including recognizing their safe lifting limits when lifting and carrying. Heavy objects in kitchens should be stored at lower levels, whereas smaller items that are used regularly should be stored between waist and chest level to avoid unnecessary bending and lifting. Periodic inspections should be made in these areas to ensure that lifting and overexertion hazards are minimized. However, this is more difficult to do for work outside the food preparation area(s). Pay attention to how food and equipment is delivered and set up at event sites. It can be very difficult to use good lifting and carrying techniques such as bending over knees and avoiding twisting when loading and unloading vans and delivery trucks. Employees should be provided with dollies and hand trucks to minimize hazards in these areas.

Ergonomics is ensuring that equipment and processes used on the job do not exceed the physical limitations of employees. When they do, such as using equipment or utensils that require repeated operations or excessive strain, it can lead to cumulative trauma injuries such as carpal tunnel syndrome, elbow tendonitis, or shoulder strain. Employers in the catering industry should inspect their workplaces and employees to identify equipment and methods that could lead to these injuries. Ways to mitigate them may include such things as process redesign to minimize strain, equipment substitution, or job rotation. Often a solution can be as simple as not doing repetitive activities during food preparation all at one time, but rather taking a break to perform some other necessary task, and then return to complete the cutting or chopping. Tasks that require prolonged standing can strain the knees, back, and shoulders. Discomfort and injury can be minimized in stationary locations with the use of shock-absorbing rubber mats to reduce shock to the bones and joints. Good shoes that provide support and comfort are one of the most important pieces of equipment to the caterer, in particular when working long days at events.

Electrical Hazards. Although electrical hazards in kitchen and food preparation areas have already been addressed, of equal or greater concern to the caterer is avoiding these hazards in the often unpredictable environment they encounter at events. Before arriving at the event, possibly when first meeting with the client to prepare the bid, the caterer should inspect the location to determine that it has adequate electrical service available. Particularly if using portable electric equipment, lighting, or sound systems, it is essential to determine that the electric service has the proper amperage and circuits. Beyond the potential for injury to employees or patrons, the caterer doesn't want to deal with circuits continually tripping because they are inadequate for their needs. In the pre-event inspection, the caterer should also plan the layout of extension cords to ensure they are of adequate length and can provide power to all devices used. Do not forget to consider the potential tripping hazards extension cords pose. When necessary in traffic areas they must be taped down where possible, and at outdoor events, clearly marked. Sometimes they can be rerouted in a different direction so it is advisable to have extra long cords. Finally, when using electrical equipment in outside wet areas, a ground fault circuit interrupter (GFCI) must be used. As noted earlier, a GFCI detects unbalanced electrical current in an electrical device and opens the breaker to prevent electric shock. Portable GFCIs can be used to attach to extension cords outside if outlets used to supply power at an event are not equipped with them.

Motor Vehicle Accidents. According to OSHA, motor vehicle accidents are the number one cause of death at work, so any business that requires their employees to drive during the performance of their job duties needs to have a safe driving program. It starts with ensuring that motor vehicles are in a safe operable condition. Particularly if deliveries involve large trucks, equipment needs to be inspected to ensure that brakes and tires are in good condition, all lights are operable, and mirrors are adjusted to minimize blind spots, particularly when backing. All items in the vehicle need to be carefully secured to prevent movement during transport, including items in the occupant compartment.

However, even when operating safe equipment, the majority of motor vehicle accidents are caused by driver's actions, so a critical element of a catering safety program is an effective drivers safety training program. It is recommended that the caterer use resources such as those available from the National Safety Council, National Highway Safety Council, or other vendors that provide training programs. However, the following driver's safety tips are a good start:

- Always follow posted speed limits, including when driving in urban and residential areas where the caterer may be delivering to an event.

- Allow a safe distance between you and vehicles ahead, at least one vehicle length miles per hour travel speed and two to three when driving a large vehicle.

- Never operate a vehicle while under the influence of drugs or alcohol. The risks of operating a motor vehicle while under the influence of alcohol or illegal drugs are well known. However, studies have found that driver safety can also be significantly influenced by the use of both prescription drugs and over-the-counter medications such as those for treating cold and allergies. Driving can also be impaired when operators are extremely tired. This could be a particular problem for the caterer when working events late at night or using part-time employees who may be working other jobs. Caterers should pay close attention to their employees to ensure they appear capable of performing their jobs, particularly when it involves driving.

- Practice defensive driving at all times, scanning 3–5 seconds ahead to observe conditions and environments that pose the potential for an accident. Particular attention should be paid when approaching intersections. Drivers should watch traffic lights and be prepared to stop if they turn yellow. Far too often accidents occur when a driver speeds up to get through the intersection before the light changes red. A few minute delay while waiting at a red light is nothing compared to the potential for injury and damage from an accident, not to mention the financial impact from product loss and failure to provide the service at a catering event!

- Finally, drivers should minimize distractions while driving. This includes obvious distractions such as texting or talking on a cell phone while driving. If it is necessary for the driver to communicate over a cell phone, they should use a hands-free device and avoid talking in congested or high traffic areas. However, GPS units, radios, eating, or drinking, and even passengers can cause a distraction so the driver should exercise caution and recognize that full attention needs to be focused on the difficult task of driving.

It is a good practice for the caterer to ride along with employees occasionally to observe their driving practices. Sometimes drivers do not realize that they are engaging in unsafe driving practices and a simple suggestion or reminder about these and other safe driving habits can go a long way toward preventing a serious motor vehicle accident.

Infectious Diseases. Health care settings carry the greatest risk for exposure to infectious diseases, including bloodborne pathogens such as HIV and Hepatitis B and C viruses. However, this risk should be addressed in all workplaces, particularly in an industry like catering, with its exposure to the general public, the use of knives and cutting utensils, and the handling of food. Bloodborne pathogens are spread by direct contact with infected blood, so the best prevention is to avoid accidents in the workplace that cause this exposure. An effective safety and health program that addresses hazards with the potential for cuts and punctures will limit exposure. However, if they do occur, it is important to have an exposure control developed and communicated to all employees so that the risk of spreading disease is limited. In these events, minimizing exposure starts with having proper first aid equipment available and training employees in its proper use. Universal precautions must be followed, including wearing protective latex gloves to treat injuries involving blood or other potentially infectious diseases, proper disposal of bandages and other exposed material, and good sanitation and hygiene in cleanup.

There are other infectious diseases that, while less deadly than bloodborne viruses, should be addressed in the safety and health program. Airborne diseases such as influenza can be present anywhere but their spread can be limited by taking precautionary measures. A proper hand washing procedure should be paramount in the food preparation business, and it is also the simplest and most effective way to minimize the spread of infectious diseases. Good sanitation practices, particularly involving serving utensils used by the public, is also essential. Another simple method to reduce exposure is to cough or sneeze into the hands, and once again wash hands frequently. Finally, getting influenza vaccinations is highly recommended. Since there is benefit to society from this practice, vaccines are readily available from a number of sources at relatively low cost. The caterer may find it to be a wise investment to pay for the cost of the vaccination if it minimizes the likelihood of key employees not being available for an important event due to illness.

Workplace Violence. Workplace violence can be categorized into four types: situational, occupational, occupational/personal, and personal/occupational. The situational category includes random violence by strangers against employees that occurs as a result of the nature of their work, such as driving a taxi or working late in a retail establishment. Occupational workplace violence involves verbal, physical threats, or behavior against employees by customers or clients, common among occupations such as bus drivers, hospital staff, or social workers. The last two categories occur when personal conflicts occur at work (occupational/personal) such as between coworkers or supervisors and subordinates, or (personal/ occupational) when someone an employee has a personal relationship with confronts them at work. While no workplace is immune from conflict, some occupations have increased risk for workplace violence due to the nature of work. Employees working at events in the catering industry may be exposed to situational and occupational workplace violence, so several safety and security practices should be taken into consideration. Working late at night in unknown areas carries the risk for random situational violence. Vans and delivery trucks should be parked in well-lit areas and kept locked when unattended. If possible, doors at event locations should be locked after the event during tear down and cleanup. For events taking place in areas that are more prone to criminal activity, the caterer should consider having at least two people traveling together at all times. While catering employees have less exposure to the general public or situations that could result in violence than many other occupations, the nature of their work can put them in environments where conflict with customers and event attendees can occur, so they should be prepared for it. This can be of particular concern when working at events where alcohol is present and consumed at a considerable rate, such as weddings, class reunions, and so forth. Recognizing conflict before it escalates and using proven techniques to minimize it are paramount to preventing violence at work. Refer to Chapter 16, Conflict Resolution, in this text for specific conflict resolution techniques. The best prevention for workplace violence from relationships at or away from work is for the caterer to know their employees and intervene when necessary before conflict erupts in violence. Whether it is a disagreement between several employees or an employee who is in a disruptive relationship away from work, it is important to recognize and deal with it early on. Conflicts between catering personnel can be dealt with and resolved internally while those occurring away from work may require referrals to agencies or social services that offer these services to employees.

Unpredictable Work Environments. A number of hazards have already been addressed that are related to the fact that the caterer is often working in unpredictable and difficult-to-control environments. The caterer may be using another facility's equipment and activities taking place at the event can make planning for safety difficult. The best way to ensure a successful event without accident or injury is to include safety and health in the event planning. When the caterer talks to the client and visits facilities to consider table locations and flow, spotting and preparing for hazards should be a part of that activity. It can be as simple as determining where extension cords will be placed to identifying electrical service requirements for equipment. Planning for emergencies such as fires should include locating fire extinguishers and identifying emergency exits (Figure 14.4). Generally, a good catering plan will account for the unexpected and have measures ready in the event they occur.

Courtesy of Stephen B. Shiring, Jr.

Figure 14.4 Knowing the location of fire extinguishers helps to ensure quick action in an emergency.

Safety Committees

Safety committees can be an effective component of a safety and health program, particularly for the employer that is large enough to have the personnel to do it, yet does not have the resources to employ a safety professional. An effective safety committee can be involved in all aspects of the program: hazard identification and inspections, hazard control, training, and accident investigations (Figure 14.5). There are certain factors the caterer should consider before establishing a safety committee. General group dynamics suggest that optimal committees have between four to seven members. If different interests are being represented by the committee, ensure that members from each are serving on it. See that a chair is elected and provide him or her with the resources and time to effectively lead the committee. An issue unrelated to safety that must be considered by the caterer when establishing a safety

ELEMENTS TO CONSIDER FOR A SAFETY CHECKLIST

- Operation of all equipment
- Flow of food through the operation, from loading dock to the customer, with emphasis on proper handling of all materials including lifting and carrying of supplies and equipment
- Storage areas, including dry, frozen, refrigerated, and nonfood supplies; cooler and freezer temperature storage alarms to alert the caterer to potential equipment malfunctions
- Work stations, including the use and care of knives
- Kitchen floors and aisles, with an emphasis on reducing slips and falls.
- Work procedures, including proper lifting techniques and prevention of slips and falls
- Outside areas, including keeping the perimeter of the building clean to prevent the infestation of insects and rodents
- All management personnel and employees trained in first-aid and CPR; access to first-aid kits for both on-premise and off-premise activities; local emergency telephone numbers, and standard procedures to respond to and report fires, including periodic fire drills
- Off-premise location(s)—buffet lines built on nonslip floors
- Defensive driving
- Housekeeping area
- Client services, including handicap accessibility and safety measures
- Maintenance of equipment and their records
- Implementation of security systems, such as video-surveillance systems; limited access to keys or electronic controls for valuable inventory storage areas; security procedures for the client and employee
- Warewashing area
- New employee orientation must include safety, fire emergencies, floods, storms, tornados, hurricanes, power failures, telephone failure, hazardous material spills, and automobile/truck accidents

Figure 14.5 The catering safety management team should create a safety checklist for inspecting all areas of the operation.

safety management team A group of employees who continually monitor the environment to identify and correct potential risks, ensuring the proper safety of the employees and guests.

committee is to ensure that they do not run afoul of labor relations laws. The National Labor Relations Act prohibits employers from creating employee representation entities that could be construed to be acting in place of an employee union.

There are several things to consider before establishing a safety committee or any other employee representation team in the workplace. First, the group must be given very clear guidance about what it can and cannot do. They must not engage in discussing or proposing to management any activity or proposal related to wages, hours, benefits, or other conditions of employment. The group cannot be dominated by management, and in fact should be comprised of a majority of non-management employees. Employees should select their representatives rather than management choosing who will be on the committee. Besides complying with labor relations mandates, these guidelines should result in a more effective committee.

Occupational Safety and Health Administration (OSHA)

A common misconception exists that OSHA standards do not apply to small employers. This misunderstanding most likely is due to the fact that employers with 10 or less employees are exempt from *the record-keeping requirements for OSHA only*. There are records that must be kept and posted by larger employers from which OSHA exempts very small businesses. This section will provide some very basic information for OSHA compliance as well as include several free resources the caterer can use for meeting their requirements.

All employers must post what is known as the OSHA Job Safety and Health Poster, which informs employees of their rights under the act. Employers with 11 or more employees also must comply with the record-keeping requirements under OSHA, including an annual posting of injuries and illnesses. In addition to the "general duty clause" to provide employees a safe and healthful workplace, OSHA has promulgated a comprehensive list of regulations, known as "general industry standards," that apply to the caterer depending on the nature of his or her work. Standards such as personal protective equipment, bloodborne pathogens, fire and emergency evacuations, and so forth, are but a few examples. While large corporations typically employ a staff of safety professionals to review and determine how to comply with these regulatory requirements, most catering professionals do not have the resources to have that kind of in-house expertise. However, they ignore this agency or its requirements at their peril, because fines for violations of the OSHA standards can be prohibitive, particularly for a small employer.

One of the best resources for the caterer or other small business is the OSHA website at http://www.osha.gov. It contains a wealth of information, including a number of programs and guides for small businesses. Another excellent resource for small companies is the OSHA Consultation Assistance Service. An extension of OSHA, it offers consultants through state government agencies or universities employing professional safety and health consultants. At no cost to the employer, these services provide compliance consultation to identify violations of OSHA standards without penalty or citations. As long as the employer abates the violation, no other action is taken. For more information and a list of agencies available throughout the country, visit http://www.OSHA.gov/consultation.

Accident Investigation

One of the important elements of an effective safety and health program is a process for reporting and investigating accidents occurring at work. When an accident occurs, it must be investigated to determine the cause so that measures can be taken to minimize the likelihood of it reoccurring. In addition, workers compensation laws (see next section) require employers to complete reports of the incident, and a wise employer will want to conduct a thorough investigation to protect themselves from claims that are not work related. Accident investigation begins with a process for reporting injuries and accidents resulting from work. The caterer should review the procedure for reporting incidents at work with all employees, including whom to call and how to get emergency assistance or treatment. Accident report forms, including the necessary insurance paperwork, should be readily available in the caterer's vehicles in the event they are involved in a motor vehicle accident. Once the employee has been treated, or in the event of a motor vehicle or other property damage accident the scene secured, an investigation into what happened should begin immediately. The investigator should gather basic information about what happened, where did it occur, who was involved, how did it happen, and so forth.

A variety of techniques exist for conducting accident investigations, but one thing they all have in common is the need to get beyond immediate or superficial reasons for the accident and identify root causes. "Why" questions can help identify the basic or root causes. As an example, in a rear end collision, asking why the accident occurred could reveal that the employee failed to stop in time and struck a vehicle making an emergency stop in front of them. Asking why they failed to stop could bring the response that they were following too closely. When asked why the employee was following too closely could bring the response that they were late for an event. The answer to asking why they were running late for an event could be that the chef did not have some of the necessary materials to prepare the order. And finally, one of the root causes (and there are often several) could have been identified as not sufficient refrigerated storage space for the size and frequency of events. This example was dramatically simplified but is intended to illustrate the need to get beyond the unsafe employee action that directly resulted in the accident. Safety committees can be a very effective tool in the accident investigation process.

Workers Compensation

The caterer needs to be familiar with the specific workers compensation requirements in his or her state, since these programs are administered on a state-to-state basis, resulting in significant differences. A basic tenet of all workers compensation programs, however, is that they are a no fault system for compensating employees who are injured on the job, while providing limited liability to employers. When there are disputes, they generally are regarding disagreements over whether the injury resulted from an incident that "arose out of employment" and/or during the "course of employment." If there is doubt about the origin of an injury, for example a lower back injury, there may be disagreements about whether it happened on the job or not. The caterer certainly cannot or should not be paying compensation for injuries unrelated to the job. Not only can the initial cost be substantial, but the rates the employer pays for insurance is based on part of the workers compensation claims for their employees compared to employers of similar size in the same business. Referred to as an experience modification rate, it can raise or lower the rates paid by the employer for workers compensation insurance. A good source for assistance and resources is a reputable workers compensation insurer. Working closely with them, the caterer can develop an effective safety and health program for preventing accidents and injury on the job, as well as ensuring that their workers compensation costs are kept at a minimum.

Insurance

A catering **crisis management team** can help resolve the immediate needs of the situation. However, a well-designed **insurance program** will help protect the long-term interests of the caterer. When establishing the right insurance program for the organization, a caterer must:

1. identify and analyze the exposures or potential causes of loss (Figure 14.6).
2. know the options to address the exposures, and choose the best alternative for the organization.
3. monitor the insurance program and make incremental adjustments to the overall package.

A caterer will want an insurance policy that provides liability coverage and property coverage for the building and its contents. The package may include coverage for a caterer's loss of business income, extra expense, and ordinance.

Addressing Risk

Insurance coverage is not the only option for a caterer to address risk. A caterer may **avoid**, **reduce**, or **transfer risk**. A caterer can implement a plan to avoid risk by eliminating all circumstances that cause it (Figure 14.7).

crisis management team Group of homogenous management and hourly employees who can quickly respond to an unforeseen crisis with the purpose of protecting the interests of the guest and the organization.

insurance program The complete package written by a professional carrier to protect the caterer against the potential of loss.

avoid risk The catering management processes meant to eliminate all circumstances that may cause a risk to materialize. One example is the creation of a safety team whose purpose is to monitor the environment to identify and correct potential risks to ensure the safety of the employee and guest.

reduce risk A process, procedure, or tangible element specifically designed to reduce the element of risk. One example is the installation of a sprinkler system to reduce the risk of a fire.

transfer risk The caterer may assign the ownership of the risk to another party. One example is for a caterer to rent a facility rather than owning it.

BENEFITS OF A SAFETY SURVEY

A safety survey:

1. documents an active commitment to creating a positive safety record.
2. creates safety procedures that become standard operating procedures.
3. identifies training needs.
4. documents guest's comments and accidents related to safety issues.
5. provides for the continuous inspection and monitoring of the operation.
6. develops effective emergency procedures designed to protect the guest and the employee (Figure 14.7).

© Cengage Learning 2014

Figure 14.6 Safety surveys can be used as a development tool and to help create a better work environment.

1. In case of an emergency, keep calm.

2. Determine if emergency assistance is required. Do not attempt a rescue if it could result in an injury.

3. Determine if the area is safe for rescue personnel. Check for fire (heat), smoke, exposed electrical lines, and chemicals.

4. Dial 911. Stay on the phone with the 911 operator until told to do otherwise.

5. Know the location. Provide the name of facility, address, phone number, and your name. Speak slowly and wait for confirmation.

© Cengage Learning 2014

Figure 14.7 Employee orientation should include review of the organization's emergency procedures.

Reducing Risk

Risk can also be reduced. A caterer can have a sprinkler system or a central alarm system to reduce the risk of fire. A caterer can also transfer the risk of loss by renting a facility instead of owning the building. Some companies use a cross-agreement with a competitor that basically states, "If you have an emergency, I will help you, and if I have an emergency, you will help me." Although this type of agreement is not commonly used, it can be effective. The point to remember is that insurance is only one option against risk. A complete, integrated plan can help avoid risk. A caterer can also reduce risk by the implementation of a safety program.

INSURANCE SERVICES OFFICE (ISO)

Standard insurance policies are written on forms created by the **Insurance Services Office (ISO)**. Generally, insurance companies file their rates with the Insurance Commissioner's office in states where they desire to conduct business. They may also file a policy form that deviates from the standard ISO form to add coverage(s), making their product more appealing to their clients and prospective catering businesses. It is recommended that the caterer, to be an informed consumer of insurance, find out on what form the insurance company's proposals are written, and note any differences that may exist from the standard form.

Insurance Services Office (ISO) The property/casualty insurance industry's leading supplier of statistical, actuarial, underwriting, and claims information.

INFORMED CONSUMER

Becoming an **informed consumer** of insurance is very important to maintaining a healthy catering business. Caterers must be educated about the loss-control services offered by their insurers to take full advantage of the right mix for their organization.

Loss-control services offered by a caterer's insurance company focus on the goals they both share, to reduce the frequency and severity of losses/claims. When a claim is made, the insurance companies take note and it is reflected in the insurance cost. However, caterers with low losses are rewarded with lower costs. Therefore, it is important to protect the insurance record.

informed consumer A caterer educated about the loss-control services offered by an insurance carrier. The mix of loss-control services includes basic coverages for property, liability, and workers compensation.

An insurance company will typically inspect the caterer's operation each year, but if not, a loss control inspection can be requested. The individual conducting the inspection will be highly trained in safety science. Upon completion, the caterer will receive a detailed report regarding any hazards or deficiencies that require corrective action. Some operators may view this as one more problem to deal with, but the best business managers understand the correlation between attention to loss control and the success of their operation.

Property Insurance

property insurance
This insurance provides protection against the loss of property.

A caterer has a few options regarding the coverage of **property insurance**. One choice is to have the building and contents covered on a replacement cost (RC) basis. An insurer will only pay the caterer the replacement cost when the property is actually replaced. Or if the caterer does not intend to replace the property, an actual cash value (ACV) option can be used. A common formula used is:

$$ACV = RC \text{ less depreciation}$$

A caterer will also have options regarding the different levels of coverage with regard to causes of loss. These options are basic, broad, and special. The special cause of loss form is the broadest of the three and usually worth the extra cost. The special cause of loss covers all causes of loss except those specifically excluded. The insurer must prove a claim is specifically excluded under the policy language in order to deny payment to the caterer.

Liability Insurance

liability insurance
Premise/operations coverage to protect a caterer against claims arising from the ownership, maintenance, or use of the premise and of the caterer's operations in-progress.

Liability refers to other people and their property. Three steps have to be proven for a claim to be successfully made against the caterer. First, there must exist a *duty owed* such as a safe environment and uncontaminated food. Second, there must be a *breach of that duty*. Last, there must be measurable *damages* as a result of the breach of the duty owed.

There are two aspects to liability coverage for a caterer. The first is a premise exposure at locations he or she owns, leases, or occupies. The second aspect is the products and completed operations exposure. Here is a simple analogy to aid in clarifying the differences:

Premise Exposure: a customer slips on a wet floor that should have been barricaded or clearly marked with a warning sign. The damages are the injuries the customer sustains as a result of the negligence of the caterer.

Product Exposure: a customer contracts foodborne illness after eating the caterer's food and has medical bills, pain, and suffering.

Personal and Advertising Injury Liability

personal and advertising injury liability
Insurance coverage to protect against claims alleging false arrest, libel, slander, and false advertising if the caterer had no knowledge of the falsehood.

Personal and advertising injury liability will protect the caterer against claims alleging false arrest, libel, slander, and false advertising if the caterer had no knowledge of the falsehood.

Fire Damage Liability

fire damage liability
Insurance coverage for a caterer's legal liability arising from fire damage to structures rented to the caterer.

Fire damage liability provides coverage for the caterer's legal liability arising from fire damage to structures rented by the caterer.

Medical Expense Coverage

Medical expense coverage will reimburse all reasonable medical expenses incurred by anyone, except the caterer or the caterer's employees, as a result of an accident without regard for the caterer's liability. This gives the insurer some money to offer an injured party without concluding an investigation. This flexibility to respond quickly helps control the claim costs by settling claims early without delay.

medical expense coverage This insurance will provide reimbursement for all reasonable medical expenses incurred by anyone, except the caterer or caterer's employees, as a result of an accident, without regard for the caterer's liability.

Automobile Insurance

Laws regarding **automobile insurance** vary depending on the state in which the caterer is conducting business. It can be observed in the same light as property and liability coverages. Even if a caterer does not own a company vehicle, the caterer must have hired and nonowned liability coverage to be protected from liability imputed by the actions of an employee owning an automobile. A caterer can be named in a lawsuit resulting from an automobile accident involving an employee if the employee is found to be on a mission for the caterer, even if the caterer had not directed the employee's action as a result or purpose of the trip.

An employee stops on the way to work and purchases lettuce for the caterer. As the employee turns into the parking lot, he hits a pedestrian. Even though the caterer did not ask the employee to purchase lettuce, technically, and in the eyes of the law, the employee is on a mission for the caterer. This is reinforced if the caterer had ever, in the past, sent anyone anywhere for anything. Legally, this imputes liability to the caterer. This coverage also pays for the attorneys and their legal defense. Hired and nonowned liability coverage is very inexpensive, but very important.

automobile insurance Insurance to protect the caterer from liability imputed to him by the actions of an employee. Laws regarding insurance for vehicles vary depending upon the state in which a caterer is conducting business.

Employment Practice Liability

This is a very hot topic in insurance, due to the high profile of some sexual harassment cases. **Employment practice liability** coverage has many options for deductibles and limits to help a caterer tailor a policy to fit the needs of the organization. It is recommended for a caterer to reference some of the excellent materials available to help prevent a claim of this nature. It is also important to obtain an estimate for this type of coverage to get as much information as possible before a decision to purchase or decline it is made.

employment practice liability Coverage of day-to-day activities in the workplace.

SELECTION OF INSURANCE

The most desirable program for a caterer is one that addresses all possible causes of loss with a combination of insurance, safety practices, and sensible transfers of risk at the least expense to the caterer.

Before a caterer can purchase the policy, he or she must design the best program to provide the maximum coverage for the business. To help make intelligent decisions regarding the purchase of an insurance policy, a caterer must answer the following questions. The answers will help build a strong foundation for an effective insurance program.

1. What is required by the law? Most states require a caterer to carry workers compensation to cover the employees for medical expenses and wages if hurt in the course of employment.
2. What is required by a bank or lienholder for financed property or vehicles?
3. What must be covered to ensure survival in the event of a claim or loss?

An insurance grid will help a caterer to understand the process of designing the best program providing maximum coverage for the business (Figure 14.8).

INSURANCE CHART

RISK	NON-INSURANCE	INSURANCE
Building	Rent instead of own Install central alarm system Install sprinklers Use fire resistive material	Insure at replacement or actual cash value if no intention to rebuild Special cause of loss form
Contents	Separate flammables Safe storage Have alternate supplier	Insure at replacement cost Special cause of loss form
Loss of Income	Cross agreement	Business income coverage Include extra expense and consider ordinary payroll
Boiler and Machinery	Boiler inspections Back-up power supply Surge protection	Some packages include this to cover cooling equipment, electric equipment
Liability	Keep certificates of insurance on file for subcontractors and use hold-harmless agreements in contracts	Coverage to meet a caterer's organization's needs Protect company and personal assets
Automobile	Drug testing Check MVR and conduct safety meetings	Liability, physical damage, medical Hired and nonowned liability is a must, even if the organization does not own a vehicle
Workers' Compensation	Safety committee (some states require insurers to give a discount) Drug-free workplace	Required by law A caterer may need employer's liability
Umbrella	Incorporate to protect personal assets	Sits over top of a caterer's liability Very broad coverage to protect against large awards

© Cengage Learning 2014

Figure 14.8 Caterers can use an insurance chart to design an insurance program that best meets their organization's needs.

A caterer must also be aware of **throw-ins**, which are added to policies by insurance companies to make their policies more competitive. Throw-ins are extra coverages at no extra cost to the caterer. Salespeople, called **producers**, will point out these throw-ins to a caterer to make their proposals more attractive than their competitor's policy.

throw-ins A term used in the insurance industry to describe when extra coverage is given at no additional charge to make the policy more competitive in the marketplace.

Insurance Expense

A caterer trying to balance adequate coverage and the cost of insurance is considered to be making, at best, an educated guess. Therefore, here are some basic truths about insurance coverage. Higher deductibles, higher coinsurance clauses, low losses, if any, and competitive quotes will keep the cost of insurance down. The most important consideration is making sure a caterer has the right coverage to fit the needs of the business at a competitive rate. The caterer must learn about claims procedures by meeting with a representative and asking questions. The loss control services being provided should also be clearly understood.

producers A term used in the insurance industry to describe the individuals who sell insurance.

The relationship between the caterer and the agent must be built on trust. When shopping for the best coverage, the caterer should look for an agent who would be trusted with a key to the business, because to some degree, this is what a caterer will be doing. The caterer should request credentials and expect honest and clear explanations. Agents should have a reputation of integrity, and the caterer should check references.

Tips from the Trade

In a proposal, I always write an explicit and detailed explanation regarding pricing. Prices will differ depending on the type of event. Prices differ depending on the day of the week and the duration the space is to be rented. Here, at The Chestnut Ridge Golf Resort & Conference Center, we cater Galas, Fundraisers, Charity Benefits, Proms and Homecomings, Fraternity and Sorority Events, Sports Banquets, Retirement Parties, Reunions, Bar and Bat Mitzvahs. We own two golf courses, and each has its own unique pricing structure. Next, I will write a detailed description of the food packages we offer, the hotel room rental, our staffing options, and the room setup services we can provide.

For the contract, I always make sure the start and end times are explicitly identified. All pricing is explicitly detailed. This includes the cost of the food and any associated fees, such as equipment rentals (china, linens, chair covers, wine or water glasses, silverware, or disposables), staffing services, room rentals, service charges, sales tax, and the gratuity. I include our cancellation policy so if the client decides to cancel the event they will know if they should expect to get their deposit returned or if it is forfeited.

Natalie Dunlap, Catering Sales Manager, The Chestnut Ridge Golf Resort & Conference Center, Blairsville, Pennsylvania

CONTRACTS

A caterer does not need to have an elaborate contract, but the contract must spell out the important details. Drafting the right contract is but a matter of identifying the basics, using good judgment, and following common sense. Figures 14.9, 14.10, and 14.11 illustrate various contractual arrangements.

JARDINE'S CATERING

Monroe Road • Sarver, Pennsylvania Phone number • Fax number • E-mail address

ORGANIZATION NAME: _____ (Client's Name)

ENGAGER: _____

ADDRESS: _____ STATE/ZIP _____

CITY: _____

PHONE: _____ FAX: _____

E-MAIL: _____

METHOD OF PAYMENT: _____ (cash, credit card)

WHO IS MAKING PAYMENT: _____ (e.g., wedding—bride/groom's family,

social event—Elizabeth 50% + Samantha 50%, celebration—Stephen 100%)

DAY: _____ DATE: _____ (function's day & date of execution)

FUNCTION: _____ (e.g., wedding, birthday, picnic, family reunion)

SPECIAL REQUEST: _____ (e.g., Tammie's birthday, Laurie & Tisha's graduation)

HOURS: _____ (exact starting and ending time)

LOCATION: _____ (exact location of function and directions)

APPROXIMATE NUMBER OF GUESTS: _____ (best estimate, based on historical data)

MINIMUM GUARANTEE: _____ (minimum guest count for this contract)

*FINAL GUARANTEE: _____ (guest provides in writing, attachment, guest will

guarantee to pay caterer for this number, regardless if fewer attend function)

*Final guarantee number will be charged unless adjusted prior to 1:00 P.M. on _____

(last day for guest to adjust final count without penalty)

MENU REQUIREMENTS: (All menu details as agreed upon with client)

Price Per Guest: $(_____) (If quote per person, amount specified in this contract)

All food and beverage subject to (_____%) sales tax and (_____%) service charge.

ENTREE AND SIDES: _____ (exact menu, portion size)

SERVICE STYLE: _____ (explicit description of service responsibilities)

BEVERAGE SERVICE: _____ (nonalcoholic/alcoholic beverages and service)

SET UP REQUIREMENTS: _____ (any special requests, floor plan and seating chart)

CHEFS: a flat $(_____) labor charge will be assessed for each chef required for buffet-line carving stations.

OTHER:

LINEN: Jardine's Catering will provide white linen from its inventory. Special requests for linen will incur an

additional charge.

AUDIOVISUAL: Jardine's Catering recommended audiovisual company (_____) can handle any range

of specialized audiovisual requirements.

FLORIST: Jardine's Catering recommended florist (_____) will arrange to meet your individual needs.

PHOTOGRAPHER: Jardine's Catering recommended photographer (_____) will arrange to meet your individual needs.

SPECIAL DECORATIONS AND SERVICES: Jardine's professional catering staff can enhance your event with ice sculptures, hand-carved centerpieces, individualized flower arrangements, and thematic decorations. SECURITY: Jardine's Catering will not assume any responsibility for damages, loss, or stolen articles of clothing. ITEMIZED INVOICE: Attachment, an itemized list of all function-related expenses incurred executing the function.

Engager: _____ Date: _____ Jardine's Catering: _____ Date: _____

Witness: _____ Date: _____ Witness: _____ Date: _____

Attorney's Signature: _____Date: _____ (if reviewed)

Figure 14.9 Jardine's Catering sample contract.

Courtesy Bill Jardine

TERMS AND CONDITIONS

Figure 14.10 Hyatt Orlando sample contract.

All reservations and agreements are made upon, and are subject to, the rules and regulations of the Hotel and the following conditions:

In arranging for private functions, the attendance must be definitively specified and communicated to the Hotel by 12:00 noon, forty-eight (48) hours (2 working days) in advance. This number will be considered a guarantee, not subject to reduction, and charges will be made accordingly. The Hotel cannot be responsible for identical services to more than five percent (5%) over the guarantee for parties up to 500. For parties over 500, we will prepare for 25 additional guests. Guarantees for Saturday, Sunday, and Monday are due by 12:00 noon on the preceding Thursday. Guarantees for Tuesday are due by 12:00 noon on the preceding Friday. If a guarantee is not given to the Hotel by 12:00 noon on the date it is due, the lower number on the contract will automatically become the guarantee.

All federal, state, and municipal taxes which may be imposed or be applicable to this agreement and to the services rendered by the Hotel are in addition to the prices herein upon, and the patron agrees to pay them separately.

No food or beverages of any kind will be permitted to be brought into the Hotel by the patron or any of the patron's guests or invitees.

For private parties with groups of twenty (20) or less, the Hotel will charge a $60.00 labor charge.

Performance of this agreement is contingent upon the ability of the Hotel management to complete the same and is subject to labor troubles; disputes or strikes; accidents; government (federal, state, or municipal) requisitions; restrictions upon travel, transportation, food,

(continues)

(continued)

beverages, or supplies; and other causes whether enumerated herein or not, beyond the control of management that may prevent or interfere with performance. In no event shall the Hyatt Orlando Hotel be liable for the loss of profit, or for other similar or dissimilar collateral or consequential damages, whether on breach of contract, warranty, or otherwise.

Payment shall be made in advance of the function unless credit has been established to the satisfaction of the Hotel, in which event a deposit shall be paid at the time of signing the agreement. The balance of the account is due and payable twenty-one (21) days after the date of the function. A deposit of twenty-five percent (25%) of the total balance of social functions is required at the time of booking; balance payable forty-eight (48) hours prior to the event.

Prices are subject to all applicable service charge and taxes; currently, 19% service charge and 7% sales tax.

The prices herein are subject to increase in the event costs of food, beverage, or other costs of operation increase at the time of the function. Patron grants the right to the Hotel to increase such prices or to make reasonable substitutions on the menu with prior written notice to the patron, providing, however, patron shall have the right to terminate the agreement within seven (7) days after such written notice from the Hotel.

The Hyatt Orlando does not accept any responsibility for the damage or loss of any merchandise or article left in the Hotel prior to, during, or following your function.
Patron agrees to be responsible and reimburse Hyatt Orlando for any damage done by patron or patron's guests of the Hotel.

The Hotel reserves the right to advance approval of all outside contractors hired for use by a convention group. The Hotel will, upon reasonable notice, cooperate with outside contractors. Hotel facilities are available to outside contractors to the extent that their function does not interfere with use of the facilities by other guests. Under such arrangements, the Hotel receives a ten percent (10%) commission from any outside contractors coming into the Hotel.

The Hotel has the following policy with respect to signs in the banquet and meeting areas:

The Hotel reserves the right to approve all signage. All signs must be professionally printed. No signs are allowed on the guestroom floors and main lobby areas of the Hotel or building exterior. Printed signs outside function rooms in the Convention Center only should be free standing or on an easel. The Hotel will assist in placing all signs and banners. Depending on labor and equipment involved, a charge for the services may apply.

Function rooms are assigned by the Hotel according to the guaranteed minimum number of people anticipated. Room rental fees are applicable if group attendance drops below the estimated attendance at the time of booking. The Hotel reserves the right to change groups to a more suitable room at the Hotel's discretion, and with notification, if attendance drops or increases.

The Hotel reserves the right to make the final decision regarding outdoor functions as follows:

a) The time to make the decision on whether the function will be outdoors or indoors;
b) Once the Hotel makes the decision, it is final.

Client Signature   Date

Courtesy Dianne Herzog, Catering Manager, Hyatt Orlando, Kissimmee, FL

ALL OCCASION CATERING, INC.

534 Clever Road
Robinson Township, PA 15136
(412)787-5266

Banquet Contract
Terms and Conditions

1) All prices are guaranteed at time of original deposit received.

2) All menu selections must be submitted 2 weeks prior to your scheduled function.

   At this time we should already have an approximate number of guests expected to be at your function, if you have not given us the number you must at this time.

3) The guaranteed number of people must be provided 48 hours in advance of your function.

   This final guarantee is not subject to reduction. All charges will be based on this guarantee or the actual number of guest served whichever is greater.

Deposits and Payments

Dates

1) $100.00 deposit will be required to hold reservation if booked outside of 90 days, otherwise the following steps 2 or 3 will apply.   _____

2) One third of total is required 90 days prior to functions   _____

3) Second one third is due 30 days prior to function.   _____

4) Balance is due 2 days prior to function,   _____

Cancellation Terms of Contract

Dates

1) Full deposit will be refunded 3 months before scheduled function.   _____

2) 50% of total deposits returned if function is canceled

   within _____ (90 days) to _____ (30 days) prior to your scheduled date.

3) Total deposits retained if function is canceled less than 30 days prior to the date of function.

All Occasion Catering, Inc. Banquet Contract

Name of Party: _____   Type of Function: _____

Address: _____   Date of Function: _____

_____   Est. # of People: _____

For All Occasion Catering Use:

Home Phone: _____   Deposit Received: _____

Date of Deposit: _____

Work Phone: _____   1st. Payment Due: _____

2nd. Payment Due: _____

Location of Function: _____   Balance Due: _____

Signature: _____

Figure 14.11 All Occasion Catering sample contract.

Permission of John R. Smith

contract The legal agreement between the client and caterer outlining details of an event. It does not have to be elaborate, but should cover the basics including time, date, menu items, number of guests, the price and payment policy, and provisions for extenuating circumstances beyond the caterer's control.

engager The client or person who is contracting the services of the caterer.

To clarify the significance, it is important for a caterer to understand some basic business activities that involve a contract. A **contract** is a binding agreement between two or more parties. This may also be defined as an agreement creating an obligation. The importance of a written contract involves the statute of frauds, which may render a contract void or voidable if it is not in writing.

The caterer is obligated to provide the food and service promised. The other party, referred to as the **engager** or client, is obligated to pay for food and specific services, if satisfactory. If either party fails to fulfill its side of the obligation, the other party may have a cause of action. Every job a caterer agrees to execute, regardless of the party, requires a contract. One exception where no binding agreement is required is when the caterer supplies catering services as a gift. This might include providing food and service for weddings, birthdays, and similar events for friends and family.

Execution of a contract enables a caterer to establish a firm business policy. Furthermore, putting agreements in writing ensures compliance with the statute of frauds together with smooth and pleasant client relationships. A well-written contract will prohibit additional services demanded by the client to be provided by the caterer during the implementation stage of the function. It will also enable the client to better understand the services they are receiving.

Contracts are used to protect the hotel and the client. Contracts outline legalities such as cancellation fees, force majeure for cancellation (force majeure is a legal clause freeing the hotel or the client from its obligation or liability when an uncontrollable event or circumstance renders the event impossible) without any type of cancellation fee, indemnification, and dispute resolution to name a few. By outlining the terms in the agreement prior to a situation occurring, the outcome has already been agreed upon by the hotel and the client.

Contracts outline the service the hotel agrees to provide and the revenue the client is committed to spend. The hotel's event space is in high demand. In order to reserve this space, a client must agree to meet a revenue minimum of food and beverage and/or meeting room rental. These minimums are outlined in the contract along with the deposit schedule.

Suzy Miller, Senior Sales Manager, Sheraton Station Square, Pittsburgh, Pennsylvania

Contracts are also valuable business assets for the caterer. They can be used as collateral to borrow money to meet short-term cash needs and are considered tangible assets in the sale of a catering business. Most contracts require customer signature and acceptance.

The creation of a contract is an important element in the establishment of any relationship with a catering customer. The initial stage of such a relationship will usually involve exploratory discussions as the prospective client shares their event idea with the caterer. Once the parties decide that the idea is feasible and that the planning should proceed, the next step is to negotiate a contract covering the details of the event.

Contracts are by far as important as the quality of food and service we are providing. If a contract is too strong you could lose business, if it is too soft you could end up with an event that is not profitable and could quite possibly take advantage of your business and its resources. **Please understand that this business is based on time. There is no way to ever return or exchange it; once it is consumed, you will never get it back.** It is very important to include the following items in every contract: date and time of event, number of people, type of event, cancellation policy, and all pertinent hotel policies and procedures. I always include a minimum dollar amount, which must be met during the event. This minimum is determined by the type of event and its total estimated revenue. The hotel will be financially covered if the client's guarantees were to drop, or their budget were to decrease. Example: Let's plan a Christmas party for 500 people at an estimated charge of $40 per person. This party is on a Saturday in December. (Note: There are only three good Saturday nights in December for holiday parties, so this is prime space.) I have a $1,000 deposit and the client is paying by credit card. What if 10 days before the event, the group's guarantee drops to 300 people? If there is no minimum dollar amount in your contract you will be losing $8,000. That's $8,000 you will never be able to get back.

Dianne Herzog, Catering Manager, Hyatt Orlando, Kissimmee, Florida

A contract that clearly defines the expectations of both parties in reasonable detail will help ensure a positive relationship throughout the planning, organizing, and implementation stages of the event. Failure to address important aspects of the relationship may lead to dissatisfaction, destruction of goodwill, and even lawsuits. Failure to create a legally enforceable contract may result in significant financial loss. It is advisable to consult with an attorney before entering into a contract with the client.

A contract is a legally enforceable agreement between two or more parties. It is a legal relationship created by one of the parties making an offer that is accepted by another party. There is also a requirement that the party against whom enforcement of a contract is sought have gained something from the agreement; this is known as "consideration." The court will find the consideration to be inadequate when the party making the promise received nothing of value, or of any benefit, in return for the promise. For example, in a catering contract, the consideration motivating the caterer is usually the payment of money, and the consideration motivating the client is the provision of the catering services.

A "meeting of the minds" is the common way of understanding what a court will look for in determining whether an agreement was reached. Anything about which the parties did not agree bilaterally will not be enforced as part of the contract. Such a determination can sometimes be very difficult, and the discussion that follows covers some of the rules that have been adopted by the legal system to aid in that determination.

An agreement need not be elaborate nor must it contain esoteric legal terms to be legally binding. The most important aspect of the agreement is that it must accurately reflect items that were mutually agreed upon by the parties. If the contract contains terms that the client reasonably failed to understand, and which were not adequately explained to the client, it is possible that the court will not enforce them against the client. Another concern is whether the client might be deemed to lack the capacity to enter into an enforceable contract due to intoxication, status as a minor, or serious mental deficiency.

The importance of reducing any catering agreement to a written form signed by the parties cannot be overstated. While it is possible to prove an oral agreement, it is not easy. The caterer should always ensure that any significant cost items or matters that may give rise to a legal dispute are covered in a written document. The creation of the written document prevents use of oral representations made prior to the execution of the written agreement as evidence. This is known as the parol evidence rule. This rule does not, however, exclude evidence of oral agreements made after the writing. Because of this it is essential that written addendums to modify the agreement be created if the client asks for modifications after the execution of the original agreement. Another contract enforcement rule, known as the statute of frauds, requires that contracts which cannot be completed within one year be reduced to a writing signed by the parties, along with several other specific types of agreements.

The length and content of the agreement are dictated by the circumstances. A contract for a relatively small event with simple arrangements being planned for the near future may require a very basic document. On the other hand, a large, complex event that will require many months of planning and will be very costly may merit a much more detailed contract than the caterer normally creates. An addendum document may be created to supplement the caterer's usual contract form.

The contracts in Figures 14.9, 14.10 and 14.11 illustrate the fact that the contract must reflect the specific nature of the enterprise. In addition to specifying basics such as the parties to the agreement, the services to be provided, the time of performance of the services, and the payments to be made, the contracts contain features to address the allocation of risk for various contingencies that may arise. It is important to coordinate the features of the contract with the risk coverage, or exclusions, found in the caterer's insurance.

In Figure 14.9, Jardine's Catering specifies that requests for linen that is not white will incur an extra charge and also that it will not be responsible for "damages, lost or stolen articles of clothing." All Occasion Catering (Figure 14.11) includes a policy covering "Cancellation Terms of Contract." Over time, these types of agreements tend to evolve into lengthier and more detailed documents reflective of the previously unforeseen and troublesome contingencies that have occurred during previous events. A good set of basic contract stipulations is provided in Figure 14.12.

In the event that difficulties arise during the performance of the contract and the dispute ends up in court, the complaining party will usually be seeking compensatory (i.e., monetary) damages for any losses sustained. It will be important that accurate records were maintained, whether for the purpose of proving or for defending against a damage claim.

Basic Contract Stipulations

A contact must cover a standard set of basic contract stipulations or details (Figure 14.12). Before entering into a contract with the client, an attorney should be consulted to review its specific contents.

BASIC CONTRACT STIPULATIONS

1. The exact number of people who will be served must be stipulated.

   A stipulation requiring the final guarantee as to the number of guests attending this event to be given by 12:00 noon no later than (_____) business days in advance of the function. Once given, this guarantee is not subject to any reduction. The caterer will permit a 15% increase if advised by 12:00 noon (_____) days prior to the date of the function. The caterer will provide seating for an additional 5% beyond the guaranteed number at no extra charge. If, however, unexpected attendance exceeds 5%, then a $(_____) per person surcharge will be applied.

   If no guarantee is received at the appropriate time, the caterer will attempt to contact the engager. If, after two documented attempts go unsuccessful, the caterer will assume that the original engager's expected count will be the guarantee, and all charges will be applied to this number.

2. The exact menu to be served.

   In order for the caterer to assure the availability of the menu items selected, final confirmation of the menu selections must be submitted (_____) weeks prior to the date of execution. However, unforeseen market conditions may require the caterer to make professional substitutions on menu items. Speciality and theme menus will be designed to meet individual needs and tastes.

3. The type of service to be provided at the event by the caterer and staff.

4. The exact amount of time for each activity.

   Time limits are especially important. If the caterer runs into overtime, this must be carefully spelled out in advance on the contract. The caterer and client will agree to an exact beginning and ending time. Many caterers will include a clause granting the client permission to continue the celebration past the contracted ending time. If permission is granted, an overtime charge would be applied against the client.

5. The exact price.

   The caterer may stipulate that all printed catering menu prices are subject to change without notice. In addition, all contracted prices would be honored. However, for contracted events at least six months in advance, the following stipulation would be included: This is an approximate price; the client grants the caterer the right to adjust the price based on unforeseen market conditions. The caterer will provide the final price (_____) days before the function date.

6. Payment Policy.

   A minimum deposit of 33 1/3% of the total bill is required when the contract is signed. Another 33 1/3 % of the total bill is required no later than (_____) day(s) prior to the date of the event and the remainder of the final bill is due (_____) day(s) prior to the event.

7. Deposit and Refund Policy.

   All deposits are nonrefundable. Each event is different and if a function is canceled, it remains the judgement of the caterer to make this decision.

8. Cancellation and Refund Policy.

   The caterer reserves the right to cancel this agreement without penalty and notice in the event of breach of contract by the client.

9. Method for Counting Guests.

   An accounting method for tracking the number of guests must be determined. When the caterer is being compensated per guest, this is extremely important, especially if catering large events, such as a 1500-guest picnic. Techniques used may involve tickets, plates issued, bundled or rolled silverware with a napkin issued, an employee and guest assigned to each "count," and monitor attendance.

Figure 14.12 Every contract should include a standard set of contract stipulations and details

INDIANA HOLIDAY INN

1395 Wayne Avenue
Indiana, PA   15701
Telephone: (724) 463-3561 Toll-Free: (800) 477-3561
Fax: (724) 463-8006   E-Mail: IndianaSale1@CrownAm.com

BEO #:
Page 1 of 1
Date Created:

Banquet Event Order

Group Information

Account:	Event Date:
	Contact:
Post As:	Phone:
	Fax:
Address:	On-site Contact:
	Phone:
	Fax:
Deposit:	Booked By:
	Catering Manager:

DATE	TIME	FUNCTION	SETUP	ROOM	EXP #	GTD	RENT

Menu Requirements	Beverage & Break Requirements
Meal Time:	Time:

Billing Requirements	Set Up Requirements

Miscellaneous Arrangements	Audio Visual Requirements

Figure 14.13 (a) Sample banquet event order form (front).

Additional Information

Guaranteed count of attendance is due by 11:00am three (3) business days in advance of the function or _____ ; *(list exact date)* if no count is received, the original count is considered the guarantee for billing purposes. Should your event cancel, deposit and payments are non-refundable.

All food and applicable beverage charges are subject to 16% Service Fee and 6% State Tax. All audio visual equipment is subject to 6% tax. Meeting room rental is subject to 6% tax.

Meeting room rental and set-up fees are subject to an additional charge should there be more than a 15% reduction in the contracted number of attendees.

Meeting/Banquet rooms are assigned by the number of people anticipated. We reserved the right to change groups to a room suitable for the attendance. We will make every effort to contact you in advance should this occur.

All food and beverage to be consumed in any public area must be purchased from the hotel and must be consumed on premise. The scheduled event time cannot be changed without prior approval by the hotel management.

In the event that the attendance exceeds the guaranteed minimum, the Hotel will make every reasonable effort to accommodate the extra number of guests with the same or comparable arrangements.

Any special dietary requests must be made 24 hours prior to the function.

All banquet checks must be signed by the person in charge or a designated representative at the completion of each function. Any discrepancies in counts or charges should be identified and resolved at that time.

Organization must obtain prior approval from Hotel for all activities which are planned for the event. The premises shall be used only for those approved activities. Organization agrees to assist Hotel in prohibiting any violation of this provision if Hotel deems it necessary.

The person executing this Agreement as Organization's representative expressly represents that he or she is over eighteen (18) years of age. Where the Organization is a corporation, an un-incorporated association, partnership or other legal entity, this Agreement shall be binding on such legal entity, its successors and assigns. The person executing this Agreement as the Organization's representative expressly represents that he or she is authorized to execute said Agreement on Behalf of the Organization.

Organization Authorized Signature

Hotel Representative Signature
on behalf of the **Indiana Holiday Inn**

Date

Date

Owned and Operated by Crown American Hotels

Courtesy of Indiana Holiday Inn (Crown American Hotels)

Figure 14.13 (b) Sample banquet event order form (back).

BANQUET EVENT ORDER

banquet event order (BEO) This form is a multipurpose catering management tool used internally to communicate the details for execution of an event to the appropriate personnel.

The **banquet event order** (BEO) is a multipurpose catering management tool used internally to communicate the specific details for execution of a catering event to the appropriate personnel (Figure 14.13). It simultaneously functions as an indirect control document because the BEO establishes accountability and assigns managerial responsibility by launching a concrete paper trail that is easily audited and confirmed. The BEO is often used by a hotel catering department to coordinate each catering event through communicating to the appropriate personnel or departments what participation is needed.

Summary

Catering management decisions regarding insurance and legal issues will help protect a successful catering business. *Ingredient for Success 41* reminds us *"The creation and maintenance of the right insurance and legal package, based on the mission of the organization, will protect the caterer against any unpredictable crisis."* A well-designed insurance program will help protect the long-term interests of the caterer. In addition to the appropriate insurance and legal package, a well-organized catering business will anticipate a variety of potential crises that might occur. To be prepared for these unforeseen events, the creation of a crisis management team can quickly respond to any crippling crisis and attack the problem using a structured and pretested emergency plan. The caterer may also avoid, reduce, or transfer risk. The establishment of an internal safety team to continuously monitor the environment to identify and correct potential risks will ensure the proper safety of the employees and guests. Successful caterers create an organization built with a commitment towards safety, and empower each employee to become an active participant in creating their own safe environment.

Equally important as having the right insurance package, a caterer must always use a contract to spell out all of the important details for each and every event. Every contract must cover a standard set of basic contract stipulations or details. Remember, the contract will be very similar in descriptive detail to the caterer's written proposal that is accepted by the client based on exceeding their needs, wants, and demands. Before entering into a contract with the client, an attorney should be consulted to review its specific contents.

Review Questions

Brief Answers

1. Describe why insurance and legal concerns are important to the caterer.
2. Explain intrinsic and extrinsic rewards.
3. Describe why the caterer must develop and implement the right insurance and legal program.
4. Explain how a caterer can avoid, transfer, or reduce risk.
5. Explain the purpose of a crisis management team—why is this important to the caterer?

6. Explain the purpose of a safety management team.
7. Explain why a caterer needs to conduct frequent safety surveys.
8. Explain the basic insurance coverage for property, liability, and workers compensation.
9. Explain personal and advertising coverage, fire damage liability, medical expense coverage, and automobile coverage.
10. Explain why a caterer must create a contract that covers the basics.

Multiple Choice

Select the single best answer for each question.

1. Rewards the caterer experiences as a result of executing the event are _____.
   a. intrinsic rewards
   b. catering rewards
   c. customer rewards
   d. extrinsic rewards
   e. all of the above
2. A(n) _____ is a group of homogenous employees and a manager who are quickly summoned to deal with an emergency.
   a. safety team
   b. crisis management team
   c. risk management team
   d. sanitation team
   e. insurance team
3. When establishing the right insurance program, the caterer must:
   a. identify and analyze the exposures or potential causes of loss.
   b. know the options to address the exposures.
   c. choose the best alternative for the organization.
   d. monitor the insurance program and make adjustments to the overall package.
   e. all of the above.

True or False

Read each of the following statements and determine if it is true or false.

1. Caterers can use the results of the safety survey to create a better work environment.
2. Insurance policies are written on forms created by the Insurance Services Office (ISO).
3. A contract is a binding agreement between two or more parties.

Putting It All Together

Stephen's Catering is a combination restaurant and bakery. The restaurant is managed by Kendall while his sisters, Elizabeth and Samantha, coordinate the catering operations and Nick manages the bakery. Each manager supervises 10 employees.

The normal practice upon closing the restaurant is for one of the restaurant employees to turn off and clean the deep fat fryer. There's no assigned person to do this, though one of the employees typically has done it on a regular basis. One night, however, that employee was off and no one thought to take care of this very important task. As a result, the fryer oil overheated, causing the grease to catch fire. As the entire production area began to fill with smoke from the fire, a bakery employee smelled the smoke and was alerted to the fire raging in the kitchen. She called Emergency Control, who alerted the local fire department.

In the meantime, the employee grabbed a pressurized water fire extinguisher and went to put out the grease fire. As she ran to the production kitchen to try stopping the flames from spreading, the automatic sprinkler system discharged from the ceiling. The employee slipped on the wet floor and fell, spraining her ankle and injuring her ribs.

The fire department arrived shortly afterward and completed extinguishing the fire, but extensive damage was done to the production area. The employee was taken to the hospital to have her ankle and ribs x-rayed.

Who is liable in this incident? What insurance coverage is needed for the employee's injuries, the fire, damage to equipment, and loss of materials and supplies? What do you think were the root causes of this incident? What safety procedures should have been in place to prevent this string of events from happening? What apparent training deficiencies could have led to this incident? What, if any, OSHA regulations were violated? As the lead investigator, what steps would you take to ensure it doesn't occur again?

Part 3

Gaining a Competitive Edge

Chapter 15

Beverage Management

Objectives

After studying this chapter, you should be able to:

1. Describe beverage management.

2. List the job tasks of beverage management.

3. Explain why beverage management is an important component of a special event.

4. Summarize the initial information needed to successfully plan the beverage service for an event.

5. Describe why atmosphere is a key element in the life of an event.

6. Summarize the information needed to be collected from the event site prior to planning the beverage service.

7. Explain why the appropriate utilization of space is a key consideration when planning the beverage service.

8. Describe the differences between an indoor and an outdoor bar setup.

9. Explain the contents of a contract's beverage section.

10. Explain the costs associated with providing beverage service.

11. Summarize the content of a cancellation and performance refund policy.

12. Discuss the benefits of offering an all-inclusive beverage package.

13. List the equipment required for beverage service.

14. Explain why quality glassware is crucial in the delivery of all beverage service.

15. Explain the importance of having properly trained and certified employees.

UNIQUE RESPONSIBILITY

The delivery of beverage service during an event requires an attention to detail. Offering and serving guests alcoholic beverages involves a unique responsibility to both the caterer and the client. Knowledge about selling and serving alcoholic beverages is a prerequisite for success (Figure 15.1). In today's litigious world, even careful monitoring of alcoholic beverage service still brings with it potential litigation. Specific job tasks are involved when serving alcoholic and nonalcoholic beverages during a client's function.

The management of the overall beverage service in a manner most pleasing to all guests is a caterer's responsibility. The uncompromising attention to detail sets apart an amateur from the professional. Establishing a budget and exceeding customer expectations must be balanced with responsible alcohol service. Supervising bar personnel, monitoring inventory levels, establishing standards, implementing operating procedures, and learning about wines and beverages is a caterer's responsibility. Specific beverage service management tasks must be identified, learned, and practiced to ensure a successful event (Figure 15.2).

BEVERAGE MANAGEMENT

Beverage management is an important component of all successful special events. Imagine a bartender handing you a perfect martini, a fantastic glass of wine, and later, toasting the bride and groom with a sparkling glass of champagne (Figure 15.3). Now visualize sipping a martini mixed with too much olive juice, a glass of wine not at the appropriate serving temperature, and watching the server pour the last drop

beverage management
Management of the overall beverage service in a manner most pleasing to all guests with uncompromising attention to detail, establishing a budget, and exceeding customer expectations balanced with responsible alcohol service. Specific tasks include supervising bar personnel, monitoring inventory levels, establishing standards, implementing operating procedures, and learning about wines and beverages.

Figure 15.1 Knowledge about selling and serving alcoholic beverages is a prerequisite for success.

Figure 15.2 Beverage management job tasks.

1. Design and maintain a bar product/supplies inventory system for:

   a. Nonalcoholic beverage supplies and mixers

   b. Glassware

   c. Expendable paper and other supplies

2. Plan strategies to promote the beverage program.

3. Inspect and maintain the cleanliness and sanitation of bar area, glassware, and equipment.

4. Develop standard operating procedures to ensure service bars are set and operated with efficiency.

5. Maintain an adequate supply of liquor, wine, and beer through an effective inventory system.

6. Recruit, train, schedule, and supervise bar personnel.

7. Develop product/sales control systems and procedures to prevent employee theft.

8. Assures laws applicable to beverage operations are followed.

9. Work with staff to ensure efficient beverage service.

10. Develop wine and food pairing options and beverage lists.

11. Monitor financial information and take corrective action to achieve financial goals.

12. Solve client complaints and monitor suggestions.

13. Select, supervise, and evaluate service staff.

14. Implement safety, accident, and emergency policies and procedures.

© Cengage Learning 2014

beverage plan The outcome of analyzing the beverage needs for a specific function based on the customer, number attending, purpose and length of the event, location, space, budget, the knowledge of the bar, type, and kind of equipment, transportation, and staffing need requirements.

Diemo Video Picture

Figure 15.3 Mixing the perfect drink requires training and practice.

of champagne before reaching your glass. Avoiding all these situations requires diligent management of the beverage service during a special event. The ability to deliver a memorable experience delighting guests is the trademark of a skilled caterer.

To ensure the successful service of beverages during a special event, whether large or small, planning is the most important management function. The formulation of the **beverage plan** requires knowledge of the bar, type, quantity, and kind of equipment, transportation requirements, and staffing needs. The initial information to successfully plan the beverage service for an event is derived from the following questions:

(1) What is the guest count? Who are they?

(2) How long will the event last?

(3) Where is the location of the event?

(4) What type of space is available?

(5) What percent of the overall budget is allocated for beverage service?

(6) What kind of event?

(7) When is the event being held (time of year, time of day/night)?

What Is the Guest Count? Who Are They?

To accurately forecast the consumption of beverages and ice, it is crucial to know the number and demographic composition of the guests. Will all guests be of legal consumption age? Are they predominantly beer drinkers or will they request mixed drinks? Remember, unused beverages can be transported back for storage.

How Long Will the Event Last?

The length of the event will affect the amount of beverage and ice consumed. There tends to be an inverse relationship with length of beverage service and amount of alcohol consumed. Guests consume more beverages in the beginning than at the end of the event. Forecast how many drinks a "typical" guest will consume. Plan on one drink per guest per hour.

Where Will the Event Be Located and What Type of Space Is Available?

This question engages the caterer to anticipate the environment in which the beverages will be served. Will the event will be held inside, outside, or both? Will the inside area permit enough space for a bar setup (Figure 15.4)? Will the outside area be covered to protect against the elements of weather? Will there be a tent? Will the tent be with or without walls?

What Percent of the Overall Budget Is Allocated for Beverage Service?

Establish a clear cost estimate with the client. A budget quoted for the food is completely different than from behind the bar, be careful not to mix the two.

Figure 15.4 Will the area permit enough space for the bar setup?

Always be upfront and honest with the client. If the client has a $500 budget for a 150-person wedding party, realistically explain what they will receive and stress the differences from their expectations.

What Type of Event?

atmosphere Atmosphere takes into account managing the guests' senses of sight, sound, scent, and touch. All events have their own unique life to them. Atmosphere is a key element in the life of an event.

All events have their own unique life to them. **Atmosphere** is a key element in the life of an event. Understand what type of event your client anticipates and what they want the actual event to be like.

Atmosphere takes into account managing the guests' senses of sight, sound, scent, and touch. When planning the beverage service for a wedding, how will the sensory factors be managed? Using beverage service, champagne will be needed to toast the bride and groom. For a summer barbeque, the brand, amount, and quality of beer offered may be a prerequisite for success. Alcoholic beverage service for a child's birthday celebration may create a negative atmosphere. If planning a corporate event, party, or meeting, alcoholic beverage service may create a hostile environment or violate company policy.

When Is the Event Being Held (time of year, time of day/night)?

site inspection Visit the exact location for the event. Inspect the property or location. Review the available assessable space. Draw a diagram or take pictures to keep a visual readily available for future reference.

The time of the year, and whether it occurs during the day or night will affect the amount of beverages and ice consumed. Outside events held in late summer will require more ice than similar events held in late winter. In hot weather guests consume more beverages. The type of event will affect the amount of ice used and beverages consumed (Figure 15.5). Providing beverage service for a golf outing in August requires a significant amount of ice to keep beer, wine, soda, and water cold. Safely forecast enough ice for each job. The golf outing may need 5 pounds of ice per person. A wedding reception may need one pound of ice per person. On average, plan between one and one-half to 3 pounds of ice per person minimum. An event during the day will involve consumption of less alcohol than one during the evening.

Site Inspection

After the initial beverage service questions are answered, conduct a **site inspection**. Visit the exact location for the event. Inspect the property or location. Review the available assessable space. Draw a diagram or take pictures to keep a visual readily available for future reference. Use a tape measure to accurately measure

Diemo Video Picture

Figure 15.5 The type of event will affect the amount of ice used and beverages consumed.

the dimensions of the space, taking care to note the width of doors, elevators, and hallways. Visualize the placement of the bar. Diagram into the allotted space the location for the guest tables for dinner, buffet tables, dessert stations, bathrooms, and other service details. Take detailed notes showing the location for the entrance and exits and where the dance floor and band will be set.

Appropriate use of space is a key consideration when planning the bar (Figure 15.6). First, designate a "mingle area" for the guests. Second, create space to support a neat and orderly queue which will form during busy periods. Third, bigger is not always better. Will the bar be large enough to permit multiple drinks made from mul-

Figure 15.6 Appropriate use of space is a key consideration when planning the bar.

tiple bartenders? Will there be enough space for a service bar? Will speed rails fit behind the bar? Fourth, eliminate wasted space behind the bar. Wasted space creates a movement problem. It creates a larger area for the bartender to cover during service delivery. This may create a problem, depending on the number of bartenders scheduled. Fifth, plan for storage. Safely store and hide bar supplies, equipment, and inventory. Items needing to be stored during beverage service include:

- liquor bottles
- kegs and keg lines to the bar
- CO_2 tanks for kegs and soda gun
- glassware
- food or bar snacks

Recognize storage space. Visualize the height of the bar and the number of tables behind the bar. Depending on the type of bar, extra space can be found underneath it. Storage beneath the tables is also common.

Knowing the allocated space and dimensions, size and height of the bar, and number and placement of tables will assist in creating a good beverage service plan. Remember to use a tape measure to create accurate, detailed diagrams.

Event Location: Indoor or Outdoor

Depending on the event location, planning for an **indoor bar** or an **outdoor bar** will create different challenges. Regardless, plan to have the bar set up within a reasonable amount of time. Complete the set up at least 30 minutes prior to the start of service.

The simpler set up is an indoor bar. Inspect the proposed bar area for electrical outlets (electric blender). Extension cords, if needed, can be safely routed through

indoor bar A bar located inside the premise.

outdoor bar A bar located outside of the premise.

the room. Identify the type of flooring the bar will be set upon. Plan and prepare for spilled beverage on the floor. Common types of floors and considerations are:

(1) Carpeting: Can a mat be laid over top of the carpeting to protect against spillage? Is it an antique carpet? What is the standard operating practice of the property? Do they have a cover available?

(2) Wood: Is it durable? Is it a treated wood? Can spills easily be cleaned up? Is the event being held in a historic location or a cultural institution? Protect a wood floor against potential guest damage. Place protective mats over the floor. Wrap coverings on table or bar legs touching the floor. If the wood becomes damaged or scratched, the caterer will be required to pay for its restoration!

(3) Tile or concrete: Can the surface be mopped or cleaned? What is needed to prevent or clean up spills?

The outdoor bar is more difficult to plan. Why? There are more factors to consider. Will the area enclosing the service bar be covered? Does it need to be covered to support the type of event or to protect the guest from inclement weather? If covered how many guests, table tops, and supporting equipment will fit beneath the space? As more guests occupy the covered area, less space is available for guests to stand at the bar, decreasing participation or creating congestion. A portable covering for an outside event is always a nice feature.

What time of the year will the event be held? If the event is in the fall, protect the bar with a cover against falling leaves. A cold spring day or cool fall night may require portable heaters to keep guests and bartenders comfortable. Cooling fans during a warm summer day or evening are especially important for bartenders to maintain hygiene standards. Will the area be windy (Figure 15.7)? To prevent debris from penetrating the bar area, a temporary tarp works effectively well as a wall to keep the bar clean and guests comfortable.

Consider the type of flooring upon which the bar will be placed on. Typically, asphalt and concrete surfaces are commonly found beneath a pavilion or in a parking lot. Grass and mulch are a possibility. Can protective mats be placed over the asphalt or concrete surfaces? Most important is for the outside area to be level. Use a carpenter's level to verify and note any discrepancies. Always use a level, do not simply "look." The last thing wanted is a drink sliding off the bar.

Precut wood blocks or spacers work well to level the bar and tables. When dealing with a grass or mulch surface, determine if the area can easily flood or become muddy. For a brief rainstorm, tarps can be put down to prevent a muddy situation. A heavy rain, however, will easily destroy a grassy surface, especially if the guests are constantly walking on the area, creating a difficult cleanup.

Figure 15.7 Excessive wind can affect the pouring of alcohol for a drink.

Lastly, write a contingency backup plan. Most outside events are designed with a backup location within walking distance. Establish tear-down procedures to effectively move the bar inside if needed. This will save time and products from being damaged.

Accept or Reject the Event

Decide whether to accept or reject the event based on the information. Can you do it? If unsure, never take the event as this can cause loss of client and potential clients. Respectfully decline and direct the client to another professional caterer to prevent losing your credibility. Offer an explanation: perhaps the event space is too large, the guest count too high or too low, or possible equipment problems exist. This communicates to the potential client a reason and allows them to consider changes in the event. If changes are made you might be able to execute the event. If the event can be done, prepare and present a proposal.

Beverage Contract

A well-written contract is a necessity (see Chapter 14). A contract needs to cover all elements of the event. The beverage section explains in detail the beverage services provided by the caterer and those to be received by the client. Never allow the client to be uncertain of any element in the contract. Explain the specific brands, kinds, and volume of alcoholic and nonalcoholic beverages supplied by the caterer. If the client is supplying his or her own alcohol, be specific. Generic contracts can be used as a reference tool. Writing your own contract is perceived as more professional. It is easier to write unique specifications based on client needs into your own contract. The beverage section of a contract contains the following information:

- Function's date and day
- Exact starting and ending time of the beverage service
- Exact location (site) of the event; include address, descriptions, room number, and directions
- Exact room(s), specific location, and a backup location, if needed
- Minimum guarantee guest count for this contract
- Final guaranteed guest count provided in writing. Guest will guarantee to pay caterer for this number, regardless if fewer attend it
- Extra cost for additional guests. Increased guest count prior to the event, clause automatically adjusts to higher contracted fee
- Price per guest for beverage and service as specified in the beverage package chosen
- Description of the beverage package (packages explained later in the chapter)
- Specific products and guest services in the package
- Staffing requirements, including bartenders and beverage servers. Typically one bartender for every 50 guests. A bartender cannot leave the bar. It creates a risk of theft in alcohol and tips if the money is left unattended on the bar. Beverage servers are scheduled in addition to food servers

- Cost for equipment, including rental equipment
- Cost for transportation to and from the event
- Unique or specific requests from the client, management policies, or conditions
- Signature and date
- The caterer and client both sign the contract to acknowledge the mutual agreement to the terms within the contract

Cost of the Event

The basic cost for the beverage service is the client's deposit and negotiated price per attendee. Federal, state, local, and miscellaneous taxes may apply. If the client is tax-exempt, a copy of its tax-exempt status or number must be obtained and kept on file. Additional service fees may include a one-time fee for setting up and tearing down the bar, transportation charges, equipment rental, and a predetermined dollar amount including a gratuity for each bartender and server. Increased guest counts beyond the guaranteed number automatically adjust charges upward. The amount will usually depend on the type of beverage package selected by the client. Often an event will exceed the contracted ending time. If agreed to continue the beverage service beyond this time, an additional charge will apply. Finally, confirm with the client if the service employees will be allowed to receive and keep guest generated tips. Depending on the event, clients may not set a tip jar, as the gratuity has usually been calculated in the client's cost.

Cancellation and Performance Refund Policies

cancellation policy Stipulations in a cancellation policy are usually framed and guided by time and define the course of action the caterer will take, beginning at a predefined period from the event date, to before the event. The policy communicates what amount of the deposit and money will be refunded to the client.

performance refund policy A performance refund is requested by an unsatisfied client whose needs were not met. Usually caused by an operational or service defect, this breakdown occurs in any of the key activities that cause the system to malfunction. Defects include poor food quality and service.

Catering is a business based on time. **Cancellation** and **performance refund policies** must be explicitly spelled out in the contract. A cancellation terminates a prescheduled future event. The cancellation of a future event certainly affects the caterer. The potential loss of revenue, the ability to rebook the date, and a client's deposit and prepaid monies being held by the caterer are real issues to address.

A performance refund is requested by an unsatisfied client whose needs were not met. Usually caused by an operational or service defect, this breakdown occurs in any of the key activities that cause the system to malfunction. Defects include poor food quality and service.

Cancellation and performance refund policies must be explicitly stated in the contract. Have an attorney review the policy. Attempt to provide a fair and reasonable solution. Certainly, each situation has its own unique set of circumstances. Policies guide organizational decision making. Adhering to a well-designed policy treats all clients honestly and communicates a level of professionalism to the marketplace.

Stipulations in a cancellation policy are usually framed and guided by time. A common strategy is to frame the policy within a time line, anchoring the date of the signed contract to event date. A policy will define the course of action the caterer will take, beginning a predefined period from the event date, to 6 months, 90 days, 60 days, 30 days, and 2 weeks before the event. The policy communicates what amount of the deposit and money will be refunded to the client. A graduated formula is used to calculate the amount of the refund. If a client cancels one year or longer from the event date, most, if not all of the deposit, may be returned. A cancellation one year prior permits the caterer enough reasonable time to rebook the date. If the event is cancelled 90 days, 60 days, 30 days, 2 weeks, or the day before, the policy must specifically communicate the amount to be returned. Standard practice, if a guest cancels within 2 weeks of an event, depending on the circumstances, the caterer will keep the deposit and the entire prepaid amount.

Always include those elements in the beverage section of the contract. Be sure to explicitly cover every specific detail. If it is not covered in the contract and a problem arises, the caterer is at fault. This can cost the caterer money, a client, and future business.

Beverage Packages

A common sales strategy is to define beverage service framed in an all-inclusive **beverage package** based on a guaranteed price per person. Optional packages are written to explain in detail the amount of beer, wine, mixers, juices, garnishes, service staff, and other items available. Include a section to describe the complimentary items being provided at no extra cost to the client. Be creative. Monitor client requests to differentiate their event from others. Compile these requests into a list of complimentary products or services. Complimentary items create excellent marketing strategy and deliver value. Items may include colored linen, chair covers, overlays, decorations, waiving setup or breakdown fees, potato chips or other snacks, or engraved champagne glasses. Many caterers maintain a prop room stocked with reusable unique trinkets, candles, glassware, and other props. To create atmosphere or to enhance the theme, offer the trinkets to decorate tabletops, walls, hallways, or room columns. Use the complimentary products to create a unique event while differentiating your service from the competition.

> **beverage package** A common sales strategy used to define beverage service is written to explain in detail the amount of beer, wine, mixers, juices, garnishes, service staff, and other items available.

Packages enable a client to better understand the atmosphere of the event. A typical client will not be aware a cherry is needed to garnish a Manhattan cocktail. By bundling together beverage products and services into a complete package, the client is guided by the caterer to make the "right" decision.

Most caterers offer a minimum of three different packages: a basic package, a brand name package, and a premium package. Beverage packages provide the caterer continuity and standardization in planning an event. An all-inclusive package is a negotiating tool. Certainly, a client can select one of the packages as is, or, add or subtract products or services to customize it to meet their needs. It is easier to have the client select an existing package with little or no alterations; however, flexibility in creating the right client package is a key to success. If changes in the package are agreed upon, the special requests need to be communicated to the beverage staff to ensure they will be remembered.

Basic Package

The basic package is the foundation upon which the other options are built. The basic package offers fewer products and a limited choice of beer, wine, and liquor. The basic package will include:

1. Beer
   a. Between two and four types of bottled beer and one type of draft beer

In the state of Pennsylvania, alcohol is not allowed to be provided by the limousine company. The company will usually supply unlimited water and ice along with some decorative glass beakers that may be used for whiskey and other beverages. If the client brings their own alcohol and decorations, we will happily use our best skills to make the decorations fit nicely in the limousine, or assist the client with them (Figure 15.8).

A good way to reserve your limousine is to personally visit the company. Limousine companies may offer a variety of different vehicles. Check the comfort, pricing options, and availability of the vehicles. Extra amenities can always be added for any occasion. Services, such as a red carpet service, where a red carpet is literally rolled out before opening the limousine door before entering or exiting the vehicle can be provided. Although somewhat more old-fashioned and perhaps outdated these days, some clients still do request it. Various types of glasses are offered in almost every type of limousine. If beverages are to be served in the limousine, verify beforehand to assure there are glasses provided.

At Unique, we have limousines, not limos; we have chauffeurs, not drivers. We have an extensive training program for our chauffeurs and only once they are trusted driving the owner's family, friends, kids, and grandkids, then and only then are they trusted with our clients and their families and friends.

Ben Cavallaro, Unique Limousine, Harrisburg, Pennsylvania

2. Wine
   a. Two types of wine, including a red and a white, providing an option to add an additional fee for sparkling

3. Liquor
   a. Stock all generic liquor, such brands as Jaquine's, Burnett's, or Banker's Club
   b. Only vodka, gin, rum, tequila, and whiskey will be offered

4. Bar mixers and liquors
   a. Triple-sec, grenadine, and a sour mix

5. Juices
   a. Orange juice, cranberry, pineapple, and lime juice

6. Mixers
   a. Four will be available: cola, lemon-lime, ginger ale, and soda water

7. Garnishes
   a. Lemons, limes, oranges, and cherries.

A basic package will inexpensively cover most types of special events. One recommendation, add a scotch or brandy to satisfy older guests.

Figure 15.8 A limousine may offer enough space for beverage service.

Brand Name Package

The brand name package is typically the most popular package. Competitively priced, it delivers higher guest satisfaction, provides a better value, and is more prestigious for the client. Guests appreciate a higher grade of alcohol. This package features recognizable liquors and brands. A typical brand name package will include:

1. Beer
    a. Four to seven types of bottled beer, two types of draft beer
2. Wine
    a. Red: two types
    b. White: two types
    c. Sparkling: one type
3. Liquor

    Liquor offered in this package is of a higher quality. It is referred to as "call brand liquor." The following are examples of call brand liquor:

    a. Vodka
        i. Absolut
        ii. Stolichnaya
    b. Gin
        i. Beefeater
        ii. Tanqueray
        iii. Bombay
    c. Rum
        i. Bacardi—a recommended choice since the Bacardi brand provides a popular silver and dark rum
        ii. Captain Morgan
        iii. Malibu
    d. Whiskey

        When choosing whiskey for the brand name package, select a bourbon, blended and scotch whiskey. Know the differences of the three different types

        i. Bourbon
            1. Wild Turkey
            2. Jim Beam
        ii. Blended
            1. Crown Royal
            2. Seagram's VO
        iii. Scotch
            1. Johnnie Walker Red
            2. CuttySark
    e. Tequila
        i. Jose Cuervo Gold
        ii. Sauza Gold
        iii. Dos Reales

4. Bar mixers

    a. Sour mix, cream, pina colada mix, margarita mix, daiquiri mix, vermouth (used in martinis and manhattans), bitters, grenadine, and Bloody Mary mix if needed.

5. Mixers

    a. Four available: cola, lemon-lime, ginger ale, soda water.

6. Juices

    a. Lime juice, orange juice, cranberry, and pineapple juice

Premium Package

The premium package offers greater variety, better options, and is the most expensive. A premium package delivers the "wow" factor to an event. When the premium package is chosen, schedule the best professional bartenders who have the expertise to maximize the inventory to deliver and to exceed customer expectations.

1. Beer

    a. Seven to 10 types of bottled beer, three types of draft beer

2. Wine

    a. Red: three types

    b. White: three types

    c. Sparkling: one type, option for a second but one type of either red or white must be dropped

3. Liquor

top shelf brand liquor
Highest quality and brand named alcoholic beverages.

Liquor offered in this package is of a higher quality. It is referred to as **top shelf brand liquor**. Examples of top shelf brand liquor are:

    a. Vodka

        i. Grey Goose

        ii. Belvedere

    b. Gin

        i. Beefeater

        ii. Tanqueray No. 10

        iii. Bombay

    c. Rum

        i. Bacardi Superior—a recommended choice since the Bacardi brand provides a popular silver and dark rum

        ii. Captain Morgan

        iii. Mount Gay

    d. Whiskey

    When choosing whiskey for the premium package, select a bourbon, blended, and scotch whiskey. Again, be familiar with the differences of the three different types.

        i. Bourbon

            1. Wild Turkey

            2. Jim Beam

      ii. Blended
         1. Crown Royal
         2. Jack Daniel's or Gentleman's Jack, Jack Daniel's premium whiskey
      iii. Scotch
         1. Johnnie Walker Green, Blue an optional upgrade
         2. Macallan 12 or 15

  e. Tequila
      i. Jose Cuervo Gold
      ii. Patron

  f. Cordials
      i. Jagermeister
      ii. Bailey's
      iii. Frangelico

4. Bar mixers
  a. Sour mix, cream, pina colada mix, margarita mix, daiquiri mix, vermouth (used in martinis and manhattans), bitters, grenadine and Bloody Mary mix

5. Mixers
  a. Five available: cola, lemon-lime, ginger ale, soda water, and cream

6. Juices
  a. Lime juice, orange juice, cranberry, and pineapple juice

Use the tangible benefits and the intangible prestige factor to show the premium package. The guest will enjoy a higher quality beverage, and the package affords more variety, choice, and drink-mix options. This package delivers an atmosphere for a highly prestigious event. Let the package sell itself.

Finally, be very explicit in a detailed itemized description of the beverages and services provided in each package. Concise language keeps everyone honest. Be sure the client understands every detail of the complete package. Review the services, beverages, and pricing policies, gratuities, time, day, and date. It cannot be emphasized enough to communicate an accurate understanding of the package. Require the client to initial each itemized description to fully acknowledge their complete understanding of the product and service being provided.

Equipment List

Beverage service begins with the plan and the plan includes an equipment checklist. Using an equipment checklist avoids problems and keeps everyone organized. If it is an off-premise event, the checklist saves time and ensures the collection of all of the equipment. Checklists account for each piece of equipment. Although never a big deal to make an extra trip if the event is down the road, if something is forgotten, it may be difficult to return and retrieve it. Crucial time is lost and fuel is consumed when a caterer must travel across town or a significant distance to retrieve the forgotten item.

There will be multiple checklists. First, a checklist of the equipment inventory and its location will start the process. A specific equipment checklist will be created based on the type of beverage service to implement the event. A third checklist can be used to check off each item as it is loaded into the truck for transportation to the site. A fourth checklist is used to check off the equipment as it is loaded back on the truck at the conclusion of the event for its return to the facility. A final checklist is used to check off the clean equipment as it is placed back into storage (inventory).

The following equipment is needed to support beverage service for a special event.

Bar Top

If the event location does not have a bar available, a bar top is then needed. Pack items to level out the bar. This should be noted on the checklist after the site inspection has been completed.

Tables

These tables are for the bar area or if the client has requested them. Tables consume a large amount of space in transportation, so the less the better.

Bins for Storage

To utilize space in transportation, fill the bins with other equipment off the checklist. Place cleaning supplies in one bin, bar equipment in another. Do not mix alcohol with other items in transportation. This is an easy way to lose items. If alcohol is left unattended during setup, it creates a high risk of theft.

Three-Bay Sink

If the special event site does not have a dishwasher, a three part sink or three sanitary washing bins are needed. Include a washing and sanitizing solution.

Behind the Bar

A standard set of equipment to support the bartender's effort behind the bar is required for a typical event. Most of these items can easily be forgotten. Some items can be disregarded depending on the type of beverage service. Typically, it is best practice to pack the following back bar equipment for each event.

1. 30 oz. mixing tin. This will be used for making mixed drinks, shots, martinis, and manhattans. Pack more than one—the required number depends on the event size and the number of bartenders.
2. Pint glasses (16 oz.) mixing glasses. Although these will be brought to the event, pack a few extra to use for mixing drinks.
3. Strainer. When making certain drinks it is used to strain the liquid from the ice. Pack more than one, depends on the size of the event.
4. Bar spoon. This spoon is needed for layering and stirring drinks.
5. Muddler. Wooden muddler or the back of a large wooden spoon for mashing herbs, fruit, and so forth—only needed if drinks such as a mojito are being served.
6. Jigger. A jigger (1 1/2 ounces) measure with easy-to-read half-and quarter- ounce measures. Most bartenders do not care to use a jigger when serving drinks. If the caterer requires all drinks to be measured, then pack a few jiggers.

7. Beer speed opener (large bottle opener). Used when serving large numbers of bottled beer. Use a speed opener to save time by opening multiple bottles of beer and to avoid cutting one's hand when opening hundreds of beer bottles.

8. Ice bin and scoop. An appropriate size ice bin is needed behind the bar. Even if there is an ice machine, an ice bin is used to store and transport ice for the event. Always use an ice scoop for sanitary reasons to fill glasses with ice. Never use a glass to scoop ice from a bin due to the potential risk of breaking the glass.

9. Waiters wine key. If serving wine, a wine key is needed. There are multiple types of wine openers; the preferred type is called a "2-step." A 2-step wine opener features a standard cutter used to open the bottle and a 2-step hinge to ease the opening of the bottle.

10. Blender and glass rimmer. These two items go together. The rimmer is used to add salt or sugar on the outer rim of a glass, as requested by a guest. The blender is used to mix drinks, such as daiquiris and margaritas.

11. A knife and cutting board is needed for the bartender to cut garnishes, such as lemons and limes, for drinks if not precut before service. It is recommended to bring a knife and cutting board to cut more garnishes (Figure 15.9).

12. A bar caddie. Bar caddie contains small plastic trays used to separately store precut garnishes. A bar caddie has a lid to cover the garnishes during slow periods.

13. Garbage bins. Typically the event site will have garbage bins available. If the location is outside or away from a banquet area, estimate two large trash bins for every 50 guests. Place one large or two medium garbage bins behind the bar. This is based on the number of bartenders and size of the event. If the trash bin is too large, hauling it to a dumpster may make be difficult.

14. Coasters or napkins—used for two important reasons. First, they protect the surface of the bar against spilled liquid or surface chipping from glassware being placed down. Second, a coaster is used to mark a guest letting other bartenders know the guest has already been waited on.

15. Measuring spoons

16. Can opener

17. Large pitchers

18. Recipe guide

19. Additional items. Large and small straws for drinks, toothpicks to put cherries and olives together for drinks

Figure 15.9 A knife and cutting board is needed for the bartender to cut garnishes, such as lemons, for drinks.

Figure 15.10 Quality glassware, clean and unchipped, is crucial in the delivery of all beverage service.

Glassware

Quality glassware, clean and unchipped, is crucial in the delivery of all beverage service. Match the type of drink with its appropriate glass (Figure 15.10). For a standard event, beer, wine, mixed drinks, whisky, and brandy will be served in a glass. Beer is served in a standard mug (12 to 16 oz) or a pilsner (10 to 16 oz) glass. Since most events do not allow a guest to carry a glass bottle, plan for additional glasses, as these are needed to serve the bottled beer. Depending on the event, plan to have a minimum two glasses per guest inventory.

Wineglasses (6 to 11 oz) range from simple to extravagant depending on the event. A standard wineglass can be used to serve both white and red wines. Specifically, red wine is served from a glass having a larger bulb at the bottom, known as a larger "tulip" shape. This shape allows the bouquet of the red wine to find the guest's nose. White wine is served from a glass having a smaller "tulip" and tends to be thinner at the bottom of the bulb. This minor distinction is important to a serious wine drinker and may offend them if the wine is not served in the correct glass. If hosting a wine tasting event, use the proper glassware for serving both red and white wines.

Mixed drinks are served in either a 5 or 7 oz rocks glass. This glass is used for a standard drink, such as rum and cola. A glass called a "highball" is used for mixed drinks; these glasses tend to be a few ounces larger to hold additional ice or a mixer. Martini glasses are used for both martinis and for manhattans. A margarita glass can be used if there are not enough pint glasses available; these glasses add flare and style, pleasing guests. A champagne flute (4 to 6 oz) is used for sparkling wine. Lastly, coffee and Irish coffee are served in a hot drink mug (10 to 12 oz).

For all glassware a plastic or disposable option is available. A disposable plastic container makes for an easier cleanup but is wasteful and produces more trash at the end of an event. If possible, suggest biodegradable containers for less of an environmental impact.

Transport glassware in proper carriers. These carriers serve a dual function: they are used to safely transport glassware and for use in a warewashing machine.

Some catering halls may provide glassware. If so, count each type to verify the complete inventory. Determine from the count if the specific type, such as a brandy glass, and number needed is available.

Beverage Service Employees

Serving alcohol requires all employees, servers, and bartenders to follow specific guidelines. All employees serving alcohol to a guest must be 18 years old. Everyone

Figure 15.11 A bartender checks the guest's identification to confirm he is 21 years old.

consuming alcohol must be 21 years old or older, a standard law for all 50 states. A bartender or server must know how to recognize false identification. Guests may attend from other states or from other countries. Beverage staff needs to be trained to recognize different forms of identification and to find the person's date of birth (Figure 15.11).

Most catering companies require all employees serving alcohol to be certified either by TIPS (Training for Intervention ProcedureS; http://www.gettips.com) or ServeSafe (http://www.servsafe.com) training programs. These server training programs provide need-to-know information regarding all aspects of alcohol service. The alcohol-training program teaches the proper procedural steps to handle an intoxicated guest, to recognize when to stop serving a guest, and to determine if the guest needs alternative means of transportation home or to a hotel.

When hiring a bartender, a caterer will require the candidate to be tested. A talented bartender will properly pour and serve beer, liquor, and wine, as well as make shot, martinis, margaritas, and blended drinks. A bartender must be able to stand for extended periods of time, have ability to lift a certain weight, and move equipment (Figure 15.12). Employees must comfortably handle and count money for cash transactions. Never settle for an employee who may not be trusted or is not completely qualified as this will have an impact on the event and a caterer's reputation.

Figure 15.12 A bartender's job requires them to lift, carry equipment, and bar supplies.

The number of bartenders for an event will vary. A standard rule of thumb to follow is one bartender for every 50 guests. However, this number will change depending upon the following factors:

What is the guest count? Who are they?

How long will the event last?

Where is the location of the event?

What type of space is available?

What percent of the overall budget is allocated for beverage service?

What kind of event?

When is the event being held (time of year, time of day/night)?

Summary

Beverage management is a crucial part of a special event. The successful delivery of beverage service during a special event is accomplished by the beverage staff, who diligently work to set up, clean, and provide outstanding service to guests.

Review Questions

Brief Answers

1. Describe beverage management.
2. List the job tasks of beverage management.
3. Explain why beverage management is an important component of a special event.
4. Summarize the initial information needed to successfully plan the beverage service for an event.
5. Describe why atmosphere is a key element in the life of an event.
6. Summarize the information needed from an event site prior to planning the beverage service.
7. Explain why the appropriate utilization of space is a key consideration when planning the beverage service.
8. Describe the differences between an indoor and an outdoor bar setup.
9. Explain the contents of a typical contract's beverage section.
10. Explain the costs associated with providing beverage service.
11. Summarize the content of a cancellation and performance refund policy.
12. Discuss the benefits of offering an all-inclusive beverage package.
13. List the equipment required for beverage service.
14. Explain why quality glassware is crucial in the delivery of all beverage service.
15. Explain the importance of having properly trained and certified employees.

Multiple Choice

Select the single best answer for each question.

1. The formulation of the beverage plan requires knowledge of the following:
   a. physical bar
   b. type, quantity, and kind of equipment
   c. transportation requirements
   d. staffing needs
   e. all of the above

2. Appropriate utilization of space is a key consideration when planning the bar. Which of the following is not a key consideration?
   a. designate a "mingle area" for the guest
   b. create space to support a neat and orderly queue or line
   c. the bigger the bar, the better the service
   d. eliminate space wasted behind the bar
   e. plan for storage

3. The following bar equipment is needed for the beverage service in a special event:
   a. bar top
   b. storage bins
   c. three-bay sink
   d. behind the bar equipment
   e. all of the above

True or False

Read each of the following statements and determine if it is true or false.

1. Since catering is a business based on time, cancellation and performance refund policies must be explicitly written in the contract.
2. A common sales strategy is to define beverage service for a client as framed in an all-inclusive beverage package based on a guaranteed price per person.
3. Atmosphere takes into account managing the guest's senses of sight, sound, scent, and touch.

Putting It All Together

Create three beverage package options for a client's New Year's Eve event. Explain the amount of beer, wine, mixers, juices, garnishes, and other service items offered per package. Summarize how each package will help to set the atmosphere for the event.

Chapter 16
Conflict Resolution

Objectives

After studying this chapter, you should be able to:

1. Define conflict.
2. Describe the process of resolving conflict.
3. Define the issue dimension of a conflict.
4. Define the position dimension of a conflict.
5. Understand how emotions can prevent a resolution of a conflict.
6. Explain the two basic elements in a conflict.
7. Explain why there are two sides to every story.
8. Discuss why each party in a conflict should identify alternative options that provide mutual gain for each side.
9. Identify industry standards common to the catering industry that can be used to create options in resolving conflict.
10. List the negative styles of resolving conflict.
11. Explain why one should aim for mutual gain and satisfaction and not a total victory when resolving conflict.
12. Describe principled negotiation.

KEY TERMS

conflict

conflict resolution strategy

interests

issue dimension

negotiation

position

positional bargaining

principled negotiation or negotiation on the merits

DIMENSIONS TO RESOLVING CONFLICT

Conflict, it happens. Conflict is the disagreement caused by the tension between two or more parties.[1,4] No matter how hard a caterer tries, sooner or later an uncontrollable factor will escalate a situation into an unpredictable conflict scenario. The potential for conflict always exists, no matter how detailed an event plan or how well-managed an event. The ability to positively resolve conflict through negotiation influences the success or the failure of a business. **Negotiation**, as a management tool, is a back-and-forth communication process between opposing sides sharing a common interest that is designed to arrive at a mutually agreeable alternative.[2,3,5]

A professional conflict resolution style creates a reputable persona that precedes the caterer into the marketplace. The conflict resolution style can either positively or negatively influence the long-term success of the business.

In most cases, conflict is viewed from a negative perspective. Conflict is seen as a fight or a battle having a winner and a loser. A **conflict resolution strategy** following this approach is simplistic; either win the conflict or ignore the conflict until it disappears. Conflict is likely to happen regardless of how hard it is avoided; this is especially true in catering, as the caterer is trying to make money while the client is trying to get the highest quality food service at the lowest price. Both parties (the caterer and the client) have very different interests in this relationship. When one side believes their individual interests are not being met, the potential for conflict is likely to increase.

Take for example an actual conflict witnessed firsthand at a catered event. The local caterer was hired for a wedding reception. Renowned, he was the exclusive caterer for many prominent families and corporate accounts in the community. His catering facility was recently renovated by a contractor to improve its air conditioning system and air circulation quality. However, problems in the new air conditioning system were recurring, as the new control monitoring system would unexpectedly shut off, causing the banquet room to become excessively warm. This particular wedding reception was booked one year in advance, and prior to the renovations. The bride and groom, their family, the catering staff, and the guests were all excited to be the first event in the newly remodeled hall. The bride and groom's guest list nearly exceeded the capacity rating for the banquet room. The outside temperature was exceedingly hot, even for a typical summer day. The caterer prepared a delectable sit-down four course meal and baked an extravagant assortment of petit fours. The focal point of the room, positioned in front of the head of the bridal table, was a magnificent three-tiered wedding cake set against a mountainous chocolate fountain.

As the guests arrived, they entered using the four double doors leading directly from the parking area into the banquet room. The four double doors were propped

conflict Conflict is the disagreement caused by the tension between two or more parties.

negotiation Management tool consisting of a back-and-forth communication process between opposing sides sharing a common interest that is designed to arrive at a mutually agreeable alternative.

conflict resolution strategy The way to effectively resolve conflict in a situation regardless of the client, setting, environment, or relationship.

[1]Fairhurst, G. T., & Sarr, R. A. (1996). *The art of framing: managing the language of leadership.* San Fransisco: Jossey-Bass Publishers &

[2]Fisher, R., Ury, W., & Patton, B. (1991). *Getting to yes: negotiating agreement without giving in (2nd ed.).*London: Penguin Books,

[3]Furlong, G. T. (2005). *The conflict resolution toolbox: models & maps for analyzing diagnosing, and resolving conflict.* New York: J. Wiley & Sons Canada

[4]Lebedun, J. (1998). *Managing workplace conflict.* Virginia Beach: Coastal Training Technologies Corp.

[5]Ury, W. (2007). *Getting past no: negotiating in difficult situations (Bantam pbk. reissue. ed.).* New York: Bantam Books.

open to accommodate guest flow as they arrived for the reception. The open doors and outside temperature may have triggered the new air conditioning system to overload and eventually shut off. As a result, the ambient room temperature rose, causing an uncomfortable temperature for the seated guests. With all eyes focused on the best man, as he toasted to the health and wealth of the bride and groom, the fondant icing on the wedding cake began to melt. Suddenly, the beautiful cake collapsed onto itself, hurling the upper tier directly into the chocolate fountain with a splash.

The caterer has several options to resolve this scenario. First, simply refuse to bargain over the issue. Since the caterer was not directly responsible for the fall of the cake, demand full payment of the contract. Second, give in to the demands of the client and refund a substantial amount. Third, do nothing; hope no one saw the incident and assume the client will understand the issue. Fourth, blame the contractor. Since the faulty renovations were the cause, insist the client seek retributions from the contractor. Regardless of the caterer's approach to this situation, their action or lack of action dealing with the conflict may have severe repercussions on the caterer-client-guest relationship.

Knowing how effectively to resolve conflict in a situation regardless of the client, setting, environment, or relationship is a prerequisite for the long-term survival of the a business. Particularly important is the appropriate way to handle a client who has just experienced a conflict in their event. Catering is largely influenced through referral connections. Most guests will likely form an independent opinion of the catered service. If impressed with the food and beverage service, they may ask for a referral. If the guest is not impressed, they will certainly want to avoid using the caterer. Again the question becomes: "Who catered this event?"

Consider the phenomenon known as the Six Degrees of Separation. This is the belief that any one person can be linked to another person in six steps. This is particularly relevant in today's society with the ubiquity of social media sites. The cake fiasco in the earlier wedding scenario will negatively influence the client's attitude of the caterer. It is unlikely the conflict will stay contained among the caterer, the client, the bride and groom, and the 425 guests attending the event. The immediate outreach of social media sites (see Chapter 5), such as YouTube and Facebook, can propel this singular event into a highly viewed conflict situation.

It is possible the client will acknowledge the faulty air conditioning system in the banquet room caused the excessive temperature to melt the icing on the wedding cake, collapsing it into the chocolate fountain, and not blame the caterer. However, it is more likely the client will reason the caterer should have known about the faulty air conditioning system and should have done something to prevent it from happening.

If it is believed everyone can be linked within six steps, it is possible to comprehend the entire world will know of the caterer's inability to bake and present a cake that can remain intact during a wedding reception.

The remainder of this chapter will focus on how a caterer can follow steps to resolve a conflict situation.

RESOLVING CONFLICT: OVERVIEW

How does a caterer effectively resolve conflict situations? The Harvard Negotiation Project has identified a four point model of resolving conflict through negotiation.

The following four propositions comprise the tactic called **principled negotiation** or **negotiation on the merits.**

- People: separate the people from the problem
- Interests: focus on interests, not positions
- Options: brainstorm a variety of alternatives before deciding on a course of action
- Criteria: base alternatives on an objective standard

Using the tactic of principled negotiation, the caterer then proceeds through three successive stages to arrive at a mutually acceptable alternative to resolve a conflict situation. These three stages are:

1. Analyzing the conflict and discovering why
2. Planning for mutually satisfying options
3. Discussion and agreement based on industry standards

There are two basic elements in a conflict: its dimensions and the story. First, conflict has two dimensions, the issue and the emotions. Second, there are two sides to every story. To effectively resolve all conflict situations, understanding of these two basic elements is essential, as it helps to move forward in resolving the conflict and to prevent the reactions of those involved from amplifying the conflict.

Once analyzed, each party must recognize the options that satisfy their own individual interests in the dispute. Next, each party should identify those alternative options that provide mutual gain in meeting each party's interests. Industry standards identify options that have the best chance of working.

When negotiating with people involved in a conflict, always treat them as a person. Negative styles of conflict resolution, such as winning the fight or ignoring the conflict, may make the person part of the problem. This strategy is counterproductive in resolving conflict. Once the parties have reached a resolution, shake hands and move forward.

Conflict happens no matter how hard one attempts to avoid it. All conflict will not be resolvable. Resolving a conflict will strengthen the relationship between the parties. In a referral business, such as catering, the ability to effectively resolve conflict will improve the ability to attract more clients.[6]

Analyzing the Conflict: The First Dimension of the Conflict

The **issue dimension** is typically the source of the conflict. Referring to the wedding reception introduced earlier in the chapter, the fall of the top tier of the wedding cake into the chocolate fountain is the cause of the conflict. When conflict happens, too often the parties involved create a defensive position. Valuable time is wasted in a useless exercise spent trying to convince the other side their position is wrong.

Individuals expert in conflict resolution recommend analyzing the conflict from all perspectives. Roger Fisher and William Ury define this as going to the "balcony" and looking down upon the conflict to see it from all sides. In the wedding cake example, it is evident that this conflict cannot be solely blamed on the caterer. On the other hand, the client is likely to be horrified because their special day may now be ruined.

principled negotiation or negotiation on the merits A four point model of resolving conflict through negotiation developed by the Harvard Negotiation Project.

issue dimension Typically is the source of a conflict between two or more people.

[6]Yarbrough, E., & Wilmot, W. (1995). *Artful mediation: constructive conflict at work*. Boulder:Cairns Publishing.

Why spend time analyzing the conflict? Both parties, particularly the caterer, need to understand what caused the situation. Understanding how the conflict occurred, knowing how the parties feel about the conflict, and knowing what the potential ramifications are will better prepare those involved to resolve the conflict.

Put the Emotions into Neutral: Controlling the Second Dimension of the Conflict

The second dimension of the conflict is concerned with the emotions invested in the issue. This dimension focuses on personal feelings and reactions. Imagine how a bride would feel after watching the top tier of her wedding cake fall into the chocolate fountain. Certainly, her wedding is the most important day of her life, and it was ruined by a falling cake. While the issues may be complicated, if used in a negative tone, the emotions invested in the situation can make the issue even more difficult to resolve.

Uncontrollable emotions can negatively influence a conflict situation. Most theorists agree that controlling one's emotions in a conflict situation will help to create a win-win outcome. The participants' emotional outburst will interfere and compound the issues inherent in the conflict. How can this happen? Picture the conflict situation, a wedding cake submerged in a chocolate fountain. If the caterer immediately directs an emotional outburst at the client, viewable by all in attendance, stating that he could not prevent the cake from toppling, then the caterer has not acted professionally. How then, would the client react to the caterer's ill-advised outburst?

Tips from the Trade

The key factors in delivering a catering event are organization and detail orientation. The catering manager is responsible for preplanning each defined detail of an event. It is important to synchronize with the management team to make certain each department correctly understands their role in implementing the designed event plan. Here, at The Chestnut Ridge Golf Resort & Conference Center, I personally work with the Chef, the Banquet Manager, and the Restaurant Manager to ensure our quality exceeds the client's expectations. For example, take a wedding reception. I will confirm with the Chef the final guest count, ensure the Banquet Manager has set the room correctly and double-check that each of the finer details as requested from the client are completed. I personally inspect all of the food, such as the appetizers and entrees, to ensure they were made correctly, are served quickly and served hot. Should a problem arise, I try to correct it as best as I can. At times, I have to handle an emotionally upset client. My first response is to always listen to the client. They will tell me what their problem is. Next, I always respond in a calm manner, and using my best judgment, to correct that situation in a mutually beneficial way.

Subcontractor agreement: wrote chapter:
David Piper, Ph.D.

An emotional response to a stressful situation is a natural, human reaction. Care must be taken to not allow one's emotions to get the better of oneself. Good conflict resolvers:

- recognize emotions as a natural response
- acknowledge and take ownership of their emotional energy
- remain calm unemotional

An understanding of basic psychology is beneficial in understanding conflict situations. When a person is confronted with a stressful situation, they responded by deploying a fight or flight approach. These responses are categorized as negative styles of resolving conflict. They are negative because fighting about or fleeing from the conflict will hamper the ability of the parties to amicably resolve the conflict. Negative styles of conflict resolution will not help to set a productive climate for resolving conflict. A successful conflict resolver creates a positive environment by controlling their emotions and limiting the use of a negative conflict resolution style to resolve conflict.

Two Sides to Every Story: The Second Element in a Conflict

There are two sides to every story, and each side believes their version of the conflict is the correct one. It is beneficial to recall the philosophical phrase "perception is reality." The person engaged in a conflict is behaving according to their perception of the conflict. Arguing to convince the other side they are wrong on the issue can be a negative style of conflict resolution. A more advisable strategy is to abandon the need to prove the other party wrong and focus instead on how each party views the conflict. This will create a set of alternatives to address the issue of the conflict.

Returning to the wedding reception, what would the customer's likely response be after the caterer demanded full payment, claiming the room temperature was the entire reason the cake was destroyed? Is the client likely to pay the full bill? Will the client readily accept the explanation for the cake's fall because the banquet room's faulty environment controls are to be blamed? Or is it more likely that the hysterical bride, the angry mother-of-the-bride, and the father-of-the bride (who has to go home with these people), will refuse to pay the entire bill (assuming they are responsible for the costs) for the catered event?

In this scenario, it is easy to see how both sides of the conflict believe they have a legitimate issue. Too much time arguing over who is right will only deepen the conflict between the client and the caterer. It is certainly in the caterer's best interest to explain to the customer how the heat caused the cake to collapse. The issue is whether the customer should bear the responsibility to pay the full cost of the cake. If the caterer acknowledges the customer has the right to be upset and explains how he will look for an amicable solution, then this will most likely redirect the conflict into a discussion on who should bear the financial consequences of the ruined cake. This should also prevent the escalation of the conflict into other issues surrounding the event.

Proving You are Right May Be All Wrong

Never use a negative style of conflict resolution to convince the other party your side of the story is the only correct version, as it is natural for each party in the conflict to feel their side is right. This is human nature and a product of our competitive society. No one likes to lose, regardless of the issue. If too much time is spent arguing, the other party may stop arguing and find another way to get their point across to you.

Back at the reception, the caterer is a competitive person with an intimidating body appearance, and is now arguing his position with the father-of-the-bride that the cake's destruction was not his fault and that he is not responsible for the financial burden. This is not a productive method to find a solution to the problem as the father-of-the-bride has alternatives. He may decide not to argue during the reception and quietly seek his own way to resolve the issue. First, he may stop payment on the check. Second, he can send a check without an endorsing signature for payment after the event. Third, he may decide to arbitrarily deduct a dollar amount from the bill for the cake, including his own discount for the caterer's rudeness, his embarrassment, and his loving daughter's intangible cost of her ruined day. Now the conflict has grown and it is up to the caterer to find a solution.

Arguing over who is right often is counterproductive to resolving conflict. Instead, talk about the situation and the potential options for resolution. Searching for alternatives and options having mutual gain for both sides will be received more positively than fighting over who is right and who is wrong.

Know the Interests of the Parties: Don't Focus on Positions

interests Demands of those parties engaged in a conflict.

position The interests of the parties engaged in the conflict and stated as their demands in the form of a position.

positional bargaining When people engaged in a conflict take a position and argue for it.

Before looking for alternatives and options, understand the **interests** of the parties engaged in the conflict. In conflict people often state their demands in the form of a **position. Positional bargaining** happens when people take a position and argue for it. Concessions from this position are made to reach a compromise. Interests, on the other hand, fuel the energy behind a position. William Ury describes interests as the intangible motivations that lead one to take a position. This could be one's needs, desires, concerns, and fears. Focusing on positions in a conflict rather than the interests usually will not lead to the best resolution of a conflict.

Using the wedding reception, the positions and interests of both parties may be very different. The position and interest of the caterer are pretty similar: he does not want to bear the financial responsibility for the destroyed cake. The caterer may also have a bigger interest in wanting to maintain a respected reputation in the catering industry.

The positions and interests of the customer may not be exactly the same. It is likely their position will be not to pay for the cake. Their interest may be for another cake. The bride and groom will want to be photographed in the traditional cake cutting ceremony. If another cake is provided, the bride and groom can still symbolically perform their first task together as husband and wife. They can potentially salvage this part of the reception, including capturing the precious moment in a picture.

Looking at alternatives and options that focus on the interests of both parties, and not merely compromising on positions, could help create a more positive resolution to the conflict. Resolving conflict in a positive manner will help to restore the relationship between the parties. If the client knows the caterer will resolve the conflict in a manner to satisfy their best interests, he will be more inclined to hire the caterer in the future.

Understand the Alternatives, Yours and Theirs

In conflict there are only three real ways to reach a resolution. The first is having the power to force a resolution. Second, the parties can utilize their rights and sue each other. While the use of legal action to sue the other party is valid, there are potential consequences of pursuing such an action. Once the conflict is turned over to a third party (judge or jury) the control of the resolution is no longer in your hands. The judge or jury will decide the solution and both parties must accept the decision. Remember, if unable to resolve a dispute, both parties have the option to sue each other. The final option is to find a mutually acceptable solution to resolve the dispute.

As in all conflict situations, the caterer and the bride and groom have alternative solutions available to resolve the issue between them. It is unlikely either party has the power to force a resolution, unless the client is extremely influential and can ruin the caterer's reputation. The most likely alternatives are to either be sued or to resolve the dispute themselves. If resolving the dispute themselves, the next step will be to create alternative solutions.

Consider the wedding reception from the caterer's perspective. Knowing the interests of those involved is an aid in negotiating a resolution, by helping the caterer to generate and select alternatives. For example, if the caterer is made aware of the bride and groom's desire to still cut their cake, several options present themselves. If the cake can be salvaged, then use the remaining sections for the cake cutting ceremony. If not, take time during the meal service to resolve the issue with the wedding party. Alternatively, if the father-of-the-bride berates the caterer and escalates the situation into an international incident, the caterer may simply inform him that a replacement cake is unavailable and that his daughter must forgo the cutting ceremony.

Discussion Stage: Look for Options that Provide Mutual Gain—The More the Better

Options provide opportunity to resolve the conflict. Brainstorming options together is an excellent strategy for both sides. Seeking mutual resolutions by creating ideas to satisfy the largest number of interests in the dispute do work. When seeking a common resolution to the conflict, consider the following two factors. First, when brainstorming options, no commitment should be enforced unless both sides agree. Second, always consider options that best satisfy the interest of both sides. Before a dispute can be settled, both sides must agree on an acceptable option.

Back at the reception, the caterer and the bridal party are reviewing each other's interests. The client is not interested in paying for a ruined wedding cake, but the client is interested in participating in the traditional cake cutting ceremony. The caterer is interested in limiting the financial loss and the potential loss of new referrals. Therefore, what options exist to resolve this conflict?

One option is produce a replacement cake for the cutting ceremony. The following suggestions were provided by local caterers:

1. Purchase another cake from a local bakery. Create a "newer tier" for the bride and groom. Use this tier for the cake cutting ceremony.

2. Repair some of the fallen wedding cake by redecorating it to camouflage the defects.

3. Reconfigure the tiers and construct a smaller wedding cake.

4. Bake small cupcakes during the meal service for the cake cutting ceremony.

When developing alternative options to resolve a conflict situation, seek to answer this question: "What is the caterer's biggest interest in the resolution of this conflict?" In this example, is it to receive full payment for all services rendered? Is it to mitigate the potential loss in reputation? Is it to limit the long-term damage from this incident? Once a caterer's interest in the resolution is known, then one can decide the best option that will satisfy both the caterer and the client's needs.

Utilize Standards When Determining Options

Using industry standards is one technique employed to formulate a mutually agreeable option. Industry standards provide instant credibility to a resolution. Standards establish a framework by which a resolution can take shape. If an option for a resolution is supported by the standards commonly used in the industry, then a sense of justice is likely to be implied. Such standards set a benchmark for a potential option, provides each party with a justifiable frame of reference and a guarantee that they will not be taken advantage of in the resolution. It creates a sense of security assuring both sides equal and fair treatment.

For example, in the field of labor negotiations, most wage issues are settled when both sides use cost of living as the benchmark industry standard. By using this standard, the employees know they are getting paid similar increases as other employees in the area, while the employer knows they are not paying a higher wage than their competitors. By using industry standards, each side of the conflict knows they are being treated in an impartial manner, allowing the participants to view the settlement as fair. A caterer can suffer negative consequences, such as a tarnished reputation, if the client does not view the resolution as fair.

In the wedding reception example, the caterer should apply standard catering industry practices to resolve the conflict. A simple thing to do is to refund services which may not "cost" the caterer a substantial amount of money, but were added to the wedding reception to create value for the client. Potential costs to refund include:

*   colored linens
*   chair covers
*   set up or tear down
*   table rental
*   china rental
*   limousine service
*   valet parking

- photographer
- champagne for the bride and groom's toast
- engraved champagne glasses
- cake cutting
- chocolate fountain rental
- chocolate and accessories for dipping

Additionally, the caterer can offer a more substantial refund or a discount to the client, however, this option takes money out of the caterer's pocket. These may include:

- money refunded for the wedding cake
- a discount for a future event
- coupons for future events

A final possibility is to offer the client complimentary services beyond the wedding reception, such as:

- pay to have the bride's dress professionally cleaned and boxed for storage after the wedding
- pay the first night's honeymoon hotel accommodation

Deal with People Using People Skills

When dealing with conflict, the issue is usually straightforward. In the wedding reception, the fallen wedding cake is the issue. People involved in the conflict are the other variable. When conflict occurs, expect emotions to trigger. While it's natural for both the caterer and client to have emotions, try to prevent them from influencing a negative style response to conflict resolution, as discussed earlier in the chapter.

To prevent the people issue from becoming the bigger problem in the conflict, always use appropriate human relation skills and behave as a rational human being. The first tactic in resolving a conflict situation is to be prepared. Always expect the customer (who may not have read this chapter) to engage in the negative styles of conflict in response to a caterer's emotions. Instead of reacting to the client's negative attitude, try to neutralize it. Understand a person uses an

Tips from the Trade

While it is certainly understandable that some of the issues in a conflict situation may not be the fault of the caterer, focusing one's negative emotions toward the customer is never a good idea. Nowhere else is this more true than in catering. It is a consumer-oriented business. It is not always correct to say the customer is never right, but it is more accurate to say the customer never feels they are wrong. Knowing this, the ability to treat the client as a rational person will likely diffuse negative emotions. The ability to communicate and your willingness to help the customer by keeping their overall interest in mind rather than hindering the process will help to resolve the dispute with less suffering and less damage to your professional and personal reputation.

Helped David Piper write chapter: Leah Riegel;
Contributed Some portion of the Chapter 16

emotional outburst as a communication attempt. Picture the wedding cake conflict and this response from the client: "Oh my goodness, my daughter's wedding cake is ruined!" This statement is likely to be made in an adverse tone. Now picture the client's reaction after the caterer retorted: "Well, it's not my fault. It wasn't my bright idea to have this reception on the hottest day of the year in a nonclimate controlled environment!" How would the client react if the caterer responded in this manner instead: "Oh, this is not good. I can understand your concern. Let me see what my staff and I can immediately do to make this situation right for you and your daughter."

Resolve, Shake Hands, Forgive, and Move On

Once both sides have formulated mutually proposed and acceptable options based on agreed upon industry standards, the next step is to formulate a resolution with the client. This can be as simple as saying, "Are you in agreement with what has been proposed?"

Remember, client-generated options give a client a stake in the settlement. It is beneficial to ask the client for their ideas or suggestions regarding the outcome. However, if the client's option is outside of the acceptable industry standards, acknowledge this, and then explain how this option would not necessarily be fair for the caterer to implement.

The trick is to know when one has enough information on an agreement to move forward in the dispute. In the wedding reception case, the caterer should not get the client to sign a written agreement to the resolution while the bridal party is in the middle of dinner. More likely, the course of action to be pursued will be to seek a verbal confirmation of the agreed upon option along with a handshake. A handshake is not a full guarantee of a promise, but it is a huge symbolic gesture of agreement.

Good conflict resolvers follow a basic rule: forgive and move on. When parties resolve conflict, the purpose should be to strengthen the relationship. Never use the agreed upon resolution as a mechanism to destroy the relationship. Never hold the client hostage by using the resolution against him in the event. The customer will likely remember this selfish act more than anything else. Do not carry this as a grudge against the client and conspire "to get even" with him or her at a future event.

The easy part of the special event catering business is to have a perfectly executed event. However, a time will invariably come when conflict happens. The most successful caterers are able to resolve conflict in such a way that the client feels good about the resolution and will hire the caterer again in the future.

Learn from the Situation

When a situation turns from conflict to resolution it should become a learning experience for the caterer. Use the situation as an exercise with the staff. Debrief the conflict. Learn how the problem was started, how the problem was resolved, and what steps need to be done to prevent the problem from recurring in the future.

The wedding cake scenario is no different. The following is a list of lessons the caterer may have learned from this situation:

- Continuously monitor and check the temperature in the banquet room
- Know the location of the breaker box and which breaker controls the air conditioning
- Keep a frozen wedding cake as a backup
- Do not place the wedding cake next to the chocolate fountain
- If you notice the room temperature rising, place the top tier on a "fake cake" foundation featured on a skirted table
- If the room is humid, place a "fake fondant cake" on display and use presliced sheet cakes during the dessert course of the reception.

Summary

Stay in business long enough and it is inevitable that a situation will arise that causes conflict. Some issues may directly be the caterer's fault, others may be beyond anyone's control. Regardless of whose fault the issue may be, the caterer will likely have to fashion a resolution that will be acceptable to the client. The more conflict resolution skills you possess, the better you will be able to meet the buffet of challenges conflict will present to you.

Remember it is important to:

- not make rash decisions
- prevent emotions from taking control
- broaden options before and after a catered event
- acknowledge the client's point and offer an apology if appropriate
- satisfy unmet interests
- not overlook basic human needs and not dismiss them as irrational
- aim for mutual gain and satisfaction, not victory
- listen to the client
- offer and employ sincere empathy

Review Questions

Brief Answers

1. Define conflict.
2. Describe the process of resolving conflict.
3. Define the issue dimension of a conflict.
4. Define the position dimension of a conflict.
5. Explain how emotions can interfere in resolving a conflict.
6. Explain the two basic elements in a conflict.
7. Explain why there are two sides to every story.
8. Discuss why each party involved in a conflict should identify alternative options that provide mutual gain for each side.

9. Identify industry standards common to the catering industry one can use to create options to resolve conflict.

10. Explain the negative styles of resolving conflict.

11. Explain why one should aim for mutual gain and satisfaction and not a total victory when resolving conflict.

Multiple Choice

Select the single best answer for each question.

1. In most cases, conflict is viewed by each party from a _____ perspective.
   a. positive
   b. negative
   c. neutral
   d. winnable
   e. all of the above

2. There are two basic dimensions in a conflict, and these are:
   a. issue and emotions in the conflict
   b. story and emotions in the conflict
   c. issue and story in the conflict
   d. both a and c
   e. none of the above

3. In conflict, people often state their demands in the form of a:
   a. position
   b. issue
   c. emotion
   d. standard
   e. all of the above

True or False

Read each of the following statements and determine if it is true or false.

1. Using industry standards is one technique employed to formulate a mutually agreeable option in a conflict situation.

2. To prevent the people from becoming the bigger problem in the conflict, always use appropriate human relation skills and behave as a rational human being.

3. Good conflict resolvers follow a basic rule: forgive and move on.

Putting It All Together

Interview a caterer. Ask them to describe a conflict situation from an event. How did the caterer effectively handle the conflict situation? What were the dimensions of the conflict; specifically what were the issue and the emotions in the conflict? What was the story in the conflict? What was the final solution offered? Were alternative solutions evaluated? Were these solutions based on industry standards? If yes, what were the standards? Did the resolution help keep the client as a long-term customer?

Chapter 17

Sustainable Catering: One Ecological Step at a Time

Courtesy Eat'n Park Hospitality Group

Objectives

After studying this chapter, you should be able to:

1. Define sustainability.

2. Identify greenwashing.

3. Explain how to integrate sustainable business practices into your catering company.

4. Discuss how to evaluate sustainable business practices in your catering company.

5. Explain how a caterer can communicate successful sustainable business practices with their target market.

6. Provide an example of a sustainable "Best Practice" in a catering operation.

7. Using Moore's Model of Sustainability, design a sustainable catering business.

8. Discuss why sustainable business practices must be realistic and profitable.

9. Forecast future sustainable green business practices and their impact on the caterer, customer, and environment.

KEY TERMS

Community Supported Agriculture (CSA)

Eat'n Park Hospitality Group (EPHG)

EcoSteps

Energy Star

FarmSource

greening

greenwashing

LEED (Leadership in Energy and Environmental Design)

National Restaurant Association's Conserve Solutions for Sustainability

Pennsylvania Association for Sustainable Agriculture (PASA)

Slow Food

strategic sustainable green zones

sustainability

Sustainable Catering Association

CREATING A SUSTAINABLE BUSINESS MODEL

What Is Sustainability?

A concrete awareness of how a caterer's business practices impacts the environment is emerging as one of the most important customer-driven forces in the food service industry today. The proactive attention to **"greening"** a business—use of renewable resources and lessening of the environmental impact of operating a catering business—is the single most significant force driving competitive change in the catering industry (Figure 17.1). In the daily life of caterers, everything they touch can present sustainable environmental challenges for them. To remain competitive in a changing industry, caterers need to understand the concept of sustainability, become proactive and knowledgeable about how to implement sustainable business practices, be able to measure its success, and effectively and successfully communicate these sustainable accomplishments with their target audience.

"Greening" is a term used to describe a process or an outcome from the implementation of a business practice whose purpose is to improve the environment through efficient utilization of resources in day-to-day operations. This can be accomplished in multiple ways, including: conserving energy; recycling; buying locally grown foods; composting; reducing resource usage, such as using energy-efficient equipment; adopting alternative fuels, such as solar power; and conserving water. Specific business practices by a caterer can target green initiatives in their operations. A client, as well, can adhere to environmental friendly initiatives by requesting or agreeing to specific "green" products and services from the caterer. **Greenwashing** refers to a situation where a customer has been deceived by the caterer into believing that a green initiative has been implemented when in fact it hasn't.

A caterer can work in a **LEED** certified environment (Figure 17.2). LEED is an acronym for Leadership in Energy and Environmental Design (http://www.usgbc.org/leed).

greening The use of renewable resources and lessening the environmental impact of operating a catering business.

greenwashing A situation where a customer has been deceived by a caterer into believing that a green initiative has been implemented when in fact it has not.

LEED An acronym for Leadership in Energy and Environmental Design.

Figure 17.1 Smiley at the recycling center.

Figure 17.2 LEED certified Eat'n Park Restaurant with wind turbine.

Courtesy Eat'n Park Hospitality Group

Developed in March 2000 by the United States Green Building Council (USGBC), "LEED provides building owners and operators with a framework for identifying and implementing practical and measurable green building design, construction, operations, and maintenance solutions."[1]

Caterers can use energy efficient equipment certified by the **Energy Star** label (http://www.energystar.gov). Energy Star is a joint program of the US Environmental Protection Agency (EPA) and the US Department of Energy. Introduced by the EPA in 1992, the Energy Star label identifies and promotes energy-efficient equipment. Energy Star qualified commercial kitchen equipment includes dishwashers, fryers, griddles, hot food holding cabinets, ice machines, ovens, refrigerators and freezers, and steam cookers.[2]

Sustainability is when today's current users of resources consume them in such a way as to not jeopardize or harm the environment. Positive decisions today will ensure future generations' access to a similar or a better quality of life. According to the **Pennsylvania Association for Sustainable Agriculture (PASA)**:

> Sustainable agriculture means building farms that can sustain healthy soil, produce healthy food and be profitable as well. The farm then becomes a vital economic part of the community, enhancing open space, providing community access to fresh, healthy food, and keeping the money spent on that farm in the community. Methods of sustainable agriculture seek to be environmentally and socially responsible without sacrificing its ability to earn profit. It also strives for harmony with the natural environment, while considering human health as well as societal and economic well-being. Each sustainable farmer produces what works best on their farm so you will find that there is a lot more diversity of food products in a community that has these kinds of farms.[3]

The genesis of sustainability can be linked to the release in 1962 of Rachel Carson's *New York Times* bestseller *Silent Spring* and subsequently to April 22, 1970, when the United States celebrated its first Earth Day. Momentum from these two

Energy Star Energy Star is a joint program of the US Environmental Protection Agency (EPA) and the US Department of Energy to identify and promote energy-efficient equipment.

sustainability A concrete awareness of how a caterer's business practices impact the environment.

Pennsylvania Association for Sustainable Agriculture (PASA) The largest statewide, member-based sustainable farming organization in the United States, its mission is to work to bring farmers together to learn from each other, and to build relationships between those farmers and consumers looking for fresh, wholesome, locally and sustainably produced food.

Figure 17.3 Jamie Moore, director of sourcing and sustainability, Eat'n Park Hospitality Group.

significant events carried forth the creation of the EPA and the passage of the Clean Air, Clean Water and Endangered Species Act.[4] Today, as a result of this lineage, caterers are responding to consumers in emerging markets demanding sustainable business policies, procedures, and practices. Sustainability has become imbedded in our society as a social and ethical conscious thought. Sustainable practices are being driven by enlightened and educated consumers who are aware of environmentally sustaining practices, and these sustainable practices are having economic implications for everyone.

Planning for Sustainable Business Practices

One of the foremost proactive authorities in the United States hospitality industry on the concept of sustainability is Jamie Moore, director of sourcing and sustainability, Eat'n Park Hospitality Group (EPHG). Moore defines sustainability as "keeping the earth the way it is for future generations" (Figure 17.3). Moore encourages others to seek his advice and welcomes the adaption of his operationally proven sustainable business practices into their own business model.

EPHG is now acknowledged as the leading company within the family dining industry when it comes to sustainability.[5] The EPHG had its beginnings in 1949 as a family car-hop restaurant in Pittsburgh, Pennsylvania. It has evolved into a regionally powerful diversified company operating in Pennsylvania, West Virginia, Ohio, Maryland, New York, Connecticut, and Michigan. As a diversified company, it has five related strategic business units: Eat'n Park, a regional chain of about 72 restaurants and over 100 on-site catering operations, consisting of 50 Parkhurst Dining Services (1996; universities, colleges, business, and industry, including specialty markets such as cultural institutions and fine dining accounts), 52 Cura Hospitality operations (1996; hospitals and retirement homes), and the Six Penn Kitchen (2005), a neighborhood American bistro located in the cultural district in Pittsburgh.[6] In November 2011 the newest concept to open is called "the Porch." At lunch, the restaurant emphasizes quick and casual service. Patrons order from a cashier, but food is brought to their tables. The menu includes salads, sandwiches, a soup and pizzas, with daily specials to augment the seasonal offerings. Then, at 4:30 p.m., they bring out a host stand and switch to full service for dinner. A strategic business unit (SBU) must meet the following four characteristics: (1) each is independently planned and has operational autonomy from the other SBUs, (2) each has its own manager capable of making independent decisions, (3) each has its own unique set of competitors, and (4) each has its own mission and purpose. The SBUs in the EPHG meet these criteria.

Sustainable Business Practices: The Model

EPHG's business model has evolved by embracing a guiding long-term strategy focused on sustainable strategic business practices. EPHG has built a competitively sustainable focused business model by using the following main strategic components: mission statement, strategic vision, core values, objectives, and corporate and business-level strategies and tactics (see Chapter 3).

A mission statement defines the purpose of a caterer's organization. The vision defines the future direction of what a caterer would like to become. Core values state guiding principles a caterer will follow in conducting business. Objectives set measurable and definable benchmarks to be accomplished in a specific time frame. Strategies are used to navigate the corporate and business-level operations in day-to-day actions. Tactics are used to accomplish the objectives while adhering to the core values in the mission in pursuit of the long-term vision.

The architect of the EPHG's sustainability model is Jamie Moore. Moore began his career as the manager of purchasing for their on-site brands (Parkhurst and Cura Dining Services) in 2000. A strategic initiative to develop innovative programs to provide a competitive advantage was launched to position their SBUs for growth in a mature, competitive industry.[7] Moore's vision, leadership, and personal passion for sustainability led to the strategic initiative to integrate a clear, defined, long-term sustainable strategy and tactics into EPHG's business model. As a result, EPHG formulated both corporate and local measurable sustainability standards with a commitment to environmental issues into their mission.

In 2002, sustainability at EPHG was defined in a strategic initiative called **FarmSource**. FarmSource is an initiative to locate and to partner with local farmers and food producers as a sustainable source of food. Today, this connects EPHG to growers within a 125 mile radius of local distributors, based on the location of the restaurant or catering operation. As a result of FarmSource, 20 percent of total food purchases within the EPHG are now sourced from local providers (Figure 17.4). This initiative is recognized in the contract food market as being one of the best executed local purchasing programs.

FarmSource An initiative to locate and to partner with local farmers and food producers as a sustainable source of food by EPHG.

EPHG furthered its commitment to sustainability by creating a specific corporate-level management position in sustainability within the organization's hierarchy. Moore was promoted in 2007 to the position of director of sourcing and sustainability. Moore's role in this position has evolved in response to changing industry demands. He serves both in line and staff functions within the company, and he provides external consultation to the local community. "He is responsible for educating senior management and business clients on the 'real cost' of greening a facility; biodegradable products, organic waste recycling, carbon neutrality, and reduction of waste."[7]

According to Moore, the implementation of a strategic initiative required building a distinct competence around sustainable practices in the business model and the company's

Figure 17.4 Locally grown apples.

Courtesy Eat'n Park Hospitality Group

EcoSteps Created by Jamie Moore to describe EPHG's continuous improvement process toward sustainability.

continuous proactive pursuit of it. Moore coined the term **"EcoSteps"** to describe this continuous improvement process inching the company toward sustainability. Moore says, "It's our ecological steps toward sustainability. It is steps we are taking. Yes, I would like to have all of our locations composting our leftover food but let us be realistic. We will probably have a few units at a time come along, but as each unit begins to compost its food, that is an EcoStep. Ultimately we are reducing the amount of waste that is going into our landfills. We are not doing this all at once; we are doing it in bits and pieces." (J. Moore, personal communication, July 9, 2011). Moore has designed an EcoSteps logo to bring attention and highlight the ecological improvements being accomplished by the company. The logo is followed by a short narrative describing what EcoSteps were done to help reduce their ecological footprint of the operation. The EcoSteps logo is a branding tool used to vocalize and to communicate specifically to EPHG's market audience, reinforcing its mission and image of being a sustainable company.

Community Supported Agriculture (CSA) A direct connection between the farmers and the final consumers. Members who join a CSA buy a share of the season's harvest. A member's share guarantees security for the farmer, knowing he or she has been prepaid for a portion of the harvest.

The ability to partner with local growers within a 125 mile radius is accomplished by bringing the local growers together with operators, who then design their menus featuring freshly harvested foods. The advantages of using locally grown foods include reduction in energy costs to transport product from grower to user, less use of pesticides, support of the local farming community, and fresher, healthier, tastier, food (Figure 17.5). To make this happen, Moore built a series of strategic partnerships with other organizations and groups within the market. Moore has partnered with purveyors and distributors in the local markets to provide the logistics of moving locally grown foods from the small grower to the user. He has joined with groups such as PASA and other **Community Supported Agriculture** groups, **(CSAs)** to form a partnership among the small farmers, distributors, caterers, and restaurateurs.

Figure 17.5 Locally grown watermelon.

Sustainable Spotlight: Organizations Offering Sustainable Resources

Pennsylvania Association for Sustainable Agriculture (PASA)
http://www.pasafarming.org

PASA's mission is to work to bring farmers together to learn from each other, and to build relationships between those farmers and consumers looking for fresh, wholesome, locally and sustainably produced food. As the largest statewide, member-based sustainable farming organization in the United States, PASA seeks to provide economic viability, environmental soundness, and social responsibility of food and farming systems in Pennsylvania and across the country. A concerted effort is made to build bridges between broadly diverse participants in the agricultural industry, from "farm to fork."[8]

Community Supported Agriculture (CSA)
http://www.localharvest.org

Community Supported Agriculture is a direct connection between the farmers and the final consumers. Members who join a CSA buy a share of the season's harvest. A member's share guarantees security for the farmer knowing he or she has been prepaid for a portion of the harvest. The farmer's "community" participates in how and where their food is grown. This direct connection between member and farmer puts the face and place of the grown food in full view for everyone to see. Before the start of the season, when the farmer is planning the upcoming year, shares are sold to members of the community at a fixed price. The farmer plans the plantings to meet the shares that have been sold. Every week throughout the season, the CSA community receives a box of food consisting of that week's harvest. Most of the local CSAs will deliver to several convenient area locations for pickup. CSAs encourage the community to come to the farm, and even to participate in the growing of their food.[9]

Slow Food
http://www.slowfood.com

Slow Food is a global, grassroots, nonprofit member-supported organization having supporters in 150 countries around the world. Their common bond is linking the pleasure of good food with a commitment to their community and to the environment. Slow Food was founded in 1989 to counter the rise of fast food and fast life, the disappearance of local food traditions and people's dwindling interest in the food they eat, where it comes from, how it tastes, and how food choices affect the entire world.[10]

National Restaurant Association's Conserve Solutions for Sustainability
http://www.conserve.restaurant.org

The **National Restaurant Association's Conserve** initiative is designed to initiate and inspire actions that improve a company's bottom line, but also are good for people and the planet. Conserve explores conservation efforts being adopted by restaurants around the nation and offers suggestions and resources to help people reduce the cost of running their operation—both to their bottom line and the environment.[11]

Slow Food A global, grassroots, nonprofit member-supported organization having supporters in 150 countries around the world. Their common bond is linking the pleasure of good food with a commitment to their community and to the environment.

National Restaurant Association's Conserve Solutions for Sustainability Designed to initiate and inspire actions that improve a company's bottom line and are good for people and the planet. Explores conservation efforts being adopted by restaurants around the nation and offers suggestions and resources to help reduce the cost of running a food service operation.

(continues)

(continued)

Sustainable Catering Association
http://www.sustainablecateringassociation.org

Based in Portland, Oregon, the **Sustainable Catering Association** is a membership-based trade association that works with enterprising caterers to enhance and further integrate sustainable practices into their business model. Since its founding in 2008, the Sustainable Catering Association has embraced the principle of Triple Bottom Line, advocating initiatives in the areas of People, Planet, and Profit. Its mission is to provide high value-added education and training for caterers, vendors, legislators and other regulatory bodies, and other interested stakeholders, who wish to understand the benefits inherent in sustainable practices within the catering industry.[12]

The force binding all of this together is the continued education and relationship-building of the members in the infrastructure. Moore works to educate the members of the sustainable infrastructure network he has created to make this a successful win-win venture. Moore, in his role as an external consultant, lends his expertise to first finding the small farmers who are willing to grow and package chickens and cattle, fruits and vegetables, and produce dairy products according to USDA standards so they can be used by commercial caterers and restaurateurs (Figure 17.6). Second, he educates the members of the infrastructure how to become a contributing partner in the sustainable network. He needs the distributors to participate, since they play a major role in the sustainable infrastructure. He makes it known to the distributors the importance of buying locally grown products.[13]

To replicate sustainable practices in a catering operation, Moore recommends using his model, adapting similar strategic initiatives and following tactics by:

Figure 17.6 Moore inspecting local farm.

(1) Creating a vision to define a future direction describing what sustainability means to you as a caterer.

Courtesy Eat'n Park Hospitality Group

(2) Writing your purpose, as a sustainable caterer, into your mission statement.

(3) Identifying core values to guide sustainable practices and following them in conducting your catering business.

(4) Establishing measurable and definable sustainable objectives and setting benchmarks to be accomplished in a specific time frame.

(5) Pursuing strategies to navigate the corporate and/or business-level operations in day-to-day actions, working toward sustainability.

(6) Using tactics to accomplish the sustainable objectives.

Take an "EcoStep"

Committing to Moore's structured sustainable business model is the first step towards becoming a sustainable caterer. Next plan the plan and design a greener sustainable catering business by answering each question in the model. After that, review the whole company to identify and benchmark existing sustainable practices. Subsequently work with employees, associations, government agencies, purveyors, equipment suppliers, and other groups to help identify ways to become more sustainable. "Sustainability means to think about your business being around for the future. I think that helps you swallow the word 'sustainability' a little easier, because if you are not going to be around in the future, what are you going to do? I do not know the answer to that question."

What does being a sustainable caterer mean (Figure 17.7)? According to Moore, it means breaking down the business into **strategic sustainable green zones.** Then strive to make each zone as sustainable as realistically possible. Strategic sustainable green zones can be created by using a number of different methods. One easy way to identify sustainable green zones is to follow the flow of food through an operation. Green zones, for example, can be organized by the following: the building housing the catering business, source of food, purveyors, receiving, storage, preparation, hot food production, cold food production, final preparation, customer service, warewashing, transportation, garbage, and solid waste removal. Work within each green zone to identify current sustainable practices and to then unlock ways to become more sustainable. Take your EcoSteps incrementally, one at a time.

A caterer should be realistic when pursuing sustainable business strategies. A balance between a green application and the long-term economic survivability of each business involved must be mutually beneficial. Green initiatives must be profitable for them to work.

Buying locally grown food and knowing where all the proteins and vegetables are coming from is realistic. Cooking in a LEED certified facility may be cost prohibitive and not realistic for the small business caterer. Purchasing or replacing old equipment with energy-efficient equipment is realistic. Recycling fryer oil, all bottles and cans, and composting leftover food is realistic. Replacing incandescent lightbulbs with compact fluorescent light bulbs is realistic. Serving food and then putting the waste into a landfill is not the right thing to be doing if you are a sustainable caterer.

One of the challenges Moore faced when creating the **EPHG** sustainability business model was to bring together the caterer, the chef, or someone in food service with the local person growing the product. He needed support from the local purveyor to make it happen. At first, the local purveyors were not happy. They were resistant to creating a distribution infrastructure to link the local grower with the commercial food service operator (Figure 17.8).

Eat'n Park Hospitality Group (EPHG) Beginning in 1949 as a family car-hop restaurant in Pittsburgh, Pennsylvania, it has evolved into a regionally powerful diversified company operating in Pennsylvania, West Virginia, Ohio, Maryland, New York, Connecticut, and Michigan.

strategic sustainable green zones By mapping the flow of food through a catering operation (i.e., the building, source of food, purveyors, receiving, storage, preparation, hot food production, cold food production, final preparation, customer service, warewashing, transportation, garbage and solid waste removal) identification of current sustainable practices and how to unlock ways to become more sustainable within each zone are discovered.

Figure 17.7 Locally grown peppers.

Courtesy Eat'n Park Hospitality Group

Figure 17.8 Moore with locally grown pepper in the distributor's warehouse.

Moore explains why the distributors have now embraced the sustainable model (J. Moore, personal communication, July 9, 2011; full quotation in Tips of the Trade at end of chapter):

It is profitable not only for us but also for the food service distributor. The food service distributor sees a market. It is an untapped market. The market has all of a sudden been handed to them because of a larger customer demand for locally grown foods. . . . Our distributors had to adjust their business model from buying products from a single, large supplier having a continuous global steady source of product available year-round to adjusting their processes to the demands of working with small local producers whose products were being harvested in short growing seasons.

Moore provides two examples when a green initiative is not realistic. He says (J. Moore, personal communication, July 9, 2011; full quotation at end of chapter):

. . . Are you willing to pay $7 for a hamburger if I put grass-fed beef on the menu? For one hamburger I am going to charge you $7. Well, how does that make sense? I am paying $1 right now for my ground beef and for me to move to pastured or grass-fed I've got to pay $4 per pound. . . . Grass-fed beef takes longer to raise, costs more to process, and costs more to find a home for all of the different cuts. I was just on a conference call this morning talking about the concept of moving more sustainable proteins into a hospital. . . . Are you going to feed the patients and/or residents pastured beef? Or pastured poultry? Or cage-free eggs? Is that realistic? And do you think a hospital will pay more for this? . . . Awesome they want to do it, but let us be realistic. . . .

Future of Sustainability

Sustainability is an ongoing, evolving, open process influenced daily by the adoption of new technologies, the acceptance of new greener methods, the creation of greener products, and the introduction of green practices into the catering industry. Standards driven by government oversight, independent third party testing, customer demand for greener business practices, a growing awareness and a heightened focus by the consumer on sustainability is making everyone look towards tomorrow with a greener outlook. Caterers are being encouraged to respond to these challenges by taking small, incremental steps, dubbed EcoSteps, toward becoming sustainable businesses.

Moore says (J. Moore, personal communication, July 9, 2011; full quotation at end of chapter):

The biggest piece of this is that in 40 years from now we are going to have 9.5 billion people on this earth and the conventional and sustainable farming methods need to work together to be able to feed this earth. I would consider that to be sustainable. . . . [R]ight now we have barriers between the organic world and the conventional world, and I do believe they need to figure out how to work together. . . . We have to start thinking about technology and science. I do not want to have food that is a chemistry set but I do want to have food to feed this country.

Looking out into the future . . . I see probably more of a LEED standard, of how we are doing construction, making sure we are not disturbing the earth. I see food sourcing will ultimately change to be a little bit more local. I think a local synergy will come together and start some additional processing facilities tied into the other local growers. I do think alternatives to current fuel sources will be developed. I think we are going to start to see more electric cars. We are going to see a lot more influx of alternative means of transportation. I think there is going to be a heightened awareness of where our food is coming from the general public. . . . I think those are the four things we are ultimately going to see. And I think the fifth is really just finding a way to limit the amount of waste, food waste specifically, going into our landfills. We will ultimately find a way to recover that food waste and possibly find a way to generate energy from it. . . . [T]here are small farms, small dairy farms, running their entire farms off of their own waste from the cow manure.

Tips of the Trade

One-on-one conversation on "Sharing Best Practices in Sustainability" with Jamie Moore, director of sourcing and sustainability, Eat'n Park Hospitality Group (J. Moore, personal communication, July 9, 2011):

S. Shiring: When I came to you, I had a limited working knowledge of the concept of sustainability. Is being green and being certified as a LEED business the same as being a sustainable operation?

J. Moore: I do not know. It's a toss up. I think that definition is going to have to go through some fine tuning. Not only by me but by others as well. I think being green and being certified as a LEED business would be a separate category. LEED certification is more of operations.

S. Shiring: You were one of the first to integrate the sustainability concept into your hospitality business model. Your whole concept of sustainability is ahead of the market.

J. Moore: It is!

S. Shiring: So now you are moving light speed but everyone is trying to catch up to you. You are creating a sustainable business model for your company as you continue to move forward.

J. Moore: I call it EcoSteps. I have coined a term called EcoSteps. It is our ecological steps toward sustainability. It is steps we are taking. We are not taking leaps, we are taking steps. Yes, I would like to have all of our locations composting our food but let us be realistic. We will probably have a few come along but each one of those that comes along is an EcoStep. Ultimately we are reducing the amount of waste that is going into our landfills. But we are not doing it all at once, we are doing it in bits and pieces.

S. Shiring: Is sustainability a social or cultural movement rather than a business trend?

J. Moore: I think it's an awareness. I think more people are becoming more aware with a heightened focus on sustainability. They are aware if your company is a sustainable company. Are you going to be around 50 years from now? If you are not, you probably have to look at the core values of your company to make sure you will be around for 50 years. You know if you are using up all of your resources, whatever those resources might be, they will be harder to come by and to pull those resources in. If, for example, I am developing a specific widget requiring a lot of resources, and I know those resources are hard to come by, and it is more difficult for me to pull those resources in to make it, I probably am not going to be sustainable. I need to really focus on something

(continues)

(continued)

else. You need to evaluate your whole company. I think sustainability means to think about your business being around for the future. I think that helps you swallow the word sustainability a little easier because if you are not going to be around in the future, what are you going to do? I do not know the answer to that question.

S. SHIRING: When I was a little boy growing up, everyone in my small town planted their own garden in their backyard. It seems along the way during my lifetime, people got away from having a garden. Do you see sustainability as getting back to reeducating and teaching people how to grow food again? Except for the farmer and the Amish, from whom you purchase food from for your operations, most people today do not have a garden.

J. MOORE: I think it is more of an awareness of knowing where your food comes from. The farmer and the Amish understand it, they have been doing this for years, they got it! I think the education or reteaching old habits is a piece of it. I think people now want to know where their food is coming from, such as vegetables. I still get the question "where is our local pineapple" but it happens, what are you going to do? I think also promoting and working with other organizations, such as the Pennsylvania Association for Sustainable Agriculture (PASA) and Slow Food, is another reason. Slow Food is an international movement started by Carlo Petrini in Turin, Italy. It originally was begun as a revolt against "fast food" companies' entry into the European market. They formed a nonprofit organization called Slow Food. Slow Food is basically going back to the old world ways of cooking food, trying to preserve the old world flavors and cooking procedures. Slow Food holds an annual conference each year and rotates the location between the United States and Italy. Their meetings held in Turin, Italy, are called Terra Madre. I think this is something a caterer could feature on their menu. Explain a little part on Slow Food—basically cooking in the old world way, cooking from scratch, not cooking from fully prepared products. Explain we are active members of Slow Food.

S. SHIRING: Does being a sustainable company purchasing foods from local sources mean you are obtaining a more nutritious and healthier food?

J. MOORE: Health is a big part of sustainability. Where I think sustainability ties in if you are buying local, you have a little less crop residue, less fertilizer might be on some of your vegetables just because the farmer is not using so much. There are other aspects of it certainly. Cooking from scratch, certainly one. If you are buying local, you will be cooking from scratch. You are not going to be buying bagged lettuce to put out for your salad, you will be buying fresh lettuce and chopping it. This is one reason why Eat'n Park operations are so successful with locals because they make everything in-house. We do not buy bagged lettuce, we do not buy sliced tomatoes, we do not buy chopped onions, we do not buy most things other restaurants are buying, we are chopping all that in-house. We do not buy a fully prepared coleslaw. We take cabbage, we take carrots, and we make coleslaw. That is what we do.

S. SHIRING: What you are doing today is just how food service operations were when we all started in this field way back when, but then something happened?

J. MOORE: Something happened! Labor is what happened! To find skilled labor is the challenge. Really, it is the way it is supposed to be. We are not supposed to be buying a bunch of prepared food. Prepared food is no good. Sodium and the other ingredients that go into prepared foods are no good. I think an understanding is, if you are sustainable, you better not be buying prepared foods. I think that is a broad spectrum of what you need to think about. To be a sustainable caterer buying prepared foods is not something that makes you a sustainable caterer. Why? The biggest reason is that you may not know exactly all the sources of your food, and there is certainly more to it than that!

S. SHIRING: One of the keys to creating your sustainability business model was trying to bring together the caterer or the chef or someone in food service with the local person growing the product. Is that the challenge?

J. MOORE: It is!

S. SHIRING: Your distributors were not happy at first when you began to build the infrastructure to support your sustainable business model but now they are, why?

J. MOORE: Gosh, it is working! It is profitable. It is profitable not only for us but also for the food service distributor. The food service distributor sees a market. It is an untapped market. The market has all of a sudden been handed to them because of a larger customer demand for locally grown foods. It has somewhat changed the mentality of the focus of that distributor. Can that happen in a catering venue, sure, it can happen anywhere. Did we have growing pains? We did! The growers had to learn the commercial distribution side of moving their product to market. Issues such as packaging, sizing and growing the right kinds of products, adhering to sanitation procedures, and building long-term relationships to make this work were challenges to overcome. Our distributors had to adjust their business model from buying products from a single, large supplier having a continuous global steady source of product available year-round, to adjusting their processes to the demands of working with small local producers whose products were being harvested in short growing seasons.

S. SHIRING: The caterer can be buying from those same vendors.

J. MOORE: Right! Jump on the band wagon.

S. SHIRING: As a result, the distributor can be servicing yet another customer.

J. MOORE: I think there are a few different pieces going on here. I think outlining what you want in a catering menu is important. So I have different tiers for my catering menu. You have something that says here is a sustainability section. Maybe it is a sustainability note that goes on the bottom of each of the different sections that you might be talking about. You can market sustainability to capture some additional customer segments. Use different terms on your menu to describe your products. Use existing terms such as free-range eggs and pasture poultry. These terms are more sustainable than battery chicken and confinement beef and all those bad terms. Write the better terms into your menu. Tell your potential client this is what we are doing! Have them available, cage-free, for example, always make them available for those customers who want them. Upsell the sustainable products. I always think there is a big potential for capturing a higher dollar from that guest. Ultimately being more profitable for you. That is key and that is great. Granted it might take a little bit more work because now I have to source it, find it.

S. SHIRING: In your sustainable model, you set and work within explicit parameters to define what local means to you: you are within a 125 mile radius of local procurement of food and 20 percent of your food budget is purchased locally.

J. MOORE: For us, that is the definition.

S. SHIRING: You strongly encourage and recommend others to make sustainability a part of their business mission and to integrate it into their business model. First, a caterer needs to identify and define their customer as a starting point. You recommend the caterer needs to define for their customer what their definition of sustainability is and how the business implements sustainable practices. Next, the caterer needs to work within those parameters to communicate with their clients the sustainable definition and what the caterer has to offer.

J. MOORE: I think defining it and putting a true definition to either the word local or to anything you may be putting out there is important. If I put the term pastured poultry out there does the layperson necessarily know what it means? Do we need to define what that means?

S. SHIRING: Is being a sustainable caterer mean you are educating your guest or client?

J. MOORE: It is an education as well as knowing the source of where that product came from. Be specific on the menu. I am using Joe's chicken from. . . . Writing your catering menu saying where that chicken came from means something to someone. For example, we can do a quarter chicken buffet for you. If you want a quarter chicken from Bob's farm, it is going to cost you extra money. We can also do this regular one, but call the farmers out you are going to use. Honestly, that

(continues)

(continued)

means so much to that one guest or client when you identify the local source of your food. But you might begin to see a trend where everyone will want to see and want that local product. I do not know if you will see that or not. Maybe, rather than just serving a specific market segment, you become a full-fledged sustainable caterer! We are a sustainable catering operation. Wow! What does that mean? We know where all of our proteins are coming from. We know where most of our vegetables are coming from and we really try to support local. Okay, you are supporting local, that is great. What else are you doing? We are cooking in a LEED certified facility. We are recycling our fryer oil. Recycling all of our bottles and cans. We are composting our leftover food. Serving food and then putting the waste into a landfill is not the right thing you should be doing, if you are a sustainable caterer.

S. SHIRING: Just like your prototype operational restaurant unit in Fox Chapel, Pennsylvania.

S. SHIRING: When I was in college, I served my internship as the head chef, in charge of the kitchen, at a mountainous Boy Scout camp in Boswell, located near Johnstown, Pennsylvania. My friend and I served 300 scouts breakfast, lunch, and dinner for each day over a 10 week summer program. Every Wednesday, the number for dinner would swell as parents and family would join their scouts for an evening campfire program. The Wednesday evening dinner consisted of a 1/2 charcoal-roasted chicken. We must have been ahead of the curve, because we would go to a local farmer and buy our chicken. We would drive off the mountain, pick it up in a truck. It came in fresh, boxed, and on crushed ice.

J. MOORE: It was beautiful! How do you promote sustainability? A market for being a sustainable caterer? I do not know. I think it is really an open topic. I do not think there are a lot of sustainable caterers out there. It would be a new trend. So, to go down that new trend, or path, of being a sustainable caterer. What does that mean? What does that entitle you to? You better know the source of where your foods are coming from, that is very, very important. You have to live and breathe sustainability. If you are going to live and breathe it, you probably are not going to greenwash—a term I think you need to know. Sort of lying to your customers about some of the green initiatives you have done or falsifying buying or exaggerating maybe the truth. Be conscious of that. Whatever you end of doing in reference to a catering manual or a catering menu be true to your customer and be true to whatever you are saying that might come back and bite you. I am still trying to gain what this business is, catering? Who is in the catering business? It is hotels, universities, not a lot of independent caterers out there.

S. SHIRING: Are there sustainable caterers?

J. MOORE: Certainly not promoting sustainability. Who would be a sustainable caterer? Buffets in a fire hall is not the market we are going after here. This is a market that might be a little more well educated. If you do not have a sustainable caterer in a high end hotel, then shame on you. I think defining your customer base in reference to sustainability is important, it is not for everyone. You can be sustainable. You can be a sustainable caterer and you can still do those mom and pop type events at the local fire hall, but it does not go hand in hand.

S. SHIRING: Are clients focused solely on price?

J. MOORE: Focused on price? Eat'n Park Restaurants are focused on price points. However, we are perceived as sustainable. We source local. Sourcing local is a little bit more sustainable than what is happening on the national scene.

S. SHIRING: This reinforces what you said earlier, do what you can as a caterer with sustainability within your target market, know your customer within a competitive price point.

J. MOORE: That is what we are doing.

S. SHIRING: You offer great advice. It gives you, as a sustainable caterer, a competitive advantage in the marketplace. A distinct competence to carve out a niche in the marketplace.

J. MOORE: Definitely a huge competitively advantage. Live and breathe it!

S. SHIRING: How would you recommend for someone to get started?

J. MOORE: I think you need to first define who your customers are and what your customer base is. If you know what customer base you want to gravitate towards, I know you want to gravitate toward a customer who cares about where their food is coming from, then I think finding realistic sources of your supply are going to be a vital part of what you are going to charge the customer. Where to get started? I think first is knowing the source of your food or supplies is important. Second, how do I start a menu? If I am going to develop a menu, then I need to make sure what I am going to pay for my supplies. If I am going to pay $3.50 per pound for my chicken, I better make sure I write my menu accordingly. I do not want to write a menu to charge a customer $6.99 per person where the chicken is just half the cost. Be aware of that, understanding where the source of your supply comes from at this point.

S. SHIRING: Can a caterer tap into PASA and Slow Food?

J. MOORE: Absolutely. Yes, to help you buy fresh, buy local, go to www.buylocalpa.org. This is a good source. If looking for pastured beef or cage-free eggs you can find it.

S. SHIRING: How do you see your role in the Eat'n Park Hospitality Group? You have an individual passion for sustainability. And then the company has given you the opportunity to be engaged in this concept.

J. MOORE: I can grow it as fast as they let me. I have held back on a lot of things. And rightly so, I think they should hold me back. I think my actions need to follow the mission of the organization, or that might hurt us. I see this position evolving more into a consulting type of position than more of a doer type of position. Today, the position is more of a doer.

S. SHIRING: I think part of being a doer is your knowledge of sustainability. People are just hungry for it. You have created a model that is working.

J. MOORE: They are hungry for knowledge and they are hungry for hopefully the right information. I think a lot of people are misguided by reference to reality. I ground students quite a bit and put them back to reality to say just not feasible. Yes, you talk a great game and you want Fair Trade coffee, and you want pastured poultry, and you want grass-fed beef, but let us be realistic. Are you willing to pay $7.00 for a hamburger if I put grass-fed beef on the menu at this university? For one hamburger I am going to charge you $7.00. Well, that does not make sense. Yes it does! I am paying one dollar right now for my ground beef and for me to move to pastured or grass-fed I got to pay $4.00. Are you willing to pay $7.00 for a hamburger? It just takes longer to raise it, cost more to process it, and find a home for all of the different cuts. For example, I was just on a conference call this morning talking about the concept of moving more sustainable proteins into a hospital. I like their energy behind the concept, but let us be really realistic. Are you going to feed the patients and/or residents pastured beef? Or pastured poultry? Or cage-free eggs? Is that realistic? And do you think a hospital will pay more for this? Let us be realistic. Are you willing to pay for it? Awesome they want to do it, but let us be realistic. Is realistic a term that will be going to get out there? Becoming more associated with the concept of sustainability is being realistic. This is very, very important and it goes back to knowing who your customer is and the other things we discussed.

S. SHIRING: Where do you see the future of sustainability? 3, 5, and 10 years out because this is not going to go away. It is like an avalanche. You have a little snowball, a few snowflakes, and all of a sudden it is a big blizzard and here it comes!

J. MOORE: I see this to some extent. The biggest piece of this is that in 40 years from now we are going to have 9.5 billion people on this earth, and the conventional and sustainable farming methods need to work together to be able to feed this earth. I would consider that to be sustainable. What does that mean? Does that mean we are going to have to have chemical-ridden food? Or chemically developed food? No, I do not think it is that. I think there is a happy medium that right now we have barriers between the organic world and the conventional world and I do believe

(continues)

(continued)

they need to figure out how to work together. And is technology going to be incorporated into growing food? Yes! We have to start thinking about technology and science. I do not want to have food that is a chemistry set but I do want to have food to feed this country. Looking out into the future, I do see construction being a little bit different, how we construct or erect buildings. I see probably more of a LEED standard, of how we are doing construction, making sure we are not disturbing the earth. I see food sourcing will ultimately change to be a little bit more local. I think a local synergy will come together and start some additional processing facilities tied into the other local growers. I do think alternatives to current fuel sources will be developed. I think we are going to start to see more electric cars. We are going to see a lot more influx of alternative means of transportation. I think there is going to be a heightened awareness of where our food is coming from the general public. I think we are beginning to see that now. I think those are the four things we are ultimately going to see. And I think the fifth is really just finding a way to limit the amount of waste, food waste specifically, going into our landfills. We will ultimately find a way to recover that food waste and possibly find a way to generate energy from it. It is a nitrogen source, there is a lot of energy behind it. I think the food waste can ultimately go to better use. Biodigesters are the first ones that come to my mind. And there are small farms, small dairy farms, running their entire farms off of their own waste from the cow manure. So that is a model that is going to start others to follow.

Courtesy Eat'n Park Hospitality Group

Summary

A concrete awareness of how a caterer's business practices impacts the environment is emerging as one of the most important customer-driven forces in the food service industry today. The proactive attention to "greening" a business, the use of renewable resources, and lessening the environmental impact of operating a catering business is the single most significant force driving competitive change in the catering industry. To remain competitive in a changing industry, caterers need to understand the concept of sustainability, become proactive by implementing sustainable business practices, be able to measure its success, and effectively and successfully communicate these sustainable accomplishments with their target audience.

Today caterers, such as the Eat'n Park Hospitality Group, are responding to consumers in emerging markets by creating sustainable business policies, procedures, and practices. Sustainability has become imbedded in our society as a social and ethical consciousness. Consumers make purchasing decisions based on cause-related issues such as sustainability. Sustainable practices are being driven by an enlightened and educated consumer who is aware of environmentally sustaining practices having economic implications for everyone.

Review Questions

Brief Answer

1. Identify and discuss how you can implement sustainable business practices into an on-premise catering and off-premise catering operation.
2. Define sustainability. Discuss and provide best-case examples from the Eat'n Park Hospitality Model of sustainability.

3. Discuss how a caterer can differentiate their business by being a sustainable caterer.

4. Identify five reasons how a caterer can benefit from being a sustainable caterer.

5. Discuss if sustainability is a business trend or social or cultural phenomenon.

6. Explain the term "greenwashing." Give an example of "greenwashing."

7. Identify why a caterer should be implementing sustainable business practices into their operation.

8. Discuss the role the small local grower, the distributor, and the commercial end user play in the sustainable model presented in the chapter.

9. What are the key questions a caterer must ask themselves before becoming a sustainable caterer?

10. Explain why sustainable business practices are good for the environment.

Multiple Choice

Select the single best answer for each question.

1. LEED is an acronym for:

    a. Leadership in Energy and Environmental Design

    b. Leadership in Eating and Environmental Digestion

    c. Lying Environmental Ecological Design

    d. Low Environmental Energy Design

    e. Leadership in Environmental Eating Digestion

2. A nonprofit member-supported association, _____ was founded in 1989 to counter the rise of fast food and fast life, the disappearance of local food traditions and people's dwindling interest in the food they eat, where it comes from, how it tastes, and how our food choices affect the rest of the world.

    a. Slow Food

    b. Recreational Dining

    c. Fast Food

    d. Global Restoration

    e. World Catering Network

3. EPHG has built a competitively sustainable focused business model by using the following main strategic components:

    a. strategic vision

    b. mission statement

    c. core values

    d. objectives, strategies, and tactics

    e. all of the above

True or False

Read each of the following statements and determine if it is true or false:

1. A concrete awareness of how a caterer's business practices impacts the environment is emerging as one of the most important customer-driven forces in the food service industry today.

2. "Greening" is a term used to describe either a process or an outcome from the implementation of a business practice whose purpose is to improve the

environment through efficient utilization of resources in the performance of day-to-day operations.

3. Slow Food is a global, grassroots organization with supporters in 150 countries around the world who are linking the pleasure of good food with a commitment to their community and the environment.

Putting It All Together

Partner with a local caterer. Guide the caterer to a long-term strategy focused on sustainable business practices by using the following strategic components: mission statement, strategic vision, core values, objectives, and corporate and business-level strategies and tactics. Next, review the whole company to identify and benchmark existing sustainable practices. Subsequently work with employees, associations, government agencies, purveyors, equipment suppliers, and other groups to help identify ways to become more sustainable.

End Notes

1. US Green Building Council. What LEED Is. Retrieved July 5, 2011, from http://www.usgbc.org/.

2. US Environmental Protection Agency and US Department of Energy. Find Energy Star Products: Appliances. Retrieved July 31, 2011, from http://www.energystar.gov/.

3. Pennsylvania Buy Fresh Buy Local. Glossary. Retrieved July 21, 2011 from http://www.buylocalpa.org/.

4 Earth Day: The History of a Movement. Earth Day Network. Retrieved July 5, 2011, from http://www.earthday.org/.

5. Phillips, V. (October 9, 2009). Eat'n Park's director of sustainability passionately connects farms and forks. *Pittsburgh Post-Gazette*. http://www.post-gazette.com/.

6. No author. (2010). About Jamie Moore, director of sourcing and sustainability. Parkhurst Dining Services. Retrieved June 16, 2011, from http://www.parkhurstdining.com/.

7. No author. (2010). About Jamie Moore, director of sourcing and sustainability. Parkhurst Dining Services. Retrieved June 16, 2011, from http://www.parkhurstdining.com/.

8. Pennsylvania Buy Fresh Buy Local. Glossary. Retrieved July 21, 2011, from http://www.buylocalpa.org/.

9. Pennsylvania Buy Fresh Buy Local. Glossary. Retrieved July 21, 2011, from http://www.buylocalpa.org/.

10. Slow Food. About Us. Retrieved July 21, 2011, from http://www.slowfood.com/.

11. National Restaurant Association's ConSERVE Solutions for Sustainability. Retrieved September 11, 2011, from http://www.conserve.restaurant.org/.

12. Sustainable Catering Association. Retrieved September 11, 2011, from http://www.sustainablecateringassociation.org/.

13. Petrucci, J. (October 22, 2009). Q&A: Jamie Moore, Eat'n Park. Keystone Edge. Retrieved June 16, 2011, from http://www.keystoneedge.com/.

Chapter 18

Human Resources Management

Permission of John R. Smith

Objectives

After studying this chapter, you should be able to:

1. Define human resources management.

2. Understand federal employment laws.

3. Explain why human resource management practices are integrated into a catering operation.

4. Discuss the procedures for employee recruitment.

5. Summarize the tools used to gather background information on employment candidates during the recruitment process.

6. Describe a bona fide occupational qualification (BFOQ).

7. Explain the components of a job analysis.

8. Describe a progressive discipline policy.

9. Explain why employee benefits are important for recruiting and retaining employees.

10. Understand employee health care benefits are a significant cost for the employer.

11. Understand the concept of "hours worked."

12. Summarize the collective bargaining process.

13. Understand the process involved when negotiating a labor agreement.

KEY TERMS

Age Discrimination in Employment Act (ADEA)

Americans with Disabilities Act (ADA)

bona fide occupational qualification (BFOQ)

child labor laws

collective bargaining

Consolidated Omnibus Budget Reconciliation Act (COBRA)

distributive bargaining

employee benefits

employment at will

essential job functions

Fair Labor Standards Act (FLSA)

Family and Medical Leave Act (FMLA)

Health Insurance Portability and Accountability Act of 1996 (HIPAA)

hybrid approach to negotiations

integrative or interest-based bargaining

job analysis

job description

job specification

labor contract

National Labor Relations Board (NLRB)

negligent hiring

offer of employment

progressive discipline policy

Title VII of the 1964 (1990) Civil Rights Act

violation of confidentiality

wage and hour calculations

workers compensation

EMPLOYMENT LAWS ALL CATERING PERSONNEL SHOULD KNOW

Employment policies and practices are rooted in several key federal laws (Figure 18.1). Compliance with federal law is facilitated by an understanding of their basics. State law is prominent in professional certification and collective bargaining of public sector employees, but federal law is the primary driver of employment policy in most other human resource areas. Prominent federal laws in the area of employment include the following:

Age Discrimination in Employment Act (ADEA): This act, passed in 1967 and currently enforced by the Equal Employment Opportunity Commission (EEOC), prohibits discrimination in employment against individuals age 40 and older. The law addresses employment practices, including failure to hire, discharge, denial of employment, and discrimination because of an individual's age within the protected age group. Anytime a pool of qualified candidates includes individuals over the age of 40 and a person under the age of 40 is hired, it sets the stage for a potential ADEA complaint. Hiring the best overall candidate is the best defense to a potential ADEA claim.[1, 7, 21]

Americans with Disabilities Act (ADA): This act, passed in 1990, targets employers with 15 or more workers and was developed to protect current and potential employees from discrimination based on a person's disability. The act requires employers to make reasonable accommodations to the essential functions of the job for known physical or

Age Discrimination in Employment Act (ADEA) This act, passed in 1967 and currently enforced by the Equal Employment Opportunity Commission (EEOC), prohibits discrimination in employment against individuals age 40 and older.

Americans with Disabilities Act (ADA) This act, passed in 1990, targets employers with 15 or more workers and was developed to protect current and potential employees from discrimination based on a person's disability.

Law	Targeted Area of Employment Law
Age discrimination in Employment Act (ADEA)	Protects employment rights of individuals age 40 and over.
Americans with Disabilities Act (ADA)	Protects employment rights of disabled persons.
Consolidated Omnibus Budget Reconciliation Act (COBRA)	Creates employee rights to purchase group health care after termination.
Fair Labor Standards Act (FLSA)	Creates compensation rights of hourly employees; equal pay guarantees; child labor law.
Family and Medical Leave (FMLA)	Grants leave days for personal or family illness.
Civil Rights Act	Establishes employment rights of protected minorities.
HIPAA	Protects privacy of medical information; guarantees insurability with new employer.
Workers Compensation	Guarantees payments for injured workers.

© Cengage Learning 2014

Figure 18.1 Summary of significant federal labor laws.

[1]Belton, R., Avery, D., Ontiveros, M.L. & Corrada, R.L. (2004). Employment discrimination law: Cases and materials on equality in the workplace. St. Paul, MN: Thomson-West.

[7]Jones, J.E., Murphy, W.P., & Belton, R. (1987). Cases and materials on discrimination in employment. St. Paul, Minnesota: West.

[21]Walsh, D.J. (2007). Employment law for human resource practice (2nd Ed.). St. Paul, NM: Thomson-West.

mental disabilities. It prohibits the employer from using a disability as the reason not to hire or to terminate an employee if a reasonable accommodation could be made, allowing the employee to carry out the essential functions of the job. Reasonable accommodations can include things such as making a facility accessible to disabled people, acquiring equipment or devices to be used by a disabled person, and modifying or restructuring work schedules to accommodate a disabled person.

Consolidated Omnibus Budget Reconciliation Act (COBRA): COBRA requires employers to offer group health coverage to employees and dependents if a qualifying event terminates their medical coverage. This coverage is only required if the employer provides medical coverage as part of a fringe benefit program. Qualifying events include separation from employment, divorce, or loss of dependent status (child turns 23) for a period between 18 and 36 months. The employer must provide the coverage to the covered recipient for no more than 102 percent of the employer cost. During times of economic crisis, the federal government has extended COBRA coverage and provided tax incentives to employers for paying a portion of a qualified employee's medical insurance coverage when involuntary separation from employment has occurred.

Fair Labor Standards Act (FLSA): In general, the law with the most reach for catering individuals would be FLSA. This law provides the minimum hourly rate paid to a worker (currently at $7.25 per hour) and covers other aspects such as 1 ½ payment for hours worked over 40 in a week, equal pay, and Child Labor Laws. The equal pay component of the act prohibits discrimination in employees' pay rates on the basis of gender. The act states that employees of the opposite sex shall be paid equally if the job requires equal skill, effort, and responsibility, and are performed under similar working conditions. The act allows for wage differences if the wage is based on seniority, merit, quantity and quality of production, or a differential due to any factor other than sex.[8, 16, 18]

Family and Medical Leave Act (FMLA): Passed in 1993, FMLA requires employers who employ 50 or more workers to provide up to 12 weeks (or 26 weeks—see below) of unpaid leave for qualifying circumstances, including the birth of a child, placement of a son or daughter for adoption or foster care, care for an immediate family member with a serious health condition, medical leave because of a serious health condition or to facilitate care for a veteran of recent military action or pending military deployment. To qualify for the leave, an employee must have worked at least 1,250 hours over the previous 12 months. While on leave, the employer must continue to pay all health benefits it would normally pay if the employee continued working for a period of 12 weeks. In cases dealing with the care of military personnel who are seriously ill or injured while on active duty, FMLA leave is extended to 26 weeks of coverage.[12]

Title VII of the 1964 (1990) Civil Rights Act: This act was one of the most influential pieces of discrimination legislation in American history. It states that it shall be unlawful to discriminate in the employment arena based on an individual's race, color, religion, sex, or national origin. The 1990 amendments to the Civil Rights Act allowed plaintiffs to sue for punitive damages in discrimination claims.[19]

Health Insurance Portability and Accountability Act of 1996 (HIPAA): This act not only protects the confidentiality of health related issues of an individual, but it also provides protection in health insurance coverage for employees and their dependents upon

Consolidated Omnibus Budget Reconciliation Act (COBRA) COBRA requires employers to offer group health coverage to employees and dependents if a qualifying event terminates their medical coverage.

Fair Labor Standards Act (FLSA) In general, the law with the most reach for catering individuals would be FLSA. This law provides the minimum hourly rate paid to a worker and covers other aspects such as 1 ½ payment for hours worked over 40 in a week, equal pay, and Child Labor Laws.

Family and Medical Leave Act (FMLA) Passed in 1993, FMLA requires employers who employ 50 or more workers to provide up to 12 weeks (or 26 weeks) of unpaid leave for qualifying circumstances, including the birth of a child, placement of a son or daughter for adoption or foster care, care for an immediate family member with a serious health condition, medical leave because of a serious health condition, facilitation of care for a veteran of recent military action, or pending military deployment.

[8]Keagy, D.R., & piper, D.M. (2007). The elements of human resources (3rd Ed.). Harrisburg Pennsylvania: Pennsylvania Association of School Business Officials.

[12]Martocchio, J.J. (2003). Employee benefits. New York: McGraw-Hill Higher Education.

[16]Noe, R.A., Hollenbeck, J.R., Gerhart, B., & Wright, P.M. (2006). Human resource management: Gaining a competitive advantage (5th Ed.). Boston: McGraw-Hill, Irwin.

[18]Piper, D.M., & Keagy, D.R. (2006). Federal wage and hour law: The Fair Labor Standards Act (2nd Ed.). Harrisburg, Pennsylvania: Pennsylvania Association of School Business Officials.

[19]Player, M.A. (1992). Federal law of employment discrimination: In a nutshell. St. Paul, MN: Thomson-West.

Figure 18.2 Hire the best people and let them do their job.

Title VII of the 1964 (1990) Civil Rights Act It states that it shall be unlawful to discriminate in the employment arena based on an individual's race, color, religion, sex, or national origin.

Health Insurance Portability and Accountability Act of 1996 (HIPAA) This act protects the confidentiality of health related issues of an individual and provides protection in health insurance coverage for employees and their dependents upon moving from one employer to another.

workers compensation Compensation is a required form of insurance paid by the employer. It provides payment of medical bills and lost wages to employees hurt in the course of employment.

moving from one employer to another. It limits rights of new employers to deny coverage because of preexisting conditions and enhances portability of coverage upon leaving one insurance program and enrolling in another.

Workers Compensation: Workers compensation is a required form of insurance paid by the employer. It provides payment of medical bills and lost wages to employees hurt in the course of employment. In exchange for this insurance and compensation protection, employees cannot sue their employer for damages unless they can prove gross negligence caused their injury.

HIRING

One of the most important responsibilities of the human resource function is recruiting and hiring high quality employees (Figure 18.2). Much of modern management science is found in variations of the simple advice, "Hire the best people and let them do their job." Because of an increasingly litigious environment, the safest and most effective approach to hiring is to involve the human resource department early and often. The law of employment and hiring is extremely complex and violations are subject to potentially severe penalty; this participation should be undertaken in partnership with a qualified human resource professional. In the absence of such a person, this participation should be undertaken with great care.[5]

Recruiting

Recruiting methods vary with employee classification, geographic area, and personal preference. Some caterers might prefer to initiate a statewide search for a specialty position, but a local search for servers and basic cooks. But one main goal exists in all hiring: hire "the best."

Posting positions: in the catering industry, the hiring process typically begins with a job posting announcing an available position. While no statutory requirements exist for such postings, sometimes it is necessary to post a job to a job board to recruit the best candidates. Regardless of requirements, job postings are an important beginning to the recruiting process for practical reasons. "Word-of-mouth" and "network" hiring is very common in the catering industry. Once a catering company caters a successful event for a large number of people, recruitment will be easier due to the superior reputation the company now possesses. A caterer must be able to hire employees based on qualifications and without personal connections or bias. Internal postings are important within large catering operations, allowing for the continued growth of current employees within the company. This also encourages current employees to demonstrate their credentials. The only time not to use job postings is when an in-house candidate is overwhelmingly the best applicant for the job. Larger caterers can use job fairs, websites such as craigslist, and/or personal websites. The local county employment agency might also provide qualified applicants for open positions.

Job posting requirements: a job posting should define the position that is open, where an applicant can receive information regarding the job, the deadlines for

[5]Desler, G. (2004). Human resource management (10th Ed.). Upper Saddle River, New Jersey: Prentice Hall.

submitting an application, and a contact person. Sometimes a posting will include a brief summary of the job responsibilities and a salary range. Since the inception of the Americans with Disabilities Act (ADA), it is now common to see more detailed information regarding the job in a posting advertisement. In order to determine if a disabled person is qualified to do the job and to comply with ADA requirements, more and more job postings are defining the "essential functions" of the position—what the person is required to do. This will include physical attributes such as the amount of weight a person is required to lift, the amount walking or being on their feet, and the required cognitive abilities needed for the position. ADA requires that reasonable accommodations be granted to disabled candidates.

GATHERING INFORMATION ON POTENTIAL EMPLOYEES

Different positions within the catering industry sometimes call for differing approaches to application documentation. Recruiting for a catering manager is likely to involve a letter of interest with resume, references, credentials, formal application, and perhaps a sample cooking or leadership exercise. The process for hiring a cook or a waitress is probably more direct. However, all (Figure 18.3) involve collecting information from potential candidates.

Resumes are needed when hiring for any position to fully understand the experience a potential employee possesses. Most recruiting and hiring decisions begin with the receipt of an applicant's resume. Some attorneys and HR professionals have concerns with resumes because they can provide information that may be protected under law, such as age, religion, race, sex and marital status. When the applicant discloses protected information, it is not an illegal act by the employer unless the employer further explores the protected information in an interview or uses the protected information as a reason not to hire the individual. A carefully designed application is purged of improper questions, such as date of birth, race, and so forth. As a result, a standard employment application designed to prevent the disclosure of protected information, as opposed to a resume, is the preferred means of collecting applicant information. Employment applications or interview questions should not solicit the following information:

Newspapers	Support positions such as servers tend to come from local labor pools; newspaper advertising is an effective tool.
Internal posting	Often required if a labor contract is in force; useful because it generates "word-of-mouth" publicity
Job fairs	Effective for recruiting specific specialty positions such as sushi chef.
Websites	Catering or general information websites such as craigslist should include a link to employment opportunities
"Word of mouth"	Potential hires may be customers of a previously successful catering event.

© Cengage Learning 2014

Figure 18.3 Recruiting staff.

- Questions about race, sex, religion, national origin or sexual orientation are never relevant unless a **bona fide occupational qualification (BFOQ)** (Figure 18.4) is present. A BFOQ is an exception to discrimination claims when a particular job requires a unique physical attribute, such as gender or height, to fulfill the duties of the job. In some occupations, such as a restroom attendant or a center on a basketball team, sex and height may be a BFOQ. The employer must demonstrate that a BFOQ is a requirement for the job and not just a preference for the position.

- Age or questions that would indicate age, such as high school graduation dates, should not be asked. Because of (federal form) I-9 requirements, it is permissible to ask about citizenship.

- Height and weight questions should not be asked unless a (BFOQ) is present.

- Marital status, child care situations, or pregnancy are also issues that should not be addressed on an employment application or during an interview. However, one could, and should, ask whether or not any situations would prevent a person from completing the requirements of a job. For example, the fact that a pregnant woman is expected to deliver during the time of a temporary short term vacancy is sufficient cause to reject candidacy for that position (since the vacancy is temporary and the potential employee would be unable to work for a majority of the vacancy). A similarly pregnant women would be entitled to protection if they were applying for a long-term permanent position but came to the interview pregnant. Here the employer would be guilty of violated the pregnant women's rights if the reason for dismissing the candidate for employment is pregnancy. Care should be taken to ensure the stated reason for the rejection is the lack of required availability, and not the pregnancy.

- Questions about education should not be asked unless they are part of the job specifications. Most job descriptions **do** specify a minimum education requirement; however, such questions can only be asked if the educational attainment is necessary to be successful in the job. Minimum educational requirements cannot be the manifestation of a desire to have "smart" people working in the organization. The education must either be (1) needed to do the job or (2) be a good predictor of job success and does not disproportionately discriminate against a protected class of individuals. Dates of graduation should not be required. However, proof of graduation, degree, or certification can be required if the underlying education is a bona fide job requirement (Figure 18.4).

- Pursuant to the requirements of the Americans with Disabilities Act (ADA), questions about a handicap or disability, except to ask whether an accommodation would be needed to complete the essential functions of the job, should not be asked. Therefore, focus on the applicant's ability to perform the essential functions of the job "with or without a reasonable accommodation." The job description (discussed later) plays a critical role in defining essential functions of a position. It is the candidate's responsibility to identify any aspect of the essential functions of the position that would require a reasonable accommodation. The candidate must be made aware that he or she must make this request.

- Do not ask for photographs of the applicant.

In response to growing litigation over age, race, and national origin discrimination, the use of phone interviews at the first level is becoming very popular with large private employers and some federal government agencies.

Diemo Video Picture

Figure 18.4 State, county, and city laws determine the legal age of a bartender.

INTERVIEWING

Some HR professionals consider the traditional interview process to be low in reliability and very subjective. In a society riddled with litigation exploiting the results of unreliable selection methods, care must be taken to strengthen the validity and reliability of the interview process. Interview reliability and validity can be strengthened by including the following suggestions:

- Multiple interviewers (if available) should be used to reduce potential bias.
- Include select employees and supervisors (if you have them) in the interview process.
- Develop standardized questions to be asked of all candidates and submitted for approval prior to the interview.
- Ask questions that deal with specific situations likely to arise on the job. Use situational questions that are experienced based and future oriented (Figure 18.5).
- Questions should be reviewed to ensure that protected information is not being asked of the candidates (race, sex, children, etc.).
- Interviewers should evaluate applicants' answers to each question. Further, each interviewer should rank all candidates.
- When possible (especially with cooking positions), an actual demonstration of specific skills needed for the job should be utilized as a valid method of rating candidates. Requiring cooking candidates to prepare a sample meal to certified chefs is an appropriate and reliable mechanism to determine the applicant's skill level.
- Proficiency tests—written and practical—may be used in the selection process provided the assessments are relevant to the position and job description.

Interview Questions NOT to Ask: here are some questions that should not be asked on an application or during an interview. There is a potential for subsequent legal action if these

EXAMPLES OF EXPERIENCE-BASED AND FUTURE-ORIENTED QUESTIONS	
Experience-based:	
Motivating employees	"Think about an instance when you had to motivate an employee to perform a task that he or she disliked but that you needed to have done. How did you handle the situation?"
Resolving conflict	"What was the biggest difference of opinion you ever had with a coworker? How did you resolve that situation?"
Overcoming resistance to change	"What was the hardest change you ever had to bring about in your past job, and what did you do to get the people around you to change their thoughts and behaviors?"
Future-oriented:	
Motivating employees	"Suppose you were working with an employee whom you knew greatly disliked performing a particular task. You needed to get this task completed and this person is the only one available to do it. What would you do to motivate that person?"
Resolving conflict	"Imagine that you and a coworker disagree about the best way to handle an absenteeism problem with another member of your team. How would you resolve that situation?"
Overcoming resistance to change	"Suppose you had an idea for a change in work procedures that would enhance quality, but some members of your work group were hesitant to make the change. What would you do in this situation?"

© Cengage Learning 2014

Figure 18.5 Examples of experience-based and future-oriented questions.

questions are asked during an interview or solicited on the application form. When conducting group interviews, care must be taken to ensure that all participants understand the rules for questions (Figure 18.6).

Job Analysis

job analysis
Encompasses a job description and job specification for each position.

job description Defines the essential tasks, duties, and responsibilities of a job.

essential job functions The essential functions of the job define the major tasks expected from the employee.

Job Descriptions: some catering companies may lack formal job descriptions for some positions within the catering entity. One reason for this is the lack of trained HR professionals who have experience in writing effective job descriptions. Another reason is the perceived fear that some employees will only work to the job description and nothing more. However, a job description is a vital component of the employment process.

The passage of the Americans with Disabilities Act (ADA) has increased the importance of effective and accurate job descriptions. Job descriptions should contain two components: a description of the job and the specifications needed for the job.
Essential Job Functions: the job description should define the essential tasks, duties, and responsibilities (TDRs) of the job. It is important to understand the term "essential," because it is these functions of the job that require a reasonable accommodation under ADA. The essential functions of the job define the major tasks expected from the employee. It is important to make a distinction between essential and nonessential functions of the job. The job description should be specific to the

EXAMPLES OF IMPROPER INTERVIEW QUESTIONS	
Question	**Problem**
What year did you graduate?	Age discrimination
Do you have any health-related issues or handicaps?	Civil rights violation—sex, Americans with Disabilities Act
Are you or will you be getting married?	Civil rights violation—usually asked of women
What is your family heritage?	Civil rights violation—national origin
Do you have any physical handicaps?	Violation of Americans with Disabilities Act
What is your maiden name?	Civil rights violation—national origin
Do you have any children? How old are they?	Civil rights violation—sex and age
What child care arrangements have you made?	Civil rights violation—sex—question usually asked of women
Are you pregnant, or do you have a family?	Civil rights violation—sex—question usually asked of women
How many years have you been out of school? How long have you been working?	Civil rights violation—age

© Cengage Learning 2014

Figure 18.6 Examples of Improper Interview Questions

essential functions, yet broad enough to protect the employer's interest in facilitating an efficient operation. "Other duties as assigned" is a useful phrase found in many job descriptions.

> Meaningful job descriptions are the basis for justifying essential job functions and basic qualifications of employment. They benchmark the requirement for reasonable accommodation and establish a basis for testing and work sampling. They are the starting point for effective screening and hiring practices.
>
> *David Piper, Employment and Labor Relations, Indiana University of Pennsylvania, Indiana, Pennsylvania*

Job Specification: the job specification should also list the education/knowledge, skills, abilities, and other characteristics needed to perform the job. It is important to stress that the required education/knowledge, skills, and abilities should define those requirements that are needed to be successful in the job. Requiring knowledge, skills, and abilities above the requirements for a job poses threats because of the potential for discrimination claims.

job specification Lists the education/knowledge, skills, abilities, and other characteristics needed to perform and be successful in a job.

Checking References

Reference checking is problematic from both sides—one as a **potential** employer and one as a **current** employer. There have been cases where individuals have successfully sued their previous employer because of defamation of character claims. When giving and receiving references, the operative key concept is, "The truth is always defensible," as long as the truth is well documented. Some employers limit release of information to dates of employment and average salary. Obviously, being unable to obtain good references presents problems as well. Regardless of the frustration level associated with obtaining references, employers must be diligent in seeking this information.

negligent hiring When an employer knew or should have known about dangerous or incompetent propensities and still hires an individual for a position in which he or she may repeat the conduct.

- **Negligent hiring:** an employer has a duty to use reasonable care to hire safe and competent employees. When an employer knew or should have known about dangerous or incompetent propensities and still hires an individual for a position in which he/she may repeat the conduct, it is deemed as negligent hiring. A good question to use in determining if a "negative employment past" may exist is to ask the previous employer, "Would you hire this person again?" Prior experience is often important in making a hiring decision and should also be verified. A potential employer is not limited to checking listed references.

violation of confidentiality As a current employer, one must always speak truthfully about the employee. The truth should be backed up by documentation. If the truth cannot be verified, the opinion should not be shared.

- **Violation of confidentiality:** as a current employer, one must always speak truthfully about the employee. The truth should be backed up by documentation. If the truth cannot be verified, the opinion should not be shared. There have been legal actions taken for slander or defamation as the result of remarks made during a reference check. For this reason, responses to reference checks are often formally limited to confirmation of employment period, duties performed, and rates of pay.

As an inquiring employer, gathering useful information during a reference check is more of an art than a science. Remember, the individual on the other side of the conversation is operating in the same environment of caution. As stated earlier, a good way to get a grasp of the overall worth of the individual to his/her previous employer is to ask whether or not they would "hire the individual again."

The Offer of Employment

offer of employment An offer to be employed to a candidate. Once an offer of employment is extended to a candidate, the employer has the right to make the offer of employment contingent upon the passing of a medical exam, including drug testing. If an employer uses this process, it cannot be used in a discriminatory manner. It must be used for all hires.

Once an **offer of employment** is extended to a candidate, the employer has the right to make the offer of employment contingent upon the passing of a medical exam, including drug testing. If an employer uses this process, it cannot be used in a discriminatory manner. It must be used for all hires.

Pre-employment Documentation

Every employee must be able to demonstrate they are legal to work in the United States of America. Therefore each employee must complete and provide to the employer an signed I-9 form complete with the evidence confirming legal employment status. The employer must maintain this documentation for up to 7 years after the employee leaves service with the caterer. Employees are also required to complete federal W-4 forms identifying their preferred taxation reporting status (single or married) and the number of dependents they plan to claim. Documentation must be received before a potential candidate can officially work for the caterer.

Termination/Resignations/Employment at Will

Employment in most situations is considered to be "**Employment at will.**" This doctrine states that either party can sever the relationship for good reason, bad reason, or no reason at all as long as neither party violates any statutory law or in violation of protected classes. What does this mean? As an employer, if you discover that one of your employees has a bad attitude that is hurting your customer service based operation, you can sever the employment relationship. Likewise, if an employee is fed up with the banquet stress on any given night, they can end the employment relationship at that moment without giving a 2-week notice. What cannot be done is for the employer to decide they are going to terminate the employment of an individual who just turned 50. It is always best to sever employment relationships that do not promote the quality of service the caterer expects; but caution needs to be given anytime the need for firing a person exists (see next section). Realize that the employment-at-will doctrine exists for the employee too, and understand that a last minute resignation, while uncomfortable to the caterer, isn't a violation of law. What you may want to consider is when a person "resigns" from a position, their resignation can be used as a defense when the same person tries to file unemployment compensation, so try and get the resignation in writing or confirm a person's resignation in writing by sending them a confirmation document with their last paycheck.

employment at will This doctrine states that either party can sever the relationship for good reason, bad reason, or no reason at all as long as neither party violates any statutory law or in violation of protected classes.

Documentation Needed for Disciplinary Action When Collective Bargaining Agreement (CBA) Exists

Unfortunately, there are times when an employee does not adapt well into catering operations or engages in behavior that requires discipline. This is extremely important if the caterer is covered by a collective bargaining agreement. If employee discipline is subject to arbitration most arbitrators and judges are going to be looking for certain aspects in order to determine whether or not the discipline was just. These include the following:[11, 14]

- Did the employee carry out the act the employer claims? Is there evidence?
- Did the employee know the act was in violation of rules, procedure, or contract?
- Has the employer engaged in progressive discipline if dismissal or suspension is the action sought? (The underlying principal in disciplinary matters is for corrective action, not punitive measures).
- Have similar actions by other employees resulted in similar discipline?
- Does the discipline fit the crime?[17]

Understanding the methods by which an arbitrator will make his/her decision helps supervisors determine what information or documentation they need

[11]Lewicki, R.J., Saunders, D.M., & Saunders, D.M, (2006). Negotiation, 5th Ed.). Boston: McHraw-Hill.

[14]McPherson, D.S., Gates, C.J., & Rogers, K.N. (1987). Resolving grievances: A practical approach (2nd Ed.). Reston, Virginia: Reston Publishing Company.

[17]Nolan, D.R. (2007). Labor and employment arbitration: In a nutshell. St. Paul, MN: Thomson-West.

to provide. Written documentation is always the best form of documentation, especially if the information was reviewed with the employee. Documentation that should be maintained for disciplinary purposes includes the following:

- Date, time, and location of the incident, including the witnesses or individuals involved in the situation.
- Written documentation defining how the incident was investigated and what information the investigation provided.
- Notice to the employee that an infraction or violation of law might have occurred and the establishment of a meeting time for the employee to address the situation.
- Notes taken during the meeting in which the employee provided his/her side of the story, including names of individuals who were present during the meeting.
- Written letters from witnesses who saw the infraction or who are making the complaint.
- Copies of the rules, procedures or guidelines that define the infraction or action as a violation of policy.
- Documentation acknowledging that the employee should have known his or her actions violated the rules and procedures of the employers.
- Documentation of warnings or other disciplinary actions relating to the employee.
- Documentation relating to similar treatment of other employees violating similar policies.

Progressive Discipline Policy

progressive discipline policy Progressive discipline is a system of penalties that increase in severity following repeat offenses. Progressive discipline attempts to ensure that the employee understands that he or she is violating policy or not performing up to standards, has been given a chance to correct deficiencies, and is aware of the consequences of future violations or inadequate performance.

Employee discipline can be a very complicated issue in catering operations. In cases where an employee is covered by a collective bargaining agreement or where there is a policy on discipline, a "just cause" provision may apply. "Just cause" requires the employer to have legitimate reasons for taking actions and to act appropriately and fairly when disciplining an employee. Discipline must be corrective in nature and not punitive. In essence, the discipline must fit the crime. Arbitrators will sustain and uphold most employee termination cases that result from numerous infractions or violations of policy if the arbitrator believes progressive discipline has been used. Progressive discipline is a system of penalties that increase in severity following repeat offenses. Progressive discipline attempts to ensure that the employee understands that he or she is violating policy or not performing up to standards, has been given a chance to correct deficiencies, and is aware of the consequences of future violations or inadequate performance.

Progressive discipline is usually a consistent sequence as follows:

1. An oral warning
2. A written warning, defining potential actions for future offenses
3. Various degrees of suspensions—3 days, then up to 30 days
4. Move for termination

Written documentation of disciplinary actions should be maintained in the employee file and, beyond the oral warning, a document (copy) should be sent to the employee summarizing the incident and the disciplinary action. The possibility and nature of future actions should be noted.

It also should be understood that certain serious infractions should not follow the progressive discipline path. They should result in a suspension of duties and/or action for termination.

- Assaulting a supervisor or coworker or gross insubordination
- Assaulting or corrupting a minor
- Stealing company property

INTRODUCTION TO EMPLOYEE BENEFITS

Employee Benefits

Employee benefits are becoming an increasingly important item for employees, but for different reasons. The issue of benefits is a required issue of negotiations and in some cases is likely the main sticking point in contract negotiations. However, if a catering operation does not have a collective bargaining agreement, then there are less restrictions when it comes to providing benefits. With the rising cost of health insurance and the increase of employee benefits other than health insurance in government regulation to provide some benefits, the total costs for a benefit plan could range anywhere from 30 percent to 50 percent of the payroll costs. As economic resources continue to tighten, employers will need to be more prudent and cost effective with the administration of employee benefits programs.[13, 15]

Health Insurance: Since the late 1980s, health insurance is the most discussed benefit issue at the negotiations table. Currently, health care insurance is the single most expensive benefit provided to employees in terms of total cost.

Health insurance plans generally fall into two types, fee-for-service and managed care. Fee-for-service plans, also known as indemnity plans, provide benefits for health expenses such as hospital, surgical, and physician charges if these expenses were incurred as a result of a covered medical condition. Fee-for-service plans sometimes provide a major medical benefit that provides comprehensive coverage outside of the specific charges of hospital, surgical and physician expenses. Under a fee-for-service plan, the plan participants can choose to see any medical specialists without a referral and have a choice regarding the medical facility they wish to use for any medically covered procedure.

Under an indemnity plan arrangement, the employer pays a fixed fee to the insurance company and the insurance company pays all medical expenses incurred by the participants covered under the plan. The plan is likely to contain deductibles and copayments, and some services like routine checkups will not be covered. In a fee-for-service arrangement, the insurance company will negotiate discounted payment rates with health care providers in their network. These providers are known as participating providers. When using a

employee benefits Benefits offered to a candidate as conditions of employment, including health insurance, dental insurance, life insurance, vision insurance, and retirement packages.

---

[13]Martocchio, J.J. (2001). Strategic compensation: A human resource management approach (2nd Ed.). Upper Saddle River, New Jersey: Prentice Hall.

[15]Milkovich, G.T., & Newman, J.M. (2005). Compensation (8th Ed.). Boston: McGraw-Hill, Irwin.

participating health care provider, the provider accepts the fee paid by the insurance company as payment in full and is not allowed to bill the participant for the remaining difference between the provider's charge and the fee paid to the provider by the insurance company.

Managed care plans technically try to control costs by limiting the employee's choices of health care providers. Managed care plans basically come in three types, health maintenance organization (HMO), preferred provider organization (PPO), and point-of-service (POS) plans. In an HMO the participants of the plan must select a primary care physician (PCP) and it is only by referral of PCP that a participant gets specialized medical treatment. Most HMO organizations limit the hospital facilities in which participants can use for medical treatment. Payments for medical services of an HMO provider are covered by the insurance plan and may require nominal copays by the participants, but payments for medical services outside the HMO network are not covered by the health insurance plan.

In a PPO, the health plan defines a network of physicians and hospital providers with plan participants free to seek medical services from any provider within the network without the need of a referral from the PCP. PPOs also require nominal copays for all services, but unlike an HMO, the network or provider is usually larger in scale and the PPO does not require a referral of the PCP for participants to see specialists. A POS plan is similar to a PPO, but it differs in allowing participants to seek medical treatment outside the network. However, reimbursement rates for medical services outside the network are lower than the reimbursement rates for medical services inside the network and require the participant to pay the difference in cost for using out of network providers.

Two ways exist in which an employer can purchase a health care plan—buy a fully funded plan or self-fund the plan. In purchasing a fully funded plan, the employer pays the insurance company a set fee and the insurance company pays all claims. In a self-funded plan, the insurance company acts as a third party administrator with health care providers and the employer pays the health care costs of the employees. In self-funded plans, usually the employer will purchase a secondary "stop-loss" plan that either caps individual claims to a certain dollar amount, caps total claims to a certain dollar amount, or both. The difference between these funding plans is which party absorbs the risk of paying for health care, the employer or the insurance company.

Regardless of the type of health insurance plan used, the cost of health care is dependent solely upon the utilization of the plan. The more the participants use the plan, the more expensive the plan is going to be. As medical procedures continue to advance, drug prices continue to increase, and the employees continues to age, the concern regarding the affordability of employer paid health care will continue into the next generation.

Dental Insurance: Dental insurance can range from plans that provide basic dental services such as cleanings and filling cavities to plans that provide orthodontic services. Dental insurance plans are not as complex as health insurance plans and the costs of these plans have increased at a more conservative rate than health insurance.

Vision Insurance: This benefit provides insurance coverage for eye exams and needed vision corrections. Most vision plans do not cover eye surgeries such as eye correction services (Lasik surgeries) performed by an opthalmologist but rather routine services performed by an optometrist.

Life Insurance: Life insurance plans are inexpensive plans for any employer with a reasonable number of employees. Group term life insurance is a relatively inexpensive benefit to provide employees. Life insurance plans also may provide additional coverage for accidental death and dismemberment claims. The IRS does limit the amount of nontaxed life insurance an employer can provide to $50,000 per employee. The cost for life insurance premiums above $50,000 is taxable income to the employee and must be shown on the employee's W-2 form.

Social Security: Social Security and Medicare taxes are paid equally by the employer and the employee. A Social Security tax of 6.2 percent of the employees wage is paid by both the employee (4.2 percent for 2012) and employer up to a capped level that is adjusted each year by the federal government. Medicare tax of 1.45 percent of the employees wage is paid by both the employee and employer and is paid on all salary amounts; it is not capped.

Retirement: Employers can offer a wide variety of retirement options. Most offer tax-deferred IRS qualified retirement plans in which the employee contributes into their own retirement plan and the employer has the option to match the employees' contribution up to a certain level or decide not to contribute to the plan as well. As the viability of Social Security continues on an uncertain path, tax-deferred retirements plans will continue to increase in usage by employees.

Workers Compensation: Workers compensation is a required benefit for employers to provide medical coverage and replacement of wages for employees who are injured on the job. Workers compensation coverage pays for all medical bills related to the work injury, including rehabilitation, and compensates the employee roughly two-thirds of their salary on a tax-free basis while the employee is off work due to the injury. Compensation starts after the employee misses 7 days of work and continues until the employee is able to return fully to active duty. The trade-off on workers compensation is that when an employee is hurt on the job, the employee's medical bills and lost wages are compensated in exchange for the employee not suing the employer for the accident.

Flexible Spending Accounts/Cafeteria Plans: With the increased cost of health insurance and the resulting cuts in health care coverage, the popularity of flexible spending accounts is gaining ground. Any employer can utilize agencies like Colonial Insurance or AFLAC to provide flexible spending accounts for their employees to contribute money from each paycheck tax-free into an account that can be used during the year for certain qualifying expenses. These expenses can range from reimbursements for payment of health-related purchases to payments for child care.

INTRODUCTION TO FLSA

The **Fair Labor Standards Act (FLSA)**, sometimes called the "Wage and Hour Law," was enacted in 1938 to guarantee fair treatment of workers and aid economic recovery during the Great Depression. While its initial significance was in establishing a minimum wage ($.25 per hour at the time), it now has more of an impact in governing an employee's right to overtime pay and defining compensable time. In 1985, a landmark Supreme Court ruling, *Garcia v. San Antonio Metropolitan Transit Authority*, determined public employees **are** also subject to the FLSA. Every owner, supervisor, and manager must have a basic understanding of an employer's responsibilities under the FLSA to guide them through dangerous waters. The most recent wage and hour legislation at the federal level was enacted in 2004—The "Fair Pay" overtime initiative—redefined the employees covered by the act and those exempt from its protections. The legislation was in the form of amendments to the FLSA.

Fair Labor Standards Act (FLSA) Sometimes called the "Wage and Hour Law," was enacted in 1938 to guarantee fair treatment of workers and aid economic recovery during the Great Depression. While its initial significance was in establishing a minimum wage ($.25 per hour at the time), it now has more of an impact in governing an employee's right to overtime pay and defining compensable time.

Salary Status

There are two salary tests: a salary level test and a salary status test. The level test is fairly easy to determine, $455 per week for example. The status test is more difficult to understand and has a more complex compliance matrix.

In addition to meeting certain criteria regarding job responsibilities and duties, employees must be paid on the basis of a fixed, periodic salary in order to be considered exempt under the FLSA. In the context of the FLSA, "salary" and "hourly" have specific meanings, and there are important distinctions between them. A salaried employee is one who, regardless of the number of hours worked, receives full salary for any workweek (or predefined period) in which he or she performs work. In other words, a salaried employee, whose compensation is defined to be $1,000 per week, will receive that salary on a weekly basis regardless of the work that was required of him or her during that week.

Overtime payment requirements cannot be waived by agreement between the employer and the employees. An employee's right to compensation for overtime hours worked cannot be ignored, even if the employer announces that overtime work will not be permitted or that overtime work will not be paid for unless prior authorization has been established.

wage and hour calculations Employees covered by the FLSA must receive overtime/premium pay for hours worked in excess of 40 in a workweek. The premium time pay can be no less than 150 percent of the regular pay rate.

Wage and Hour Calculations

The importance of correct classification (covered or noncovered) becomes clear after studying FLSA minimum wage and overtime requirements. And it becomes apparent why employers see an economic advantage to treating employees as noncovered and why federal legislation and oversight is necessary to curb abuse.

Concept of Minimum Wage and Hourly Pay: As of 2012 the FLSA established minimum wage rate of $7.25 per hour; each state also sets a minimum wage rate. Following the principle that federal law establishes a minimum level of benefit unless superseded by a state law that offers a greater benefit, the established minimum pay rate for a covered employee would be the higher of the two established minimum pay rates. For instance the minimum rate of pay established by Georgia is $5.15 per hour. Since the federal rate is higher, workers in Georgia must be paid $7.25 per hour. The minimum rate established by Oregon is $8.80 per hour and is adjusted yearly for inflation. Therefore the worker in Oregon must be paid a minimum of $8.80 per hour since the state rate is higher. A sub-minimum wage can also be established for the employment for an employee less than 20 years of age in some locations. As discussed previously, wages of computer workers have a special place in federal wage and hour law. There is no special minimum wage for computer workers, but if the hourly wage rate is at least $27.63 an hour, then the computer worker is exempt from the FLSA overtime pay requirement.

Basic Premium Time/Overtime Calculations: Employees covered by the FLSA must receive overtime/premium pay for hours *worked* in excess of 40 in a workweek. The premium time pay can be no less than 150 percent of the regular pay rate. There is no limit as to the number of hours an employee may work in any given workweek as long as they are age 18 or older (16 or older for nonhazardous jobs). Overtime

---

Overtime Pay Calculation Example

Given: An employee's hourly rate is $10 and he or she works 50 hours in a workweek.

Calculation: 40 hours times $10 equals $400 in basic pay. To this amount is added $10, times 1.5, times 10 (hours) or $150 in premium pay. The weekly wage for this employee is $550.

pay is not required for work on Saturdays, Sundays, holidays, or regular days of rest if the employee has not *worked* in excess of 40 hours during the defined workweek. Collective bargaining agreements or employer policy may require special treatment, like double-time for work on holidays or differential pay for second or third shift work, but there is no such requirement under the FLSA or the minimum wage acts of each state.

The "Workweek": At the core of the overtime calculation is the concept of the 40-hour workweek. The premium calculation applies to hours worked over 40 hours in the defined workweek, and the definition of "workweek" must be predetermined; it cannot float. Further, an employee cannot avoid the application of premium time by averaging time worked over an 80-hour biweekly pay cycle. For example, an employee working 50 hours in week one and 30 hours in week two of a biweekly pay cycle is entitled to 10 hours of premium time pay, even though the average hours worked per week was 40.

Fixed Weekly Amounts

It would appear that "salary" has no place in a discussion of "regular rate." Rate of pay implies hourly employment, and hourly employment implies "covered" status. Employees who are identified as nonexempt (meaning that they are covered by certain key provisions of the FSLA) should be paid on the basis of a preestablished and understood hourly rate.

This is a major trouble area and the law is often misapplied. Some think the quick fix to overtime issues is just to pay their employees a salary each week or pay-period and thereby exempting employees from coverage. This is not so. The duties of the employee establish the compensation method, not an agreed amount arrangement. Fixed weekly amounts can be used, but the hourly rate then floats. The federal minimum wage test applies and the employee is still obligated to keep time records.

The concept of "salary," however, is addressed in the context of minimum wage and premium time in the FLSA. When an employee, who is determined to be covered, is paid as a salaried employee, DOL will determine "regular rate" as follows:

> The regular rate for an [FLSA covered] employee paid a salary for a regular or specified number of hours a week is obtained by dividing the salary by the number of hours for which the salary is intended to compensate. If, under the employment agreement, a salary sufficient to meet the minimum wage requirement in every workweek is paid as straight time for whatever number of hours is worked in a workweek, the regular rate is obtained by dividing the salary by the number of hours worked each week.

The concept becomes more readily understood in the context of previous discussions about salary if "agreed weekly payment amount" is substituted for "salary."(Figure 18.7). In this way, there is a clearer connection between "salary" and "exempt employees."

The employer cannot avoid the requirement to pay covered employees minimum wage or premium time by arbitrarily converting a nonexempt position to a "salaried" position. Further, the imposition of a fixed weekly amount obviously does not eliminate the need to maintain weekly time records.

While it may be true that many employers compensate hourly employees at fixed weekly amounts with no time records, it is also true that these employers are in violation of FLSA, for doing so and would be subject to punitive fines and back pay if discovered.

- An employee's hours vary each week, but he/she agrees to be paid $420 per week, regardless of the number of hours worked.
- In a 50-hour week, the regular rate of pay is $8.40 ($420/50 hours). In a 40-hour week, the regular rate of pay is $10.50 ($420/40 hours). In a 30-hour week, the regular rate of pay is $14.00 ($420/30).
- The minimum wage requirement must be satisfied at all times after this calculation is performed.
- The requirement to pay premium time for hours worked over 40 must also be met.
- In the 50-hour week example, the employer is required to pay the employee for 10 hours at $4.20 (the premium attributed to a $8.40 rate) in addition to the $420 base. The weekly pay is $462.

Figure 18.7 Example of regular rate calculation from a "salary" agreement.

Definition of "Hours Worked"

Employers must pay covered employees for hours worked (Figure 18.8). A covered employee's compensation cannot be determined without the calculation of the total hours *worked* during a pay period. Generally speaking, hours worked

Figure 18.8 Hours worked includes all the time spent by the employee performing his or her job duties during the workday.

includes all the time spent by the employee performing his or her job duties during the workday. An underlying principle of the FLSA and the Wage and Hour Division's enforcing of it lies in its definition of "employ," which includes being permitted to work."

Thus the definition of "workday" for the purposes of compensation is "the period between the time on any particular day when such employee commences his/her principal activity and the time on that day at which he/she ceases. . . ." The principles are fairly straightforward. It is in the application of these principles where the complexities arise.

The principles present a particular problem for an employer working in a culture with strict budget constraints and the potential for emergency situations that must be dealt with regardless of the limitations of the defined workday. The compensatory time bank is helpful, but "working off the clock," particularly among the field staff, is not uncommon (Figure 18.9). Uncommon or not, an employer requiring or condoning time worked off the clock represents a clear violation of the FLSA. Employers engaging in this practice are, in the extreme, subject to fines, penalties, and sanctions. Employees subjected to this practice are entitled to back pay, and sometimes are also awarded penalties.

Wage and hour division compliance guidelines are specific: reasons and intent are immaterial. Hours worked are compensable.

1. Nonexempt employees cannot "volunteer" to do their employers work on "their own time." All such work must be compensated. (There is an exception for work totally unrelated to employers duties; for example, a caterer's employee can be an unpaid server for their child's sports banquet, if the caterer is not charging for this service or event and is not requiring the employee to help.)

2. The employer cannot claim lack of knowledge of employees working "off the clock." The employer is deemed to have an understanding of the amount of time required to complete assigned work.

3. The employer is responsible for advising employees of the employer's policy for recording time.

4. The employer is responsible for disciplining employees who violate the time recording policy.

© Cengage Learning 2014

Figure 18.9 "Off the Clock" work issues.

The employer is deemed to know if the employee is working "off-the-clock" hours (Figure 18.10). A mutual understanding that the employee will not be paid for the unclocked time is an admission of wrongdoing by the employer. There can be no such understanding under the terms of FLSA.

Usually Classified as Work Time	Usually Classified as Personal Time
Time spent traveling as a part of the workday.	Commuting to and from work.
Mandatory attendance at lectures, meetings, and training programs.	Voluntary professional and personal development.
Preparatory time spent prior to the start of the workday that is required in order to perform the job.	Normal movement to place of work and wardrobe preparation.
Rest periods and coffee breaks shorter than 20 minutes.	Lunch or dinner breaks of 30 minutes or longer.
"On call" time where the employee is required to remain on premises.	"On call" time where the employee is granted personal freedom.
Time where the employee is engaged to wait—time between tasks during the workday.	Time where the employee is waiting to become engaged—time before or after an early punch in, for example.

© Cengage Learning 2014

Figure 18.10 Examples of work time and personal time.

Child Labor Laws

child labor laws Child labor laws were enacted to provide for the health, safety, and welfare of minors. The law restricts the type of work certain minors can perform, the number of hours per week a minor can work, and other conditions of employment.

An employer must be aware of **child labor laws** when it employs students as workers within the school entity (Figure 18.11). Child labor laws were enacted to provide for the health, safety, and welfare of minors. The law restricts the type of work certain minors can perform the number of hours per week a minor can work, and other conditions of employment.

The FLSA includes restrictions on employment of children, as does almost every state law. The provisions listed here are those generally applicable in Pennsylvania and enforced by state agencies and school entities. FLSA and state law covers additional areas, such as association with alcohol, work in the entertainment industry, newspaper delivery, and so forth.

- Youths 18 years or older may perform any job, whether hazardous or not, for unlimited hours.
- Youths 16 and 17 years old may perform any nonhazardous job.
- Youths 14 and 15 years old may work outside school hours in various nonmanufacturing, nonmining, or nonhazardous jobs under the following conditions: no more than 3 hours on a school day, 18 hours in a school week, 8 hours on a nonschool day, or 40 hours in a nonschool week. Also, work may not begin before 7 a.m., nor end after 7 p.m., except from June 1 through Labor Day, when evening hours are extended to 9 p.m.
- Minors under the age of 18 are not permitted to work more than 6 consecutive days in any one-week period or more than 44 hours in the same one-week period.
- Minors under the age of 16 are not permitted to work on scaffolding, nor in any heavy work in the building trades, or in any tunnel.

Permission of John R. Smith

Figure 18.11 Monitoring the schedules of minors ensures compliance to the child labor laws.

- Minors under the age of 18 are not permitted to work more than 5 consecutive hours without a 30-minute lunch period.
- No minor under the age of 18 can be permitted to work between the hours of 12:00 a.m. and 6:00 a.m if the minor is enrolled in a "regular day school." Minors 16 and 17 years of age can be employed until 1:00 a.m on Fridays and Saturdays and on days preceding a school vacation.
- No minor under the age of 18 is permitted to work with paint that contains lead, nor are they permitted to prepare compositions which are considered dangerous, including leads, acids, dyes, and explosive material.
- Minors under the age of 18 must receive either an employment certificate or, if 16 years or older, a transferable work permit from an appropriate issuing official.

OVERVIEW OF COLLECTIVE BARGAINING

Introduction

One of the more contentious aspects of hospitality management involves the negotiating of a **collective bargaining agreement.** While most individuals have negotiated at some point in their life, negotiating wages, hours and other terms and conditions of employment with a union can be demanding. While some negotiations can be cooperative, others might be extremely contentious and may damage the relationships between the parties. Tight economic conditions of management and unrealistic demands of the union only make this process more difficult. Future managers should recognize that

collective bargaining The purpose of collective bargaining is to give employers and employees a voice in wages, hours, and other terms and conditions of employment

distributive bargaining
This approach uses a more adversarial approach to negotiations in which each party uses inflated proposals full of many different issues and positions to secure the items most wanted by each party.

National Labor Relations Board (NLRB) Certifies, after assuring a majority of those voting cast affirmative ballots, that a particular labor organization is the exclusive bargaining agent for a particular classification of employee.

results of collective bargaining will likely influence, either in a positive or negative way, the labor-management relationship between the employer and its employees.

It is important for upcoming managers to understand how to negotiate with their employees, even if they hire a professional negotiator to negotiate the labor contract; the process of negotiation continues after the labor agreement is signed. Therefore, it is important to understand how to use **distributive bargaining** and **integrative bargaining** and to recognize the options of both parties when a disagreement regarding a condition of employment exists.[3, 6, 10]

The emphasis of collective bargaining is on the rights of employees to organize into bargaining units with "an identifiable community of interest." In the private sector, this right is granted to employees through the National Labor Relation Act. The **National Labor Relations Board (NLRB)** certifies, after assuring a majority of those voting cast affirmative ballots, that a particular labor organization is the exclusive bargaining agent for a particular classification of employee.[4]

Once identified as a member of a certified bargaining unit, the employee is covered by the terms and conditions of the collective bargaining agreement negotiated between the management and the bargaining unit, regardless of whether the employee chooses to join the bargaining unit as a dues paying member. Further, the bargaining unit has the duty to fairly represent all covered bargaining unit members, regardless of whether the employee joins the bargaining unit.

Collective Bargaining Agreement

The purpose of collective bargaining is to give employers and employees a voice in wages, hours, and other terms and conditions of employment. Many labor relations theorists believe that the way in which the parties negotiate a labor agreement will determine how the parties interact during the term of the collective bargaining agreement. If the employees feel that they didn't get a fair contract, it is likely that the number of grievances during the contract will increase.[9, 20]

Once a union is certified, management must meet with the union to bargain over wages, hours, and other terms and conditions of employment. Employers do, however, have inherent rights that are not subject to bargaining unless they allow them to be bargained into the contract. These inherent management rights include the rights to operate, to determine how work will be done, and to hire and direct the workforce. It is important to understand that if the union is able to get management to agree on bargaining over an inherent employer right, it then becomes a term and condition of employment and is now a mandatory subject of bargaining in future negotiations. The most common inherent rights lost by managers include the right to hire, and the right of directing the workforce.

[3]Brommer, C., Buckingham, G., & Loeffler, S. (2002). Cooperative bargaining styles at FMCS: A movement toward choices. Pepperdine Dispute Resolution Law Journal 2(465), pp. 465–490.

[6]Fisher, R., Ury, W., & Patton, B. (1991). Getting to yes. New York, New York: Penguin Books.

[10]Lewicki, R.J., Barry, B., & Saunders, D.M. (2007a). Essentials of negotiations (4th Ed.). Boston: McGraw-Hill Irwin.

[4]Budd, J.W. (2005). Labor relations: Striking a balance. Boston: McGraw-Hill.

[9]Hall, L. (1993). Negotiation: Strategies for mutual gain. Newbury Park: Sage Publications.

[20]Ury, W. (1993). Getting past no: Negotiating your way from confrontation to cooperation. New York: Random House.

In negotiations, the representatives from both sides will engage in discussions with the intent to ratify a labor agreement. There are many ways in which this process may unfold, and experienced negotiators are familiar with a variety of negotiation strategies. Primarily, each side will come to the negotiation table with a list of essential issues that will need to be addressed. Negotiators refer to these as "interests" of each side. Interests are the items that each side "needs" in order for them to agree on a labor contract. In most cases the interests of both parties center around wages and benefits; the difference being that management has an interest in keeping wages and benefits low, while the union's interest is to maximize the wages and benefits of its members.

Typically, parties use "positions" or things that they say they want in negotiations as the mechanism to carve out the interests they need if they are going to agree on a contract. Successful negotiators are able to uncover the priorities of the other union and what they are willing to accept—their bottom line—if they are going to agree on a contract. Therefore negotiators work very hard to determine what the "interests" of the parties are and what positions they will use to get to these interests. Negotiators understand that in order to get a contract agreement you must get a simple majority, 50 percent plus one vote of those casting votes to favor contract ratification and at times will package contract proposals to favorably influence the majority of potential union voters.

During negotiations, the parties will likely engage in distributive bargaining, integrative or interest-based bargaining, or a combination of the two. Most often, the negotiations will use distributive bargaining techniques unless the parties have a history of more integrative styles of bargaining or management proposes a switch to the interest-based approach. The reason for this is that in most negotiations, the union is the group requesting a new labor agreement and therefore the first to present its proposal to management. It is unlikely that a union will want to open negotiations with an interest-based bargaining proposal unless it is certain that management will not take advantage of knowing exactly what the union must have in the contract prior to submitting management's initial proposal. It is important for those who will have an interest in the outcome of labor negotiations to understand the different styles of bargaining and recognize when each style is appropriate for use.

Distributive Bargaining

Distributive bargaining is probably the most common form of negotiation and is used widespread in almost all facets of bargaining; from negotiating labor agreements with a union to buying a used car from a salesmen. This approach uses a more adversarial approach to negotiations in which each party uses inflated proposals full of many different issues and positions in order to secure the items most wanted by each party. Both parties will use whatever form of coercion they have at their disposal to force the other side into an agreement with their proposal. The reason this approach is used most often is that it is the most familiar negotiation style for all participants. It is easy to learn and is likely practiced by the participants in other facets of their lives. The approach is also used when one side needs to get a concession from the other side or when limited monetary resources for negotiations prevents the parties from using more collaborative styles of bargaining.

The winning philosophy behind distributive bargaining is to maximize the gains for your party without sacrificing too much in return. This is a popular approach by both sides primarily for its adversarial nature.

Negotiations using distributive bargaining strategies will likely be done with each side exchanging offers and communications through the use of a chief spokesperson. In distributive bargaining, the side likely to win is the one with the most negotiating power, that is, the side that has the better ability to influence the other side should an agreement not be reached.

To win at distributive bargaining, the negotiator must first uncover the other party's resistance points or bottom lines. If the bottom line is within the settlement range; then settlement is very easy. If the other party's bottom line is not within the settlement range, then the negotiator must influence the resistance point either by changing the perception that the bottom line is obtainable or realistic on both sides, or by influencing either party to the negotiations that the alternative to not settling (potential strike) is a worse option.

While distributive bargaining may be the most popular model used in most negotiations, there is the concern that it may strain the relationship between the parties. Because the approach focuses on an adversarial model, the tendency is to see each party in the negotiations as the enemy. If the parties are unable to reach an agreement and an impasse turns to a strike, the relationship between the parties will likely remain strained in the future.

Integrative Bargaining

integrative or interest-based bargaining Using this style of bargaining, the parties work collaboratively with each other to come to an agreement on a new labor contract. The parties work to form an agreement in which each side feels they have maximized their interests in the negotiation.

Integrative or interest-based bargaining provides a different approach to collective bargaining. Using this style of bargaining, the parties work collaboratively with each other to come to an agreement on a new labor contract. The parties work to form an agreement in which each side feels they have maximized their interests in the negotiation. Under the interest-based bargaining model, the wish list of negotiable items is limited to a set number for each side (usually 10 at most), requires the parties to share all information they have regarding the open issues on the table, and work together for consensus type solutions for each "real issue" brought by both sides.

Unlike distributive bargaining, interest-based bargaining requires full participation from all members of the two bargaining teams, no chief spokesperson is used. It also facilitates the use of brainstorming to provide many different solution options while utilizing industry standards as a fair settlement mechanism for negotiable items such as salary demands and cost of living percentages as the basis for settling salary issues. The main difference between the two approaches is distributive bargaining views the other side as an adversary while interest-based bargaining views the other side as a collaborative partner. Unlike distributive bargaining, interest-based bargaining, when used successfully, can strengthen the relationship between the parties and is likely to reduce workplace tension between the two parties. As a result, fewer grievances are filed once the contract has been approved.

Hybrid Approaches

There will be times in negotiations in which it may not be possible for the parties to use interest-based bargaining approaches on every negotiable issue. This is especially true when rough economic times limit the employer's ability to offer comparable wage requests or other hot button issues (such as health care insurance) impede acceptance of the contract by one side or the other. In these situations, using a hybrid approach to negotiations may be the best approach.

A **hybrid approach to negotiations** mixes some of the collaborative styles of interest-based bargaining with some of the traditional styles of distributive bargaining during a negotiation. For example, during a contract negotiation an employer might use interest-based bargaining styles on nonmonetary "housekeeping" issues while using the distributive style approach on the monetary issues of salary and benefits.

There are many variations of the hybrid approach, but the two most popular include modified traditional bargaining and timed mediation. Modified traditional bargaining got its start when introduced by the Federal Mediation and Conciliation Service as a bargaining style that bridged the gap between the adversarial nature of distributive bargaining and the collaborative style of interest-based bargaining.

Recognizing that many parties would feel uncomfortable fully committing to a complete interest-based bargaining approach, modified traditional bargaining combines the collaborative mindset of the interest-based style with the proposal-counterproposal format of distributive bargaining. Under this model, the parties limit the number of issues brought to the table and begin negotiations with an open interest-based discussion on all issues, followed by a brainstorming session on options to address each issue. Upon completion of this process, the parties begin sharing proposals and counterproposals on any unresolved issue with the goal to settle all of the issues brought by the parties.

Because of the initial interest-based discussion and brainstorming session, this approach is likely to produce proposals within the realistic settlement range much earlier in the negotiations process. Many variations of this approach have emerged over the years with the difference being how much the amount of collaboration will be included in the bargaining model. Some models limit the use of interest-based techniques to include a certain number of the issues to be negotiated, along with the recommendation to explain why each issue is being brought to the negotiation table, and then allow the traditional method of distributive bargaining to settle all the issues.

Timed mediation is a bargaining approach in which management and the union set a compressed schedule for negotiations, with the goal being to settle as many issues as possible during this time frame. The typical timed mediation approach is usually over a 2-day period in which the bargaining teams seclude themselves in a hotel and spend the next 48 hours negotiating all remaining open issues in the negotiation. This method works much better when the parties limit the number of issues they plan to discuss during the timed mediation and it does not require the open collaborative approach of interest-based bargaining. Because the parties negotiate constantly, the open issues get resolved primarily because the number of proposals that are exchanged over the 2-day bargaining session move the open items into a settlement range.

Negotiating a Labor Agreement

The first time a person sits at the table actively negotiating a **labor contract** can be a very interesting time. It is suggested that prior to beginning this experience, managers should attend a negotiations workshop to understand how the process

hybrid approach to negotiations Mixes some of the collaborative styles of interest-based bargaining with some of the traditional styles of distributive bargaining during a negotiation.

labor contract An agreed upon outcome of the collective bargaining process between management and workers to determine the terms and conditions of work environment works. Negotiating a new labor agreement will take preparation, time, energy, and on occasion, a sleepless night or two. In some negotiations, tensions will run high. In others, the process is well established and bargaining is just another event in the fiscal year cycle. Regardless, how management prepares and conducts its negotiations will go a long way in how successful it will be in meeting the objectives established.

Prepare, Prepare, and Prepare—successful negotiators win at negotiations by being well prepared at the table. For management, this means researching recent labor agreements not only in and around the area, but statewide. Reviewing recent labor contract agreements will provide the employer with a settlement range that will likely guide the current negotiations. Management should review the current labor agreement for issues that need addressed in the current collective bargaining agreement. This may include reviewing past grievances during the current labor agreement to determine if specific language in the contract may need to be changed. It is also advisable to create a comparison matrix of surrounding hospitality agents to have accurate information on what other companies are doing. Finally an understanding of current contract agreements of other industries within the area, outside of hospitality, may be beneficial in getting an idea of the potential settlement ranges for the upcoming negotiations. This information will provide the employer with sense of comparison that will help it develop a compelling negotiations strategy. It is likely that the other side will also gather similar information that will help them in their negotiations strategy.

Formation of a Negotiations Team—a negotiations team should be assembled and a determination will need to be made regarding the hiring of a professional negotiator. In most negotiations, the decision to hire a professional negotiator will likely be determined by the skill of current managers in contract negotiations and whether the union decides to negotiate the contract with the assistance of their representative. Because of the adversarial relationships of distributive bargaining and the need for management to have good working relationships with employees, the hiring of a professional negotiator may be a good idea; the "hired gun" can be seen as the adversary, instead of the manager being seen as the adversary.

Establish Management Objectives—before going into negotiations, the employer must establish a set of objectives that they plan to accomplish during the negotiations. One of the primary issues in this phase is to establish a desired settlement range on monetary issues. Most important is to determine management's "bottom line." The importance of the bottom line number is that it represents the employer's strike number; if the salary demand is higher than management's bottom line, then the employer is willing to accept the strike. Successful negotiators hold onto the bottom line firmly and very rarely move from this number because doing so weakens the negotiator's credibility and the strength of the bottom line aspect. If a bottom line continues to move upward, then the wrong message may be sent to the other side in that the bottom line is always negotiable. In most cases, the bottom lines should be something that is discussed with the governing board prior to and during the negotiations with an emphasis on what will happen if the salary demand exceeds the bottom line.

Frame Your Words and Proposals—when negotiating, it is important to remember that you should use people skills with the opposing negotiations team and problem solving skills on the negotiations issues at the table. At times, when tensions are high, negotiators need to be very careful of words used at the negotiations table; any derogatory remarks about members of the bargaining unit or the negotiations team will likely be bulletin board material for the union. Furthermore, when negotiations proposals from the union must be rejected, the stated reason behind the rejection should be "limited economic resources" and not "the employees do not deserve any more money."[2, 22]

Use All Negotiations Tools Available—negotiation tools include the use of technology and third parties to help narrow the issues toward resolution. When beginning a negotiation, the key issues for both sides will likely be monetary issues such as salary and benefits. Using computer programs such as Excel will provide management with the opportunity to develop a cost spreadsheet that will determine the total cost of a proposed settlement. To accomplish this, management needs to know the number of pay steps, the number of employees on each pay step, and the number of years in the new agreement. It is also very important that management know this information in order to determine the net cost of a new labor contract. Mediators are also good tools to use in negotiations, especially when the differences between the union's and management's proposals are large with little progress gained in the negotiation sessions to date. State mediators are adept at refocusing unrealistic negotiation expectations into a more realistic picture for both sides.

Tentative Agreements—as the bargaining sessions continue through the negotiations process, the parties will begin to agree on certain terms and conditions on the new labor agreement. When this occurs, it is very important that the parties acknowledge the agreement and tentatively sign off on the agreed terms. It is then useful to keep a running log of agreed upon terms. Most negotiators like to start new bargaining sessions with a review of previously agreed upon terms. The parties should try to avoid reopening settled terms because it is counterproductive to the goal of reaching a final agreement between the parties.

Keep Copious Notes—one member of the negotiations team should be responsible for maintaining a list of notes during the negotiations sessions; especially proposals and counterproposals made by both sides. Knowing who made what proposals and counterproposals in the new labor agreement can be a very valuable source of information should a grievance be filed regarding the interpretation of a new provision in the collective bargaining agreement. The arbitrator of the case is usually very interested in how the provision was negotiated and whose version of the language was adopted, the union's or management's.

Working towards Agreement

As stated earlier, negotiating a labor agreement can be a very daunting task and will require a dedicated effort in order for the process to conclude with a favorable outcome. Realize that even though both sides in the negotiations are looking for different things, this doesn't mean that the process has to be adversarial. Some of the basic reasons why parties cannot come to an agreement on a collective bargaining agreement may have more to do with how the negotiations are handled rather than the substance of the agreement. For instance, some sides may reject a

[2]Branson, R. (1988). Coping with difficult people: The proven effective battle plan that has helped millions deal with the troublemakers in their lives at home and at work. New York, New York: Dell Publishing.

[22]Yarbrough, E., & Wilmot, W. (1995). Artful mediation: Constructive conflict at work. Boulder, Colorado: Cairns Publishing.

proposal, simply because it is not their idea. Therefore, when the proposals are very close to the settlement range, some negotiators feel it prudent to accept the offer of the union rather than have the union accept the employer's last offer. It is very difficult for the union as a whole to reject the contract, if the final version accepted is the union's offer.

Remember, information is key to negotiations. When proposals are submitted by the union, ask appropriate questions about why the union feels this proposal will work. Likewise, ask for criticism regarding proposals submitted by management. This exchange of information at the bargaining table provides management with an opportunity to determine the bargaining unit's main interest areas in the negotiation. Also, input and choices help promote buy in. Frame responses correctly and don't dismiss proposals and ideas as irrational. Rather, consider them options to the negotiation for a new agreement.

Also, remember that it is likely that the union negotiating team has probably made promises to members of the bargaining unit regarding what they will likely accomplish at the bargaining table. With this in mind, it is important for managers to understand the importance of allowing the negotiations team to "save face" when a final agreement is reached. A simple press release on the diligence and effort of the union negotiation team to get the best deal possible for their bargaining unit members will go a long way in how the team will present the offer to the membership and also the outcome on future negotiations between management and the union.

Summary

Employment policies and practices are rooted in several key federal laws. Compliance with federal law is facilitated by an understanding of their basics. State law is prominent in professional certification and collective bargaining of public sector employees, but federal law is the primary driver of employment policy in most other human resource areas.

One of the most important responsibilities of the human resource function is recruiting and hiring high quality employees. The law of employment and hiring is extremely complex and violations are subject to potentially severe penalty; this participation should be undertaken in partnership with a qualified human resource professional.

Employee benefits are becoming an increasingly important item for employees, but for different reasons. The issue of benefits is a required issue of negotiations and in some cases is likely the main sticking point in contract negotiations. With the rising cost of health insurance and the increase of the cost in all of the other benefits, the total costs for a benefit plan will range anywhere from 30 percent to 50 percent of the payroll costs. As economic resources continue to tighten, employers will need to be more prudent and cost effective with the administration of employee benefits programs.

The Fair Labor Standards Act (FLSA), sometimes called the "Wage and Hour Law," was enacted in 1938 to guarantee fair treatment of workers and aid economic recovery during the Great Depression. While its initial significance was in establishing a minimum wage, it now has more of an impact in governing an employee's right to overtime pay and defining compensable time.

A caterer must be aware of Child Labor Laws when employing students as workers within the school entity. Child Labor Laws were enacted to provide for the health, safety, and welfare of minors. The laws restrict the type of work certain minors can perform, the number of hours per week a minor can work, and other conditions of employment.

One of the more contentious aspects of hospitality management involves the negotiating of a collective bargaining agreement. It is important for a caterer to understand how to negotiate with their employees. The emphasis of collective bargaining is on the rights of employees to organize into bargaining units with "an identifiable community of interest." During negotiations, the parties will likely engage in distributive bargaining, integrative or interest-based bargaining, or a combination of the two.

Review Questions

Brief Answers

1. Define human resource management.
2. Explain key federal employment laws.
3. Explain why human resource management practices must be integrated into a catering operation.
4. Describe the process of recruiting employees for a catering business.
5. Summarize the tools used to gather information on potential employees in the recruiting process.
6. Describe a bona fide occupational qualification (BFOQ).
7. Explain the components of a job analysis.
8. Describe a progressive discipline policy.
9. Explain why employee benefits are important for recruiting and retaining employees.
10. Why are employee health care benefits considered the single most important benefit in terms of total cost to the caterer?
11. Define the concept of "hours worked."
12. Summarize the collective bargaining process.

Multiple Choice

Select the single best answer for each question.

1. What act, passed in 1967 and currently enforced by the Equal Employment Opportunity Commission (EEOC), prohibits discrimination in employment against individuals age 40 and older?
   a. Age Discrimination in Employment Act (ADEA)
   b. Title VII of the 1964 (1990) Civil Rights Act
   c. Family and Medical Leave Act (FMLA)
   d. Americans with Disabilities Act (ADA)
   e. All of the above are correct.

2. What doctrine states that either party can sever the relationship for good reason, bad reason, or no reason at all as long as neither party violates any statutory law or is in violation of protected classes?

   a. off-premise catering

   b. negotiating a labor agreement

   c. The Fair Labor Standards Act (FLSA)

   d. employment at will

   e. none of the above

3. When giving a reference or speaking for an employee, the truth should be backed up by documentation. If the truth cannot be verified, the opinion should not be shared. Which of the following protects an employee against false or untruthful statements being made from an employer:

   a. negligent hiring

   b. violation of confidentiality

   c. progressive discipline

   d. The Fair Labor Standards Act (FLSA)

   e. collective bargaining agreement

True or False

Read each of the following statements and determine if it is true or false.

1. The passage of the Americans with Disabilities Act (ADA) has increased the importance of effective and accurate job descriptions.

2. A job posting should define the position that is open, where an applicant can receive information regarding the job, the deadlines for submitting an application, and a contact person.

3. Once an offer of employment is extended to a candidate, the employer has the right to make the offer of employment contingent upon the passing of a medical exam, including drug testing.

Putting It All Together

Visit an independent caterer, the catering department of a hotel or restaurant, a health care facility, college/university, or a home-based caterer. Identify and discuss the challenges of managing their human resource area. What are the challenges they confront? How do they adhere to the child labor laws? What employee benefits do they provide? Do they operate with a labor agreement? How do they attract applicants for their staffing needs? Write a short report summarizing your visit.

Glossary

Age Discrimination in Employment Act (ADEA) This act, passed in 1967 and currently enforced by the Equal Employment Opportunity Commission (EEOC), prohibits discrimination in employment against individuals age 40 and older.

American service Food is preplated and brought out to the guests. Sit-down dinners are considered American service where portion control is maintained, keeping food costs low.

Americans with Disabilities Act (ADA) This act, passed in 1990, targets employers with 15 or more workers and was developed to protect current and potential employees from discrimination based on a person's disability.

amusement park catering This is a dimension of corporate catering. The management of an amusement park may cater their own functions internally or may outsource the responsibility of providing the food and related service for all on-premise catering events to an independent caterer.

appropriate personnel The human resource standard as defined by the caterer to describe the required individual needed to accomplish the specific task.

architects Architects work with the caterer to determine equipment needs, including writing equipment specifications based on need, request for bid to equipment dealers, and installation.

atmosphere Atmosphere takes into account managing the guests' senses of sight, sound, scent, and touch. All events have their own unique life to them. Atmosphere is a key element in the life of an event.

automobile insurance Insurance to protect the caterer from liability imputed to him by the actions of an employee. Laws regarding insurance for vehicles vary depending upon the state in which a caterer is conducting business.

avoid risk The catering management processes meant to eliminate all circumstances that may cause a risk to materialize. One example is the creation of a safety team whose purpose is to monitor the environment to identify and correct potential risks to ensure the safety of the employee and guest.

back-of-the-house (operations) Physical, mechanical, and financial activities performed by a caterer that the customer generally does not get to witness.

balance sheet The statement of financial position that shows the accounting equation: total assets = liabilities + owner's equity.

banquet event order (BEO) This form is a multipurpose catering management tool used internally to communicate the details for execution of an event to the appropriate personnel.

barriers These include obstacles that inhibit or challenge the caterer. The two main types of barriers include operational barriers and human resource (or communication) barriers.

base recipe A standardized recipe changed by adding additional ingredients to create another menu item to complement the menu mix.

benchmarks predetermined standards. A caterer establishes these standards to compare against actual operational performance.

beverage management Management of the overall beverage service in a manner most pleasing to all guests with uncompromising attention to detail, establishing a budget, and exceeding customer expectations balanced with responsible alcohol service. Specific tasks include supervising bar personnel, monitoring inventory levels, establishing standards, implementing operating procedures, and learning about wines and beverages.

beverage package A common sales strategy used to define beverage service is written to explain in detail the amount of beer, wine, mixers, juices, garnishes, service staff, and other items available.

beverage plan The outcome of analyzing the beverage needs for a specific function based on the customer, number attending, purpose and length of the event, location, space, budget, the knowledge of the bar, type, and kind of equipment, transportation, and staffing need requirements.

blogging Similar to a newspaper column; a blog is typically maintained by an individual with regular entries of commentary, descriptions of events, or other material. Popular blogging sites include: Wordpress, Blogger, and Blogspot.

blueprint A detailed outline of a plan used to guide organizational behavior.

bona fide occupational qualification (BFOQ) Is an exception to discrimination claims when a particular job requires a unique physical attribute, such as gender or height, to fulfill the duties of the job.

bone china A hard-paste porcelain containing bone ash, making it easier to manufacture, stronger, not chipping easily, and with an ivory-white color that lends itself to decoration.

branded menu items Food items produced by a principal, backed by its name to guarantee a consistent level of quality.

broadline distributor A market intermediary who bundles a number of specialized product lines, such as food, nonfood, equipment, chemical, and cleaning supplies together.

budget A financial, tactical, single-use plan used to set the parameters for each event.

buffet service A common style of service used to serve food. The distinguishing characteristic of buffet service is that customers actively participate in supplying part of the service by serving themselves from an organized table offering a variety of food.

bundle of tasks The catering management procedure to identify and group all similar employee tasks together based on the event's tactical plan. It is used to assign or delegate tasks to the appropriate employee for their execution.

business growth plan A strategic plan based on the answers to key questions used to identify a caterer's market niche that provides for controllable growth in the appropriate direction as established by the caterer.

cancellation policy Stipulations in a cancellation policy are usually framed and guided by time and define the course of action the caterer will take, beginning at a predefined period from the event date, to before the event. The policy communicates what amount of the deposit and money will be refunded to the client.

capital resources Includes the facility, equipment, land, and inventories of raw materials managed by the caterer to exceed customer expectations.

cash and carry businesses Equipment is stocked at store locations. Buyers are invited to visit these cash and carry locations. If a decision to make a purchase occurs, then they go on their way with product in hand.

cash flow The uninterrupted series of cash installments by the client to the caterer for executing the catering function.

caterer's market The group of all actual and potential customers in a caterer's geographic service area who have an unmet need, want, or demand requiring the service of a caterer.

catering management Tasks of planning, organizing, influencing, and controlling each activity involved in the preparation and delivery of food, beverage, and related services at a competitive, profitable price that meets and exceeds the customer's perception of value.

ceramic plates Plates classified according to their body type: a flint body, an alpha alumina body, or as bone china. Ceramic plates are bone china, stoneware, earthenware, and vitreous china (e.g., porcelain).

child labor laws Child labor laws were enacted to provide for the health, safety, and welfare of minors. The law restricts the type of work certain minors can perform, the number of hours per week a minor can work, and other conditions of employment.

client-based pricing method This pricing method bases the cost of a function on the client's perceived value rather than the direct food and labor costs to produce the event.

code of ethics A formal statement used to describe the caterer's philosophy regarding an employee's professional conduct and behavior.

collective bargaining The purpose of collective bargaining is to give employers and employees a voice in wages, hours, and other terms and conditions of employment.

commercial segment Traditionally considered the "for-profit" catering segment, it includes the independent caterer, the restaurateur and caterer, and the home-based caterer whose financial goals include a profit gained from revenue minus expenses.

communication barrier(s) A type of barrier (also called a human resource barrier) caused by the staff that disrupts the elements of a catering event. These may include human error, lack of communication, and deviation from standard operating procedures.

Community Supported Agriculture (CSA) A direct connection between the farmers and the final consumers. Members who join a CSA buy a share of the season's harvest. A member's share guarantees security for the farmer, knowing he or she has been prepaid for a portion of the harvest.

competitive-based pricing method This pricing method bases the cost charged to a client for a function on the relative cost charged by competitors in the market, rather than on direct food and labor costs or demands.

conflict Conflict is the disagreement caused by the tension between two or more parties.

conflict resolution strategy The way to effectively resolve conflict in a situation regardless of the client, setting, environment, or relationship.

Consolidated Omnibus Budget Reconciliation Act (COBRA) COBRA requires employers to offer group health coverage to employees and dependents if a qualifying event terminates their medical coverage.

consultants Experts who work with the caterer to determine equipment needs, including writing equipment specifications based on need, request for bid to equipment dealers, and installation.

contract The legal agreement between the client and caterer outlining details of an event. It does not have to be elaborate, but should cover the basics including time, date, menu items, number of guests, the price and payment policy, and provisions for extenuating circumstances beyond the caterer's control.

controlling One of the most important catering management functions. Ensures the effective and efficient utilization of the caterer's resources in the process of producing food and beverage to accomplish organizational goals.

control point Any point in a specific food system at which loss of control does not lead to an unacceptable health risk.

convenience foods Manufactured or processed by a principal and delivered to the caterer in a ready-to-eat or ready-to-cook form.

convention catering One of the most profitable types of catering events. Distinguishing feature is the ability to simultaneously prepare and serve food and beverages to support professional, business, and social activities of a large group of people. These events are held in a closed environment, at a hotel or convention facility, using multiple meeting rooms and/or a large banquet or ballroom.

corporate catering The professional caterer's target market is a clientele of corporate and business accounts such as meetings, ceremonies, anniversaries, recognition dinners, training sessions, seminars, conventions, and other related events.

cost-based pricing method Adding a standard markup to the direct labor and food cost to determine the client's final cost for a function.

cover The complete place setting for one guest at the start of the meal including the service plate, flatware, napkin, and water glass.

creativity Combination of imagination, ability, and understanding customer needs to create excitement, wonder, and anticipation for the client attending a catering event.

crisis management team Group of homogenous management and hourly employees who can quickly respond to an unforeseen crisis with the purpose of protecting the interests of the guest and the organization.

critical control point (CCP) As defined in the Food Code, means a point at which loss of control may result in an unacceptable health risk.

critical limit(s) As defined in the Food Code, means the maximum or minimum value to which a physical, biological, or a chemical parameter must be controlled at a critical control point to minimize the risk that the identified food safety hazard may occur.

customer appeal Professional expertise, such as proper food preparation techniques, sanitation procedures, attractive thematic presentations, and related amenities offered by the professional caterer.

customer base A solid foundation consisting of current and potential clients upon which a caterer continuously builds to support the catering business now and in the future.

customer-satisfaction objectives These objectives are developed by the caterer specific to the client's needs and wants for each individual event. Exceeding these objectives should be the goal.

delegate The assignment of responsibility and authority to an appropriate employee to execute a "bundle of tasks" or a job in the catering operation.

demands Derived from the client's needs and wants, demands also include the client's ability to purchase them.

deviation The failure during the implementation of the HACCP plan to satisfy a required critical limit for a critical control point.

distinct competence This is achieved when a caterer defines their target market exclusively and hones their skills to enable them to do something uniquely better than the competition. It also provides a competitive advantage that is difficult to copy or penetrate.

distributive bargaining This approach uses a more adversarial approach to negotiations than the integrative and hybrid approaches to bargaining, in which each party uses inflated proposals full of many different issues and positions to secure the items most wanted by each party.

distributor (or purveyor) These individuals purchase items directly from the principal (manufacturer or farmer). They set up huge warehouses to handle large volumes of food and supplies for a specific geographic region. (see specialty distributor; broadline distributor).

distributor sales representative (DSR), supplier sales representative, territory sales manager, merchandising associate Terms used interchangeably to refer to a purveyor's sales representative, the contact between the caterer and the distributor.

dual restaurant catering When a restaurant operator evolves into catering services to strategically increase the efficiencies of the base operation.

earthenware Less strong, easily chipped, and more porous than stoneware, but its low cost compensates for these deficiencies. Due to its higher porosity, earthenware must usually be glazed to be watertight.

Eat'n Park Hospitality Group (EPHG) Beginning in 1949 as a family car-hop restaurant in Pittsburgh, Pennsylvania, it has evolved into a regionally powerful diversified company operating in Pennsylvania, West Virginia, Ohio, Maryland, New York, Connecticut, and Michigan.

EcoSteps Created by Jamie Moore to describe EPHG's continuous improvement process toward sustainability.

employee benefits Benefits offered to a candidate as conditions of employment, including health insurance, dental insurance, life insurance, vision insurance, and retirement packages.

employee work schedule The catering management task of assigning tasks to be completed by the employees predicated on the production schedule and event plan.

employment at will This doctrine states that either party can sever the relationship for good reason, bad reason, or no reason at all as long as neither party violates any statutory law or in violation of protected classes.

employment practice liability Coverage of day-to-day activities in the workplace.

Energy Star Energy Star is a joint program of the US Environmental Protection Agency (EPA) and the US Department of Energy to identify and promote energy-efficient equipment.

engager The client or person who is contracting the services of the caterer.

equipment Caterers determine equipment needs based on the menu, service requirements, type and location of the event, and any special needs of the client.

equipment auction Sites that offer used food service equipment for purchase based on a bidding process.

essential job functions The essential functions of the job define the major tasks expected from the employee.

event planner A person who directly coordinates for a client the planning, organizing, implementation, and control of their event.

exclusive caterer A caterer owns the sole rights to all catering functions held at a specific facility.

execution of tasks The physical action by an employee to accomplish predetermined goals defined as tasks.

extrinsic rewards The tangible rewards gained from executing a successful catering event, such as earning a competitive salary.

Fair Labor Standards Act (FLSA) In general, the law with the most reach for catering individuals would be FLSA. This law provides the minimum hourly rate paid to a worker and covers other aspects such as $1\frac{1}{2}$ payment for hours worked over 40 in a week, equal pay, and Child Labor Laws.

Family and Medical Leave Act (FMLA) Passed in 1993, FMLA requires employers who employ 50 or more workers to provide up to 12 weeks (or 26 weeks) of unpaid leave for qualifying circumstances, including the birth of a child, placement of a son or daughter for adoption or foster care, care for an immediate family member with a serious health condition, medical leave because of a serious health condition, facilitation of care for a veteran of recent military action, or pending military deployment.

family-style service In this self-service type of catering, food is delivered to the table on platters or large serving dishes with enough for everyone seated. The guests pass the platters and help themselves.

FarmSource An initiative to locate and to partner with local farmers and food producers as a sustainable source of food by EPHG.

field testing Procedure of serving food, prepared from a new recipe, to an unbiased sampler to ascertain its fit in the caterer's menu mix.

financial catering activities Back-of-the-house catering activities. Procedures that help to accomplish predetermined profit objectives by controlling operational resources in the daily execution of catering tasks.

financial objectives These are based on the needs of the client and developed from the event budget. They're crucial to the initial planning process and will vary with every event.

financial resources The management process of procurement, allotment, investment, and control of monetary resources by the caterer to provide a desired financial return with its appropriate investment.

fire damage liability Insurance coverage for a caterer's legal liability arising from fire damage to structures rented to the caterer.

flowchart Shows how a plate physically moves through the catering operation. Describes the work being done at each subsequent fundamental operational step.

flow of food This concept refers to the order in which food will travel through a catering operation, from receiving, to storage, to preparation, to production, and finally to service.

food broker A market intermediary whose fundamental task is to bring the caterer and the principal together in the marketplace to facilitate a sale. Brokers identify trends, conduct training programs, educate caterers to new ideas, products, and culinary techniques, and build recipes by bundling product lines together.

formal payment policy The explanation and guidelines created by the caterer to describe for the client how payment is made. Creates a positive cash flow into the organization.

formal structure Created by the caterer, its purpose is to help allocate and control organizational resources while supporting its evolving strategy as determined by the mission statement and outlined in the catering plan.

formulating (a plan) To design a specific plan of action to meet the client's needs based on the proposal and contract.

French service An elaborate style of service where food is prepared at table-side using a gueridon (a small table with wheels) and a rechaud (a pan set over a heating element).

front-of-the-house (operations) Extremely visible, customer-driven service activities designed primarily to please the guest in the dining area, where customer expectations and a caterer's performance intersect.

fund-raising events Usually catering services are required to support various fund-raising events sponsored by the corporate community. These provide excellent business opportunities for a caterer.

greening The use of renewable resources and lessening the environmental impact of operating a catering business.

greenwashing A situation where a customer has been deceived by a caterer into believing that a green initiative has been implemented when in fact it has not.

hazard As defined in the Food Code, it means a biological, chemical, or physical property that may cause an unacceptable consumer health risk.

Hazardous Analysis and Critical Control Point plan (HACCP) A HACCP plan, as defined in the Food Code, means a written document that delineates the formal procedures for following the HACCP principles developed by The National Advisory Committee on Microbiological Criteria for Foods.

Health Insurance Portability and Accountability Act of 1996 (HIPAA) This act protects the confidentiality of health related issues of an individual and provides protection in health insurance coverage for employees and their dependents upon moving from one employer to another.

hidden costs Any unknown (to the client) costs levied against the caterer for providing food and related services in a third-party owned catering hall.

high school/elementary school catering An on-premise catering service offered by the food service director exclusively for the school's own population.

home-based caterer A caterer who operates from their home facility.

hospital catering Primarily on-premise catering operation that occurs within a hospital's environment servicing internal associations and/or a department's special needs.

human resources Skill levels, knowledge base, experience level, and maturity (length of service) of the caterer's employees.

human resource barrier(s) A type of barrier caused by the staff that disrupts the elements of a catering event. These may include human error, lack of communication, and deviation from standard operating procedures. Also called a communication barrier.

hybrid approach to negotiations Mixes some of the collaborative styles of interest-based bargaining with the some of the traditional styles of distributive bargaining during a negotiation.

implementing (the plan) The catering management processes of using effective communication skills to launch a plan into action.

income statement The statement of revenues, expenses, gains, and losses for the accounting period.

indoor bar A bar located inside the premise.

informal structure The interpersonal relationships that emerge as a result of employees working together to accomplish a common goal.

informed consumer A caterer educated about the loss-control services offered by an insurance carrier. The mix of loss-control services includes basic coverages for property, liability, and workers compensation.

insurance program The complete package written by a professional carrier to protect the caterer against the potential of loss.

Insurance Services Office (ISO) The property/casualty insurance industry's leading supplier of statistical, actuarial, underwriting, and claims information.

integrative or interest-based bargaining Using this style of bargaining, the parties work collaboratively with each other to come to an agreement on a new labor contract. The parties work to form an agreement in which each side feels they have maximized their interests in the negotiation.

interests Demands of those parties engaged in a conflict.

intrinsic rewards The internal satisfaction or feelings of achievement a caterer experiences as a result of executing a successful catering event.

issue dimension Typically is the source of a conflict between two or more people.

job analysis Encompasses a job description and job specification for each position.

job description Defines the essential tasks, duties, and responsibilities of a job.

job specification Lists the education/knowledge, skills, abilities, and other characteristics needed to perform and be successful in a job.

key activity (subsystem) Part derived from the whole catering management system. Common subsystems of the catering operation include purchasing, receiving, storage, production, transportation, service, and cleanup.

labor contract An agreed upon outcome of the collective bargaining process between management and workers to determine the terms and conditions of work environment.

LEED An acronym for Leadership in Energy and Environmental Design.

legal concerns All activities and specific obligations the caterer must meet, including adhering to the legality of a contract, charging appropriate sales tax, understanding differences between an employee and independent contractor, and identifying and pursuing legal recourse against a client who fails to pay.

liability insurance Premise/operations coverage to protect a caterer against claims arising from the ownership, maintenance, or use of the premise and of the caterer's operations in-progress.

life cycle of customer events The cycle of lifetime celebrations: bridal shower, wedding reception, anniversary, birthday, baby shower, baptism, prom, sporting banquet, college graduation, marriage, and death that requires the services of a caterer. The cycle repeats itself.

manufacturer's agent A market intermediary who is employed by the principal and has direct responsibility for accomplishing sales goals for each product in an assigned geographical sales area. Does not take title to the goods, issue invoices, or set prices.

market-penetration pricing strategy This pricing strategy sets a low initial price to penetrate a new segment or to gain an overall market share.

market-skimming pricing strategy This pricing strategy sets a rather high initial price to skim profit from the market.

master menu Standard lists offering a variety of both entrees and side dishes based on the caterer's skill level from which a client selects to create his or her own menu based on individual needs and budgetary requirements.

mechanical catering activities A back-of-the-house catering activity that focuses on the effective and efficient use and maintenance of the equipment.

medical expense coverage This insurance will provide reimbursement for all reasonable medical expenses incurred by anyone, except the caterer or caterer's employees, as a result of an accident, without regard for the caterer's liability.

melamine A plastic, a durable synthetic polymer used in the manufacture of plates.

menu This is the most important factor in the catering plan and is built around client needs and wants, availability of products, and the caterer's financial objectives and capabilities.

menu development The process of defining the function of a menu; forecasting, pricing strategies, and item popularity and mix.

merchandising associate, supplier sales representative, distributor sales representative (DSR), territory sales manager Terms used interchangeably to refer to a purveyor's sales representative, the contact between the caterer and the distributor.

micro blogging Sending blogs with messages of 140 characters or less. Typically, people subscribe to follow others and receive their messages. Popular micro blogging sites include Twitter, Pounce, tumblr, and Jaiku.

military segment The catering segment that encompasses all catering activities involved in association with the armed forces and/or diplomatic events. Traditionally operates on a break-even basis, with revenue equaling expenses.

mission statement A written statement to define why a caterer is currently in business and communicate this purpose to stakeholders in the marketplace. A caterer's guiding light.

mobile catering A caterer who employs one or a fleet of trucks specially equipped to support an assortment of food and beverages for customers located at diverse locations, such as construction sites.

monitoring step The planned sequence of observations, or measurements of critical limits, designed to produce an accurate record and intended to ensure that the critical limit maintains product safety. Continuous monitoring means an uninterrupted record of data.

multitasking equipment Food production equipment that offers the ability to be used for multiple procedures or processes in the preparation of food. For example, a tilting braising pan can perform multiple cooking duties such as braising, frying, roasting, thawing, and hot or cold holding.

napperon (overlay) A small tablecloth placed over the larger one to help protect it and accent it with additional color.

National Labor Relations Board (NLRB) Certifies, after assuring a majority of those voting cast affirmative ballots, that a particular labor organization is the exclusive bargaining agent for a particular classification of employee.

National Restaurant Association's Conserve Solutions for Sustainability Designed to initiate and inspire actions that improve a company's bottom line and are good for people and the planet. Explores conservation efforts being adopted by restaurants around the nation and offers suggestions and resources to help reduce the cost of running a food service operation.

needs The complex set of human needs that include the need for food, beverage, and related services.

negligent hiring When an employer knew or should have known about dangerous or incompetent propensities and still hires an individual for a position in which he or she may repeat the conduct.

negotiation Management tool consisting of a back-and-forth communication process between opposing sides sharing a common interest that is designed to arrive at a mutually agreeable alternative.

negotiation on the merits or principled negotiation A four point model of resolving conflict through negotiation developed by the Harvard Negotiation Project.

noncommercial segment Traditionally considered a "not-for-profit" catering segment that operates on a break-even basis where revenue equals expenses. Catering and services are provided as an adjunct service to complement the catering required by a business and industry account, college and university account, health care facility account, recreational food service account, school account, social organization account, or transportation food service account.

nonprofit (or private) caterers These caterers provide the hall, food, beverage, and servers for an occasion. Usually, the events are held on-site since many nonprofit caterers lack the expertise and equipment to handle off-site events. Catering is used as a supplement to their internal financial budgets.

objectives Framed by the mission statement, they are established to serve as benchmarks against which actual performance can be measured against a predetermined target.

offer of employment An offer to be employed to a candidate. Once an offer of employment is extended to a candidate, the employer has the right to make the offer of employment contingent upon the passing of a medical exam, including drug testing. If a employer uses this process, it cannot be used in a discriminatory manner. It must be used for all hires.

off-premise catering The caterer transports all of the food, equipment, and personnel to an external location to execute the event.

one-stop shop catering A full-service catering operation that supplies the client with a choice of a variety of services designed to satisfy their needs, wants, and demands.

on-premise catering When all of the tasks, functions, and related services that the caterer executes in the preparation and implementation of food and service for the client are done exclusively within the caterer's own facility.

open stock Plates held by the manufacturer or equipment supplier for immediate delivery.

operational barrier(s) A barrier that disrupts the physical elements of a catering event and may include human error, accidents, time constraints, and Act of God disturbances.

operational task(s) A singular, identified activity that must be executed in order to accomplish an objective.

operations A term used by a caterer to describe the task of implementing and executing the daily elements of a catering plan.

ordering The catering management process of communicating the exact needs to a purveyor.

organizing (function) The catering management function of formally creating a structure to support the efficient and effective execution of each delegated task in the accomplishment of stated objectives.

outdoor bar A bar located outside of the premise.

overhead The cost of operating the catering business regardless of the type or number of functions executed. It describes indirect labor, utilities, indirect material costs, insurance, taxes, depreciation, and the repair and maintenance of equipment.

overlay (napperon) A small tablecloth placed over the larger one to help protect it and accent it with additional color.

Pennsylvania Association for Sustainable Agriculture (PASA) The largest statewide, member-based sustainable farming organization in the United States, its mission is to work to bring farmers together to learn from each other, and to build relationships between those farmers and consumers looking for fresh, wholesome, locally and sustainably produced food.

performance refund policy A performance refund is requested by an unsatisfied client whose needs were not met. Usually caused by an operational or service defect, this breakdown occurs in any of the key activities that cause the system to malfunction. Defects include poor food quality and service.

personal and advertising injury liability Insurance coverage to protect against claims alleging false arrest, libel, slander, and false advertising if the caterer had no knowledge of the falsehood.

personality conflicts An unexplainable dislike of the client based on the intuitive feeling of the caterer, formed by the initial interview, that causes the caterer to refuse the function.

photo sharing Websites that allow users to upload, maintain a library of their personal photos online, and permit users to share their library with friends and family. Popular photo sharing sites include Flickr, shutterfly, SmugMug, and photobucket.

physical catering activities The back-of-the-house interrelated management activities of purchasing, receiving, storage, preparation, and transportation.

planning The process of detailing and outlining all tasks required to accomplish an objective. Planning is the first of seven catering management functions.

plate presentation The arrangement of good tasting food to heighten the attractiveness of the plate through its colorful and attractive display on the serving plate.

position The interests of the parties engaged in the conflict and stated as their demands in the form of a position.

positional bargaining When people engaged in a conflict take a position and argue for it.

preventive measure An action to exclude, destroy, eliminate, or reduce a hazard and prevent recontamination through effective means.

primary caterer Handles approximately 75 percent of a client's total catering need.

prime cost(s) The sum of the direct food cost plus the direct labor cost to produce a menu item for a client.

principal A common term used in the hospitality trade to denote a source who manufactures or processes food.

principled negotiation or negotiation on the merits A four point model of resolving conflict through negotiation developed by the Harvard Negotiation Project.

private (or nonprofit) caterers These caterers provide the hall, food, beverage, and servers for an occasion. Usually, the events are held on-site since many private caterers lack the expertise and equipment to handle off-site events. Catering is used as a supplement to their internal financial budgets.

private-party catering Many restaurants have separate rooms that can accommodate small groups for private parties such as bridal showers or retirement and award dinners. Off-premise caterers can service private parties at an individual's home.

producers A term used in the insurance industry to describe the individuals who sell insurance.

professional sales staff Based on need and budgetary requirements, this team's purpose is to represent the caterer in the target market by communicating to potential clients a caterer's skills and capabilities to satisfy customer needs, wants, and demands.

professionally trained full-service equipment supplier A fully integrated food service design and build consultation firm featuring a professionally trained staff able to provide turn-key operations, from concept to opening.

progressive discipline policy Progressive discipline is a system of penalties that increase in severity following repeat offenses. Progressive discipline attempts to ensure that the employee understands that he or she is violating policy or not performing up to standards, has been given a chance to correct deficiencies, and is aware of the consequences of future violations or inadequate performance.

property insurance This insurance provides protection against the loss of property.

proposal A communication tool used to effectively inform and educate the prospective client about everything the caterer can do for them during the particular event.

prospecting strategies Methodologies used by a caterer to introduce himself or herself to a prospective client with the purpose of building a sustainable customer base.

psychographic segmentation The process of segmenting a catering market by variables such as lifestyle, social class, or personality characteristics to identify a target group of customers based on these characteristics.

purveyor (or distributor) These individuals purchase items directly from the principal (manufacturer or farmer). They set up huge warehouses to handle large volumes of food and supplies for a specific geographic region. (See specialty distributor; broadline distributor.)

receiving The catering management task of the following specific procedures to inspect, verify, and confirm the delivered item meets the caterer's needs by checking it against a set of written specifications. It includes receiving, storage, and the internal distribution of raw materials to meet production needs.

recipe Specific plan or formula used to describe the preparation of a certain food.

recipe development Process of creating new recipes in response to changing consumer trends and tastes. Function of a caterer's love of food, experience, and the application of the basic knowledge of food preparation.

recipe research Begins the process of recipe development by seeking to understand the relationship between a client's needs and a caterer's skill level.

reduce risk A process, procedure, or tangible element specifically designed to reduce the element of risk. One example is the installation of a sprinkler system to reduce the risk of a fire.

referral(s) When a satisfied customer recommends a caterer to others.

relationship The bond that connects the caterer with a client based on mutual respect for each other.

reputation The character of the caterer, whether favorable or not, that is held by a customer. A customer's expectations predicated on the past performance of a caterer. One of the most important considerations a client uses to select a caterer.

retail grocery store Caterers who shop for their goods and services here should be careful to purchase the specific quantity needed. It would also be wise to negotiate a fixed markup or pricing formula rather than pay consumer prices.

rethermalization (retherm) The process of taking a prepared product, either prepared from scratch or purchased in a prepared state, that was either chilled or frozen, and applying heat to bring it to a desired serving temperature. Depending on the item, final rethermalization temperature is based on HACCP-recommended procedures for reheating prepared foods. For example, a temperature of 165°F is required to retherm a poultry product before serving it.

risk An estimate of the likely occurrence of a hazard or the change of loss, damage, or injury.

risk management A complete analysis of the potential causes of loss inherent in a caterer's business and the appropriate defense to provide protection or to avoid, reduce, or transfer the risk.

Russian service This formal and elegant style of service distinguishes the use of silver serving platters, the skillful handling of the serving utensils, and the arrangement and presentation of the food.

safety management team A group of employees who continually monitor the environment to identify and correct potential risks, ensuring the proper safety of the employees and guests.

scheduling The catering management task to balance a precise number of employees against a given volume of work.

scratch foods Menu items prepared on-premise by the caterer's staff using standardized recipes.

seasonal niche Special events that may occur during a specific time or season of the year. One example is a county fair.

secondary caterer This caterer manages approximately 25 percent of a client's catering needs. Often maintained to back up the primary caterer.

segment The part or submarket derived from the total of all potential catering customers. Members of these various submarkets have similar, identifiable needs, wants, and demands.

sensitive ingredient(s) Any ingredient historically associated with a known microbiological hazard that causes or contributes to production of a potentially hazardous food as defined in the Food Code.

service Caterers define service as it applies to their mission statement. Their reputation is built on delivery of service so developing hiring and recruiting strategies should complement a caterer's service objectives.

service standards Predetermined levels based on the organization's mission established to gauge an employee's performance.

severity The degree of seriousness of the consequences of a hazard if it were to become an actuality.

signature menu item Special or unique food giving the caterer a distinct recognition as the sole supplier of this specialized item.

signature recipe(s) A recipe that has been tweaked or adjusted to be unique to a specific caterer (e.g., adding a unique seasoning or marinade, adding an additional preparation step that alters the recipe in some unique way).

silencer/silence cloth (undercloth) A cloth placed beneath the tablecloth to prevent it from sliding. It also protects the table surface, provides cushioning for the tablecloth, reduces the noise of placing or moving china and glassware, and brings out patterns on the tablecloth.

sit-down dinner A very elegant event where the caterer must be well organized and have a good plan. Typically, the food costs are lower than with a buffet dinner because the caterer prepares a set portion per guest with a slight (2 percent to 3 percent) overage.

site inspection Visit the exact location for the event. Inspect the property or location. Review the available assessable space. Draw a diagram or take pictures to keep a visual readily available for future reference.

Slow Food A global, grassroots, nonprofit member-supported organization having supporters in 150 countries around the world. Their common bond is linking the pleasure of good food with a commitment to their community and to the environment.

small wares The additional service items placed on the table including sugar holders, salt and pepper shakers, ashtrays, pitchers, creamers, ice buckets, and compote dishes.

social catering A distinct field of catering which provides food and service to clients engaged in social events such as weddings, birthdays, and similar events. A distinguishing facet is that the event is usually held in someone's home.

social media Websites that enable a caterer to communicate with and interact with friends, family, customers, and potential clients including MySpace, Facebook, and Twitter.

social networking Websites that provide a hub for communication and interaction. Popular sites include Facebook, Linkedin, and MySpace, and emerging rapidly is Twitter.

social news Websites where people and businesses can share news stories, press releases, links to their websites, and bookmarks to web pages. Similar to social networking, popular social news sites include: digg, StumbleUpon, and delicious.

speciality distributor Basic type of market intermediary who specializes in the distribution of one product category, such as produce, cleaning supplies, or chemicals.

speciality wholesaler A specialized market intermediary. This wholesaler furnishes the food service industry with a specialized line of products, such as produce or chemicals.

specifications Concise statements communicated internally and externally, of the exact products needed by a caterer in the operation to maintain standards and exceed a client's needs, wants, and demands.

speed scratch cooking Foods that are made from scratch and finished off in the caterer's kitchen with little preparation.

staffing The catering management task of identifying the correct number of employees needed to execute an event.

stakeholders Anyone who has a direct relationship with the catering business, including employees, suppliers, clients, guests, community, neighbors, competitors, or government agencies.

standardized menu Exact listing of the type of food, beverage and related service offered by the caterer without a client's option to modify, change, or make substitution.

standardized recipe A specific plan. A standard operating procedure that communicates how to use the exact ingredients in the preparation of a specific food. It delivers a consistent quality, exact yield, and portion size each time it is produced. The achievement of financial objectives is supported by ensuring consistency, controlling costs, and preventing foodborne illness.

stoneware A hard pottery made from siliceous paste, fired at high temperature to vitrify (i.e., make glassy), the body is heavier and more opaque than porcelain and differs from terracotta in being nonporous and nonabsorbent.

storage The correct placement of all items on-premise in the storeroom, refrigerators, and freezers. Providing protections from spoilage, pilferage, and theft are some key tasks of the storage function.

strategic plan Plan established to guide the entire catering organization over the long term, 3 to 10 years into the future.

strategic sustainable green zones By mapping the flow of food through a catering operation (i.e., the building, source of food, purveyors, receiving, storage, preparation, hot food production, cold food production, final preparation, customer service, ware washing, transportation, garbage and solid waste removal) identification of current sustainable practices and how to unlock ways to become more sustainable within each zone are discovered.

strategic vision A long-term outlook that focuses on where the business is headed over the next 10 years. All possible demands that may exert pressure on the business during this time are also identified.

subplan Plan developed for each individual catering function derived from the parameters of the caterer's master or strategic plan and the specific needs of the client.

subscribe To pledge, such as signing an agreement, a subscription.

supermarket catering A traditional supermarket prepares food in their deli department. The customer will purchase this food and carry it themselves to the event location.

supplier sales representative, distributor sales representative (DSR), territory sales manager, merchandising associate Terms used interchangeably to refer to a purveyor's sales representative, the contact between the caterer and the distributor.

sustainability A concrete awareness of how a caterer's business practices impact the environment.

Sustainable Catering Association Based in Portland, Oregon, a membership-based trade association that works with caterers to enhance and further integrate sustainable practices into their business model.

SWOT analysis A strategic management tool used by a caterer to match their business strengths to market opportunities. An acronym that stands for identifying internal strengths and weaknesses, and the external opportunities and threats.

tabletop This includes any items placed on the table that are needed by guests for their dining experience.

tableware Dinnerware (i.e., dishes), glassware, and flatware used in setting a table for a meal.

tactical plan Specifically created to provide the caterer precise short-term guidance as required for each catering event. This requires precise detail and precision execution.

teamwork A collective staff working together to implement the catering plan. A necessity to executing any event successfully.

territory sales manager, supplier sales representative, distributor sales representative (DSR), merchandising associate Terms used interchangeably to refer to a purveyor's sales representative, the contact between the caterer and the distributor.

throw-ins A term used in the insurance industry to describe when extra coverage is given at no additional charge to make the policy more competitive in the marketplace.

Title VII of the 1964 (1990) Civil Rights Act It states that it shall be unlawful to discriminate in the employment arena based on an individual's race, color, religion, sex, or national origin.

top shelf brand liquor Highest quality and brand named alcoholic beverages.

transfer risk The caterer may assign the ownership of the risk to another party. One example is for a caterer to rent a facility rather than owning it.

undercloth (silencer or silence cloth) A cloth placed beneath the tablecloth to prevent it from sliding. It also protects the table surface, provides cushioning for the tablecloth, reduces the noise of placing or moving china and glassware, and brings out patterns on the tablecloth.

university/college caterer On-premise catering service primarily responsible for providing food and related services to the students, faculty, administrators, and guests.

upgrading the event To enhance the delivery and showmanship of the food and/or service by tweaking elements of the event package to exceed a client's basic needs. These professional suggestions may be based on the caterer's expertise.

verification step The methods, procedures, and tests used to determine if the HACCP system in use is in compliance with the HACCP plan.

video sharing Allows a caterer to post video to the Internet. Popular video sharing sites include YouTube, phanfare, Metacafe, and Break.

violation of confidentiality As a current employer, one must always speak truthfully about the employee. The truth should be backed up by documentation. If the truth cannot be verified, the opinion should not be shared.

vitrified china "Vitreous" means the material has an extremely low permeability to liquids, is nonporous, therefore there is no absorption.

wage and hour calculations Employees covered by the FLSA must receive overtime/premium pay for hours worked in excess of 40 in a workweek. The premium time pay can be no less than 150 percent of the regular pay rate.

wants A client's basic needs as communicated to the caterer.

"what if" scenarios The caterer's plan should include provisions for unanticipated or unexpected problems. (e.g., "What if" the equipment fails? "What if" the weather conditions don't complement an outside event?) By determining these problems in advance, the caterer will have a backup plan in place should they occur.

wholesale clubs A large warehouse stocked with a variety of bulk foods, equipment, clothes, and other items. A membership fee is required for the privilege to purchase at the warehouse location. Caterers may find it advantageous to become a member and purchase food at these clubs.

word-of-mouth advertising A type of referral when a satisfied customer recommends the caterer to others.

work production schedule A communication tool used to guide the appropriate behavior of the caterer's staff in the execution of tasks.

workers compensation Compensation is a required form of insurance paid by the employer. It provides payment of medical bills and lost wages to employees hurt in the course of employment.

workstation Areas in the production kitchen influenced in design by three basic dimensions: method of preparation, type of cooking method utilized, and volume of food produced. Common workstations include preparation, hot food, cold food, final preparation, warewashing, and transportation.

Index